MASTERY MOTIVATION: ORIGINS, CONCEPTUALIZATIONS, AND APPLICATIONS

ADVANCES IN APPLIED DEVELOPMENTAL PSYCHOLOGY VOLUME 12

VOLUME EDITORS

ROBERT H. MACTURK
GALLAUDET UNIVERSITY

GEORGE A. MORGAN
COLORADO STATE UNIVERSITY

SERIES EDITOR

IRVING E. SIGEL
EDUCATIONAL TESTING SERVICE

 ABLEX PUBLISHING CORPORATION
NORWOOD, NEW JERSEY

Printed in the United States of America

ISBN: 1-56750-146-X (cl) 1-56750-203-2 (pap)
ISSN: 0748-8572

Ablex Publishing Corporation
355 Chestnut Street
Norwood, New Jersey 07648

TABLE OF CONTENTS

PREFACE

Irving E. Sigel

During the last decade there has been a shift in research with young children from social–emotional questions to cognitive developmental ones. Noteworthy as these changes have been, and, in fact, still are, it is time to renew our acquaintance with some basic issues in motivation. Motivation is a topic within the confines of the social emotional domain simply because it is central to all living creatures, including humans. What we do, how, why, and when are central for understanding the course of human development in any living society.

Mastery motivation, or whatever the final label applied to phenomena of persistence and mastery of any task, is the study of how individuals become sufficiently engaged so they strive to persist in mastering a task. Whichever way the construct is finally defined, the problem addressed in this volume under the rubric of "mastery motivation" is important. Its importance is largely due to its prominent place in the culture of the United States. The motive to persist in the face of difficulty and to have the inward drive to master whatever one undertakes is usually viewed as a social good. In fact, the definition of a successful person is one who is imbued with the motivation to master whatever task he or she undertakes. As one thinks about this entire subject in our society, it almost has the markings of a moral question. For example, one should be motivated to engage in activities deemed proper to achieve in any field one is in, such as school or the work place, and for which one accepts responsibility for his or her actions.

This volume edited by MacTurk and Morgan reflects this interest in their search for understanding mastery motivation. The authors of the chapters in this volume engage the issues of what mastery motivation is, how it evolves among different populations of children, and how it will be studied now and in the future. There is also some attention paid to intervention that again reveals the importance of enhancing such motivation. Of course, embedded in the intervention process is another confirmation of the idea that mastery motivation is a social and personal good.

The significance of mastery motivation as a requisite to fulfill oneself in our society is paramount because society requires such a motivational disposition in each of us. This is not the place to argue about the philosophical justification of such a social requirement; rather, we all recognize it as a social value generally shared in our U.S. social fabric. We seem to take it for granted. In view of the social requirement for practical purposes, it follows that the more that can be learned about the origins, conceptualizations, and applications of what is known and should be known about mastery motivation, the more the field of developmental psychology can contribute to a social good.

However, as is noted in this volume, the editors welcome dialogue and do engage in discussions about the definition of method of assessment and the place in the psychological firmament of important constructs. The welcome engagement of dialogue bodes well for the future, because progress can only come with continued reflection and discussion. Further, the fact that educators recognize that mastery motivation is not an isolated phenomena, but rather is related to other central psychological functions such as cognition and conation, places the questions of mastery motivation in a broader social psychological context. By so doing, the editors acknowledge that humans are not fractionated organisms, but rather functionally unified in their humanity.

MacTurk and Morgan have provided an invaluable service by presenting an important problem in a reflective, constructive manner that should stimulate further thought and work in this field.

FOREWORD

Frank A. Pedersen

Many of the contributors to this volume can trace a signifi-cant influence on their professional development to Leon Yarrow. Leon was my mentor as well, and I worked with him at the National Institute of Child Health and Human Development for 16 years. I shared authorship on some of the early publications that stimulated interest in issues identified with the field of mastery motivation. Moreover, I remember vividly many spirited discussions with Leon's collaborators (often postdoctoral fellows) who were mounting a variety of research projects targeted to increase understanding of this construct. It is the fruition and elaboration of these projects that form a core of the chapters in this volume. These investigators, in turn, have enlisted colleagues; and, as mastery motivation research has attained greater scientific visibility, a consensus on some issues has emerged, and new questions have been articulated.

It is possible to trace a diversity of influences that has lead to the early interest in studying the motivational characteristics of infants and young children. Formal attribution is most often given to Robert White (1959), who is frequently cited as the spiritual inspiration of the mastery field. In *Motivation Reconsidered: The Concept of Competence*, White's ideas were first and foremost an effort to direct attention to alternatives to drive-reduction theories of motivation that were derived from Hullian behaviorism and psychoanalysis. It may be difficult for contemporary psychologists to appreciate the hold that drive-reduction theory had attained, but White's influence was one of several that advanced conceptual alternatives. Another name frequently identified with the area is Joseph McVicker Hunt. One of Hunt's publications, *Intelligence and Experience* (1961), highlighted the role of intrinsic motivation as a factor influencing cognitive and intellectual development. In addition to the above "classic" citations to the origins of mastery motivation, there is another reference that is relevant yet frequently overlooked: Wenar's (1976) study of "executive competence" (p.192) of one-year-olds. Wenar conducted observations in the home setting and scaled the length of time, degree of involvement, and level of complexity of toddlers' self-initiated transactions with their physical environments. He attempted to capture some of the same dimensions in the natural setting that Yarrow's colleagues focused on in more structured play observations. His discussion of findings anticipated some current issues, such as the relationships between attachment behavior and executive competence.

It is possible that there were also informal influences that contributed to the conceptualization of mastery motivation. For example, another theorist who even earlier proposed an alternative to drive-reduction theory was Kurt Lewin, with whom Yarrow studied with as a young graduate student. We may speculate that some of Lewin's conceptualizations concerning field theory and self-directed behavior of school-age children were incorporated into Yarrow's reflections on mastery motivation. It is also interesting to note that Yarrow and Hunt worked closely together on a White House Task Force in the mid-1960s that, with other distinguished collaborators, attempted to set forth a scientific rationale for an intervention directed to children of poverty which evolved into the Head Start program. It is likely that their informal discussions influenced the crystallization of mastery concepts.

Although to some the work inspired by Yarrow may seem narrow in scope, restricted as it was to the infancy period, its conceptualization was in the forefront of innovative thought for its era. It is likely that developments identified as the "cognitive revolution" and ethologically-inspired attachment theory have become the dominant alternatives to drive-reduction theory, but there are elements of common conceptual heritage shared by these areas with that of mastery motivation.

Among the more recent advances in mastery motivation research, there has been a refinement and elaboration of its definition. Mastery motivation was originally conceived of as simply the amount of task-directed behavior that infants displayed when engaged with toys that posed challenging problems, a definition highlighting primarily persistence. A crisper definition describes mastery motivation as a psychological force (called perhaps more aptly a 'disposition' by McCall, this volume) "that stimulates an individual, in a focused and persistent manner, to attempt to master a skill or task that is at least moderately challenging for him or her" (Morgan, Harmon, & Maslin-Cole, 1990, p.319). The underlying rationale and implication of this definition are addressed in several chapters in this volume. While earlier studies of mastery behavior were concerned with manipulation and exploration of inanimate objects, current interests have been broadened to include the social domain as well. Moreover, the markers of mastery motivation are seen to include both instrumental, task-directed activities and expressive behavior. The latter includes affective displays of pleasure and pride.

A second advance has been the casting of mastery motivation into a larger developmental perspective that spans from infancy through the preschool years. Three phases have been identified by Barrett and Morgan (this volume). Phase 1, from birth to 8 or 9 months, focuses on the importance of contingency awareness, a preference to control events rather than be a passive observer, and a preference for relatively novel stimuli. Phase 2, from 8–9 months to 17–22 months, highlights the centrality of learning and internalizing externally imposed standards of behavior when engaged with challenging tasks; affective aspects of mastery motivation (i.e., pleasure at completing a task) also are more readily observed. Phase 3, from 17–22 months to 32–36 months, especially involves self-appraisal skills and the ability to execute a sequence of behaviors to attain a goal.

A third advancement may be identified as the specification of conditions associated with different levels or degrees of mastery motivation. Addressing individual differences is distinct from charting ontogeny, yet each contributes to the validation of the mastery concept. Research has taken two directions: Group comparison studies have been done, evaluating children identified as atypical or at risk for developmental delays who are contrasted with normal children. These investigations have sought to validate the construct by its success in differentiating groups and to further our understanding of the behavioral characteristics of the groups in question. A second strategy has been to address individual differences within normal and atypical samples. These findings are basically correlational relationships. Particular attention has been directed to maternal behaviors that are thought to support or optimize mastery motivation, including provisioning the environment with interesting play materials and maternal responsiveness to the child's self-directed behavior. The latter focus upon maternal contingencies draws upon social learning principles and has highlighted the subtlety of distinctions between maternal intrusiveness and an optimal support for mastery behaviors.

Developmental studies in behavioral genetics have encouraged some shift in emphases on the relative significance of environmental vs. heritable factors affecting individual differences. Recent theorizing on mastery motivation also has addressed the possibility of it having an important genetic loading. This appears especially plausible when one views mastery motivation in an ethological perspective, a framework that often claims a biological underpinning to behavior and directs attention to its adaptive significance. Studies with designs sensitive to genetic variance, such as comparisons of identical twins, fraternal twins, natural siblings, and adoptive siblings, are needed to advance this area.

In speculating about the path that new mastery motivation research will take (or should take), one is reminded of the ancient Chinese saying: "Prophesy is very difficult, especially about the future." If concepts of mastery motivation are incorporated into more comprehensive developmental theory, and that would seem a fruitful course, one possibility will be an integration with cognitive theory.

Finding an alliance with cognitive theory would be consistent with one of the earliest research findings that sparked inquiry into the mastery area, that early individual differences in mastery motivation were moderately strong predictors of later cognitive attainment as reflected in IQ scores (Yarrow, Klein, Lomonaco, & Morgan, 1975). Intriguing though that result is, there is a conceptual basis for avoiding undue emphasis on an association with IQ for validation of the mastery construct. Bjorklund and Green (1992) have suggested a rationale that buttresses the meaningfulness of relative *independence* of early cognition and mastery motivation. Addressing the adaptive significance of early cognitive immaturity, they suggest that the young child's relative inability to make accurate appraisals of his or her cognitive abilities actually fosters persistence and a willingness to practice skills in situations where accurate cognitive appraisal might discourage them from doing so. "Children's self-perceptions of their efficacy, whether they are accurate or fanciful, serve to mediate action" (Bjorklund & Green, 1992, p. 47).

An alternative conceptual framework within which mastery

concepts may both contribute and find fresh thought is the ethological tradition and attachment theory. Seifer and Vaughn (this volume) offer some integration along these lines, although their perspective emphasizes a grander scheme they call the "organization of competence." Nonetheless, their analysis of points of contact between mastery motivation and attachment security is worthy of special attention.

Several lines of reasoning support this integration. One possible linkage with attachment theory derives from the idea that the major function of a secure attachment relationship is to facilitate independent and autonomous exploration of the environment. In other words, the attachment relationship is in the service of mastery motivation. Under conditions of threat, risk, anxiety, fatigue, separation, or other distress states, the attachment system is activated in the infant and contact with the nurturing figure is likely. From this secure base, a well-functioning attachment relationship soon facilitates affect regulation and a return to the kinds of environmental transactions that we call mastery behavior.

A second linkage is because mastery research has highlighted the significance of early self-appraisal processes. Jennings (1993) especially addressed the development of self-conceptions that play out in transactions with the environment. These ideas are very compatible with Bowlby's (1973) idea of the internal "working model" (p. 203), the self construction that one is confident of being a lovable person and able to adapt to environment challenges in a self-reliant manner. Bowlby sees these qualities as derivatives of a secure attachment relationship. A point of convergence between mastery motivation and attachment theory is that both speak to a sense of self-efficacy as an undergirding mental structure that fosters positive transactions with the larger environment.

Since the conceptual relatedness of attachment and mastery functioning is so plausible, why have statistical relationships between attachment classifications and mastery motivation been only slightly encouraging? One possibility is a methodological reason. In the study by Riksen-Walraven, Meij, van Roozendaal, and Koks (1993), 80% of the children were classified as having a secure attachment. This leaves little room for attachment variance to express itself. Moreover, the appraisal of mastery motivation was remote in time from the attachment assessment (a difference of 18 months); this also is likely to attenuate possible relationships.

Another methodological factor concerns the usual context for appraisal of mastery motivation. Measurement situations commonly involve the child in close proximity with the mother, who is also normally the child's primary attachment figure. This paradigm probably minimizes activation of the child's attachment system and that may mask or obscure psychologically important differences. If mastery tasks are given with the mother present and immediately available, it is possible that for much of the session each child is functionally the same as a child with a secure attachment. Perhaps associations between attachment classification and mastery motivation would emerge more clearly when the appraisal of mastery involves *mild* attachment activation as might occur when the mother is not immediately available. Strong activation, however, would likely suppress mastery engagements.

Another bridge between the attachment and mastery areas may relate to their overall measurement strategies. There may be a benefit in exploring whether qualitative classifications of children's involvement with mastery challenges is a useful measurement technique, just as the qualitative grouping of children into patterns of attachment security versus insecurity has proved useful. Although there is a long tradition in psychology that favors quantification of behaviors along discrete dimensions, it is possible that configurations or patterns of behavior are ultimately more useful. One such configuration might reflect the relative balance attained in engagement involving either social or object mastery challenges.

But enough of this obsessing about details! It is time to look at larger issues. This volume, then, brings the reader abreast of recent advances in the field of mastery motivation research. It was palpably exciting for me to review these developments, and I wish the reader a similarly positive experience.

REFERENCES

Bjorklund, D. F., & Green, B. L. (1992). The adaptive nature of cognitive immaturity. *American Psychologist, 47,* 46–53.

Bowlby, J. (1973). *Attachment and loss: Vol. 2, Separation.* New York: Basic Books.

Hunt, J. McV. (1961). Intelligence and experience. New York: Ronald Press.

Jennings, K. D. (1993). Mastery motivation and the formation of self-concept from infancy through early childhood. In D. J. Messer (Ed.), *Mastery motivation in early childhood: Development, measurement and social processes* (pp. 36–54). London: Routledge.

Morgan, G. A., Harmon, R. J., & Maslin-Cole, C. A. (1990). Mastery motivation: Definition and measurement. *Early Education and Development, 1,* 318–339.

Riksen-Walraven, M. J., Meij, H. T., van Roozendaal, J., Koks, J. (1993) Mastery motivation in toddlers as related to quality of attachment. In D. J. Messer (Ed.), *Mastery motivation in early childhood: Development, measurement and social processes* (pp. 189–204). London: Routledge.

Wenar, C. (1976). Executive competence in toddlers. *Genetic Psychology Monographs, 93,* 189–285.

White, R. W. (1959). Motivation reconsidered: The concept of competence. *Psychological Review, 66,* 297–333.

Yarrow, L. J., Klein, R., Lomonaco, S., & Morgan, G. (1975). Cognitive and motivational development in early childhood. In B. Z. Friedlander, G. M. Sterritt & G. E. Kirk, (Eds.), *Exceptional infant: Assessment and intervention* (pp. 491–502). New York: Bruner/Mazel.

1

MASTERY MOTIVATION: OVERVIEW, DEFINITIONS AND CONCEPTUAL ISSUES*

George A. Morgan
Colorado State University

Robert H. MacTurk
Gallaudet University

Elizabeth J. Hrncir
University of Virginia

The purpose in this chapter is to provide an overview and introduction to the area of research usually called mastery motivation, but sometimes referred to as effectance motivation, intrinsic motivation, or competence motivation. The chapter begins with a brief historical review of the area, then discusses several definitions of the concept, and concludes with a discussion of five questions or issues that recur throughout the book. These issues, which are first raised in the historical and definition sections, are:

1. What is the relationship between mastery motivation and competence; can/should they be differentiated?

*This chapter draws on parts of an article by G. A. Morgan, R. J. Harmon, and C. A. Maslin-Cole (1990) in a special issue of *Early Education and Development* edited by E. J. Hrncir and R. H. MacTurk. Special thanks are given to Harmon and Maslin-Cole for use of some of the ideas and organization of that article. We would also like to thank Karen Barrett for helpful, critical comments on several drafts of this chapter.

2. Are there developmental transformations in mastery motivation?

3. Is mastery motivation a useful construct in domains other than the usual object/toy task mastery?

4. Are both task persistence and task pleasure indexes of mastery motivation? Are there, in fact, many facets of mastery motivation which may not be highly interrelated?

5. What factors facilitate high mastery motivation in children?

HISTORICAL BACKGROUND

Effectance Motivation

White (1959) challenged psychologists to interpret behaviors such as curiosity, play, and exploration as being motivated by a need to have an effect on one's environment through self-initiated efforts. This effectance motivation was said to derive from children's intrinsic tendency to interact with the environment and to continually adapt. Effectance motivation was thought to be maintained by feelings of efficacy or pleasure that came from recognizing one's mastery of the physical and/or social environment. White (1959) said "the urge toward competence is inferred specifically from behavior that shows a lasting focalization and that has the characteristics of exploration and experimentation . . . selective, directed, and persistent" (p. 323).

White's writings produced theoretical insights on the topic of the motivation of children's behavior, but he did not attempt to assess effectance motivation in infants or children and he paid little attention to individual differences in motivation. His aim apparently was to convince psychologists that such a motive could be used to explain certain aspects of child and adult behavior better than the then dominant drive reduction theories, such as behaviorism and psychoanalysis.

The focus of most of the recent research on mastery motivation, discussed in this book, differs in several ways from White's discussion of effectance motivation. White emphasized the universality and intrinsic nature of this motivation; current research has focused on individual differences in and possible environmental effects on the young child's mastery motivation. However, Vondra (this volume) provides an interesting exception.

In the early 1970s, two separate groups of investigators, one led by Yarrow (e.g., Yarrow, Rubenstein, & Pedersen, 1975) and one by Harter (e.g., Harter and Zigler, 1974) attempted to translate White's conceptualization of effectance motivation into specific measures and hypotheses available for empirical research. We will return to Yarrow in the next section.

Harter's (e.g., 1978) research focused on school-age children, both delayed and nondelayed. She pointed out that White's concept of effectance motivation had great appeal, but little explanatory value given the breadth of behaviors he attempted to subsume. Early in her research, Harter demonstrated that mentally retarded children, who were assumed to be lower on effectance motivation, actually did score lower on four types of mastery motivation tasks than nondelayed children (Harter & Zigler, 1974). She also found that the delayed children smiled less, as predicted, after they had solved a puzzle, perhaps indicating that they had less sense of efficacy solving the problem than did nondelayed children (Harter, 1977). Some infant mastery motivation researchers (Harmon, Morgan, & Glicken, 1984; MacTurk, Hunter, McCarthy, Vietze, & McQuiston, 1985) have also considered task-related pleasure to be an important measure of mastery motivation. Issue 4, discussed later in this chapter, and Chapters 2 and 3 of this volume discuss several aspects and measures of mastery motivation.

Harter (1981) also developed a self-report instrument to assess intrinsic versus extrinsic motivation in the classroom. This instrument was one stimulus for the development of a some-what similar adult-report questionnaire used to assess several dimensions of the mastery motivation of toddlers and preschool-age children (see MacTurk, Morgan, & Jennings, this volume; Morgan et al., 1993).

Cognitive–Motivational Variables

The other main stimulus for research on mastery motivation was the study by Yarrow, Rubenstein, and Pedersen (1975) of the environment and functioning of 5½-month-old infants. These investigators were impressed by the motivational as well as cognitive aspects of infant behavior during various testing sessions. In a follow-up study of the same sample, Yarrow, Klein, Lomonaco, and Morgan, (1975) reported that early cognitive–motivational scores, such as manipulation of novel objects, predicted Stanford–Binet IQ at 3½ years; whereas, the early Bayley Mental Development Index did not. These findings suggested that understanding and measuring individual differences in infant motivation was important.

In part because his motivational scores were mostly derived from cognitive tests, Yarrow did not at this time use the term mastery motivation but spoke of cognitive–motivational variables. These included exploration, curiosity, preference for novelty, and goal-directed behaviors. Yarrow's implicit definition of the motivation involved was quite broad and similar to White's. In contrast to Harter, who studied school-aged children, Yarrow, like White, focused on infancy and early childhood.

Yarrow's View of Mastery Motivation

When Yarrow and his colleagues began to operationalize White's concept of effectance motivation, there had been considerable theoretical discussion but little empirical research about it, especially with infants. Extensive discussion and observation led Yarrow to a structured, test-like approach to measurement. This choice of methodology was based on a preference for direct observation, in contrast to maternal report, and on the observation that young infants displayed much more task-directed behavior in a structured situation than during free play. The construct measured became known as mastery motivation, in part because the situation posed tasks or problems for the infant to solve or master. The scores, however, focused on the process or motivation to master the task rather than the child's ability to solve it.

In this early research with infants (e.g., Yarrow, Morgan, Jennings, Harmon, & Gaiter, 1982; Yarrow et al., 1983), mastery motivation was operationally defined as the duration/amount of task-directed behavior during the presentation of a set of toys that posed challenging problems. The general procedure was to begin with the tester demonstrating how to use the toy in order to minimize differences due to experience or competence. Then the toy was given to the child who had the opportunity to play with it for 3 to 5 minutes with little interference or encouragement from the experimenter or mother.

The infant's behaviors during any given task were assumed to form a hierarchy from inattention to looking to mouthing and holding (which were considered to reflect exploration not mastery motivation) to task- and goal-directed behaviors (like trying to get a toy from behind a barrier or trying to put pieces in a puzzle) which were assumed to index mastery motivation. In these early studies of infants, the duration of such task-directed behaviors, called persistence, was the primary measure of mastery motivation. This is consistent with other theories of motivation which have pointed to persistence as the defining characteristic of motivated behavior (Atkinson, 1957; Feather, 1962; Weiner, Kun & Benesh-Weiner, 1980).

In the Yarrow et al. (1982, 1983) studies all children of a certain age were given the same tasks or problems. These tasks were intended to be challenging for the average child, but due to individual differences in children's abilities, the same task could be very hard for some children and easy for others. This led to the development of the individualized tasks discussed next.

Individually-Determined Challenging Tasks

Morgan, Busch-Rossnagel, Maslin-Cole and Harmon (1992) have developed a procedure that they feel deals well with the problem of controlling for cognitive differences between individuals and also makes longitudinal analysis more meaningful. This strategy involves the use of sets of similar tasks, each of which have several levels of difficulty. The child's motivation is assessed with one level of each set of tasks that is moderately difficult for him or her individually. Specifically, the level of the task is selected so that the child can and does successfully complete at least part of it, but does not finish all parts of the task too quickly. Thus, the level chosen for a given child is challenging but not so hard that partial completion is not possible. The child's persistence and pleasure at those moderately difficult tasks are the main measures of mastery motivation. More information on this method is provided in Chapter 2 of this volume.

An assumption of this individualized method is that the chosen tasks are equally difficult or challenging for each child. While this method was certainly a change in that direction, it would be very hard to meet or even test that assumption. In addition, as with the Yarrow et al. (1982, 1983) method and most standardized tests, social orientation or desire to please the tester may also influence the mastery motivation scores.

Executive Capacity

Belsky, Garduque and Hrncir (1984) developed a quite different approach to measuring mastery motivational called "executive capacity." Their measure is based on the difference or discrepancy between the highest level of play that can be elicited from an infant in a structured situation and the highest level the infant spontaneously displays during free play as measured by the Belsky and Most (1981) play scale. The less discrepancy between the elicited and spontaneous levels of play, the higher the child's executive capacity or motivation and vice versa. The rationale is that infants who are highly motivated for mastery are more likely to perform near their optimal level than infants who are less motivated (see also Vondra & Belsky, 1991). Belsky et al. (1984) found support for the construct validity of this measure; that is, securely-attached toddlers were more motivated to play near their optimal level.

The executive capacity measure has not yet been widely adopted by other researchers, but conceptually it would seem to warrant further study, in part because measures based on free play would appear to deal well with the influence of social orientation (toward the tester) on mastery motivation scores. Several authors (Castaldi, Hrncir, & Caldwell, 1990; Vondra & Belsky, 1991; Vondra, this volume) have pointed out that in free play situations the child is free to express his or her motivation without implicit or explicit social demands from the experimenter.

DEFINITIONS OF MASTERY MOTIVATION

Although psychologists have difficulty agreeing on a definition of motivation, most agree that motivation refers to a psychological force which moves one in a direction either toward or away from a goal (Kleinginna & Kleinginna, 1981). A general definition that encompasses many of the views described above and included later in this book is: Mastery motivation is a psychological force that originates without the need for extrinsic reward and leads an infant or young child to attempt to master tasks for the intrinsic feeling of efficacy rather than because of current reward. Typically, most mastery motivation researchers (see reviews by Messer, 1993; Morgan & Harmon, 1984; Morgan, Harmon, & Maslin-Cole, 1990; Yarrow & Messer, 1983) have focused on *persistent, task-directed behaviors* that could lead to the mastery of a task. These behaviors may or may not actually result in successful mastery or solving the task. Some investigators have also used *smiles* or other indications of *positive affect,* while the child is working at the task and/or immediately after the solution, as an index of feelings of efficacy and, thus, mastery motivation.

Morgan et al. (1990) proposed a definition of mastery motivation intended to distinguish the motive to *master* from broader concepts such as curiosity or effectance motivation (White, 1959). Morgan et al. (1990), focusing on moderate challenge, defined mastery motivation as a "psychological force that stimulates an individual to attempt independently, in a focused and persistent manner, to solve a problem or master a skill or task which is at least moderately challenging for him or her" (p. 319). This definition states that the task to be mastered must be challenging *to that individual* and it has led to the individualized assessment method previously mentioned and described in Chapter 2.

Barrett & Morgan (this volume) have broadened and expanded this definition to include a broader array of behaviors, in addition to persistence at tasks, as indexing an instrumental aspect of mastery motivation. They also include a number of expressive aspects, in addition to task pleasure.

Wachs & Combs (this volume) have broadened the definition of mastery motivation in a different way to include social mastery motivation, the motivation to master not just the inanimate environment but also the social environment.

FIVE KEY QUESTIONS OR ISSUES

Mastery Motivation Versus Cognitive Competence

The studies by Yarrow et al. (1982, 1983) of mastery motivation found significant, moderate correlations between mastery motivation scores and mental development indexes. It could be that these results indicate an inseparable relationship between cognition and motivation in infancy, as some investigators have suggested (Hrncir, Speller, & West, 1985; Ulvund, 1980; Yarrow & Messer, 1983). Other investigators argue that these results could be due to the way in which both mental development and mastery motivation had been measured (Morgan & Harmon, 1984; Vondra & Jennings, 1990). For example, several Bayley mental development items, such as how many cubes the child will put in a cup, have a clear motivational component. Conversely, if we give all children the same tasks (Yarrow et al., 1982, 1983) or weight the child's behaviors by the level of maturity shown (Hrncir, Speller, & West, 1985), mastery motivation scores are very likely to be influenced, perhaps artificially, by cognitive level. On the other hand, if a task is too difficult, the child may not understand what to do. Even when the child understands the task, if it is insoluble, prolonged attempts seem inappropriate. On the other hand, to persist at a task that is so simple that it is quickly mastered does not seem to reflect the motive to *master* the task. Even doing easy tasks may, however, provide the child with gratification and, thus, indicate some motive, if not mastery.

A variety of strategies, such as mental age matching, have been used to compensate for cognitive differences between groups when the mastery motivation of dissimilar ability groups has been compared. Even when groups are matched, the delayed children may "appear" to be lower on mastery motivation because the tasks were still too hard for *them,* not due to lower motivation per se. Two studies (Barrett, Morgan, & Maslin-Cole, 1993; Redding, Morgan, & Harmon, 1988) revealed that normally developing children, given sets of tasks that varied in difficulty, persist less at those tasks that are very difficult than at either moderately challenging or easy tasks. These findings support the use of an individualized procedure that provides each child with tasks that are moderately difficult for him or her (see Chapter 2, this volume; Morgan et al., 1992). The success of this approach depends, in part, on whether the selected tasks are really moderate in challenge and not too difficult for each child tested.

Morgan et al. (1990) assume that a child's mastery motivation is assessed most appropriately during tasks that are moderately difficult for him or her. However, it may also be necessary to examine persistence at very difficult tasks in order to get a complete picture. Perhaps the children most highly motivated for *mastery* are the ones who will try to solve tasks that are quite difficult for them as well as those that are moderately challenging. A study by Redding, Harmon, and Morgan (1990), which compared nondepressed and mildly depressed mothers, provided some support for this hypothesis. They found that children of these mildly depressed mothers tended to persist relatively less at tasks that were *very challenging* for them and showed less task competence and pleasure across all tasks. Conversely, the children of mildly depressed mothers persisted relatively more at tasks that were *easy* for them.

These findings may have resulted because depressed mothers are not able to provide an atmosphere conducive to the child engaging in mastery behaviors. Or, perhaps, the children of depressed mothers focus interest on easily achievable object-oriented play and avoid challenge. This latter hypothesis is consistent with the finding that infants who are avoidant of mother explore longer but *not* more maturely than non-avoidant infants (Harmon, Suwalsky, & Klein, 1979; Hron-Stewart, Lefever, & Weintraub, 1990).

Redding et al. (1988), like others (Yarrow et al., 1982), found that persistence at tasks and the Bayley MDI were moderately correlated at one year of age. However, at 24 and 36 months the correlations between persistence and IQ were not significant. This later finding is consistent with the Jennings, Connors, and Stegman (1988) study with preschoolers that found nonsignificant correlations between task persistence and IQ. Thus, it appears that the confounding of cognitive ability and persistence may be less of a issue with older toddlers and preschoolers.

In summary, this issue has been dealt with in a number of ways. One way is to acknowledge the typical relationship of cognitive development and mastery motivation measures in infancy, and then state that the concepts are overlapping and can/should not be separated. A somewhat different approach is taken by Seifer and Vaughn (this volume) who conceptualize mastery motivation as but one aspect of a broader concept of competence that includes cognition, attachment, and other aspects. On the other hand, most of the authors in this volume take the position, explicitly or implicitly, that mastery motivation is conceptually distinct from cognitive competence and that appropriate designs and measures should try to unconfound them.

Developmental Transitions in Mastery Motivation

A number of mastery motivation investigators, including Barrett and Morgan (this volume), Jennings (1993), Messer et al., (1986), Morgan and Harmon (1984), and Seifer and Vaughn (this volume), have each proposed somewhat similar transitions in mastery motivation as children develop.

The review by Barrett and Morgan (this volume) provides indirect evidence about continuity and change in mastery motivation. These authors postulate behavioral shifts in the second half of the first, the second, and the third years of life. Barrett and Morgan point out that there are also underlying continuities across these phases. Nevertheless, mastery related behaviors of six-month-olds are quite different from those of one-year-olds. In turn, mastery behaviors of one-year-olds are quite different from those of children around two or three years of age. For example, by 9 months, infants can more clearly determine which actions are task-appropriate. For this reason, to the adult-observer these look more task-directed. Another example is that by about a year and half, toddlers begin to be able to complete a series or sequence of steps in trying to solve problems and complete tasks.

In preschoolers, persistence when the behavior is highly stereotyped and repetitive may not reflect mastery motivation. Such highly repetitive persistence at easy tasks may well be tapping some other motivation, like need for approval, rather than the motive to master. However, Barrett, Morgan, and Maslin-Cole (study 1, 1993) and Piaget's writing (1936/1952) lead us to believe that repetition of a task in children around one year old (and younger) often should be characterized as mastery motivation.

Developmental change in mastery motivation is one of the themes of this book. It will be discussed more in a number of the later chapters.

Breadth of the Construct of Mastery Motivation

Most research on the mastery motivation of young children has dealt with attempts to master toys or other objects. The resulting scores might most accurately be called indexes of object-related mastery motivation.

Social Versus Object Mastery. Several researchers have noted that the typical mastery assessment situation pits social orientation against object orientation (Combs & Wachs, 1993; MacTurk et al., 1985; Maslin & Morgan, 1985; Vondra & Jennings, 1990; Wachs, 1987; Wachs and Combs, this volume). The mastery tasks have been designed to minimize social interaction of the infant with the tester and mother. Nevertheless, some children are clearly more motivated to interact with other people than with objects.

Maslin-Cole (Maslin & Morgan, 1985; Morgan, Maslin-Cole, Biringen, & Harmon, 1991) observed several patterns or styles that children showed when presented with mastery tasks. (Some showed high task persistence with the objects to the exclusion of interest in social interaction. For these children, affect tended to be flat or reflect intense engagement.) Other children, however, combined high persistence at object-oriented tasks with brief but recurrent distance interaction with their mothers and these social interactions across the room did not seem to detract from their mastery attempts, but rather seemed to enhance the child's pleasure and willingness to continue working at the task. While the first pattern (above) of high object orientation to the exclusion of social interaction is consistent with traditional views of high mastery motivation, the second pattern suggests an ability to coordinate two potentially competing orientations and could be seen as reflecting a different type or level of mastery motivation than high object orientation alone. (Still other children showed low independent interest in objects with moderate to high motivation for social interaction, especially proximity or contact seeking. Such children often appeared to be dependent and clingy and would traditionally be scored low on mastery motivation.)

However, as Wachs (1987; Wachs and Combs, this volume) has suggested, the strong and frequent social bids seen in the last pattern may reflect high social mastery motivation. (While this may be the case, the typical structured mastery tasks do not seem to provide a optimal setting for assessing social mastery motivation or comparing the relative strength of object mastery motivation and social mastery motivation.) It also seems possible that some of what Wachs called social mastery motivation is more akin to social referencing or to social orientation.

Morgan et al. (1993) have measured children's social mastery motivation with a scale of the Dimensions of Mastery Questionnaire (DMQ). This technique is discussed in Chapter 2 of this volume, and Morgan et al. (1993) provides an extensive review of studies using this questionnaire.

Gross Motor Mastery Motivation. Parent and teacher ratings (see Chapter 2, this volume; Morgan et al., 1993) and anecdotal observations of young children's play suggest that the gross motor domain should be added to the object and social domains of mastery motivation. Factor analyses of both parent and teacher ratings of toddler and preschooler persistence at a wide variety of types of play led Morgan et al. (1993) to conclude that there are three broad domains of this multidimensional construct: object oriented, social/symbolic, and gross motor mastery motivation. These domains of mastery motivation correspond roughly to Harter's (1981) academic, social, and athletic scales of perceived competence in older children.

Instrumental and Expressive Aspects of Mastery Motivation

Barrett and Morgan (Chapter 3, this volume) argue that indicators of mastery motivation can be categorized into two major types—"instrumental" and "expressive." There are a number of instrumental aspects of mastery motivation, such as the tendency to persist at tasks that are moderately difficult, preference for one's own physical and/or cognitive control over the environment, and preference for moderate challenge and/or novelty. There are also many expressive aspects of mastery motivation; for example, pleasure, interest, pride, frustration/anger, sadness, and shame depending on the child's developmental level.

Most infant mastery motivation researchers have focused on the instrumental aspects, especially task-directed persistence, as the *key* indicator, but Barrett and Morgan suggest that persistence alone provides an incomplete picture of the development of mastery motivation.

Task Persistence and Task Pleasure. One of the puzzling results of a number of mastery motivation studies is that the two most commonly used measures (persistence at tasks and positive affect during persistence or immediately after a solution) are usually found to be not at all or very modestly correlated. These results have been found using the tasks (Barrett et al., 1993, studies 2 and 3; Yarrow et al., 1982), using semistructured play (Morgan et al., 1991), and using the DMQ (e.g., Morgan et al., 1993).

It may well be that some highly-motivated children, perhaps especially older ones, are less likely to express their feelings of efficacy than other children. Thus, one finds a lack of correlation. However, expression of pleasure when solving a task may be a sufficient, if not necessary, indicator of mastery motivation. Barrett and Morgan (this volume) have argued that mastery motivation is a multifaceted concept and that the facets are not necessarily interrelated.

Table 1.1 presents a conceptual diagram intended to help the reader organize much of the material in this and in later chapters. The table indicates, as previously described in issues 3 and 4, that measures of mastery motivation fall into two main aspects (instrumental and expressive) and that there seem to be three domains (object, social, and gross motor) or types of mastery motivation. A footnote to the table indicates how it could be expanded to include issues 1 and 2.

Determinants of Mastery Motivation

What factors seem to facilitate or depress mastery motivation in children? In contrast to the preceding four issues, this question and all of the chapters in the middle section of this book deal extensively with topics related to factors that influence individual differences in mastery motivation.

Recent research, as summarized in this volume, has produced hypotheses about some of the factors that influence a child's

TABLE 1.1.   PROPOSED ORGANIZATION OF THREE DOMAINS AND TWO ASPECTS OF MASTERY MOTIVATION IN INFANTS AND TODDLERS

Domains of Mastery Motivation	Aspects/Indicators of Mastery Motivation	
	Instrumental Aspects	Expressive Aspects
Mastery of:		
a) The Inanimate Environment (Object Mastery Motivation)		
b) The Social Environment (Social Mastery Motivation)		
c) Physical Skills (Gross Motor Mastery Motivation)		

Note. By contrasting the instrumental aspects of mastery motivation with the young child's competence or skill in each of the domains, this table could be broadened to subsume issue/question 1, distinguishing between motivation and competence. Likewise, by adding layers to the table, it could be expanded to indicate the developmental transitions/phases mentioned in issue 2 above and discussed in Barrett and Morgan (this volume).

mastery motivation (see especially the review by Busch-Ross-nagel et al., this volume). For example, intrusive parental behavior seems to inhibit a child's later independent attempts to persist at and obtain pleasure from working on difficult tasks (Harmon et al., 1984; Sarimski, 1992). In addition, children of mildly depressed mothers seem to prefer easy tasks and show less pleasure at tasks (Redding et al., 1990). Another study found that the affective or emotional quality of exchanges between mothers and infants predicted the child's mastery motivation both at the same age and two years later (Morgan et al., 1993). If mother and child showed a lot of mutually positive affective exchanges, the child was likely to be high on both task persistence and pleasure at 18 months and to remain high on persistence at 3 years. Affectively mixed interactions, where mother and infant displayed opposite emotions, seem to lead to low independent attempts to master at 3 years. When the mother–infant pair had a relatively high frequency of negative exchanges, the child was rated as less persistent and competent at 3 years.

Child behavior problems such as hyperactivity and social withdrawal can be predicted from *low* parental ratings of aspects of mastery (Morgan et al., 1993). That is, hyperactivity is related to low persistence ratings on the DMQ, and early indications of childhood depression are related to low ratings of mastery pleasure.

The question of what factors appear to facilitate or inhibit the expression and development of mastery motivation is one raised in several of the following chapters and is, thus, a recurrent theme in the book. The book also includes three chapters about mastery motivation in special groups: those with sensory deficits (Jennings & MacTurk), those born prematurely (Harmon & Murrow), and those with developmental delays (Hupp). One chapter focuses on interventions (Hauser-Cram & Shonkoff) and one (Vondra) points out that genetic and confounding factors may lead to misinterpretations of the results of these studies.

CONCLUSION

For about 20 years, empirical researchers have been investigating mastery motivation in infancy and early childhood. Over this time, answers to the five questions raised at the beginning of the chapter have begun to emerge. The remaining chapters in this book provide literature reviews and analyses of these and other conceptual and methodological issues. What is known about antecedents, correlates and outcomes of mastery motivation are also described and analyzed.

REFERENCES

Atkinson, J. W. (1957). Motivational determinants of risk taking behavior. *Psychological Review, 64,* 359–372.

Barrett, K. C., Morgan, G. A., & Maslin-Cole, C. (1993). Three studies on the development of mastery motivation in infancy and toddlerhood. In D. Messer (Ed.), *Mastery motivation in early childhood: Development, measurement, and social processes* (pp. 83–108). London: Routledge.

Belsky, J., Garduque, L., & Hrncir, E. (1984). Assessing performance, competence, and executive capacity in infant play: Relations to home environment and security of attachment. *Developmental Psychology, 20,* 406–417.

Belsky, J., & Most, R. K. (1981). From exploration to play: A cross sectional study of infant free-play behavior. *Developmental Psychology, 17,* 630–639.

Castaldi, J., Hrncir, E. J., & Caldwell, C. B. (1990). Future models for the study of individual differences in motivation during infancy. *Early Education and Development, 1,* 385–393.

Combs, T., & Wachs, T. D. (1993). The construct validity of measures of social mastery motivation. In D. Messer (Ed.), *Mastery motivation in early childhood: Development, measurement, and social processes* (pp. 168–185). London: Routledge.

Feather, N. T. (1962). The study of persistence. *Psychological Bulletin, 59,* 94–115.

Harmon, R. J., Morgan, G. A., & Glicken, A. D. (1984). Continuities and discontinuities in affective and cognitive–motivational development. *International Journal of Child Abuse and Neglect, 8,* 157–167.

Harmon, R. J., Suwalsky, J., & Klein, R. P. (1979). Infants' preferential response for mother versus an unfamiliar adult: Relationship to attachment, *Journal of the American Academy of Child Psychiatry, 18,* 437–449.

Harter, S. (1977). The effects of social reinforcement and task difficulty level on the pleasure derived by normal and retarded children from cognitive challenge and mastery. *Journal of Experimental Child Psychology, 24,* 476–494.

Harter, S. (1978). Effectance motivation reconsidered. *Human Development, 21,* 34–64.

Harter, S. (1981). A model of mastery motivation in children: Individual differences and developmental change. In W. A. Collins (Ed.), *The Minnesota symposium on child psychology: Vol. 14. Aspects of the development of competence* (pp. 215–255). Hillsdale, NJ: Erlbaum.

Harter, S., & Zigler, E. (1974). The assessment of effectance motivation in normal and retarded children. *Developmental Psychology, 10,* 169–180.

Hrncir, E. J., Speller, G. M., & West, M. (1985). What are we testing? *Developmental Psychology, 21,* 226–232.

Hron-Stewart, K., Lefever, G. B., Weintraub, D. (1990, April). *Correlates of mastery motivation: Relations to mother–child problem solving, temperament, attachment and home environment.* Poster presented at the 7th International Conference on Infant Studies, Montreal, Canada.

Jennings, K. D. (1993). Mastery motivation and the formation of self-concept from infancy through early childhood. In D. J. Messer (Ed.), *Mastery motivation in early childhood: Development, measurement and social processes* (pp. 36–54). London: Routledge.

Jennings, K. D., Connors, R. E., & Stegman, C. E. (1988). Does a physical handicap alter the development of mastery motivation during the preschool years? *Journal of the American Academy of Child and Adolescent Psychiatry, 27,* 312–317.

Kleinginna, P. R. Jr., & Kleinginna, A. M. (1981). A categorized list of motivation definitions, with a suggestion for a consensual definition. *Motivation and Emotion, 5* (3), 263–278.

MacTurk, R., Hunter, F., McCarthy, M., Vietze, P., & McQuiston, S. (1985). Social mastery motivation in Down syndrome and nondelayed infants. *Topics in Early Childhood Special Education, 4,* 93–109.

Maslin, C. A., & Morgan, G. A. (1985, April). *Measures of social competence: Toddlers social and object orientation during mastery tasks.* Presented at the Biennial Meeting of the Society for Research in Child Development, Toronto, Canada.

Messer, D. J. (1993). *Mastery motivation in early childhood: Development, measurement, and social processes.* London: Routledge.

Messer, D. J., McCarthy, M. E., McQuiston, S., MacTurk, R. H., Yarrow, L. J., & Vietze, P. M. (1986). Relation between mastery behavior in infancy and competence in early childhood. *Developmental Psychology, 22,* 336–372.

Morgan, G. A., Busch-Rossnagel, N. A., Maslin-Cole, C. A., & Harmon, R. J. (1992). *Mastery motivation tasks: Manual for 15- to 36-month-old children.* New York: Fordham University, Psychology Department.

Morgan, G. A., & Harmon, R. J. (1984). Developmental transformations in mastery motivation: Measurement and validation. In R. N. Emde and R. J. Harmon (Eds.), *Continuities and discontinuities in development* (pp. 263–291). New York: Plenum.

Morgan, G. A., Harmon, R. J., & Maslin-Cole, C. A. (1990). Mastery motivation: Definition and measurement. *Early Education and Development, 1* (5), 318–339.

Morgan, G. A., Harmon, R. J., Maslin-Cole, C. A., Busch-Rossnagel, N. A., Jennings, K. D., Hauser-Cram, P., & Brockman, L. M. (1993). Parent and teacher perceptions of young children's mastery motivation: Assessment and review of research. In D. Messer (Ed.), *Mastery motivation in early childhood: Development, measurement, and social processes* (pp. 109–131). London: Routledge.

Morgan, G. A., Maslin-Cole, C. A., Biringen, Z., & Harmon, R. J. (1991). Play assessment of mastery motivation in infants and young children. In C. E. Schaefer, K. Gitlin and A. Sandgrund (Eds.), *Play diagnosis and assessment* (pp. 65–86). New York: John Wiley & Sons.

Piaget, J. (1952). *The origins of intelligence in children* (M. Cook, Trans.) New York: International Universities Press. (Original work published 1936.)

Redding, R. E., Harmon, R. J., & Morgan, G. A. (1990). Maternal depression and infants' mastery behaviors, *Infant Behavior and Development, 13*, 391–395.

Redding, R. E., Morgan, G. A., & Harmon, R. J. (1988). Mastery motivation in infants and toddlers: Is it greatest when tasks are moderately challenging? *Infant Behavior and Development, 11*, 419–430.

Sarimski, K. (1992). Ausdauer bei zielgerichteten Tatigkeiten und mutterliche Strategien in der Interaktion mit behinderten Kindern. [Persistence of intentional actions and maternal intervention style in mentally retarded children]. *Psychol., Erz., Unterr., 39.* Jg., S. 170–178.

Ulvund, S. E. (1980). Cognition and motivation in early infancy: An interactionist approach. *Human Development, 23*, 17–32.

Vondra, J. I., & Belsky, J. (1991). Infant play as a window on competence and motivation. In C. Schaefer, K. Gitlin, & A. Sandgrund (Eds.), *Play diagnosis and assessment* (pp. 11–38). New York: Wiley.

Vondra, J. I., & Jennings, K. D. (1990). Infant mastery motivation: The issue of discriminant validity. *Early Education and Development, 1*, 340–353.

Wachs, T. D. (1987). Specificity of environmental action as manifest in environmental correlates of infant's mastery motivation. *Developmental Psychology, 23*, 782–790.

Weiner, B., Kun, A., & Benesh-Weiner, M. (1980). The development of mastery, emotions, and morality from an attributional perspective. In W. A. Collins (Ed.), *Minnesota symposium on child psychology* (Vol. 14 pp. 137–202) Hillsdale, NJ: Erlbaum.

White, R. W. (1959). Motivation reconsidered: The concept of competence. *Psychological Review, 66*, 297–333.

Yarrow, L. J., McQuiston, S., MacTurk, R. H., McCarthy, M. E., Klein, R. P., & Vietze, P. M. (1983). Assessment of mastery motivation during the first year of life. Contemporaneous and cross-age relationships. *Developmental Psychology, 19,* 159–171.

Yarrow, L. J., & Messer, D. J. (1983). Motivation and cognition in infancy. In M. Lewis (Ed.), *Origins of intelligence (2nd ed.)* (pp. 451–477). Hillsdale, NJ: Erlbaum.

Yarrow, L. J., Morgan, G. A., Jennings, K. D., Harmon, R. J., & Gaiter, J. L. (1982). Infant's persistence at tasks: Relationships to cognitive functioning and early experience. *Infant Behavior and Development, 5,* 131–142.

Yarrow, L. J., Klein, R., Lomonaco, S., & Morgan, G. (1975). Cognitive and motivational development in early childhood. In B. Z. Friedlander, G. M. Sterritt, and G. E. Kirk, (Eds.), *Exceptional infant: Assessment and intervention.* (pp. 491–502). New York: Bruner/ Mazel.

Yarrow, L. J., Rubenstein, J. L., & Pedersen, F. A. (1975). *Infant and environment: Early cognitive and motivational development.* Washington, DC: Hemisphere, Halsted, Wiley.

2

THE ASSESSMENT OF MASTERY MOTIVATION IN INFANTS AND YOUNG CHILDREN

Robert H. MacTurk

Gallaudet University

George A. Morgan

Colorado State University

Kay D. Jennings

University of Pittsburgh

OVERVIEW

From the 1970s onward, there has been continuing research directed toward the selection and development of suitable procedures for the measurement of mastery motivation in young children. This research was begun by Leon Yarrow and his colleagues at the National Institute of Child Health and Human Development (NICHHD). It has been continued after Yarrow's death by MacTurk, Vietze, and others in Washington, DC, by Morgan, Harmon, and others in Colorado, by Jennings and others in Pittsburgh, and by other investigators throughout the world.

In 1984, Morgan and Harmon reviewed the research methods and findings up to that point. They summarized the evidence for the reliability and validity of the mastery tasks, which had been presented to infants and young children in a structured test-like situation (Jennings, Yarrow, & Martin, 1984; Yarrow et al., 1983; Yarrow, Morgan, Jennings, Harmon, & Gaiter, 1982). Further developments in mastery task selection, procedures, and scoring have taken place in the last decade (Jennings, Conners, & Stegman, 1988; MacTurk, Hunter, McCarthy, Vietze, & McQuiston, 1985; Morgan, Harmon, & Maslin-Cole, 1990; Wachs, 1987). These reports have shown sufficiently high levels of interrater agreement to ensure confidence in the reliability of the measures and have provided support for the construct validity of the task persistence scores.

In addition to tasks, a number of researchers have used free or semistructured play assessments to obtain somewhat similar motivational measures (e.g., Belsky, Garduque, & Hrncir, 1984; Hrncir, Speller, & West, 1985; Jennings, Harmon, Morgan, Gaiter, & Yarrow, 1979; Morgan, Maslin-Cole, Biringen, & Harmon, 1991). Belsky's procedure is quite different from the others in that it uses both free play and a structured setting to derive the motivational measure executive capacity.

Finally, Morgan and several colleagues have broadened the scope of mastery motivation measures to include a questionnaire assessment of several aspects of parent and teacher perceptions of young children's motivation. Data from 30 samples of 1- to 5-year-old children assessed with the questionnaire are summarized in a manual and review chapter (Morgan et al., 1992, 1993).

Thus, three major forms of mastery motivation assessments (structured tasks, free play, and questionnaire) have been developed and are currently used in research and clinical settings. In this chapter, we will describe examples of these approaches and what is known about their psychometric properties beyond interobserver reliability, which has been quite high in each study.

ASSESSING MASTERY MOTIVATION WITH STRUCTURED TASKS

We have divided discussion of the mastery tasks into three main types by age: for infants, toddlers, and preschoolers. For each age group, we have provided an extended description of the method used most frequently in available publications and presentations. While there are variations both within and between these three types of mastery task methods, the procedures and scoring codes have been relatively similar, except for the increasing complexity of the tasks with age.

Tasks for 6- and 12-Month-Old Infants

Yarrow, Rubenstein and Pedersen's (1975) study was the stimulus for the development of the mastery task methods. They assessed six-month-old infants' cognitive-motivational functioning as indexed by attempts to explore and master the environment, using items from the Bayley Scales of Infant Development, some additional measures of problem solving behavior, and a structured task designed to assess exploratory behavior and preference for a novel stimuli. The cognitive–motivational measures that were derived from these tasks could be predicted from early social stimulation and from responsiveness of objects in the home.

These findings were a stimulus to speculations about the role of early experience and the development of the motivation to master the environment (Yarrow & Pedersen, 1976). The findings seemed to suggest that mastery motivation could be assessed as early as six months, and that it was affected by the home environment. Moreover, early mastery motivation was a better predictor of 3½-year-old IQ than early infant mental indexes such as the Bayley MDI (Yarrow, Klein, Lomonaco, & Morgan, 1975).

Since there were no instruments for assessing infants' attempts to master the environment in the mid-seventies, Yarrow et al. (1982) began to develop procedures for assessing mastery motivation from an individual differences perspective and to examine the construct validity of these motivational measures. Several approaches to operationalizing mastery motivation were considered; however, it was decided to focus primarily on a structured situation. After pretesting a number of tasks, 11 were chosen that seemed to be interesting and challenging for one-year-olds and that were sensitive to individual differences. The tasks were presented in a standardized manner, with limited social interaction and encouragement from the experimenter so that the infant's own motivation to master the task could be observed. However, to give the child some framework and reduce differences due to the ability to understand the task, the relevant properties of the task were demonstrated and general instructions such as "make it work," or "now you try it" were given as each object was presented.

The primary measure of mastery motivation was *task persistence*, the percentage of time during each task that the child was engaged in task directed behaviors. These behaviors included all attempts, even if not successful, to produce the effect, combine the objects, or secure the goal. This measure—persistence at tasks—was based on general theories of motivation (Atkinson, 1957; Hunt, 1965; Piaget, 1952) and observations of infant behavior during the administration of standardized developmental assessments (Yarrow et al., 1975).

Task persistence has long been an index of motivation (Tolman, 1932). More recently, Atkinson (1957), Feather, (1962), and Weiner, Kun, and Benesh-Weiner (1980), have pointed to persistence as the defining characteristic of motivated behavior. It was assumed that the duration of attempts to solve a task was a valid index of mastery motivation. Looking at the toy and generalized exploratory behaviors such as touching, mouthing, and banging a toy were not scored as task-directed and thus did not count as persistence. Success, or task completion, was also not included in the persistence score as it is considered to index competence and not motivation.

The first NICHHD mastery motivation investigation yielded a number of significant findings, described in detail in Yarrow et al. (1982), Jennings et al. (1979), and Gaiter, Morgan, Jennings, Harmon, and Yarrow (1982). The results of this study indicated that it was possible to develop reliable measures of task directedness that were meaningfully related to other behavioral variables and to differences in environmental stimulation. However, the study also raised a number of psychometric questions about the tasks and measures that called for further study.

Next, Yarrow et al. (1983) refined the tasks and procedures mentioned above. Sixty-seven middle-class parents with their firstborn infants participated when their infants were 6- and 12-months old. At each age, the infants were seen in a laboratory setting three times. During the first visit, the Bayley Scales of Infant Development was administered. The next two visits were comprised of mastery motivation assessments—a battery of 12 tasks, six of which were presented during one visit and six during the other. The six tasks in each set were presented in a fixed order for three minutes each and included two tasks that tapped the three conceptual clusters of Problem Solving (PS),

Practicing Sensorimotor Skills (PSS), and Effect Production (EP). The two sets of tasks were counterbalanced by the child's sex and age, both to control for possible order effects and to permit assessments of parallel forms reliability.

The specific tasks at each age were selected during pilot testing for their ability to maintain the child's interest and to present a developmentally appropriate problem that reflected skills tapped by the three conceptual clusters. The Problem Solving cluster of tasks included a variety of situations in which an object was located out of direct reach of the infant, but within view. For the 6-month-olds, one of the problem solving tasks consisted of an attractive toy that was placed behind a clear plastic barrier. The toy could be obtained by reaching around with either hand. At 12 months, a child would be presented with a large box that had a clear plastic sliding barrier behind which a toy was placed. The child could only obtain the object by reaching around with one hand; once the object was obtained, the position of the plastic barrier was changed, so on the next trial, the child was required to use the other hand.

Effect Production tasks were those in which infants could produce an effect by their own actions. At six months, one of the EP tasks consisted of an Activity Center in which a variety of effects could be produced by turning knobs, spinning wheels, or pushing levers. The 12-month old infants were presented with a Surprise Box consisting of a series of levers, buttons and slides that released brightly colored, Sesame Street figures from under pop-up panels.

The Practicing Sensorimotor Skills cluster consisted of tasks that required the infants to coordinate perceptual and fine motor skills. An example of one of the items from the assessment at six months was a tub that contained three plastic figures. The infant's task was to remove the figures. The similar task at 12 months required the infant to remove and replace pegs in a boat.

Each mastery motivation assessment session was videotaped from behind a one-way mirror. These videotapes were subsequently coded using a Datamyte (TM) (Manufactured by Electro-General Corporation, Minnetonka, MN). The onset of each behavior change was keyed into the Datamyte while an internal clock automatically appended the time to the stored code. The resulting data set represented a time-based, sequential record of the infant's actions during the mastery motivation assessment session.

The mastery motivation coding system was divided into three general categories designed to capture the full range of an infant's behavior during a task:

1. *Object Codes:* Behaviors that were directed toward the toy.
2. *Social Codes:* Behaviors that were directed toward the mother or examiner.
3. *Affect Codes:* The infant's facial expressions of emotional state (smiling, fussing, interest, etc.).

The coding system was designed to permit simultaneous recording of any combination of behaviors in the three categories. As a rule, no two behaviors within a category can happen at the same time but may co-occur between categories; for example, in the social codes, a baby cannot look at mother and look at examiner at the same time (two social codes), but may explore the object and smile at the same time (one object and one affect code). The actual coding was performed at the individual behavior level and combined during the initial data-processing phase to yield summary measures for each toy. The durations of each coded event were summed across the full three minutes of toy presentation; then the average across the four toys in each cluster was computed to yield the measures reported here. In addition, summary scores were computed by taking the average across all of the tasks.

The measures included: (a) *Visual Attention* that consisted of only looking at the object, (b) *Exploration* that consisted of both passive (holding, touching, mouthing) and active (hitting, shaking, banging) exploration, and (c) *Persistence,* which was the primary measure of mastery motivation, and included task-related and goal-directed activities. These were behaviors that were either directed toward specific properties of the toy or directed toward mastering the toy. Several additional variables were formed that tapped the infants' lack of interest in the toys (Off-task), eagerness to engage the toy (Latency), and positive affect.

The object-related measures were considered to represent a hierarchy of Visual Attention, Exploration, and Persistence, ordered in relation to the degree of skill and goal directedness required of the infant. For example, exploring the Discovery Cottage (a 12-month toy) included such behaviors as mouthing one of the dolls, banging or pushing the cottage, or holding the object while looking at the examiner. The task-related and goal-directed behaviors, on the other hand, consisted of activities which were related to the design of the toy and directed toward a possible solution. Examples of these include attempts to open the door or roof (behind which are small dolls visible through windows), opening and closing the door or roof, or attempting to place a doll in its original position.

In a related series of analyses, the data from the 6- to 12-month study and data obtained from a parallel study of infants with Down syndrome were examined from a lag sequential perspective. This analysis draws upon White's (1959) suggestion that the element of direction is an important aspect of motivation an aspect that he described as "constantly circling from stimulus to perception to effect" (p. 322). The results of these analyses, discussed in greater detail in MacTurk, Vietze, McCarthy, McQuiston, and Yarrow (1985) MacTurk, McCarthy, Vietze, and Yarrow (1987), provide further support for the validity of the Yarrow mastery assessment model and are discussed later in this chapter.

Internal Consistency. A major goal of the Yarrow et al. (1983) mastery research was to formalize the assessment procedures and introduce some psychometric rigor into this model. As was mentioned above, the 12 objects were split into two sets of six toys with each set being presented at one of the two laboratory visits conducted within the two weeks before or after the infants' 6- and 12-month birthdays. Both sets contained two toys from each of the conceptual (EP, PS, and PSS) clusters. The following section presents the results of the reliability analysis for the three conceptual clusters at each age and the internal consistency reliability estimates for the test battery as a whole.

These results suggest that reliance on the individual clusters of mastery motivation is not supported by the data. Part of the reason for this is the small number of items (four) in each scale, a problem further compounded by the parallel forms analysis, which reduces each data point to two items. We, therefore, expected that such a scale would not demonstrate reliability figures approaching formal psychometric standards. The full-scale reliabilities are comparatively better than the component estimates; again, this increase is to be expected given the increased number of items that make up the overall mastery motivation score. This contention is particularly true for the 6-month data. At the younger age, the separate reliabilities (alphas) range from .27 to .43 with an overall reliability of .53. This latter reliability estimate implies that, at 6 months, mastery motivation is either highly differentiated or was not assessed reliably.

In contrast, the 12-month results offer some support for Yarrow's (Yarrow et al., 1983) conceptual clusters. Practicing Sensorimotor Skills demonstrated a reliability of .69, a coefficient that was greater than either of the remaining clusters or the full scale reliability. Evidence for a discrete sensorimotor component of mastery motivation is presented in the next series of analyses which examined the data from a factor analytic perspective.

Principal Components Analysis. This series of analyses examined the data in an effort to uncover the presence of discrete and interpretable components of mastery motivation. At each age, the 12 measures of task persistence were subjected to a Principal Components Factor Analysis (PCA) with orthogonal rotation. Preliminary analyses and an examination of the scree plots indicated the presence of five principal components with eigenvalues greater than 1 at each age. In subsequent analyses, the number of factors to be extracted was set to three to conform to the original conceptualization.

At six months, the three factor solution produced no interpretable results within the original conceptualization of mastery motivation. The first principal component contained five tasks, of which three were from the Effect Production (EP) component, one from the Problem Solving (PS), component and one from the Practicing Sensorimotor Skills (PSS) component. The next two principal components offered an equally mixed solution. This suggests that, while 6-month-old infants are motivated to engage with and learn about objects in their near environment, they do not display the more sophisticated organization and understanding of differential task demands that they exhibit 6 months later.

The three factor solution at 12 months yielded an interpretable first principal component that suggested the presence of a Practicing Sensorimotor Skills (PSS) cluster. Further analyses were conducted in an attempt to increase the interpretability of the three factor solution. A 2 factor solution yielded a first principal component that contained all four PSS tasks in the original Yarrow conceptualization. The second principal component contained one task from the PSS cluster and two from the EP cluster. Though this second component is empirically linked, there is no underlying conceptual justification for accepting this as representing a discrete aspect of mastery motivation.

As was to be expected, this latter set of analyses confirms and extends our results of the reliability analysis. The reliabilities for the 6-month clusters were uniformly low, and these low reliabilities are reflected in the absence of interpretable results from the PCA. A clearer picture emerges regarding the structure of mastery motivation at 12 months; of the three conceptual clusters, only the PSS cluster was confirmed by this series of analyses. With regard to Morgan and Harmon's (1984) admonition concerning the meaning of the 6-month mastery assessment, it appears that, at this age, infants' interactions with objects, while exhibiting a goal-directed quality consistent with traditional theories of motivated behavior, do not consistently tap the hypothesized discrete functional domains.

Validity.   Three approaches to addressing the validity of the mastery motivation assessment model were adopted. In the first approach, a small sample of 8- and 12-month old infants with Down syndrome (DS) were recruited to validate the mastery motivation assessments. This validation approach rests on the assumption that the measures of mastery motivation can reliably discriminate between groups of infants with known characteristics. The detection of group differences will serve as presumptive evidence for the validity of the system (Matkin, 1986).

Infants with Down syndrome are of interest because they provide the opportunity to test the validity of developmental constructs for which no formal, external performance criteria exist (Berger & Cunningham, 1981; Morgan & Harmon, 1984). Infants with Down syndrome are etiologically homogeneous and their condition is detectable at birth; this makes the monitoring of their developmental processes open to empirical inquiry virtually from the beginning. Down syndrome infants are also quite heterogeneous in terms of their physical development and intellectual functioning. Thus, by including this group of infants, who are expected to display performance decrements, and comparing them to a group of infants functioning in the normal range, support for the validity of the mastery motivation construct may be strengthened. (an analogous strategy has been employed in the development of psychodiagnostic assessments; Butcher & Keller, 1984).

Vietze, McCarthy, McQuiston, MacTurk, and Yarrow (1983) found that a sample of age-matched 6-month-old DS infants attended visually to objects for a significantly longer time prior to actively exploring them when compared to normally developing infants—a finding consistent with previous reports (Lewis & Brooks-Gunn, 1984; Miranda & Fantz, 1974). However, once physical contact was established, the DS infants displayed a similar distribution of exploratory and persistent, goal-directed behaviors, but at depressed levels. That is, their performance paralleled their nondelayed peers in terms of the relative proportions of time spent engaged with the tasks.

MacTurk, Hunter et al. (1985) investigated the relationships between object-related and socially-directed activities in a sample of 11 Down syndrome infants and 11 normally developing (ND) infants matched on cognitive level. The results suggested that the ND infants seemed to coordinate and integrate behaviors that reflect several different motivational domains and appeared to generalize more widely than the DS infants what they learn from one type of experience to other experiences. Furthermore, the amount of time the Down syndrome infants spent engaged with the toys was significantly related to their developmental level.

A second approach to examining the validity of the mastery task scores examined the sequences of the infants' behavior with the objects. This analysis tested the hypothesis that the infants would display a pattern of actions consistent with White's (1959) contention that motivated behavior is directional, in addition to persistent, and offers convergent evidence for the methods presented here. MacTurk, McCarthy, Vietze, and Yarrow (1987) found that, at both 6- and 12-months of age, infants focus their manipulative activities in a direction that leads them to the goal of successful task completion. First, there were significant transitions to and from behaviors defined as persistence and those defined as success. Second, the lack of direct paths to success from the other, less sophisticated, indices of motivated behavior supports the notion that mastery motivation may be characterized by direction in addition to persistence.

Evidence from an examination of the occurrence of positive affect lends further support to the concept of mastery motivation. At both 6 and 12 months, positive affect followed persistent, goal-directed attempts to solve the task significantly more than affect followed any of the other behaviors. White (1959) suggested that motivated behavior is maintained by positive feelings of efficacy. To the extent that these positive feelings of efficacy are accurately indexed by the frequency of positive affect, one would expect laughing and smiling to be associated with persistence more than with looking, exploration, or even success, an expectation supported by the data.

Further lag-sequential analyses addressed the patterns of mastery behavior in the sample of DS and ND infants reported on earlier (MacTurk, Vietze et al., 1985). The results found striking similarities in the manner in which DS and ND infants mastered the tasks. The overall pattern of similarities and differences suggested that social behaviors were a salient element in the attempts to master objects, regardless of infant status, but that visual attention to the objects appeared to have a different psychological meaning for the two groups.

This series of reports provides evidence for the validity of the mastery assessment model. The performance of the Down syndrome infants was systematically depressed in all measures of object engagement. They also displayed less diversity in their behavior when confronted with the competing demands of object and social activities. Thus, we see from the above reports using the 6 and 12 month tasks that the measures of mastery motivation are sensitive to individual and age differences, display a predictable pattern of changes in developmental function, and are susceptible to environmental influences (McCarthy & McQuiston, 1983; Yarrow et al., 1983, 1984). The results of the Down syndrome study add to our confidence in the task method because it detected predicted group differences.

A third approach is evidence supporting the construct validation of the persistence at tasks measure by significant correlations with other similar measures. For example, Yarrow et al. (1982) found that individual differences in persistence on the mastery tasks were significantly correlated with an independent tester's ratings of persistence during a Bayley examination at another session. Task-directed free play can also be viewed as a reflection of the infant's interest in mastering the environment. Jennings et al. (1979) found that continuity of play, which is somewhat analogous to persistence, showed significant relationships to persistence at the mastery motivation tasks. Likewise, Morgan, Culp, Busch-Rossnagel, Barrett, and Redding (1993) found significant relationships between the amount of goal-directed free play and task persistence at both 9 and 12 months of age. As predicted, significant relationships have been found between mothers' ratings of their children's persistence and the children's persistence score on a set of mastery tasks (Fung, 1984; Morgan et al., 1993; Morgan, Harmon, Pipp, & Jennings, 1983).

Validity of Task Pleasure.   This measure seems important, but the behavior is relatively rare and not well understood. Correlations between task pleasure and task persistence have typically been found to be low (Barrett, Morgan, & Maslin-Cole, 1993; Redding, Morgan, & Harmon, 1988). Mastery pleasure would seem to be conceptually, if not empirically, related to mastery motivation because it is an index of the child's pleasure during the process of attempting to master tasks. More discussion of mastery pleasure is found later in this chapter under Affect Measures.

The Individualized, Moderately Challenging Task Method

After pilot testing and preliminary use in several studies, Morgan, Busch-Rossnagel, Maslin-Cole, and Harmon (1992), described three sets of tasks (puzzles, shape sorters, and cause-and-effect toys) for 15- to 36-month-old children. Each set has six tasks that vary in level of difficulty from the easiest, which is challenging for 15-month-olds, to the hardest, which is challenging for most 36-month-olds. Each specific task has a number of parts (partial solutions) to put together or figure out in order for the task to be completed.

Administration of the Tasks.   The tasks are presented one at a time to the child, who is sitting on the floor by the examiner. The mother is seated a few feet behind the child and often occupied with a questionnaire. As with the 6- and 12-month-old tasks described earlier, social interaction among the examiner, mother, and child is minimized so that play initiated by the child can be observed. Limited interaction can also allow the examiner to score the child's behaviors as they occur.

The tester's objective is to select one task from each of the three sets that is moderately challenging relative to the tested child's developmental level. Such tasks should be sufficiently interesting enough to get the child to start working on it, not so easy that it can be completed in less than two minutes (half the trial), but not so hard that the child cannot solve at least part of it. One set of tasks is presented to the child at a time: puzzles, then shape sorters, and finally, cause-and-effect toys. Each set is begun with a task having a level of difficulty estimated to be moderately challenging for that child. Using the rules just mentioned, the tester determines whether the first task presented meets the requirement of being moderately challenging. If the child cannot solve any part of it in two minutes, the task is judged to be too difficult, is stopped, and the next easiest one in the same set is presented. If the task is judged to be too easy (i.e., all parts are completed in less than two minutes), the task is stopped, and the tester presents the child with the next most difficult task in the same set. This procedure is continued until a task meets the criterion of being moderately challenging. This moderately challenging task is then presented for a maximum of four minutes. This task may be terminated early under certain prescribed conditions (e.g., if the child's behavior is not task-directed for two consecutive fifteen-second intervals).

The importance of selecting moderately challenging tasks is indicated by two studies Morgan & Maslin-Cole—study 3 in Barrett, Morgan, & Maslin-Cole, 1993, Redding et al., 1988), which found that children persist less at very difficult tasks and may persist less at tasks that are very easy for them. Thus, since children, even of the same age, vary in ability, it is important to individualize the selection of tasks, so that all children receive tasks that are of approximately equal, moderate difficulty for them, if one wants to measure their motivation to master tasks as contrasted to their competence in solving them.

Coding and Measures. As with the 6- and 12-month tasks, object-oriented behaviors and affect were recorded. The first key score is one derived from task-directed behavior which includes trying successfully or unsuccessfully to solve the problem or master the task. The duration of task-directed behavior during the selected challenging task from each set is labelled task persistence. The second key measure is obtained from expressions of positive affect (smiling, excited vocalizations, or gestures), during task-directed behavior or immediately following successfully completing part of the challenging task. The number of intervals with positive affect has been called task pleasure. However, since this measure is quite infrequent in infants and toddlers, it may be better to use whether or not task pleasure occurred as an index of mastery motivation. More information about the use of positive affect as a measure of mastery motivation is presented in the last section of this chapter.

Interobserver Reliability.   Although coding whether a young child's behavior is task-directed may seem difficult, each of the published studies has been able to obtain good interobserver reliability. However, the early studies (e.g., Yarrow et al., 1982, 1983) were scored later from videotapes which would be assumed to produce higher reliability than live scoring by the tester.

Busch-Rossnagel, Vargas, and Knauf (1993) examined the interobserver reliabilities, scored live, using the individualized mastery tasks and procedures. The subjects were 17 Hispanic children between the ages of 16 and 38 months; 11 of the children were retested approximately two weeks later. Testing was done by an Hispanic examiner in the language with which the child was most familiar. The test was observed through a one-way mirror by a second examiner who also scored the child's behavior. The number of intervals of task-directed behavior (task persistence) showed relatively high levels of reliability, ranging from $r = .81$ for cause–effect tasks to $r = .96$ for shape-sorter tasks. Agreement on task pleasure was also relatively high (76–97% agreement), given that the observer behind the one-way mirror was not always able to see the child's face. It should be noted that scoring pleasure from video tapes is also very difficult.

Stability Over Time.   Busch-Rossnagel et al. (1993) found short-term (2 week) stability for persistence of $r = .46$ for the Hispanic toddlers previously discussed. However, relatively low stability over longer periods of time (3 months to several years) for behavioral measures of persistence has been found in several studies during infancy and early childhood, using a variety of tasks and procedures as well as the individualized method described in this section. For example, Morgan, Culp et al. (1993) found nonsignificant correlations between 9-, 12- and 25-month persistence at tasks scores. Likewise, Yarrow et al. (1983) found low and/or nonsignificant relationships between 6- and 12-month persistence scores. Others (Frodi, Bridges, & Grolnick, 1985; Maslin-Cole, Bretherton, & Morgan, 1993) also found only modest stability of persistence over parts of the second year of life.

Studies of stability from infancy to early childhood have found mixed results. Messer et al. (1986) found low stability for persistence scores from 6- and 12-months to 30-months of age. However, two other studies (Jennings, Yarrow, & Martin, 1984; Vondra, 1987) found significant correlations between mastery motivation measures for boys, but not girls, from 1 to 3½ years. One study of older preschoolers (Jennings, Connors, & Stegman, 1988) did find moderately high correlations for persistence from 3½ to 4½ years of age. Furthermore, mothers' ratings of their children's persistence are relatively stable over time (Morgan, Harmon et al., 1993).

Developmental transformations in mastery motivation probably contribute to the relatively low long-term stability in behavioral measures of persistence. This may indicate that long-term stability, especially across the transition periods discussed by Barrett and Morgan (this volume) may not be an appropriate indication of the reliability of the tests. Furthermore, motivation may well be more plastic and malleable, especially during infancy, than, for example, mental development. Perhaps this should be expected. One's motivation does seem to vary from time to time and to be influenced by environmental factors. For example, Butterfield and Miller (1984) found a significant effect of their "Read Your Baby" intervention program on infants' persistence. These findings are encouraging because they seem to indicate that a child's mastery motivation is susceptible to meaningful change that can be influenced by parents, teachers, and intervention programs.

On the other hand, several studies have shown that pleasure during mastery tasks is relatively stable over time (Barrett et al., 1993; Maslin-Cole et al., 1993). Busch-Rossnagel et al. (1993) found two-week test–retest stability of $r = .73$ for task pleasure scores using the individualized method. Furthermore, the mastery pleasure scale in the Dimensions of Mastery Questionnaire (discussed later in the chapter) has also shown stability across ages in several studies (Morgan, Harmon et al., 1993).

Scalability of the Difficulty of the Tasks.   The individualized method relies on matching the difficulty level of the task to the child's ability. Empirical evidence from two studies supports the hypothesized order of difficulty. Morgan and Maslin-Cole (study 3 in Barrett et al., 1993) studied 12 children each at 15, 20, 25, and 30 months. Each child was given five levels of each of the three sets of tasks (puzzles, shape sorters, and cause-and-effect). The assumed order of task difficulty within each of the three sets was the same as the average actual performance; older children performed consistently better than younger children on the same task and, in general, children's performance dropped as the tasks' assumed difficulty increased. From these group data, it was concluded that the sets of tasks systematically increase in difficulty, as expected.

In order to see if these group results also held for individual children's patterns of performance, a scalogram analysis for each of the three sets of tasks was completed using Green's (1956) Index of Consistency. The puzzles, with $I = .83$, were found to best meet the criterion for scalability ($I > .50$ to be labeled scalable); shapes were adequately scalable with $I = .52$. For the cause-and-effect tasks, children showed a number of reversals (mostly minor) from the predicted order of difficulty and $I = .47$, which did not quite meet Green's criterion to be labeled scalable.

In another study by Redding et al. (1988), using only the puzzle set, it was shown again to be highly scalable, with 55 out of 60 children (12, 24, or 36 months of age) showing no reversals in performance from the predicted order and $I = .90$.

Validity of Task Persistence Scores. The validity of the mastery task measures has been confirmed using two approaches. First, comparisons have been made between groups of children. One group, such as children who are at risk or handicapped, was predicted to score lower on mastery motivation measures than a normally-developing comparison group. Second, the relationship between persistence at tasks and several other measures expected to reflect aspects of the concept of mastery motivation has been examined.

Harmon and Culp (1981; Harmon & Murrow, this volume) compared the mastery motivation of very small (< 1500 grams) preterm infants with that of a full-term sample matched on gestational age. The preterm infants showed more simple, nontask-directed manipulation or exploration and less task-directed behavior (persistence) than the full-term infants. More intrusive, perhaps controlling, behavior by the mothers of the preterm infants (demonstrated during a free-play session and from interviews with them) may cause these infants to be lower on self-initiated mastery behavior and less aware of their own impact on the environment. As in the above study of very small preterm infants, Harmon, Morgan, and Glicken (1984) found lower persistence in a group of infants who had been placed in a medium-risk nursery after birth. Butterfield and Miller (1984) designed an intervention to help these mothers enhance their medium-risk infants' mastery. The nonintervention group scored lower on persistence at tasks than the intervention group, whose scores were no different from a low-risk, full-term comparison group.

Evidence supporting the construct validation of the persistence at tasks measure can be also demonstrated by significant correlations with other similar measures. For example, Yarrow et al. (1982) and others have found that individual differences in persistence on the mastery tasks are significantly correlated with independent testers' ratings of persistence during Bayley examinations. As predicted, significant relationships have been also found between mothers' ratings of their children's task persistence and the children's persistence score on a set of mastery tasks (Fung, 1984; Morgan, Harmon et al., 1993). Maslin-Cole et al. (1993), found both at 18 and 25 months of age that a first principal components factor included task persistence, mother's persistence ratings, and a tester rating of goal directedness during the Bayley exam.

Summary. The main advantage and rational for this method is that it attempts to present each child with tasks that are moderately challenging for him or her and thus, controls for the potential confounding effect of differences in cognitive ability. There are also several less central advantages to this individualized method as it has been presented by Morgan, Busch-Rossnagel et al. (1992). For example, because each type/set of tasks includes ones that vary in difficulty level, the method can be used with a group of children varying from about 15 and 36 months of mental age, not just with children of one specific chronological age. The method can also be used to compare the motivation of children who are the same age but have differing mental abilities. Furthermore, it can be used with one tester scoring the child live, without equipment except for the toys/tasks, a stopwatch, and a clipboard.

Tasks for Preschoolers

Jennings and colleagues (1984, 1985, 1988) have used both structured tasks and free play to assess mastery motivation in preschoolers and have developed tasks to assess many of the same dimensions that were assessed at 12 months. (The structured tasks will be discussed here; free play assessments for preschoolers will be discussed in a later section.) The first study on preschoolers was a longitudinal follow-up of children who had been assessed at 12 months with tasks like those described previously. Work by Harter and Zigler (1974) with school-age children was another important influence in developing these tasks. These tasks for preschoolers were modified and further developed in a second study of children seen at both 3½ and 4½ years of age. The tasks described here are from this second study (Jennings et al., 1985, 1988).

Persistence at Difficult Tasks.   These tasks required sustained or repeated effort to reach a goal. Three tasks were given at age 3½ and four tasks at age 4½. Examples of these tasks are fitting wooden cutouts of animals into a small wooden box, using a stick to obtain a toy from a narrow opening in a large plexiglass box, and catching paper fish with a magnetized fish pole. To minimize the effects of individual differences in ability, each task was designed to be interesting and fun but very difficult to complete (for example, some fish were slightly too heavy to be picked up by the magnetized fish pole). To prevent undue frustration, each task was also designed to permit non-goal-directed activity, for example, fantasy play with the fish or animal cutouts. After explaining each task, the examiner sat behind the child saying, "I have some work to do and I won't be able to help." Tasks were terminated after 5 minutes or earlier if the child repeatedly asked for help or stopped activity for 30 seconds. The persistence score was the proportion of the total possible time coded as goal-directed (as opposed to nongoal-directed) over all tasks.

Curiosity.   This was assessed with a "curiosity box," a large wooden box with manipulable gadgets on it (e.g., a door bolt and zipper) and several compartments containing different objects to be seen (by switching on lights) or felt (Banta, 1970). A different box was used at each age. The examiner placed the box before the child saying, "You can play with everything on this box; I need to sit back here and do some more work." The trial lasted 5 minutes but was terminated early if the child said he or she was finished or if the child stopped playing for 30 seconds. Three scores were summed into a composite curiosity measure: number of time units that any object was manipulated, number of different objects manipulated, and number of time units with a functional use (e.g., unlocking a latch).

Preference for a Challenging Task. Two tasks assessed preference for a challenging task at 3½ years, and three tasks were used at 4½ years. For each task a choice of three activities was given that differed only in difficulty level. For example, the examiner presented pictures of three block towers (short, medium, tall) and asked which tower the child wanted to build (Block & Block, 1980). One point was given for the easy task, two for the medium task, and three for the difficult task. The preference score was the mean over all tasks. Only the 4½-year measure appeared valid. Many 3½-year-old children seemed confused by the instructions or ignored them, that is, they made their choices either very hesitantly or impulsively before instructions were complete.

Interobserver Reliability. Interobserver reliability was high. Reliability coefficients (Pearson correlations) were .99 for persistence each year, 1.00 for curiosity each year, and .89 and .85 for curiosity (Jennings et al., 1988).

Internal Consistency. Internal reliability, or consistency, was moderate: alphas at age 3½ and 4½ were .45 and .72 for persistence, and .64 and .55 for preference.

Stability Over Time. Stability over a one-year period from age 3½ to age 4½ was assessed in both normally developing children ($n = 39$) and physically handicapped children ($n = 22$) (Jennings et al., 1988). Impressive stability was found for both persistence and curiosity even though different tasks were presented at each age. Persistence was stable in both groups ($r = .57$ and .61) and curiosity was moderately stable ($r = .39$ and .42). In contrast, a negative relationship from ages 3½ to 4½ was found for preference for a challenging task, confirming doubts about this measure's validity for 3½ year olds.

Short-term stability (over a 2-month period) was assessed for the 3½ year mastery tasks on 10 normally-developing children. As would be expected, correlations for the 2-month interval (with the same tasks) were higher than correlations for the 1-year interval (with different tasks). Correlations, however, were not dramatically higher: .65 for persistence and .61 for curiosity. The correlation for preference for a challenging task was only .32, further confirming doubts of the validity of the preference measure for the younger children.

Validity. The risk-group comparison method has been used to evaluate validity. Expected differences were found between normally-developing children (n = 39) and physically handicapped children (n = 22) (Jennings et al., 1988). Nonhandicapped children showed more persistence (F = 14.36, p < .05) at both 3½ and 4½ years of age and greater preference for difficult tasks at 4½ years (t = 2.76, p < .05). No differences in curiosity were found.

FREE PLAY ASSESSMENTS

Free Play Assessments with Infants and Toddlers

Several different approaches have used the free play behavior of infants and toddlers as a window into mastery motivation. Harmon, Morgan, and colleagues looked at the task directedness of infant's play, defined as the infant's attempts to do sustained, relatively mature, play behaviors (i.e., to produce feedback, to use toys appropriately, to combine them, and to use them in a symbolic manner). Several studies using this definition and method are summarized in Morgan et al., (1991).

Jennings et al. (1979) assessed both quantitative and qualitative aspects of infants' free play. They observed 13-month-old infants in a playroom while their mothers were occupied with an interview. Two measures that assessed the quantity of infant's exploratory play were derived. These quantitative measures assessed time spent in activities that were quite familiar and within the capabilities of all infants. First, total *exploratory play* was the number of time units in which the infant manipulated an object. Second, *production of effects* was the number of time units in which the infant produced auditory or visual effects. Two additional measures assessed the quality of the infant's play; these measures required more skill or focused attention. *Continuity of play* was the number of time units in which the infant played with the same toy as the previous time unit. *Cognitively mature play* was the number of time units of relatively high-level play.

Hrncir, Speller, and West (1985) assessed what they called *spontaneous mastery* during free play. Infants were presented with one set of toys for 15 minutes and then presented with a second set for 15 minutes. Using a highly differentiated scale of maturity of play activity, the highest level of play demonstrated by the infant in spontaneous play during each time unit was recorded. The spontaneous mastery score was the sum of these weighted scores.

Interobserver Reliability.   Interobserver reliability was high for both the Jennings et al. (1979) and the Hrncir et al. (1985) approaches. Beginning with the former, reliability coefficients (Pearson correlations) were .99 for total exploratory play, .97 for production of effects, .92 for continuity of play, and .98 for cognitively mature play. For the Hrncir et al. measure of spontaneous mastery, 92% agreement was found on highest level of play during each time unit.

Stability Over Time.   Hrncir et al. (1985) assessed stability in spontaneous mastery over a 6 month interval from 12 months of age to 18 months of age. Stability was moderate (r = .51).

Free Play with Preschoolers

Jennings et al. (1985, 1988) observed children during a regular free-play period in a nursery school setting to assess mastery motivation in a familiar, unstructured situation. They assessed three aspects of children's play. First, the *duration of play activities* was the mean number of time units per play activity. This measure reflected attention span and persistence in play. Second, *unfocused play* was the proportion of time the child was unengaged in a play activity (e.g., wandering about or passively watching others). The third measure of play assessed quality of play; different measures were used at 3½ and 4½ years of age. *Complexity of play* (measured at 3½ years) was indexed by the mean number of subactivities per play activity. For example, while painting, a child might (a) put on an apron, (b) paint circles, (c) check another child's painting, and (d) hang the painting to dry. Complexity reflected the ability to organize a sequence of actions with a single theme. The greater complexity of children's activities at 4½ years of age made recording subactivities difficult. Instead, *cognitive level* of play was assessed using Smilansky's (1968) scale. Each time unit was rated: 1 for functional play, 2 for constructive play, and 3 for dramatic play.

Interobserver Reliability.   Interobserver reliability for these free-play measures was high. Reliability coefficients (Pearson correlations) were .97 and .94 for unfocused play, .99 and .96 for mean duration of play activities, .83 for complexity (3½ years), and .84 for cognitive level (4½ years).

Stability Over Time.   Stability over a one year period (from age 3½ to age 4½) was assessed in both normally-developing children (n = 39) and physically-handicapped children (n = 22) (Jennings et al., 1988). The stability of these free play measures was low. Only unfocused play showed stability and only in the handicapped group (r = .47).

Validity.   Expected differences were found between normally-developing children (n = 39) and physically-handicapped children (n = 22) (Jennings et al., 1988). Significant differences were found on all free-play measures. Normally-developing children engaged in less unfocused play, had longer play activities, had more complex play (age 3½), and showed a higher cognitive level of play (age 4½).

ASSESSING MASTERY MOTIVATION FROM ADULT RATINGS

The Dimensions of Mastery Questionnaire (DMQ), or its predecessor, the Mother's Observation of Mastery Motivation (MOMM), has been used with over 30 samples of 1–5 year-olds, including normally-developing, developmentally-delayed, and premature children. This section, which describes the questionnaire, its use, and psychometric properties, draws heavily on the MOMM manual (Morgan et al., 1983), the DMQ manual, (Morgan, Harmon et al., 1992) and a recent review chapter (Morgan, Harmon et al., 1993). This method provides a different perspective on mastery motivation from the more typical assessments that have utilized brief behavioral observations of infants working at mastery tasks or during semistructured play. Parents and teachers observe their children over a longer period of time and in various settings. Therefore, ratings completed by parents or teachers may supplement laboratory measures of Mastery Motivation.

The DMQ provides a quicker and easier measure of young children's mastery motivation than that gained from behavioral assessments. Because the DMQ seems to produce valid measures, as discussed later, this is a significant advantage. However, parents' perceptions may be influenced not only by the child's actual behavior but also by characteristics of the parents' own personalities and by response biases. Nevertheless, parent and teacher *perceptions* of mastery motivation are important in themselves because adults' perceptions undoubtedly influence their interactions with children.

The questionnaire was designed, in part, to parallel the behavioral measures of mastery motivation from the structured tasks. Adults' perceptions could, thus, provide one method of testing the validity of the mastery tasks and vice versa. This adult perception data has also increased the generalizability of the concept by including information from natural home and preschool settings. Because the DMQ includes ratings of the child's motivation during gross motor and social/symbolic play, the scores led to a broader conceptualization of mastery motivation, as outlined in Chapter 1 of this volume.

As DMQ data were collected and the conceptualization of Mastery Motivation evolved, modifications in items were made to improve the internal consistency of the scales and to improve the readability and translatability (into Spanish) of the items (see, for example, Busch-Rossnagel et al., 1993). Much of the psychometric information summarized below comes from raw data shared by colleagues and analyzed as composite samples. See Morgan, Harmon et al. (1992, 1993) for more details.

As indicated below, the five scales of the current conceptualization are psychometrically strong and consistent with the conceptualization of Mastery Motivation provided by Barrett and Morgan (this volume). The scales include an *expressive* facet or component of Mastery Motivation, called mastery pleasure, and three *instrumental* components of Mastery Motivation (object-oriented, social/symbolic, and gross motor persistence) that roughly parallel Harter's (1981) aspects of perceived competence (i.e. academic, social, and athletic) in school-age children. Adult-perceived child competence items were also included in the DMQ because they were of general interest, but they are not considered to be an aspect of mastery motivation.

Reliability

Internal Consistency. In general, alphas for the five DMQ Scales are acceptable to good (.69 to .92) for three composite groups of raters. Teachers (n = 142) had the highest alphas. Mothers (n = 319) of normally-developing children were somewhat lower, and mothers of at-risk/delayed children (n = 83) had the lowest alphas. Perhaps the teachers were more aware or observant of the types of behaviors rated on the DMQ and thus more consistent. Because the at-risk/delayed composite group had a higher proportion of lower income and less educated mothers, lower maternal reading levels could have produced the somewhat lower alphas.

Test–Retest Reliability and Stability. A sample of 39 mothers was asked to respond to two versions of the DMQ administered three weeks from each other. For the object-oriented persistence scale, this alternate forms reliability was high: .81. The reliabilities for social/symbolic persistence, mastery pleasure, and competence scales were .54, .57, and .52, respectively, despite revisions in several items. However, due to major changes in the items, the coefficient for gross motor mastery motivation was not reliable.

Moderately high stability over time has been found for the DMQ scales. In one study the DMQ was administered at 18, 24, and 39 months. Stability correlations ranged from .32 to .80 with median coefficients of .63, .50, .37, .62, and .68 for object-oriented, social/symbolic and gross motor persistence, mastery pleasure, and competence respectively. There was no indication that stability was lower if the interval was longer. Moderately high stability was likewise found in a study of developmentally-disabled toddlers for ratings more than a year apart. Stability correlations ranged from .45 to .67 with a median of .60 (Morgan, Harmon et al., 1992, 1993).

Validity

Several approaches to assessing the validity of the MOMM and DMQ questionnaires have been used. The following sections summarize the findings.

Factor Analysis of Items. Principal components factor analyses with varimax rotation were computed for composite groups of 319 mothers and 142 teachers. The ratings by mothers yielded five clear nonoverlapping factors, which corresponded to and provided construct validity for the five DMQ scales. For teachers, similar results were found; however, the object-oriented persistence and competence factors were somewhat overlapping.

High- Versus Low-Risk Comparisons. In general, as expected, mothers of at-risk or delayed children have rated them lower in all three instrumental mastery motivation domains and competence. However, no differences have been found for ratings of mastery pleasure. These findings indicate that parents of young delayed children believe them to be lower on the instrumental, but not the expressive, aspects of mastery motivation.

The validity of the questionnaires was also suggested by the effects of an intervention program by Butterfield and Miller (1984) designed to teach parents how to "read" and respond to their baby's cues. The program seemed to raise children's motivation on mastery tasks *and* raised mothers' perception of their children's mastery motivation (Harmon et al., 1984). Because the effect on the task scores was as large as that on maternal perceptions, it appears that the mothers' ratings were largely based on observed behavior changes, not just increased expectations.

Correlations with Behavioral Assessments. Support for the criterion validity of the questionnaires has been obtained from significant, but modest, correlations of maternal mastery ratings with behavioral mastery task scores. As predicted, general mastery motivation scores were significantly correlated (r = .37) with infants' actual persistence at tasks. In another study, preschool teachers rated the usual behavior of 18 children who had also been tested, at a different time, with the mastery tasks (Morgan et al., 1983). There was a significant correlation (r = .41) between teacher ratings of the children's persistence and tester ratings of the children's task orientation (persistence).

Fung (1984) asked 38 mothers of 18-month-old infants to answer the general scales of the Dimensions of Mastery Questionnaire. Infants were also tested with the Bayley Scales of

Infant Development and a version of the mastery tasks developed by Brockman (1984). Mother's perceptions of the child's persistence were significantly related to the child's persistent behavior on the Brockman tasks (r = .33). The mother's ratings of the child's competence were correlated with the child's behavioral competence on the mastery tasks (r = .34) and also with the Bayley Mental Development Index (r = .49).

The results of a longitudinal study (Maslin-Cole et al., 1993) also provide some evidence for the validity of the DMQ. Correlations between observed task pleasure and DMQ mastery pleasure were significant. This, in contrast to Fung (1984), was evidence for the validity of the mastery pleasure scale. Like the Fung study, there were significant relationships between the Bayley Mental Development Index and the DMQ competence scale.

Sarimski and Warndorf (1991), found a significant correlation between developmental quotient and DMQ ratings of competence in a sample of mentally-retarded German children. Likewise, in a developmentally-disabled sample (see Morgan et al., 1993), a relatively high correlation (r = .56) was found between DMQ competence ratings and IQ, so mothers accurately rated the degree of their child's disability. In that same study, correlations of mothers' ratings of object-oriented persistence were significantly related to observed persistence at tasks. However, as with Fung's (1984) normally developing sample, none of the ratings of mastery pleasure were related to the small amount of observed positive affect during the tasks.

Consistency Across Types of Raters.   Another approach to checking the validity of the ratings is to examine ratings of the same group of children by two different people who have observed them in at least somewhat different contexts. Teacher–teacher, mother–teacher, father–teacher and mother–father correlations have been examined with mostly significant results.

In a study of Colorado teachers and mothers, most children had more than one student-teacher who knew them relatively well but observed them at different times of the week (Morgan et al., 1992, 1993). For these 59 children, there were significant teacher–teacher correlations for four of the five DMQ scales. Correlations ranged from .21 (*ns*) for mastery pleasure to .51 for competence, with the three instrumental domains (i.e., gross motor, social/symbolic and object-oriented persistence scales) having significant teacher–teacher correlations of .32 to .43.

Mother–teacher correlations were somewhat lower, but four of the five correlations (except object-oriented persistence) were significant. In a Manitoba preschool study, there was also general agreement between teachers and parents, with four out of five mother–teacher and father–teacher correlations reaching significance (see Morgan et al., 1992, 1993). Mothers and fathers agreed quite consistently on their ratings of the child's competence ($r = .76$), social/symbolic persistence ($r = .74$), and object-oriented persistence ($r = .53$); however, the correlations for gross motor persistence and mastery pleasure were not significant.

Summary of Psychometric Data for the Questionnaires

The DMQ provides five scales with good reliability, shown by internal consistency and stability over time. These indicators may even underestimate the questionnaire's true reliability, since some items were modified as the DMQ evolved. Construct validity is supported by a clean, conceptually meaningful factor structure, especially for the ratings of mothers of normally-developing children. Other methods of assessing the validity of the questionnaire provide some support, but not all are strong. Parents' ratings of their children correlate moderately with teacher ratings and with their children's behavior on mastery tasks and cognitive assessments. Interrater agreement was generally best for competence and social/symbolic persistence and modest for gross motor persistence and mastery pleasure. Mother–child behavior agreement, likewise, was best for competence and modest or variable for mastery pleasure and object-oriented persistence. At-risk or delayed children have generally been related lower than normally developing, low-risk comparison children on object-oriented persistence, but not different on mastery pleasure ratings.

One reason for the modest correlations between ratings of parents and teachers or between parents' ratings and observed task scores is that parents see their child in very different settings, comparing a preschool to a brief lab assessment. Thus, high correlations would not be expected even if each type of asscssment was highly valid.

Social Mastery Motivation

As indicated previously in the section on the mastery questionnaire and in Chapter 1, it seems both logical and conceptually important to measure a child's motivation to master the social environment if one wants to have a well-rounded, complete picture of early mastery motivation. There has been relatively little work in this area, in part because it is not clear what is an appropriate way to measure such motivation. In this book, the Wachs and Combs chapter is the main source of discussion and data about social mastery motivation.

Sequential Analysis

Hebb (1949), in describing motivation, contends that its defining characteristic is not arousal of. activity, but its patterning and direction. White (1959) also considered direction to be one of the defining characteristics of mastery motivation, but did not operationalize this key concept. However, his description of direction as it pertains to mastery motivation provides a clue to an empirically-testable definition as well as the appropriate analytic method. Direction was described as "constantly circling from stimulus to perception to effect" (p. 322), thus suggesting the need to preserve the sequences of infants' actions as they use various behaviors to engage with and extract information from objects.

This analytic technique involves a detailed examination of the infants' behavioral sequences (i.e., lag sequential analysis) between the various levels of mastery behaviors. This technique is well established in the ethological literature and in studies of human social interaction (Bakeman & Brown, 1977; Sackett, 1978).

The sequential measures were drawn from the Yarrow et al., (1983) raw data from the 6- and 12-month tasks (discussed previously) with three important differences. First, frequencies, rather than percentage duration, were used in order to provide independent estimates of the occurrence of each behavior. Second, the behaviors that constituted the Yarrow et al. (1983) off-task categories combined social behaviors directed toward the mother or examiner with other nontask-related activities. These two classes of behaviors were separated into discrete measures. This decision was based on the results of two reports (MacTurk, Vietze et al., 1985; MacTurk, Hunter et al., 1985) that suggested that the integration of social behaviors into the stream of object-related activities represents an important aspect of motivation. Last, success was included as a separate category in order to provide a measure of task completion.

The results support White's (1959) notion that mastery motivation may be characterized by direction, in addition to persistence. Specifically, the pattern of significant behavioral transitions suggests that at both 6 months and 12 months of age, infants focus their manipulative activities in a direction that leads them to the goal of successful task performance. This is evident not only from the significant probabilities associated with the transitions from Persist to Success, but also from the absence of any significant paths to Success from the other categories of mastery motivation.

Though there were significant age changes from 6 to 12 months in the overall frequency of each category of mastery motivation, these changes did not dramatically alter the pattern of transitions. There was a striking similarity at both ages in how the infants organized their attempts to master the objects; the only change revolved around the socially-directed behaviors. At 12 months, social behaviors seem to reflect an added dimension that was not evident at the earlier age. The older infants tend to follow social behaviors with looking at the toy before going to persist behaviors, whereas, at 6 months, social behaviors were not directly involved with task-related behaviors and did not seem to have the same salience in the context of attempting to master the environment. Because the computations involved in deriving the variables corrected for the base rates of behavior, the difference in sequence was not a function of the difference in frequency.

The change in the significant transitions from social behaviors as well as the overall increase in their frequency suggests that the relative importance of social behaviors in the context of mastery with objects changes during the last half of the first year of life. The older infant may be exhibiting a form of social referencing (Feinman, 1982) before engaging in the task again, whereas the younger child may not be as adept at integrating the social aspects of his or her behavioral repertoire into an ongoing stream of task-related activities.

Affect Measures

Another type of measure that has been assessed by several investigators of mastery motivation is the child's positive affect or pleasure while working on tasks. In a number of recent studies using the mastery tasks, specific measures of the child's affect while working on a task, and/or immediately following successful completion of a part of it, have been recorded (Barrett & Morgan, this volume; MacTurk et al., 1987; Morgan et al., 1990). These measures are thought to index an important expressive aspect of the child's mastery motivation, but must reflect a different facet of motivation than persistence at tasks because low correlations have usually been found between total task pleasure and total persistence (Morgan et al., 1990, 1991; Redding et al., 1988). However, in sequential analyses, pleasure has been found to be more likely to follow persistence than to follow a solution, or any other behavior (MacTurk et al., 1987). Thus task pleasure is considered to be conceptually, if not empirically, related to mastery motivation, and may, by two years of age, be an index of the child's pride in accomplishment.

Expressions of pleasure during the structured mastery tasks are relatively infrequent, especially for one year olds and in combinatorial type tasks (e.g., shapes). By two to three years of age, the amount of smiling contiguous with task-directed behavior increases substantially, especially in tasks that produce a noticeable audiovisual effect (Morgan & Maslin-Cole, study 3 in Barrett et al., 1993). It also seems that children show more task pleasure when playing with peers than they do while playing alone or with their mother (Morgan et al., 1991). It is likely that some of the smiles during task-directed behavior have a social component or are related to the pleasure of a sensory or audio visual effect rather than pleasure related to mastery. This has lead Morgan, Busch-Rossnagel et al. (1992) to score "other pleasure" separately from task pleasure to differentiate these concepts.

However, responses to cause-and-effect-type toys can be related to mastery motivation, perhaps especially in infancy. Barrett et al. (study 1, 1993) found results consistent with that hypothesis in a study of infant smiling during a cause-and-affect task. Two groups of 6- and 12-month-old infants participated in the study: (a) infant-contingent subjects, whose cylinder pressing activated a jack-in-the-box, and (b) infant-noncontingent subjects who had a cylinder to press and who watched the jack-in-the-box emerge at the same rate as a yoked infant-contingent subject, but whose behavior did not control the emergence of the jack-in-the-box. Infant-contingent subjects (who did control the jack-in-the-box) smiled more if they pressed more, suggesting that they experienced "feelings of efficacy." Infant-noncontingent subjects also seemed to attempt to control the jack-in-the-box, in that they pressed the cylinder more frequently if the jack-in-the-box emerged more frequently. However, these infants, who lacked control over the jack-in-the-box, did not smile more when pressing more; instead, they frequently turned to view their care givers (social referencing) with a serious look on their faces as if asking why they could not control the jack-in-the-box.

Although task pleasure, as indicated by smiling during task-directed behavior or following a solution, is not common, such scores have produced meaningful, significant correlations with other variables. This provides construct validity for task pleasure. For example, maternal reports of both 9- and 12-month varieties of play with their child were significantly related to 12-month pleasure at tasks (Morgan et al., 1992). In a study of 18-month-old children and their affect exchanges with mother (Morgan, Maslin, Ridgeway, & Kang-Park, 1988), low ratings of DMQ mastery pleasure were found in children who were relatively high on exchanges in which there were unreciprocated initiations. On the other hand, mutually positive affect exchanges with mother were related to high ratings on DMQ mastery pleasure.

Executive Capacity

Belsky, Garduque, and Hrncir (1984) developed a mastery motivation measure that is based on the discrepancy between infants' spontaneous and elicited play. They reasoned that motivated infants should spontaneously play at or near their maximum level of ability. Infants were first observed during 20 minutes of free play. Then the examiner encouraged more competent play by making verbal suggestions and/or modeling. Beginning with the level immediately above the highest level of play demonstrated during spontaneous play, the examiner suggested an activity within a play theme that the child had already shown interest in during the free play. The measure of *executive capacity* was the difference between the highest levels of elicited and of spontaneous play. This difference score was divided by the number of steps that remained above the spontaneous performance level; that is, that the child could potentially advance through during elicited play. Thus, scores can range from 0 (high motivation) to 1 (low motivation).

Summary and Conclusions

Over the last twenty years three major techniques have been developed for measuring mastery motivation; structured tasks, free play, and adult report questionnaires. By far, the most common type of measure has been the structured mastery tasks, most of which have been a variant of those developed at the NICHHD for use with infants or some variant of the individualized, moderately challenging method developed for use with toddlers and young preschoolers. The NICHHD infant tasks have been developed for use primarily in research studies with good technological and research support. This has the advantage of more precise scoring, including sequential analysis, but has the disadvantage of being less portable and less adaptable to use in the clinic or home. The individualized method also allows for testing and comparing children who are at any age or who vary in mental age. One important drawback of the structured task methodology is the experimenter-defined criteria for what constitutes persistence and success. Some children may be intensely engaged with the task but in a manner which is not (externally) defined as task persistence. This may constrain the ability to assess the full range of what may reasonably considered to be mastery motivation. Furthermore, tasks designed to assess social and gross motor mastery motivation have either not yet been developed or are not widely accepted as adequate measures of these domains.

Advocates of the free play measures argue that it is impossible to develop tasks that are not high on the characteristics of demand for compliance and cooperation with the tester. Thus, unstructured free play remains to some to be a better way to get at the child's independent, mastery motivation. A problem is that in unstructured play, infants and young toddlers show relatively few attempts to deal with or master more challenging aspects of their environment, choosing, instead, to play with toys that they appear to have already mastered.

The questionnaire assessment has the advantage of drawing on a much broader range of experiences with young children than the usually quite limited play or task sessions. However, it has the disadvantage of potential response and social desirability biases.

Despite the shortcomings inherent in the various methodologies outlined in this chapter, the existing evidence supports White's (1959) original contention that, from the earliest months of life, there is a motivation to engage with and profit from interactions with the environment. Furthermore, it is possible to accurately and reliably track the developmental course of mastery motivation both from a group difference and an individual differences perspective. The following chapters offer further evidence concerning the correlates of mastery motivation across several important areas of development and examine how mastery motivation may be influenced, both negatively, in the case of at-risk and handicapped children, and positively, by providing appropriate levels of social and nonsocial stimulation.

REFERENCES

Atkinson, J. W. (1957). Motivational determinants of risk-taking behavior. *Psychological Review, 64,* 359–372.

Bakeman, R., & Brown, J. V. (1977). Behavioral dialogues: An approach to the assessment of mother–infant interaction. *Child Development, 48,* 195–203.

Banta, J. T. (1970) Tests for the evaluation of early childhood education: The Cincinnati autonomy test battery. In J. Hellmuth (Ed.) Cognitive Studies, Vol. 1 (pp. 206–278). New York: Brunner/Mazel.

Barrett, K. C., Morgan, G. A., & Maslin-Cole, C. (1993). Three studies on the development of mastery motivation in infancy and toddlerhood. In D. Messer (Ed.), *Mastery motivation in early childhood: Development, measurement, and social processes* (pp. 83–108). London: Routledge.

Belsky, J., Garduque, L., & Hrncir, E. (1984). Assessing performance, competence, and executive capacity in infant play: Relations to home environment and security of attachment. *Development Psychology, 20,* 406–417.

Berger, J., & Cunningham, C. C. (1981). Development of eye contact between mothers and normal versus Down syndrome infants. *Developmental Psychology, 17,* 678–689.

Block, J. H., & Block, J. (1980). The role of ego-control and ego-resiliency in the organization of behavior. In W. A. Collins (Ed.),

Minnesota symposium on child psychology (Vol. 13) (pp. 294–356). Hillsdale, NJ: Erlbaum.

Brockman, L. M. (1984, May). *Mastery motivation and competence in young children.* Paper presented at the NIH Workshop on Mastery Motivation, Bethesda, MD.

Busch-Rossnagel, N. A., Vargas, M. E., & Knauf, D. E. (1993). Mastery motivation in ethnic minority groups: The sample case of Hispanics. In D. Messer (Ed.), *Mastery motivation in early childhood: Development, measurement, and social processes* (pp. 132–148). London: Routledge.

Butterfield, P. M., & Miller, L. (1984). Read your baby: A follow up intervention program for parents with NICU infants. *Infant Mental Health, 5*(2), 107–116.

Feather, N. T. (1962). The study of persistence. *Psychological Bulletin, 59,* 94–115.

Feinman, S. (1982). Social referencing in infancy. *Merrill–Palmer Quarterly, 28,* 445–470.

Frodi, A., Bridges, L., & Grolnick, W. (1985). Correlates of mastery-related behaviors: A short-term longitudinal study of infants in their second year. *Child Development, 56,* 1291–1298.

Fung, A. Y. (1984). *The relationship of mother's perception to the child's competence and mastery motivation.* Unpublished master's thesis, University of Manitoba, Winnipeg.

Gaiter, J. L., Morgan, G. A., Jennings, K. D., Harmon, R. J., & Yarrow, L. J. (1982). Variety of cognitively-oriented caregiver activities: Relationships to cognitive and motivational functioning at 1 and 3½ years of age. *Journal of Genetic Psychology, 141,* 49–56.

Green, G. (1956). A method of scalogram analysis using summary statistics. *Psychometrika, 21,* 79–88.

Harmon, R. J., & Culp, A. M. (1981). The effects of premature birth on family functioning and infant development. In I. Berlin (Ed.), *Children and our future* (pp. 1–9). Albuquerque: University of New Mexico Press.

Harmon, R. J., Morgan, G. A., & Glicken, A. D. (1984). Continuities and discontinuties in affective and cognitive–motivational development. *International Journal of Child Abuse and Neglect, 8,* 157–167.

Harter, S. (1981). A model of intrinsic mastery motivation in children: Individual differences and developmental change. In W. A. Collins (Ed.), *Minnesota symposium on child psychology, Vol. 14* (pp. 215–258). Hillsdale, NJ: Erlbaum.

Harter, S., & Zigler, E. (1974). The assessment of effectance motivation in normal and retarded children. *Developmental Psychology, 10,* 169–180.

Hebb, D. O. (1949). *The organization of behavior.* New York: Wiley.

Hrncir, E. J., Speller, G. M., & West, M. (1985). What are we testing? *Developmental Psychology, 21,* 226–232.

Hunt, J. (1965). Intrinsic motivation and its roles in psychological development. In D. Levine (Ed.), *Nebraska symposium on motivation* (Vol. 13). (pp. 189–282). Lincoln: University of Nebraska Press.

Jennings, K., Harmon, R., Morgan, G., Gaiter, J., & Yarrow, L. (1979). Exploratory play as an index of mastery motivation: Relationships to persistence, cognitive functioning and environmental measures. *Developmental Psychology, 15*, 386–394.

Jennings, K., Yarrow, L., & Martin, P. (1984). Mastery motivation and cognitive development: A longitudinal study from infancy to three and one half years. *International Journal of Behavioral Development, 7*, 441–461.

Jennings, K. D., Connors, R. E., & Stegman, C. E. (1988). Does a physical handicap alter the development of mastery motivation during the preschool years? *Journal of the American Academy of Child and Adolescent Psychiatry, 27*, 312–317.

Jennings, K. D., Connors, R. E., Stegman C. E., Sankaranarayan, P., & Mendelsohn, S. (1985). Mastery motivation in young pre-schoolers: Effect of a physical handicap and implications for educational programming. *Journal of the Division for Early Childhood, 9*, 162–169.

Lewis, M., & Brooks-Gunn J. (1984). Age and handicapped group differences in infants' visual attention. *Child Development, 55*, 858–868.

MacTurk, R. H., McCarthy, M. E., Vietze, P. M., & Yarrow, L. J. (1987). Sequential analysis of mastery behavior in 6- and 12-month-old infants. *Developmental Psychology, 23*(2), 199–203.

MacTurk, R. H., Hunter, F., McCarthy, M., Vietze, P., & McQuiston, S. (1985). Social mastery motivation in Down syndrome and nondelayed infants. *Topics in Early Childhood Special Education, 4*, 93–109.

MacTurk, R. H., Vietze, P. M., McCarthy, M. E., McQuiston, S., & Yarrow, L. J. (1985). The organization of exploration behavior in Down syndrome and nondelayed infants. *Child Development, 56*, 573–581.

Maslin-Cole, C., Bretherton, I., & Morgan, G. A. (1993). Toddler mastery motivation and competence: Links with attachment security, maternal scaffolding, and family climate. In D. Messer (Ed.), *Mastery motivation in early childhood: Development, measurement, and social processes* (pp. 205–229). London: Routledge.

Matkin, N. D. (1986). The role of hearing in language development. In J. F. Kavanaugh (Ed.), *Otitis media and child development* (pp. 3–11). Parkton, MD: York.

McCarthy, M. E., & McQuiston, S. (1983, April). *The relationship of contingent parental behaviors to infant motivation and competence.* Paper presented at the biennial meeting of the Society for Research in Child Development, Detroit, MI.

Messer, D. J., McCarthy, M. E., McQuiston, S., MacTurk, R. H., Yarrow, L. J., & Vietze, P. M. (1986). Relation between mastery behavior in infancy and competence in early childhood. *Developmental Psychology, 22,* 336–372.

Miranda, S. B., & Fantz, R. L. (1974). Recognition memory in Down's syndrome and normal infants. *Child Development, 45,* 651–660.

Morgan, G. A., Harmon, R. J., Pipp, S., & Jennings, K. D. (1983). *Assessing mothers' perceptions of mastery motivation: The utility of the MOMM questionnaire.* Unpublished manuscript.

Morgan, G. A., Busch-Rossnagel, N. A., Maslin-Cole, C. A., & Harmon, R. J. (1992). *Mastery motivation tasks: Manual for 15- to 36-month-old children.* Bronx: Fordham University.

Morgan, G. A., Maslin-Cole, C. A, Biringen, Z., & Harmon, R. J. (1991). Play assessment of mastery motivation in infants and young children. In C. E. Schaefer, K. Gitlin, & A. Sandgrund (Eds.), *Play diagnosis and assessment* (pp. 65–86). New York: Wiley.

Morgan, G. A., & Harmon, R. J. (1984). Developmental transformations in mastery motivation: Measurement and validation. In R. N. Emde & R. J. Harmon (Eds.), *Continuities and discontinuities in development* (pp. 263–291). New York: Plenum.

Morgan, G. A., Culp, R. E., Busch-Rossnagel, N. A., Barrett, K. C., & Redding, R. E. (1993). A longitudinal study of mastery motivation in infants 9 to 25 months of age (abstract). In J. E. Jacobs (Ed.), *Nebraska symposium on motivation, Vol. 40: Developmental perspectives on motivation* (p. 273). Lincoln: University of Nebraska Press. (Also presented as a poster at the Nebraska Symposium, Lincoln March, 1992.

Morgan, G. A., Harmon, R. J., & Maslin-Cole, C. A. (1990). Mastery motivation: Its definition and measurement. *Early Education and Development, 1,* 318–339.

Morgan, G. A., Harmon, R. J., Maslin-Cole, C. A., Busch-Rossnagel, N. A., Jennings, K. D., Hauser-Cram, P., & Brockman, L. M. (1993). Parent and teacher perceptions of young children's mastery motivation: Assessment and review of research. In D. Messer (Ed.), *Mastery motivation in early childhood: Development, measurement, and social processes* (pp. 109–131). London: Routledge.

Morgan, G. A., Harmon, R. J., Maslin-Cole, C. A., Busch-Rossnagel, N. A., Jennings, K. D., Hauser-Cram, P., & Brockman, L. M. (1992). *Assessing perceptions of mastery motivation: The Dimensions of Mastery Questionnaire, its development, psychometrics and use.* Ft. Collins: Colorado State University, Human Development and Family Studies Department.

Morgan, G. A., Harmon, R. J., Pipp, S., & Jennings, K. D. (1983). *Assessing mother's perceptions of mastery motivation: The utility of the MOMM questionnaire.* Unpublished manuscript.

Morgan, G. A., Maslin, C. A., Ridgeway, D., & Kang-Park, J. (1988). Toddler mastery motivation and aspects of mother–child affect communication. *Program and Proceeding of the Developmental Psychobiology Research Group Retreat,* 5, 15–16. (Summary)

Morgan, G. A., Maslin-Cole, C. A., Biringen, Z., & Harmon, R. J. (1991). Play assessment of mastery motivation in infants and young children. In C. E. Schaefer, K. Gitlin, and A. Sandgrund (Eds.), *Play diagnosis and assessment* (pp. 65–86). New York: Wiley.

Piaget, J. *The origins of intelligence in children* (M. Cook, Trans.). New York: International Universities Press, 1952. (Original work published 1936)

Redding, R. E., Morgan, G. A., & Harmon, R. J. (1988). Mastery motivation in infants and toddlers: Is it greatest when tasks are moderately challenging? *Infant Behavior and Development,* 11, 419–430.

Sackett, G. P. (1978). Measurement in observational research. In G. P. Sackett (Ed.), *Observing behavior, Vol. 2: Data collection and analysis methods* (pp. 25–44). Baltimore, MD: University Park Press.

Sarimski, K., & Warndorf, P. K. (1991). Zur Beurteilung der Ausdauer bei zielgerichteten Tatigkeiten in der Psychodiagnostik geistigbehinderter Kinder. (Assessment of persistence in goal-directed activities and psycho-diagnostics of mentally handicapped children). *Sonderpadagogik,* 21, 210–216.

Similansky, S. (1968). *The effects of sociodramatic play on disadvantaged preschool children.* New York: Wiley.

Tolman, E. C. (1932). *Purposive behavior in animals and man.* New York: Appleton-Century.

Vietze, P., McCarthy, M., McQuiston, S., MacTurk, R., & Yarrow, L. (1983). Attention and exploratory behavior in infants with Down syndrome. In T. Field and A. Sostek (Eds.), *Infants born at risk: Perceptual and physiological processes* (pp. 251–268). New York: Grune and Stratton.

Vondra, J. I. (1987, April). *Early mastery motivation: How can we measure it and what does it mean?* Presented at the biennial meeting of the Society for Research in Child Development, Baltimore, MD.

Wachs, T. D. (1987). Specificity of environmental action as manifest in environmental correlates of infant's mastery motivation. *Developmental Psychology,* 23, 782–790.

Weiner, B., Kun, A., & Benesh-Weiner, M. (1980). The development of mastery, emotions and morality from an attributional perspective. In A. Collings (Ed.), *Minnesota symposium on child psychology, Vol. 14* (pp. 327–402). Hillsdale, NJ: Erlbaum.

White, R. W. (1959). Motivation reconsidered: The concept of competence. *Psychological Review,* 66, 297–333.

Yarrow, L. J., & Pedersen, F. A. (1976). The interplay between cognition and motivation in infancy. In M. Lewis (Ed.), *Origins of intelligence: Infancy and early childhood* (pp 379–399). New York: Plenum.

Yarrow, L. J., MacTurk, R. H., Vietze, P. M., McCarthy, M. E., Klein, R. P., & McQuiston, S. (1984). Developmental course of parental stimulation and its relationship to mastery motivation during infancy. *Developmental Psychology, 20,* 492–503.

Yarrow, L. J., Rubenstein, J. L., & Pedersen, F. A. (1975). *Infant and environment: Early cognitive and motivational development.* Washington, DC: Hemisphere, Halsted, Wiley.

Yarrow, L. J., Klein, R., Lomonaco, S., & Morgan, G. A. (1975). Cognitive and motivational development in early childhood. In B. Z. Friedlander, G. M. Sterritt, & G. E. Kirk, (Eds.), *Exceptional infant: Assessment and intervention* (pp. 491–502). New York: Bruner/Mazel.

Yarrow, L. J., McQuiston, S., MacTurk, R. H., McCarthy, M. E., Klein, R. P., & Vietze, P. M. (1983). Assessment of mastery motivation during the first year of life: Contemporaneous and cross-age relationships. *Developmental Psychology, 19,* 159–171.

Yarrow, L. J., Morgan, G. A., Jennings, K. D., Harmon, R. J., & Gaiter, J. L. (1982). Infant's persistence at tasks: Relationships to cognitive functioning and early experience. *Infant Behavior and Development, 5,* 131–142.

3

CONTINUITIES AND DISCONTINUITIES IN MASTERY MOTIVATION DURING INFANCY AND TODDLERHOOD: A CONCEPTUALIZATION AND REVIEW

Karen Caplovitz Barrett
George A. Morgan
Colorado State University

In this chapter, we elaborate on a conceptual framework for the development of mastery-oriented behavior during the first three years of life, based on recent research and theory regarding mastery-related behavior in infancy and toddlerhood. Morgan, Maslin-Cole, Biringen, and Harmon (1991) proposed that there are developmental transformations in mastery motivation during the latter part of the first year of life and during the second quarter of the second year of life. Jennings (1993) also has proposed a developmental model of mastery motivation during the first 3 years of life. Here, we will expand upon previous conceptualizations, incorporating into them recent published and unpublished research from our labs as well as those of others.

Although most research on mastery motivation, per se, has concerned infants who are at least 6 months of age, it is our position that evidence of mastery motivation can be observed from earliest infancy. Moreover, strands of continuity can be observed across development. However, the *nature and complexity* of mastery motivation, as well as the conditions under which it can be observed most clearly, change markedly during infancy and early childhood, with important transition periods being observable during the second half of each of the first three years of life. In this chapter, we will describe the characteristics of the three phases defined by these transitions. We call the periods of relative stability *phases* rather than stages to highlight the fact that the characteristic behavior patterns do not emerge suddenly and replace those that preceded them. The periods of transition are expected to be quite long in many cases, with behaviors of the previous phases being common in later phases as well. The hallmark of transition and change is that the same behaviors come to serve different functions and the functions formerly served by one set of behaviors are served by other behaviors.

MASTERY MOTIVATION DURING INFANCY AND TODDLERHOOD

What are the Crucial Features of Mastery Motivation?

Before discussing the development of mastery motivation, it is important to define the domain of behavior that is developing. *Mastery motivation is viewed as a multifaceted, intrinsic, psychological force that stimulates an individual to* **attempt** *to master a skill or task that is at least somewhat challenging for him or her* (cf. Morgan, Harmon, & Maslin-Cole, 1990). We will discuss each of the key features of this definition briefly now, and rely on this definition when discussing the phases of development.

1. *Mastery motivation is multifaceted.* Indicators of mastery motivation can be categorized into two major types—*instrumental* and *"expressive."* It is important to note that instrumental aspects of mastery motivation are not devoid of affect; nor are "expressive" aspects afunctional reflections of inner states. Instrumental aspects of mastery motivation are often regulated by emotion. Similarly, expressive aspects serve important communicative functions, and may be used instrumentally.

Nevertheless, we believe that the instrumental/expressive distinction may prove fruitful in future studies. Evidence to support this belief will be presented later in the section on Phase 3 of mastery motivation.

Some important instrumental aspects of mastery motivation include: (a) a tendency to persist at tasks that are somewhat difficult, (b) an inclination/preference for one's own physical and/or cognitive control over environmental events (vs. passive observation of them), and (c) preference for at least some degree of challenge and/or novelty. Some important expressive aspects of mastery motivation include facial, vocal, postural, and behavioral communication of: (a) pleasure, (b) interest, (c) pride, (d) frustration/anger, (e) sadness, and (f) shame.

The many *aspects* of mastery motivation are *dissociable;* they are not always highly correlated, and they need not all be measured in order to investigate mastery motivation (in fact, we know of no existing studies that measure all of these features of mastery motivation). Nevertheless, we believe that studying more of these aspects will yield a more complete view of mastery motivation.

2. *Although these features are characteristic of mastery motivation at all ages, the nature of each feature changes as the child gets older.* Obviously, what is somewhat difficult or challenging, versus too difficult, for an individual changes markedly with development, but the important implications of this truism are often overlooked in the assessment of mastery motivation. We will describe some important cases in which this was overlooked later, in connection with the transition from Phase 1 to Phase 2. Furthermore, the behavioral responses available to the individual change dramatically with development, and these changes greatly affect the measurement of mastery motivation. Babies may be perfectly capable of mastering tasks that require only behaviors that are frequent in their repertoire, and that they can control;[1] however, if a task requires behaviors that they have only rarely exhibited, and over which they do not have much control, then babies will appear to lack mastery motivation. Similarly, the nature of positive and negative affective responses to mastery situations is likely to change as the abilities of the child change, because the child

---

[1]We view a baby as *controlling* a behavior to the extent that she is able to produce the behavior systematically, but is not necessarily aware of choosing the behavior.

will view the situation differently (e.g., with development, effectance pleasure may be supplemented by pride at meeting a standard; sadness at not realizing a goal may be supplemented with shame at not meeting a standard). These changes, which we will elaborate upon later, underscore that an *understanding of the capabilities of the children is crucial to understanding and measuring mastery motivation.*

3. *Mastery motivation is intrinsic to the individual.* We believe, following White (1959), that mastery motivation is intrinsic to the individual in two senses. First, mastery motivation is operative from birth; the baby need not be taught to be oriented toward mastering biologically relevant events. Second, there need not be any concurrent, extrinsic reward for the mastery behaviors; the child may engage in such behaviors in the absence of ongoing external reinforcers. It is important to note that although mastery motivation originates without the need for learning and *can* be operative in the absence of external reinforcement, the development of mastery motivation can and is affected by socialization. This point will be elaborated in our description of Phase 2. We hold that although all babies have some degree of mastery motivation, there are important individual differences in degree of motivation; and these differences most likely result from an interaction between biology and environment (see Morgan et al., 1990).

4. *Mastery motivation differs from but promotes competence.* Finally, again consistent with White (1959), we believe that mastery motivation impels children to engage in behaviors that foster competence. Mastery motivation involves behaviors *aimed* at mastery, rather than the degree of success in these attempts. However, it is expected that the child who is highly motivated to master will be more likely to learn successful strategies than will the child who cares little about mastery. Thus, it is expected that a greater degree of mastery motivation at one point in development should be associated with greater competence at later points in development. In fact, research by Yarrow and his colleagues that was seminal in fostering much of the work on mastery motivation demonstrated that mastery motivation (broadly conceived) during the first year of life predicted IQ at 3½ years of age better than did Bayley MDI (Yarrow, Klein, Lomonaco, & Morgan, 1975; Yarrow, Rubenstein, & Pedersen, 1975). Thus, although we believe it is essential to distinguish motivation from competence, we do believe that greater mastery motivation should lead children to become

more competent. We will now describe the nature of mastery motivation at different phases of development, as well as noting times at which there seem to be important developmental transitions.

THE DEVELOPMENT OF MASTERY MOTIVATION

Figures 3.1 and 3.2 summarize characteristics of the instrumental and expressive aspects of mastery motivation from birth to about 36 months of age. On the left-hand side of each figure, the approximate ages associated with each characteristic depicted in the figure, as well as with each developmental phase, are indicated. The entries in the figure are some important features of instrumental (Figure 3.1) and expressive (Figure 3.2) aspects of mastery motivation. The *top* of the box labeling each characteristic represents when, in development, the characteristic is expected to begin. Open lines indicate that although the characteristic is observable, it is not very common. Closed, narrow lines indicate that the characteristic clearly is present, but still is not frequent nor prominent. Closed, wide lines indicate that the characteristic is a prominent feature at that age. Note that developments from earlier phases continue during later phases. We will now detail the nature of mastery motivation at each of the three proposed phases, as well as the types of developments during transition periods that contribute to the observed changes.

Phase 1: Birth to 8 or 9 Months

Research has revealed surprising capabilities of even newborn babies. During the first days or even hours of life, babies can be operantly conditioned *if the response being conditioned is one they are prone to exhibit and can control* (see Rovee-Collier & Lipsitt, 1982, for a review). For example, they systematically will alter their sucking pattern so as to turn on a preferred stimulus such as their mother's voice, an interuterine heartbeat, or a familiar story (e.g., DeCasper & Fifer, 1980; DeCasper & Sigafoos, 1983; DeCasper & Spence, 1986). This indicates that even newborns are *capable* of controlling their sucking responses in order to control an environmental event, and, it

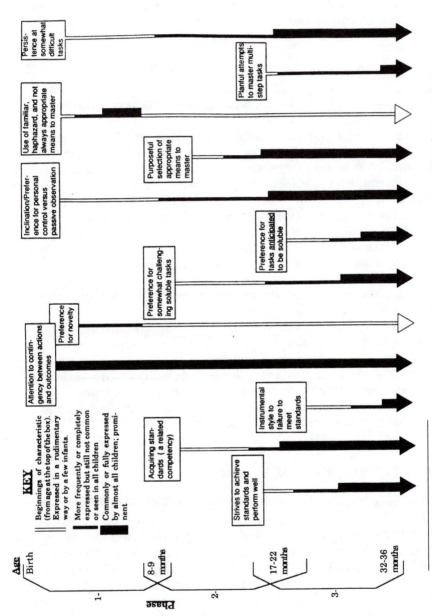

FIGURE 3.1. Instrumental aspects of mastery motivation and a related competency.

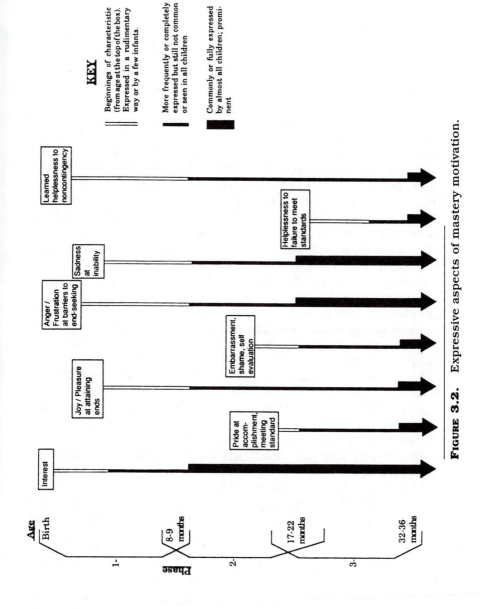

FIGURE 3.2. Expressive aspects of mastery motivation.

will be recalled, *inclination* to control is one of the important forms of instrumental mastery motivation.

Moreover, there is evidence not only that newborns are able to sense, at some level, whether an environmental event is contingent upon their behavior, but also that they prefer to control events (DeCasper & Carstens, 1981). This is suggested by the following data. First, newborns increase the frequency with which they display particular sucking patterns when such sucking patterns turn on a stimulus, but they do not increase those sucking patterns when the same stimulus is presented noncontingently with respect to their sucking. Second, infants show a *learned helplessness effect;* namely, they learn to control stimuli only if the stimuli are contingent upon their responses during their first exposure to them. If newborns first learn that events are noncontingent with respect to their sucking, they do not learn a later contingency between their sucking pattern and the stimulus presentations. Finally, newborns show evidence of increased motor activity and/or distress during a noncontingent condition when this follows the contingent condition (DeCasper & Carstens, 1981). This increased activity and distress when a previously contingent event is made uncontrollable suggests the possibility that newborn babies are preadapted to try (and prefer) to control events. Moreover, the learned helplessness-like phenomenon may provide the underpinnings for more complex helplessness phenomena that follow failure by children of older ages.

Such data regarding the newborn do *not* indicate that neonates engage in *intentional* mastery attempts. This seems highly unlikely. Nevertheless, even newborns manifest an inclination to master that does not seem to require extensive experience with reinforcement. In fact, such inclinations seem to *make it possible* for reinforcement to affect the baby (see DeCasper & Carstens, 1981).

The first phase of the development of mastery motivation extends well beyond the neonatal period, moreover, and studies with somewhat older infants have provided more complete information about the nature of mastery motivation during the period from birth to 8 or 9 months. First, there is stronger evidence that infants who are aged 2 months and older are aware of contingencies between their behavior and outcomes, and that they prefer to control events rather than to have events occur noncontingently with respect to their behavior. Again, however, in order to demonstrate babies' sensitivity to contingency and control, it seems crucial to make events contingent upon a frequently occurring, familiar behavior that the baby can control.

Alessandri, Sullivan, and Lewis (e.g., Alessandri, Sullivan, & Lewis, 1990; Lewis, Alessandri, & Sullivan, 1990) studied 2–8-month-old infants who were able or unable to control the activation of a slide/music display by moving one arm. Infants who could control the display learned the contingency, and smiled and showed interest much more frequently during the contingent period than during an extinction period. Moreover, they showed an angry facial pattern, fussing/crying, and increased movement of the conditioned arm during the extinction period, as though they were trying, unsuccessfully, to again activate the stimulus. On the other hand, babies who received the same stimulus at the same rate, but whose arm pulls were unconnected to the display of the stimulus, did not increase arm pulls nor show differential emotional responses. The investigators found no age differences in these phenomena (Lewis et al., 1990).

Interestingly, about 20 percent of the Lewis et al. (1990) babies did not show angry faces during extinction, and the majority of these babies showed sad facial patterns instead. Moreover, whereas the angry babies *increased* their arm pulling during the extinction period, those with sad facial patterns tended to *decrease* their rate of arm pulling, as if they were giving up (see Lewis, in press). These individual differences are reminiscent of individual differences in helplessness versus mastery orientations described in older children (see Dweck, 1991). It seems possible that the angry babies who continue to try to control the stimulus will become mastery-oriented children, whereas those who show sadness and stop trying will become helpless and/or shame-prone children when they get older. We will describe these distinctions among older children in more detail in connection with Phase 3.

In another study of contingency learning in infancy (Study 1 in Barrett, Morgan, & Maslin-Cole, 1993), 6- and 12-month-olds were able to control the emergence of a jack-in-the-box (contingent condition), using a cylindrical manipulandum. An additional 12 6-month-olds and 12 12-month-olds were provided the same manipulandum, and were exposed to the same number and rate of jack-in-the-box emergences (they were yoked to subjects in the contingent condition), but manipulandum activation did not affect jack-in-the-box activation (noncontingent condition). Babies could activate the manipulandum by light pressure of their hand and/or mouth.

Infants in both conditions seemed to strive to control the jack-in-the-box; children in both groups activated the manipulandum frequently, and noncontingent infants touched it more frequently if their jack-in-the-box emerged more frequently. However, only contingent subjects smiled more if they pressed more. In contrast, smiles of noncontingent subjects were nonsignificantly correlated with their manipulandum pressing. Finally, noncontingent subjects gazed at their mothers more than did contingent subjects, as if asking why the manipulandum "didn't work" or asking for assistance in making the jack-in-the-box jump up. These babies, like those in the Lewis, et al., (1990) study, seemed to have some awareness that they could or could not make the stimulus event occur, and they seemed to want to control the stimulus (see also Watson, 1972).

Another aspect of mastery motivation about which there are some, limited data is preference for novelty and/or challenge. During this initial phase of the development of mastery motivation, we believe that *preference for novelty seems to serve similar functions to preference for challenge at later ages.*

Babies' assessment of the degree to which various tasks are *challenging* probably is not possible during Phase 1, because *challenge* involves difficulty level of a task *relative to one's ability.* Purposeful *selection* of tasks on the basis of degree of challenge would thus require some awareness of one's abilities and of task difficulty. During Phase 1, the child's level of awareness of what she or he is doing is probably very limited, and awareness of the difficulty level of a task is probably even more limited. The child does not yet seem able to purposefully try new behaviors to bring about a desired end, nor to determine which behaviors would be sensible for effecting a particular end (cf. Piaget, 1952). Nor would a young infant be expected to truly evaluate, in advance, his or her competence to execute a particular task. For a baby of this age period, efficacy probably involves success at obtaining the desired end, rather than knowing that one had executed a difficult behavior or solved a tough problem (Piaget, 1952). Thus, babies are probably incapable of selecting tasks on the basis of their ability to challenge themselves.

However, *young babies may be preadapted to challenge themselves by virtue of a preference for novelty.* Although there is some debate about whether or not neonates prefer novelty (cf. Olson & Sherman, 1983), it is clear that by 2 months of age, infants prefer to look at novel stimuli. (It is possible that lability of state and/or poor visual acuity compromise researchers' ability to assess novelty preference prior to 2 months of age.) A predisposition to prefer novel stimuli would be highly adaptive, in that it would motivate babies to explore and master new stimuli and events. Such an inclination might be the forerunner of preference for challenge at older ages.

In summary, young infants show some awareness of the contingency between their actions and outcomes, and they prefer to control events rather than being passive observers. In addition, there is some evidence of individual differences in being prone to mastery versus helplessness. Finally, young infants seem to prefer looking at novel stimuli, which leads them to challenge themselves. Thus, the important elements of mastery motivation are present in early infancy. There is also evidence of social mastery motivation during this period (e.g., see Tronick, Ricks, & Cohn, 1982); however, that important phenomenon is beyond the scope of this chapter. Moreover, much change will still take place in each of these elements (e.g., preference for novelty, proneness to mastery versus helplessness). The important changes are well illustrated by findings in the literature more directly aimed at studying mastery motivation, which help demonstrate important changes during the transition from Phase 1 to Phase 2 (see Figures 3.1 and 3.2).

Transition from Phase 1 to Phase 2

In this section, we will propose an explanation for some intriguing findings in the mastery motivation literature, showing how the same operational definition of mastery motivation may capture different phenomena at different ages, and the same phenomenon (mastery motivation) must be studied differently at different ages. More specifically, we will suggest that an important transition in the middle of the second half-year of life impacts definition and measurement of mastery motivation during that period.

A series of articles regarding an investigation by Yarrow and his colleagues (e.g., Yarrow et al., 1983) highlight important changes in mastery motivation between 6 and 12 months of age. At first glance, some of these data appear to contradict the above characterization of the young baby; however, as we shall see, these contradictions are probably more apparent than real.

These investigators studied the responses of babies to 12 standard tasks when the babies were 6 and 12 months old. Several different levels of involvement with objects were distinguished: (a) simple visual attention to the task, (b) peripheral exploration (mouthing, passive holding), (c) general exploration (manipulation, examination, banging, shaking, hitting, etc.), (d) task-directed behavior, and (e) goal-directed behavior (the behaviors that actually could bring about the goal or reset the task). The first three of these levels were not considered to index mastery motivation; the fourth and fifth levels typically were summed to provide the primary measure of mastery motivation.

Tasks were classified, rationally rather than empirically, into three types—Effect Production (EP), Practicing Sensorimotor Skills (PSS), and Problem-Solving (PS)—and there often were divergent results for different types of tasks. It is therefore important to elaborate briefly on the tasks. Although infants were presented with the same *types* of tasks at 6 and 12 months, the specific tasks differed at the two ages. Most important for the present discussion are the behaviors classified as task-directed and/or required for successful goal attainment at 6 months.

Effect Production (EP) toys at 6 months produced interesting effects as a result of simple motor acts. For example, a "chime ball" and a "busy bubble" each produced visual and/or auditory effects when hit or rolled. An interesting stimulus event would be produced for all 6-month EP tasks by the infant's hitting at them, and, in all cases, hitting at the object would be considered task-directed.

On the other hand, Practicing Sensorimotor Skills (PSS) tasks at 6 months involved removing objects from containers or holes (e.g., pegs from a peg board or plastic eggs from a carton), and success at these tasks required fairly precisely coordinated grasping, picking up, and shaking. Hitting at these toys would be considered exploration, rather than task-directed behavior. Similarly, at 6 months, Problem Solving (PS) toys could not be solved by simple hitting; they required directed reaching and grasping, and classic Piagetian Stage IV behavior for solution (Piaget, 1952). Again, banging at the toys would be considered exploratory rather than task-directed activity.

At first glance, results reported in one paper from this larger investigation (Messer et al., 1986) suggest that more mastery-oriented 6-month-olds are those who are *less* task-directed in their behavior. The different categories of behaviors (i.e., visual attention, peripheral exploration, general exploration, and so on) on the different sets of tasks (EP, PSS) were correlated with McCarthy scores on the same children at 30 months of age. The prediction was that infants with greater mastery motivation would become more competent. However, the results reported in this paper indicated, surprisingly, that 6-month-olds' tendency to explore the objects (categories 2 and 3 above) was positively related to 30-month McCarthy scores, whereas tendency to engage in task-directed and goal-directed behavior was *negatively* associated with McCarthy scores (although this may, in part, have been a function of the positive correlation just described since each measure involved the amount of time spent engaging in that type of behavior and behaviors were mutually exclusive).

On the other hand, consistent with prediction (but only for girls) 12-month-olds who engaged in greater degrees of exploration of the toys tended to have *lower* McCarthy scores at 30 months, and those who engaged in more goal-directed behavior had *higher* McCarthy scores. These data suggested a developmental transformation in the nature of mastery motivation between 6 and 12 months—but how can they be reconciled with the results described earlier, indicating that Phase 1 infants are oriented toward controlling and mastering events?

One plausible explanation is that the behaviors construed as exploratory in Messer et al.'s (1986) paper (at least for PSS and PS tasks) are behaviors that are familiar to 6-month-olds and frequent in their repertoire, and that they can control (e.g., looking, banging, and mouthing). On the other hand, behaviors that would be classified as task- or goal-directed were infrequent, unfamiliar behaviors, over which infants had little control. As mentioned earlier, babies in the first phase seem to master events by engaging in well-known behaviors; they are not yet able to decide what behaviors should be effective in producing the desired effect. In the studies described earlier by Alessandri, Lewis, and Sullivan (1990), and by Barrett and Morgan in Barrett, Morgan, & Maslin-Cole (1993), successful mastery of the tasks required the same kinds of behaviors that would be considered exploration with respect to the 6-month tasks used in Messer et al. (1986).

Moreover, closer examination of Messer et al.'s (1986) results reveals that the *positive* relationships between 6-month *explo-*

ration and 30-month McCarthy scores involved only Practicing Sensorimotor Schemes (PSS) tasks; the *negative* relationships between 6 month *task-directed* behavior and 30 month McCarthy scores involved only PSS and Problem-Solving (PS) tasks. Thus, when banging toys was considered task-directed (Effect Production or EP tasks), one did not find the negative relationship; when banging and mouthing were considered exploration (PSS tasks), exploration was predictive of later cognitive competence. Messer et al.'s (1986) article pointed to an important developmental transformation in mastery motivation—a change from dependence on well-known schemes for mastering the world to the ability to select and engage in behaviors that specifically are relevant to the problem at hand.

Further support for the above interpretation can be found in the results from an earlier paper (Yarrow et al., 1983) using the same subjects as those in the Messer et al. (1986) article. In this earlier paper, the various types of mastery behaviors described in the Messer et al. article were correlated with one another concurrently at 6 months and 12 months, and over time from 6 months to 12 months. In addition, the mastery scores were correlated with Bayley scores at 6 and 12 months. We will focus on the findings most relevant to the developmental shift between 6 and 12 months—namely, the cross-age correlations.

The first set of relevant findings involved cross-age correlations between mastery behaviors at 6 and 12 months. Yarrow et al. (1983) found that persistence (duration of task- plus goal-directed activity) with EP toys at 6 months was *positively* correlated with persistence with EP toys at 12 months. Persistence with EP toys at 6 months also was related to persistence with PSS toys at 12 months. In contrast, persistence at PSS tasks at 6 months was *uncorrelated* with persistence on any task set at 12 months. Moreover, *exploration* on PSS tasks at 6 months was positively correlated with *persistence* on PSS at 12 months.

This pattern of findings makes sense if one assumes that 6-month-olds try to master tasks by haphazardly trying out familiar schemes. For 6-month effect production tasks, simple banging would produce interesting effects (and would be scored as task-directed persistence). On the other hand, those same behaviors would be scored as exploration on the 6-month PSS tasks. Perhaps infants who were most mastery-oriented at 6 months manifested this inclination by banging, arm moving, etc., regardless of task. Much of this type of activity would be classified as persistence at EP toys, but exploration at PSS, accounting for the differential relationships with persistence at EP and PSS toys at 12 months.

Similarly, exploratory behavior on PSS tasks at 6 months was positively correlated with Bayley Mental Development Index (MDI) scores at 12 months; persistence on PSS at 6 months actually was correlated *negatively* with MDI at 12 months (again, however, findings for exploratory behavior and persistence were not independent). Interestingly, 6-month persistence on EP tasks and exploration on PSS tasks were correlated positively with 6-month MDI, and exploration on PSS tasks also was correlated positively with Bayley Psychomotor index scores (PDI). Thus, 6-month-olds who responded to mastery tasks by persistently performing behaviors that were familiar to them and under their control were more competent at 6, 12, and 30 months, *regardless of whether such behaviors were classified as "exploration" or task-directed persistence.* On the other hand, 12-month-old girls who persisted in performing behaviors that were appropriate for solving tasks were more competent at 30 months, and 12-month-old girls who persisted in showing behavior that was inappropriate for solving the tasks were *less* competent at 30 months.

Additional support for a developmental transformation between the first half-year of life and the end of the first year of life is found in two other studies—Morgan, Culp, Busch-Rossnagel, Barrett, and Redding, (1993) and DiLalla et al. (1990). Morgan et al. (1993) studied subjects longitudinally at 9 and 12 months of age. At 9 months, mastery behaviors on a shape-sorter task were assessed; at 12 months, mastery behaviors on this same shape-sorter plus 8 additional tasks (2 other shape-sorters, 2 EP tasks, 2 PS tasks, and 2 symbolic tasks) were assessed. In addition, mastery behaviors were assessed during free play.

Results indicated that: (a) neither persistence at the tasks nor goal-directedness during free play was stable from 9 to 12 months, (b) task persistence at each age was positively correlated with goal-directed free play and negatively correlated with exploration in free play,[2] (c) both task-directed behavior on the

---

[2]It is important to note, however, that we see the transition as a gradual one, with infants showing Phase 2 behavior at younger or older ages, depending on the particular task. MacTurk (1993) found significant cross-age correlations in persistence from 9 to 12 months, and *positive* concurrent correlations between exploration and persistence at each of these ages; these discrepant findings may stem from differing task demands of his toys, as compared to ours.

shape-sorter and goal-directed free play increased significantly from 9 to 12 months, and (d) exploration with the shape sorter decreased from 9 to 12 months. These data support the developmental transition proposed earlier, and suggest that it takes place around 8 or 9 months of age, with some 9-month-olds already having become more able to select behaviors that are appropriate to solving a particular problem, and others still being dependent on haphazard application of known schemes. If some 9-month-olds manifest primarily the more mature (Phase 2) pattern and others the immature (Phase 1) pattern of behavior, then individual differences in level of "persistence" at 9 months might reflect whether or not infants are showing mainly mature, obviously task-related behavior versus behavior that, though aimed at solving the task, looks exploratory rather than task-directed to adult observers. Thus, individual differences at 9 months would primarily reflect an aspect of developmental level (amount of Phase 2 behavior) rather than mastery motivation. On the other hand, at 12 months, all infants would have passed through the transition period, and individual differences in persistence would stem from individual differences in mastery motivation rather than developmental level. Since there is no reason to believe that age of onset of Phase 2 behavior should be related to individual differences in mastery motivation, then individual differences in persistence should be unstable from 9 to 12 months. Since, by 12 months, all infants should exhibit mainly Phase 2 behavior, there should be increases in task-directedness from 9 to 12 months. Moreover, to the extent that a reasonable proportion of 9-month-olds showed at least some Phase 2 behavior, there should be similar relationships among task-directed persistence, exploration, and goal-directed free play at the two ages.

Interestingly, although task-directed persistence at 9 months does not predict persistence at 12 months, it does predict positive affect during task-directed behavior at 12 months (Morgan et al., 1993). Children who already have undergone the developmental transition by 9 months gain more experience with task-directed behavior by 12 months than do those who have not gone through the transformation by 9 months. Perhaps, as a result, they derive more pleasure from such activity at 12 months of age. It does not seem that competence at the tasks mediates the relationship between persistence at 9 months and pleasure at 12 months, since task pleasure and task competence are uncorrelated at 12 months (see Study 2, Barrett, Morgan, & Maslin-Cole, 1993).

A final study that provides data consistent with the proposed transformation is one directed at predicting IQ rather than specifically aimed at studying mastery motivation (DiLalla et al., 1990). However, data regarding two of the measures used are relevant to mastery motivation. Fagan's test of Infant Intelligence (Fagan & Shepherd, 1986) is relevant, since it involves preference for novelty. Moreover, Infant Behavior Record data regarding task orientation (Bayley, 1969) are relevant as well.

Results of this study (DiLalla et al., 1990) revealed that scores on the Fagan test at 7 months were virtually uncorrelated with those at 9 months. Fagan scores at 7 months were correlated with children's Stanford–Binet IQ at 3 years of age; Fagan scores at 9 months were not. On the other hand, Fagan scores at 9 months, but not 7 months, were correlated with parental IQ. Thus, individual differences in preference for novelty, as assessed by Fagan scores, were unstable from 7 to 9 months, and assessments at the two ages predicted different (but, in both cases, relevant) variables. It seems possible that these results are obtained because preference for novelty/challenge undergoes a developmental shift at about the same age as does task-directed persistence. We will elaborate why such a developmental shift would produce such results shortly. However, we will first explain why a developmental shift from preference for novelty to preference for some degree of challenge might occur around 9 months of age.

As indicated earlier, preference for moderate novelty in very young infants serves a function similar to preference for some degree of challenge in older infants and children—that of providing more events to master. Early preference for novelty should foster intellectual growth and be related to later IQ, much as later preference for challenge does, and should do so before the baby is capable of making a priori judgments as to how challenging particular tasks will be for her/him. As infants grow more aware of means–ends relations, they systematically select means to achieve ends, and they can better determine how hard it is for them to achieve success (see Phase 2, below). As a result, novelty alone may become less of a magnet for mastery attempts, as infants learn to focus mastery attempts on tasks that they can solve. For this reason, preference for soluble, but at least somewhat challenging, tasks may become more important in determining behavior than is preference for novelty, per se.

If so, the pattern of findings in the DiLalla et al. (1990) study may be explained by the same logic as were results of the Morgan et al. (1993) study, noting that this time 7 months is *prior* to the developmental transition. Perhaps at 7 months, individual differences in preference for novelty primarily reflect differences in this aspect of mastery motivation. In contrast, perhaps at 9 months, such individual differences stem from the relative mix of novelty versus means–ends challenge seeking as babies make the transition to seeking challenge. Thus, some infants who were high in novelty preference at 7 months would have become more oriented toward means–ends challenges at 9 months, while others would still primarily be interested in novelty. For this reason, individual differences in preference for novelty would be unstable from 7 to 9 months.[3] Moreover, assessing only 9-month-olds' preference for *novelty* might not enable one to predict their later intelligence, since developmental onset of preference for challenge might be uncorrelated with mastery motivation (the useful predictor of IQ). Perhaps 9 month novelty preference is associated with parental IQ for a different reason. For example, perhaps bright parents provide a wide variety of stimulating experiences for their children; thus, such children retain their interest in novelty despite their dawning awareness of difficulty level. All of this, of course, is extremely speculative, but it does provide interesting ideas that could be pursued in future studies.

The DiLalla et al. (1990) study provided additional evidence that was consistent with our hypothesized developmental transformation at about 9 months. Task orientation on the Bayley Infant Behavior Record (IBR) should provide information similar to persistence in task-directed activities, and, thus, should be a better measure of mastery motivation at 9 months than at 7 months. In keeping with this prediction, IBR Task orientation

---

[3]One might also predict a mean level decline in preference for novelty. Unfortunately, it is not possible to determine from the published version of this study whether such a decline occurred, since the measure utilized was the *percentage* of novelty preference—preference for novelty divided by total looking time. If 9-months-olds, being more interested in pursuing means–ends solutions, devoted less overall attention to the passive perceptual task used to measure preference for novelty, then scores on the Fagan test could increase from 7 to 9 months even if preference for novelty decreased (because the denominator decreased even more).

(assessed during a Bayley examination) at 7 months was uncorrelated with either parental or child IQ; however, task orientation at 9 months was correlated with both parental and child (3-year-old) IQ. Again, to the adult observer, 7-month-olds' "task orientation" is difficult to determine because of the haphazard nature of their typical problem-solving attempts. On the other hand, by 9 months, many babies look more purposeful, making task orientation a more reliable assessment.

In summary, evidence supports the possibility of an important developmental shift around 8–9 months of age. Before this shift (Phase 1), infants who are motivated to master something engage in problem-solving attempts involving poorly understood applications of well-practiced behaviors that are often inappropriate to the task, and display preference for novelty. On the other hand, after this shift (during Phase 2), motivated infants engage in more purposeful selection of appropriate means to master situations, and prefer somewhat challenging, but soluble, tasks. Individual differences at about 9 months of age primarily involve the degree to which the behaviors have undergone transition; those before 8 months of age primarily involve Phase 1 mastery motivation, and those after 9 or 10 months primarily involve Phase 2 mastery motivation. Individual differences during the transition period, therefore, are relatively uncorrelated with those before and after the transition.

Phase 2: Age 8–9 Months to 17–22 Months

In this section, we will discuss the characteristics of infants' mastery motivation during Phase 2 (see Figures 3.1 and 3.2). During this phase, infants are much better able to decide what means will accomplish particular ends. They continue to try to control events, and are beginning to determine which tasks are too difficult to accomplish. Finally, they are beginning to *learn and internalize* externally imposed standards for behavior. Eventually, toddlers will try to achieve these standards, even when others are not telling them to do so or rewarding them for doing so. At that point, which is uncommon until the transition from Phase 2 to Phase 3, behavior motivated by internalized standards will appear and feel intrinsically motivated. However, during Phase 2, babies are primarily *learning* the standards imposed by others. We will now examine each of the major characteristics of Phase 2 in greater detail.

Although Phase 1 infants were *motivated* to try to achieve desired ends, they *looked* like they were merely exploring most tasks because they knew little about how to accomplish desired ends. By the end of the first year of life, however, babies seem much more able to select means that will accomplish particular ends. At this age, task-directed persistence does seem to be related to concurrent and later competence (Messer et al., 1986; Morgan et al., 1993; Redding, Morgan, & Harmon, 1988). Moreover, as discussed earlier, infants continue to prefer to control events, rather than to passively observe them; if anything, they may increase this preference because of their greater awareness of what events they control (see Study 1, Barrett, Morgan, & Maslin-Cole, 1993).

In addition, by at least 11 or 12 months of age, infants begin to distinguish not only between overall ability to control an outcome versus lack of control (see Lewis et al., 1990), but also between levels of difficulty of tasks for them (see Morgan & Maslin-Cole, Study 3 in Barrett, Morgan, & Maslin-Cole, 1993; Redding et al., 1988). There is evidence that infants as young as 12 months of age persist longer at tasks at which they are at least moderately successful than at those that are extremely difficult (Redding et al., 1988). Thus, Phase 2 infants do seem to have a sense of which actions effect events and of which tasks that they attempt are too difficult for them. Moreover, they do persist more at tasks that are not too difficult for them. However, their understanding of their competence on tasks probably still is quite limited.

One reason for this is that they still do not understand arbitrarily imposed rules as to what constitutes success on particular tasks. Phase 2 seems to be a very important period for children's *acquiring* such externally imposed standards (e.g., I did it the right way, or *all* of the rings should fit on the ring stacker). However, it is likely that Phase 2 infants' judgments about their performance and about difficulty level of tasks *usually* are based on how much success they have in accomplishing a goal that *they* desire, and that has results they can observe clearly. They differ from Phase 1 infants in that they determine *how much* success, rather than just whether or not they control the stimulus. However, success is still not based on externally imposed standards.

We base this assertion on the following evidence: (a) Phase 2 infants react more positively to success than to failure, even though socializing agents do not, (b) Phase 2 infants rarely try to call their mothers' attention to their *accomplishments,* and (c) Phase 2 infants are less likely to manifest pride than are older infants.

First of all, at least at the beginning of this phase, infants react differently to successful mastery attempts than to unsuccessful ones, but their mothers do not. Data from a recent pilot study (Barrett, MacPhee, & Sullivan, 1992) suggest that *mothers* of 11 month olds react similarly to successful and unsuccessful mastery attempts. In both cases, they react positively, as if even an attempt is laudable. On the other hand, infants react more positively to successful than unsuccessful mastery attempts.

Mothers do not distinguish successful from unsuccessful mastery attempts, but children do. Thus, it seems likely that children at this age, like those in Phase 1, typically distinguish success from failure on the basis of failure to accomplish desired ends rather than on the basis of true, externally imposed standards for performance.

Two other pieces of evidence that Phase 2 toddlers usually do not base their judgments of success on others' standards come from the recent Stipek, Recchia, & McClintic (1992) monograph. Toddlers who were 13 to 21 months old did smile, exclaim, and clap when they succeeded. However, they did not call others' attention to their accomplishment as frequently as did older children, suggesting that they were less concerned with others' awareness of their accomplishment than were older children. Nor did they show *unambiguous pride* (a subjective rating) as frequently as did older children. Pride is often viewed as a response to meeting a standard (see Barrett, in press; Lewis, Sullivan, Stanger, & Weiss, 1989; Stipek et al., 1992). It is important to note that *some* of the younger children did call attention to their accomplishments, and some did show "unambiguous pride."

Similar findings were obtained in a recent study of children who were studied longitudinally from age 14 to 22 months (Heckhausen, 1993). As in Stipek et al.'s (1992) study, pride was observed in a few children who were as young as 14 months of age; however, the number of children manifesting pride increased steadily from 14 to 20 months. Although it is possible that toddlers who called attention to their accomplishments and/or manifested responses that communicated pride were not aware of behavior standards, their behaviors at least make it plausible that: (a) Phase 2 infants *typically* do not base their actions on appreciation of standards, and (b) Phase 2 infants are, however, beginning to learn such standards. This raises the question of how these toddlers develop an appreciation of standards, if, as suggested by the aforementioned study of 11-month-olds, mothers do not provide clear external feedback that indicates when young Phase 2 children have achieved the standard.

There are several possible ways that Phase 2 infants could acquire information about performance standards, despite the paucity of external feedback regarding successful versus unsuccessful attainment of those standards at the beginning of this phase. One possibility is that, even at the beginning of Phase 2, children are provided with *information* regarding the correct way to execute tasks (despite little feedback when they do not meet the standard). Then, they are increasingly expected to *meet* such standards as they pass through this phase. Heckhausen's (1993) recent study indicated that even mothers of 14-month-olds provide some information about the "correct" solutions to tasks such as block towers and shape sorters; however, they almost never criticize children for not attaining the standard. The rate at which mothers in that study criticized their children's unsuccessful shape sorting, however, increased very slowly from age 14 to 18 months, followed by a marked increase in such criticism from 18 to 20 months (the transition into Phase 3). Similarly, in our own work, mothers of 17-month-olds, unlike mothers of 11-month-olds, reacted more positively and less negatively to their children's successful mastery attempts than to their unsuccessful attempts (Barrett, 1993).

A second possible basis for Phase 2 infants' acquisition of achievement standards is their generalization from other types of behavior standards. Although parents do not seem to impose clear-cut achievement standards at the beginning of Phase 2, they do impose other types of standards. Externally imposed standards at this age seem usually to regard dangerous or destructive behavior (e.g., touching electrical outlets or grabbing potted plants or electronic equipment), rather than competence. At the beginning of Phase 2, infants become proficient at crawling, making it more likely that they will touch objects that are unsafe or breakable and that parents will prohibit such behaviors. Data from the pilot study of 11-month-olds mentioned earlier in this section (Barrett et al., 1992) suggest that mothers react with more negative emotion and less positive emotion to such violations of standards for appropriate behavior than to successful mastery attempts.

Similarly, by 11 months of age, infants show fewer positive responses when engaging in a concurrently prohibited behavior than when engaging in successful mastery attempts (Barrett et al., 1992). However, although babies react less positively to such standard violations than to successful mastery attempts, they do not discriminate affectively between such standard violations and *unsuccessful* mastery attempts.

It is possible that infants do not affectively discriminate between standard violations and unsuccessful mastery attempts because they do not distinguish these two classes of behavior at this age (see Stipek et al., 1992). To the child, the two classes of events are similar in some ways. In both cases, typically, a child *wishes* to effect some outcome (such as mouthing a wad of paper from a trashcan, touching an interesting button on expensive electronic equipment, putting a ring on a ring stacker or a piece in a puzzle), but is unable to obtain that end (because of prohibition or inability). In both cases, this lack of attainment of the goal may result in frustration/anger or sadness. Sometimes, an act directed at realizing a desired goal is met with a negative maternal response (standard violations); other times, the goal is prevented by inability. There is evidence that babies of this age group are responsive to others' negative affective responses (cf., Hornik, Risenhoover, & Gunnar, 1987; Klinnert, Campos, Sorce, Emde, & Svejda, 1983), suggesting that infants' attempts to engage in prohibited but desired behaviors may be stopped (frustrated) by negative maternal reactions. Regardless of the source of frustration, the child may be more affected by the lack of achievement of the desired goal, with its accompanying anger/frustration and/or sadness, than by the particular obstacle to that achievement.

Perhaps: (a) the negative responses of others enable children to learn about standards that are enforced by such responses, (b) children do not discriminate this source of negative (frustrated/angry and/or sad) affect from that caused by inanimate obstacles to goal attainment, and (c) children thus come to sense that others disapprove of nonmastery. This and other possibilities deserve further study.

Transition from Phase 2 to Phase 3

Several important changes take place between about 17 and 22 months of age, with important implications for mastery motivation. As has been mentioned already, it seems likely that by the end of Phase 2, toddlers have acquired some behavior standards. It also is likely that most children are striving to apply at least some standards during the transition from Phase 2 to Phase 3 (see also Kagan, 1981).

Moreover, these standards form the basis for another relevant development during this age period: self-evaluation. Although even very young infants have some sense of themselves and their behavior, around the middle to the end of the second year of life children seem to become self-conscious about their appearance and behavior (e.g., see Lewis & Brooks-Gunn, 1979; Lewis et al., 1989). If they see rouge on their noses when looking in the mirror, they try to rub it off;[4] if they perform in front of others, they look embarrassed; they increasingly seem proud of themselves for achieving something and ashamed for failing to do so (Lewis et al., 1989; Stipek et al., 1992).

Toddlers' increased awareness that there are standards for appearance and behavior (Kagan, 1981) improves their ability to evaluate themselves vis a vis these standards. During this transition period, and throughout most of Phase 3, toddlers probably understand only standards that concern attributes and events that are clearly and directly observable (see Stipek et al., 1992). For example, one standard that toddlers of this age might understand is that people and objects should not be dirty or messy—a messy face (rouge on nose) should be wiped. Another concrete standard that is relevant to mastery motivation is one dictating that tasks be completed (Jennings, 1993).

Children's increased tendency to evaluate their appearance and behavior probably also results from other related developments. First, toddlers are growing to *understand more and more about what they are like,* and, in particular, what they look like (e.g., Lewis & Brooks-Gunn, 1979; Pipp, Fischer, & Jennings, 1987). Second, and relatedly, they are developing concepts about their own and others' affective reactions (see Bretherton, Fritz, Zahn-Waxler, & Ridgeway, 1986). In particular, they are developing the ability to anticipate that others might react affectively to their appearance and behavior (see Higgins, 1991).

Finally, we believe that self-evaluation is not simply a cogni-

---

[4]Although toddlers are only *required* to touch their noses in order to be coded as showing self-recognition, we have found in our own work that most toddlers do attempt to rub the rouge off of their noses.

tive process that develops as a function of other cognitive developments; *evaluation* is intrinsically emotional. A crucial influence on children's tendency to engage in self-evaluation, therefore, is their *caring* about how they appear to others, and (probably beginning somewhat later in development) whether their behavior indicates that they are "good" or "bad" (see Heyman, Dweck, & Cain, 1992).

Caring (significance) is what causes thoughts about one's behavior or appearance to become evaluative. Simply knowing that one's appearance or behavior is different from usual would not necessarily imply that one should change it. Moreover, *caring* is what causes self-evaluation to affect behavior. Even knowing that people feel one *should* not look or behave a particular way would not cause one to change appearance or behavior unless one *cared* about looking appropriate and/or about that person's opinion.

Toddler's development of self-evaluation and standards has important implications for both instrumental and expressive aspects of mastery motivation. First, instrumental aspects are affected. Children's increased self-awareness and self-evaluation should cause them to select tasks and/or persist more or less at tasks on the basis of their competence to perform those tasks. However, although now the child should be better able to anticipate whether or not she or he will succeed with the task before actually trying it, *optimal challenge* (Harter, 1974) is still likely to be defined in terms of concrete outcomes such as how many pieces the child is likely to get into a puzzle. Because the standard for good performance is likely to be the existence of successes and because there is an increase in self-consciousness and awareness of others, the child may be just as motivated (or even more motivated) to engage in easy tasks as moderately difficult tasks (see Phase 3 described in the next section, and Morgan & Maslin-Cole, Study 3 in Barrett et al., 1993).

Infants' increased self-awareness and awareness of others also should further improve their understanding of just what they can and do control. During this transition period, children become increasingly motivated to "do it themselves" (cf. Geppert & Kuster, 1983; Jennings, 1993).

Expressive aspects of mastery motivation should be affected as well. Pride at successfully meeting standards, as well as shame at unsuccessful attempts to meet standards, should become increasingly common. Moreover, increasing proportions of children should manifest "helpless" styles (see Dweck, 1991) as children become more capable of determining that they have not reached a standard.

In addition to the burgeoning of self-evaluation and appreciation of standards, another relevant ability greatly improves during the transition from Phase 2 to Phase 3. This is the *ability to undertake several steps, in sequence, while keeping a goal in mind.* Several investigators have noted toddlers' improved ability to execute a sequence of actions in order to obtain a goal (see Jennings, 1993; Morgan & Harmon, 1984). This ability greatly increases the sophistication of children's efforts to attain a goal.

In summary, during the transition from Phase 2 to Phase 3, toddlers manifest increased appreciation of behavior standards and improved self-evaluation skills. These improved abilities have important implications for toddlers' tendencies to select tasks and persist at them on the basis of their competence to do those tasks, to want to "do it themselves," and to show pride and shame. In addition, during this transition period, toddlers become better able to undertake a series of steps, while keeping a more distant goal in mind. All of these abilities signal movement into the next phase of development—Phase 3.

Phase 3 (17–22 Months to 32–36 Months)

As the age guidelines for the transition from Phase 2 to Phase 3 indicate, we view the change from Phase 2 to Phase 3 as a gradual one that extends over a relatively long period of time. Most of the characteristics that distinguish Phase 3 toddlers from Phase 2 infants first become apparent during this transition period, and thus have been described in the previous section. In this section, we will describe additional published and unpublished findings regarding the relationship of mastery motivation during Phase 3 to the development of appreciation of standards, self-awareness and self-evaluation, and the ability to execute a sequence of behaviors to achieve a goal. The types of abilities and behaviors that toddlers manifest during Phase 3 really act to transform mastery motivation into achievement motivation. By the end of Phase 3, toddlers become oriented toward doing *well* at socially valued tasks (typically viewed as achievement motivation). In contrast, prior to Phase 3, babies were oriented toward simply attaining a desired end, rather than determining *how well* they performed.

Evidence has already been presented suggesting that by the end of the second year, children show awareness of performance standards. In addition to these previously discussed findings, Barrett, Zahn-Waxler, & Cole (1993) presented evidence that two-year-olds show shame-like and/or guilt-like behavior when they are led to believe they violated a normative standard (breaking another's toys). Similarly, Jennings (1992) found that during the period from 15 to 35 months, children were increasingly likely to show pride at mastery.

In addition, there is evidence that prior to Phase 3, toddlers often fail to understand the simple standard that one must *complete* a puzzle to "succeed" at it. We reexamined data collected by Pipp and Harmon[5] and found that virtually no 12-month-olds completed a puzzle, despite their competence to do so. (All pieces were the same size and shape so that if one could place several pieces in the puzzle, one would be *capable* of placing all pieces in the puzzle.) We also examined data collected by Morgan and Maslin-Cole[6] and found that even 15-month-olds almost never completed the same puzzle. On the other hand, virtually all of the older aged subjects (24-month-olds in the Pipp and Harmon data; 20-month-olds in the Morgan and Maslin-Cole data) completed the same puzzle. Similarly, as children in the Jennings (1992) study increased in age, they were increasingly likely to complete tasks, to pause after completing tasks, and to resist help on the final step of executing a task. These findings suggest that during Phase 2 children rarely appreciate the societal standard of completing tasks. On the other hand, by Phase 3, most do show some practical awareness of this standard (see Figure 3.1).

Children's growing ability to recognize and evaluate themselves is also associated with changes in mastery behavior. Pipp and her colleagues have devised a developmental sequence of 8 tasks aimed at measuring infants' level of recognition of featural aspects of the self (see Pipp, Easterbrooks, Harmon, 1992; Pipp et al., 1987). We analyzed additional data collected by Pipp and Harmon, relating this sequence of self-recognition tasks to persistence and pleasure displayed while toddlers solved puzzles that varied in difficulty level. Task difficulty was individually determined: A puzzle was considered difficult for a child if

---

[5]Other findings from this same data may be found in Pipp, Easterbrooks, & Harmon, 1992, and in Redding et al., 1988.

[6]Other findings from this same data may be found in Barrett, Morgan, & Maslin-Cole, 1993, Study 3.

that child failed to complete at least 2 pieces of it in 1 minute. A puzzle was considered easy for a child if he or she completed the entire puzzle in 1 minute. Thus, by definition, a child would perform poorly on "difficult" tasks, and would be very successful on "easy" tasks.

For 24-month-olds, we found negative correlations between level of featural self-recognition and both intervals of pleasure and persistence on *difficult* puzzles ($r = -.59$, $p < .05$ and $r = -.58$, $p < .05$, respectively; $n = 14$). These results thus suggest that toddlers who were more aware of featural aspects of the self were better able to recognize that they were performing poorly, and showed less pleasure and persistence on difficult tasks. On the other hand, for *easy* tasks, 24-month-olds who showed more advanced self-recognition skills showed significantly *more pleasure* ($r = .53$, $p < .01$; $n = 19$), but slightly *less* persistence ($r = -.15$, ns; $n = 19$). These findings suggest that 24-month-olds who are more advanced in self-recognition skills derive greater pleasure from tasks on which they are very successful than do 24-month-olds who are relatively less skilled in self-recognition. However, perhaps because they realize that they already have completed the puzzle successfully, 24-month-olds who are more skilled at featural self-recognition show a slight tendency to persist *less* at easy tasks than do toddlers who are less skilled at self-recognition.

Two other age groups were included in this study—12-month-olds and 36-month-olds. Too few subjects in these other age groups communicated *pleasure* on the difficult tasks to enable examination of the relation between pleasure and featural self-recognition. (For 36-month-olds, this was in part because only 9 subjects had even 1 puzzle that qualified as difficult, according to our criteria). However, it was possible to examine the relation between *persistence* and self-recognition on difficult tasks. Twelve-month-olds' level of self-recognition was uncorrelated with their persistence on hard tasks ($r = .04$; $n = 16$), and 36-month-olds' level of self-recognition was positively (but non-significantly, given that $n = 9$) correlated with persistence on difficult tasks ($r = .38$).

No 12-month-olds had any puzzles that met the criteria for being *easy*. For the 19 36-month-olds who found at least one puzzle easy, there was no relationship between self-recognition level and pleasure ($r = .16$, ns), but there was a significant *negative* correlation between self-recognition level and persistence on easy tasks ($r = -.48$, $p < .05$). Thus, 12-month-olds' self-recognition abilities were unrelated to persistence and pleasure on difficult tasks. On the other hand, 36-month-olds who displayed more advanced self-recognition skills were slightly *more* likely to persist on *difficult* tasks, and were significantly *less* likely to persist on *easy* tasks.

These findings converge with those of Lewis and his colleagues (Lewis, Alessandri, & Sullivan, 1992), who found that 33- to 37-month-old children showed more pride when they succeeded at difficult tasks than when they succeeded at easy tasks. Lewis and his colleagues (1992) also found that the same children showed less shame when they failed at difficult tasks than when they failed at easy ones. Unfortunately, shame and pride were not assessed in the Pipp and Harmon data. However, the two sets of results together suggest that by the end of Phase 3, children become cognizant of standards indicating that one *should* succeed at easy tasks, so that such successes are not noteworthy, and do not bear repeating multiple times. On the other hand, success on difficult tasks is noteworthy (and pride-worthy), and one should persist until success is achieved. We believe that because 24-month-olds have just completed the transition to Phase 3, those who have low levels of self-recognition have difficulty evaluating themselves, and even those with the most advanced self-recognition skills still use only a relatively unsophisticated form of self-evaluation. Such toddlers are sufficiently aware of their abilities and performance to become displeased if they see that they are performing poorly. However, they are not sufficiently sophisticated to recognize that they should feel good about *any* success on such a hard task, nor that persisting on/practicing difficult tasks is worthwhile, because this will lead to greater success (and, success on difficult tasks is pride-worthy). On the other hand, 36-month-olds, who are in the transition to Phase 4 and have more advanced self-recognition and self-evaluation skills, seem to be learning about the greater value of persisting and achieving on difficult tasks (see reanalysis of the Pipp and Harmon data previously mentioned for some relevant observations).

The third major development during Phase 3 that we wish to consider is children's ability to solve multistep problems. This, too, is an important accomplishment that is associated with changes in mastery motivation. The evidence presented earlier, indicating that Phase 3 children are more likely than are Phase 2 children to complete tasks (and to make note of such task completion by pausing and/or calling attention to it) indirectly indicates that children may be more cognizant of the multistep nature of tasks. If a child views the goal of a puzzle as successfully putting *a* piece in, then he or she has succeeded each time a piece is placed properly; there is no need to put *all* pieces in. On the other hand, if one understands that successful completion of a puzzle involves ensuring that *all* of the pieces are in the puzzle, then one views each piece as a *step* in the process of completing the puzzle.

Moreover, there is other evidence for children's increasing awareness of the multistep nature of tasks, and its effects on mastery behavior. Jennings (1992) found that, with age, toddlers manifested increasing engagement in tasks that had multiple steps. Similarly, Morgan, Culp, Busch-Rossnagel, & Redding (Study 2 in Barrett, Morgan, & Maslin-Cole, 1993) found that task-directed involvement in multipart combinatorial activities during free play at 12 months was correlated with persistence at multipart tasks at 25 months, whereas persistence at 1-step cause and effect activities during free play at 12 months was *negatively* related to both persistence and competence at multipart tasks at 25 months. Moreover, general exploration during free play at 12 months, which was *negatively* related to concurrent task persistence, was *positively* related to persistence at 25 months. Barrett, Morgan, and Maslin-Cole (1993) interpreted these findings as follows:

> Cause-and-effect toys at 12 months were straightforward, simple tasks that required a single behavior for solution. Examples included a toy toaster that popped up and a toy that made music when pushed. In order to solve these tasks, a child did not need to plan a sequence of actions; nor did s/he need to explore several possible strategies. . . . On the other hand, 12-month combinatorial toys, such as the ring stacker, could be solved completely only if the child engaged in considerable exploratory problem solving, and/or planning. These latter skills would be much more useful in preparing children to solve the 25-month tasks, which required sequences of actions for solution. Perhaps children who choose to focus on simple cause–effect toys during free play, rather than exploring and/or solving more complex toys, are less likely to acquire the requisite skills for the 25-month tasks. (pp. 96–97)

Thus, the child who shows high persistence on typical 25-month tasks seems to have developed the kinds of skills that potentiate problem solving with multistep toys.

A final set of relevant data are found in Maslin-Cole, Bretherton, & Morgan (1993). This was a longitudinal study, of instrumental and expressive aspects of toddlers' mastery motivation from 18 to 25 months. As a part of this study, component scores were derived to summarize several measures of instrumental mastery motivation at 18 and 25 months, and other component scores were derived to summarize different measures of competence at the same ages.

A component concerning 18-month-olds' *task directedness*, which included persistence on structured tasks, observers' ratings of goal directedness on structured tasks, observers' ratings of attention span on structured tasks, observers' ratings of goal directedness on the Bayley, and mothers' ratings of their children's usual persistence, was positively correlated with competence at the same age on structured tasks involving multipart toys ($r = .57$, $p < .001$). Moreover, at 25 months, a similar task directedness component was related positively to competence on structured and unstructured combinatorial tasks ($r = .48$, $p < .01$). Finally, competence on structured multipart tasks at 18 months was correlated positively ($r = .63$, $p < .001$) with a 25-month-old instrumental mastery component labeled "Overall Engrossment Plus" (engrossment, during free play, in combinatorial toys; engrossment, during free play, in symbolic toys; and maternally rated persistence). All of these findings suggest that during Phase 3, children who are most advanced at multipart tasks show greater instrumental mastery motivation during multipart tasks, both concurrently (but across different particular tasks), and over time.

Interestingly, and consistent with our belief that the 18-month assessment was made during a period of transition, correlations over time in instrumental mastery motivation measures were of low magnitude ($r = .31$ to $.38$). In addition, the exact variables making up the components, "task directedness" and "free-play engrossment," changed from 18 to 25 months, and the correlation of multipart task competence at 18 months with instrumental mastery motivation (free-play engrossment plus) was much higher ($r = .63$) than the correlation of 18-month free-play engrossment with 25 month free-play engrossment ($r = .31$). Again, individual differences *during* the transition period may have more to do with degree to which toddlers show Phase 3 versus Phase 2 behaviors than degree of mastery motivation.

In summary, improved self-recognition and self-evaluation skills, increased awareness of social standards, and increased facility with multipart tasks all seem to impact mastery motivation during Phase 3. We also believe that each of these improvements has implications for the development of *styles* of coping with mastery situations.

Earlier in this chapter, we alluded to Dweck's (1991) work highlighting individual approaches toward mastery situations. Briefly, Dweck believes that children approach mastery situations in two major ways, based on implicit theories of intelligence. One implicit theory is that intelligence is an *entity*, which can not be changed. The goal of mastery behavior is to demonstrate one's competence (and to avoid demonstrating incompetence). If one fails, this indicates incompetence, which is uncontrollable. Thus, such individuals give up when faced with failure, withdrawing and acting helpless.

On the other hand, for other individuals, the implicit theory is that intelligence is *incremental*—it can readily be increased. The goal of mastery behavior is to learn more, to increase competence: Failure implies that one needs to learn more or work harder. Thus, rather than leading to helplessness, failure leads to increased instrumental efforts (see Dweck, 1991).

Dweck and her colleagues have studied only school-aged children; however, findings from the previously mentioned study by Barrett, Zahn-Waxler, and Cole (1993) regarding toddlers' reactions to normative standard violations may be relevant. Interestingly, these two-year-olds could readily be classified into a group prone to guilt-relevant behavior (Amenders) and a group prone to shame-relevant behavior (Avoiders). Amenders, as the name suggests, quickly tried to fix the toy that they believed they had broken. In addition, they quickly told or showed the experimenter (E) about the mishap. This pattern is reminiscent of the *incremental* or mastery-oriented approach, which also may be viewed as one *instrumental* approach.

On the other hand, Avoiders were slow to repair the toy and to point out the mishap to E. Instead, they averted gaze from E and often physically avoided E after the mishap (but not before it). Avoiders smiled more after the mishap than did Amenders, and were more likely, in particular, to show "embarrassed" smiles (see Lewis et al., 1989). This pattern is quite similar to

Dweck's *entity* or helpless style, which can also be viewed as one *expressive* style.

As indicated earlier, we believe that behaviors relevant to these different styles are evident from early infancy in situations in which there is failure to accomplish a simple goal (e.g., activating an audiovisual display). During Phase 3, children seem to show these patterns in response to failure to meet normative standards. Do they also show these patterns on failing to meet *mastery or achievement* standards? Do they do so in response to failure to achieve *the final step* in a multipart task? How are these patterns related to instrumental versus expressive aspects of mastery motivation? These questions deserve further study.

It is important to note that we do not assume, based on such data, that the helpless style is the only expressive style; nor that the mastery-oriented style is the only instrumental style. Nor do we assume that all expressive styles are more maladaptive than are all instrumental styles. It is quite possible, for example, that children who display pride on attaining desired outcomes show a more adaptive response style than do those who persist at the now-mastered activity and do not show pride.

SUMMARY AND CONCLUSIONS

In this chapter, we have presented a conceptual framework for the development of mastery motivation from birth to about 36 months of age. We have argued that both instrumental and expressive aspects of mastery motivation are evident from birth, and that development in both of the major aspects of mastery is characterized by continuity in the face of change. Mastery motivation is a multifaceted phenomenon, which affects and is affected by many other developmental changes. By the time a child is 36-months old, self-evaluation and performance standards play an important role in mastery attempts, which suggests that *mastery* motivation has become almost coterminous with *achievement* motivation.

Many aspects of the model are relatively unstudied. In particular, more research is needed on Phase 3 of the model, and on continuity and discontinuity in development from Phase 3 to the elementary school years. We hope this chapter will foster attempts to test these and other aspects of the model.

REFERENCES

Alessandri, S., Sullivan, M. W., & Lewis, M. (1990). Violation of expectancy and frustration in early infancy. *Developmental Psychology, 26,* 738–744.

Barrett, K. C. (1995). A functionalist approach to shame and guilt. In J. Tangney & K. Fischer (Eds.), *Self-conscious emotions: The psychology of shame, guilt, embarrassment, and pride* (pp. 25–63). New York: Guilford Publications.

Barrett, K. C. (1993, March). Origins of social emotions and self-regulation: Appreciation of "right" and "wrong." In S. Lamb (Chair), *The beginnings of morality.* Symposium presented at the meeting of the Society for Research in Child Development, New Orleans, LA.

Barrett, K. C., MacPhee, D., & Sullivan, S. (1992, May). *Development of social emotions and self-regulation.* Paper presented at meeting of the International Society for Infant Studies, Miami, FL.

Barrett, K. C., Morgan, G. A., & Maslin-Cole, C. (1993). Three studies on the development of mastery motivation in infancy and toddlerhood. In D. J. Messer (Ed.), *Mastery motivation in early childhood: Development, measurement, and social processes* (pp. 83–108). London: Routledge.

Barrett, K. C., Zahn-Waxler, C., & Cole, P. M. (1993). Avoiders versus amenders—Implications for the investigation of guilt and shame during toddlerhood? *Cognition and Emotion,* 481–505.

Bayley, N. (1969). *Bayley scales of infant development.* New York: Psychological Corporation.

Bretherton, I., Fritz, J., Zahn-Waxler, C., & Ridgeway, D. (1986). Learning to talk about emotions: A functionalist perspective. *Child Development, 57,* 529–548.

DeCasper, A. J., & Carstens, A. A. (1981). Contingencies of stimulation: Effects on learning and emotion in neonates. *Infant Behavior and Development, 4,* 19–35.

DeCasper, A. J., & Fifer, W. (1980). Of human bonding: Newborns prefer their mothers' voices. *Science, 208,* 1174–1176.

DeCasper, A. J., & Sigafoos, A. D. (1983). The interuterine heartbeat: A potent reinforcer for newborns. *Infant Behavior and Development, 6,* 19–25.

DeCasper, A. J., & Spence, M. J. (1986). Prenatal maternal speech influences newborns' perception of speech sounds. *Infant Behavior and Development, 9,* 133–150.

DiLalla, L., Thompson, L. A., Plomin, R., Phillips, K., Fagan, J. F., Haith, M. M., Cyphers, L. H., & Fulker, D. W. (1990). Infant predictors of preschool and adult IQ: A study of infant twins and their parents. *Developmental Psychology, 26,* 759–769.

Dweck, C. (1991). Self-theories and goals: Their role in motivation, personality, and development. In R. Dienstbier (Ed.), *Nebraska symposium on motivation, 1990* (Vol. 38, pp. 199–236). Lincoln: University of Nebraska Press.

Fagan, J. F., & Shepherd, P. A. (1986). *The Fagan test of infant intelligence: Training manual.* Cleveland, OH: Infantest Corporation.

Geppert, U., & Kuster, U. (1983). The emergence of "wanting to do it oneself": A precursor of achievement motivation. *International Journal of Behavioral Development, 6,* 355–369.

Harter, S. (1974). Pleasure derived by children from cognitive challenge and mastery. *Child Development, 45,* 661–669.

Heckhausen, J. (1993). The development of mastery and its perception within caretaker–child dyads. In D. J. Messer (Ed.), *Mastery motivation in early childhood: Development, measurement, and social processes* (pp. 55–79). London: Routledge.

Heyman, G., Dweck, C., & Cain, K. (1992). Young children's vulnerability to self-blame and helplessness: Relationship to beliefs about goodness. *Developmental Psychology, 63,* 401–415.

Higgins, E. T. (1991). Development of self-regulatory and self-evaluative processes: Costs, benefits, and tradeoffs. In M. Gunnar & L. A. Sroufe (Eds.), *The Minnesota Symposia on Child Development, Vol. 23: Self-processes and development* (pp. 125–166). Hillsdale, NJ: Erlbaum.

Hornik, R., Risenhoover, N., & Gunnar, M. (1987). The effects of maternal positive, neutral, and negative affective communications on infant responses to new toys. *Child Development, 58,* 937–944.

Jennings, K. D. (1993). Mastery motivation and the formation of self-concept from infancy through early childhood. In D. J. Messer (Ed.), *Mastery motivation in early childhood: Development, measurement, and social processes* (pp. 36–54). London: Routledge.

Jennings, K. D. (1992, May). *Development of mastery motivation and sense of agency in toddlers.* Paper presented at the 8th International Conference on Infant Studies, Miami, FL.

Kagan, J. (1981). *The second year: The emergence of self-awareness.* Cambridge, MA: Harvard University Press.

Klinnert, M., Campos, J., Sorce, J., Emde, R., & Svejda, M. (1983). Emotions as behavior regulators: Social referencing in infancy. In R. Plutchik and H. Kellerman (Eds.), *Emotion: Theory, research, and experience: Vol. 2* (pp. 57–86). New York: Academic Press.

Lewis, M. (1993). The development of anger and rage. In S. P. Roose & R. Glick (Eds.), *Rage, power, and aggression: Their relationship to motivation and aggression.* New Haven, CT: Yale University Press.

Lewis, M., Alessandri, S., & Sullivan, M. (1990). Expectancy, loss of control and anger in young infants. *Developmental Psychology, 25,* 745–751.

Lewis, M., Alessandri, S., & Sullivan, M. (1992). Differences in shame and pride as a function of children's gender and task difficulty. *Child Development, 63,* 630–638.

Lewis, M., & Brooks-Gunn, J. (1979). *Social cognition and the acquisition of self.* New York: Plenum.

Lewis, M. Sullivan, M, Stanger, C., & Weiss, M. (1989). Self-development and self-conscious emotions. *Child Development, 60,* 146–156.

MacTurk, R. (1993). Mastery motivation in deaf and hearing infants. In D. J. Messer (Ed.), *Mastery motivation in early childhood: Development, measurement, and social processes* (pp. 149–167). London: Routledge.

Maslin-Cole, C., Bretherton, I., & Morgan, G. A. (1993). Social influences on toddlers' mastery motivation. In D. J. Messer (Ed.), *Mastery motivation in early childhood: Development, measurement, and social processes* (pp. 205–229). London: Routledge.

Messer, D., McCarthy, M., McQuiston, S., MacTurk, R., Yarrow, L. J., & Vietze, P. (1986). Relation between mastery behavior in infancy and competence in early childhood. *Developmental Psychology, 22,* 366–372.

Morgan, G. A., Culp, R. E., Busch-Rossnagel, N. A., Barrett, K. C., & Redding, R. E. (1993). A longitudinal study of mastery motivation in infants 9- to 25-months of age (abstract). In J. E. Jacobs (Ed.). *Nebraska symposium on motivation: Vol. 40. Developmental perspectives on motivation* (p. 273). Lincoln: University of Nebraska Press.

Morgan, G. A., & Harmon, R. J. (1984). Developmental transformations in mastery motivation: Measurement and validation. In R. Emde & R. Harmon (Eds.), *Continuities and discontinuities in development* (pp. 263–292). New York: Plenum Press.

Morgan, G. A., Harmon, R. J., & Maslin-Cole, C. A. (1990). Mastery motivation: Definition and measurement. *Early Education and Development, 1*(5), 318–339.

Morgan, G. A., Maslin-Cole, C. A., Biringen, Z., & Harmon, R. J. (1991). Play assessment and mastery motivation in infants and young children. In C. Schaefer, K. Gitlin, & A. Sandgrund (Eds.), *Play diagnosis and assessment* (pp. 65–86). New York: Wiley.

Olson, G., & Sherman, T. (1983). Attention, learning, and memory in infants. In P. Mussen (Series Ed.), M. Haith, & J. J. Campos (Vol. Eds.), *Handbook of child psychology, Vol. 2: Infancy and developmental psychobiology* (pp. 1001–1080). New York: Wiley.

Piaget, J. (1952). *The origins of intelligence in children.* New York: International University Press.

Pipp, S., Easterbrooks, M. A., & Harmon, R. J. (1992). The relation between attachment and knowledge of self and mother in one- to three-year-old infants. *Child Development, 63,* 738–750.

Pipp, S., Fischer, K. W., & Jennings, S. (1987). Acquisition of self and mother knowledge in infancy. *Developmental Psychology, 23,* 86–96.

Redding, R. E., Morgan, G. A., & Harmon, R. J. (1988). Mastery motivation in infants and toddlers: Is it greatest when tasks are moderately challenging? *Infant Behavior and Development, 11,* 419–430.

Rovee-Collier, C., & Lipsitt, L. (1982). Learning, adaptation, and memory. In P. Stratton (Ed.), *Psychobiology of the human newborn* (pp. London: Wiley.

Seligman, M. E. P. (1975). *Helplessness.* San Francisco: W. H. Freeman.

Stipek, D., Recchia, S., & McClintic, S. (1992). Self-evaluation in young children. *Monographs of the Society for Research in Child Development, 57* (1, Serial No. 226).

Tronick, E., Ricks, M., & Cohn, J. (1982). Maternal and infant affective exchange: Patterns of adaptation. In T. Field & A. Fogel (Eds.), *Emotion and early interaction* (pp. 83–100). Hillsdale, NJ: Erlbaum.

Wachs, T. D. (1987). Specificity of environmental action as manifest in environmental correlates of infants' mastery motivation. *Developmental Psychology, 23,,* 782–790.

Watson, J. S. (1972). Smiling, cooing, and "the game." *Merrill–Palmer Quarterly, 18,* 341–347.

White, R. W. (1959). Motivation reconsidered: The concept of competence. *Psychological Review, 66,* 297–333.

Yarrow, L. J., Klein, R., Lomonaco, S., & Morgan, G. (1975). Cognitive and motivational development in early childhood. In B. Z. Friedlander, G. M. Sterritt, & G. E. Kirk (Eds.), *Exceptional infant: Assessment and intervention* (pp. 491–502). New York: Bruner/Mazel.

Yarrow, L. J., McQuiston, S., MacTurk, R. H., McCarthy, M. E., Klein, R. P., & Vietze, P. M. (1983). Assessment of mastery motivation during the first year of life. Contemporaneous and cross-age relationships. *Developmental Psychology, 19,* 159–171.

Yarrow, L. J., Rubenstein, J. L., & Pedersen, F. A. (1975). *Infant and environment: Early cognitive and motivational development.* Washington, DC: Hemisphere, Halsted, Wiley.

4

MASTERY MOTIVATION WITHIN A GENERAL ORGANIZATIONAL MODEL OF COMPETENCE*

Ronald Seifer

Bradley Hospital
Brown University School of Medicine

Brian E. Vaughn

Auburn University

How is mastery motivation related to other important constructs that organize our understanding of social and cognitive development during the first years of life? This is the basic question we will address in this chapter. Mastery motivation provides us with an understanding of a discreet aspect of individual functioning during infancy and early childhood. However, full appreciation of development will only come when many discreet domains of function are integrated in larger systems that allow for understanding of complex developmental phenomena. The background against which mastery motivation will be examined is the systems approach to development

*This work was supported by grants from the National Institute of Child Health and Human Development and the National Institute of Mental Health. Ronald Seifer is at Bradley Hospital, 1011 Veterans Memorial Parkway, East Providence, RI 02915, (401) 751–8040. Brian Vaughn is at Department of Family and Child Development, Auburn University, 203 Spindle Hall, Auburn, AL 36849, (205) 842–3235.

(Sameroff & Seifer, 1983), which has been articulated to address more generic issues such as social competence (Waters & Sroufe, 1983) and developmental psychopathology (Sroufe & Rutter, 1984).

Mastery motivation has received consistent attention since the 1970s as a way of understanding an aspect of individual motivation during the first years of life. This construct is of interest because it (a) emphasizes characteristics of individual children, (b) attempts to address motivation in everyday life contexts, (c) may be conceived as an individual differences variable, and (d) is thought to be (at least partially) distinct from other measures of competence (Morgan, Harmon, & Maslin-Cole, 1990). While this precision of definition makes mastery motivation an attractive construct, that same precision also requires integration with other approaches to describing early development.

Other domains of function that have been identified as important in early development include attachment relationships with caregivers, the ability to regulate affect, solving cognitive problems, and organizing social interactions. It is important to note that all of these domains of function, including mastery motivation, have significant theoretical, definitional, and empirical overlap. However, we believe that it is useful to differentiate more precise areas of function as long as they are continually reintegrated with other aspects of early development.

In the sections that follow, we will review theoretical and empirical work regarding competence (broadly defined) during early childhood. First, we examine theoretical approaches to organizing different domains of competence during the first years of life. Next, we explore in more detail how competence may be viewed as organized patterns of behavior. This is followed by describing how another developmental domain—attachment relationships—have been viewed within this approach, since this is the area where the organizational theory has been most fully developed. We then apply the same theoretical analysis to the area of mastery motivation. The next section describes how organized mastery motivation behavior may be applied to the individual and social realms, followed by examination in the context of other domains of early competence. Finally, we present a summary and conclusion.

Competence in Early Childhood

Competence is currently defined, along the lines of Waters and Sroufe (1983), as the child's ability to use multiple behavior systems effectively in the face of developmental challenges. Prior to the 1970s, however, the major focus of development during the first years of life was in the areas of cognitive and motor accomplishments. The most obvious examples of this are developmental assessments such as the Bayley and Gesell scales (Bayley, 1969; Knobloch, Stevens, & Malone, 1980) for measuring individual differences in rates of development of cognitive and motor milestones. However, in the past 25 years, more attention became focused on perspectives that are more inclusive than cognitive competence alone (Ainsworth, Blehar, Waters, & Wall, 1978; Block & Block, 1980; Moss, 1967; Sroufe, 1979a; Waters & Sroufe, 1983; Yarrow & Pedersen, 1976), and theoretical explanations of development have been constructed to keep pace with this new knowledge. These researchers have broadened their descriptions of competence to include the domains of social/emotional behavior and motivation. In these expanded descriptions of optimal development, growth or change in one domain supports and enhances growth in others. Development is a systemic process within which growth of one function is not an isolated event, but exists as a part of a dynamic interactive matrix of abilities (see Sameroff, 1983).

One important development was the formulation of the organizational construct approach to understanding developmental phenomena (Sroufe & Waters, 1977). The hallmark of this approach was that important achievements should not be understood merely as the frequencies or rates of individual behaviors, but as the expression of systems of behavior interpreted as organized wholes. From this perspective the competent child is defined as one who is able to use effectively the personal, social, and physical resources available both to achieve current goals and to promote future development in ways that do not limit or close off the possibilities for future positive adaptations. Thus, competence at a given age cannot be described simply as achievement at or above the age norm on a single standardized test. Rather, competence must be assessed across a variety of physical and social contexts with reference to the child's coordination of behavior, affect, and cognition as these are mobilized in the face of age-appropriate developmental challenges (see Waters & Sroufe, 1983, for an article-length treatment of assessment issues).

A related theoretical advance was in the articulation of the developmental psychopathology agenda. Developmental psychopathology shares with organizational theory its emphasis on interpreting coherent behavioral systems, rather than any single behavior in isolation. Two additional aspects of this approach, which are useful for placing mastery motivation results in context, include (a) interpretation of child behavior in terms of its social–cultural context, and (b) examination of both normative and nonnormative populations. This latter point emphasizes that normative processes are essential for understanding deviations in development and, conversely, nonnormative processes enhance our understanding of normative development.

A final theoretical point that is important to consider is that there are bidirectional influences in development (Bell & Harper, 1977; Lerner & Busch-Rossnagel, 1981; Lewis & Rosenblum, 1974; Sameroff & Seifer, 1983). As noted above, it is important not to interpret individual child behavior in a vacuum—social context is always important to consider. Further, the effects that children's behavior have on the social context may serve to perpetuate that behavior. Two examples of this perspective may be found in Harter's (1981) description of mastery behavior and social reinforcement, and in Patterson's (1986) descriptions of "nattering" in conflictual families. The theoretical and empirical acknowledgment that parents and offspring are mutually influencing, but may have differing behavioral agendas and conflicting developmental goals, set the stage for the emergence of complex models for the description of actual sequences in development. In current parlance, these have come to be called transactional models of development and they have strong roots in general systems theory (Sameroff, 1975, 1983; Sameroff & Chandler, 1975).

Today, most developmental researchers consider explanations of growth and change that are not compatible with transactional models to be inadequate. Within such models, development is seen as having multiple determinants, as being organized as coherent systems, and as being potentially buffered against environmental insult (Sameroff & Seifer, 1983). Consequently, one cannot simply identify constitutional qualities or current status of individuals and expect to predict developmental outcomes; rather, individuals must be examined and understood as they grow and change within specific social and physical contexts (Vaughn, Deane, & Waters, 1985; Vaughn, Egeland, Sroufe, & Waters, 1979; Werner & Smith, 1982).

COMPETENCE AS ORGANIZED PATTERNS OF BEHAVIOR

As defined above, competence becomes a much more encompassing term than the ability to achieve developmental milestones. As a goal-oriented construct, it necessarily includes social and motivational domains not always treated explicitly in that realm. As a transactional systems construct, it is also necessary to examine the interplay among the competence domains to attain a coherent and comprehensive explanation. Within such a scheme, mastery plays a central role in defining competence in conjunction with other cognitive, social, and physical accomplishments of young children. The theoretical task is to describe the place of mastery within such a system so that it may be objectively studied and systematically related to other aspects of competence.

One example of a transactional theoretical position that has been well articulated in recent years is the organizational, ethological perspective on social–emotional development presented by Sroufe and associates (e.g., Cicchetti & Sroufe, 1976; Sroufe, 1979a, 1979b; Sroufe & Waters, 1977; Waters & Sroufe, 1983). This viewpoint has several facets that help structure an understanding of developmental change in general, and provides an example of how one aspect of competence has been integrated into a larger construct. This example will provide a basis to discuss mastery as it applies to a generalized competence construct.

First, the approach to social–emotional development by Sroufe is explicitly developmental; that is, all individuals regardless of their degree of physical/neurological intactness, are believed to advance through a predicted set of developmental "crises" (psychosocial crises in Eriksonian terms). Like Erikson (1950), Sroufe suggested that each crisis is resolved at a given life stage and that the nature of the resolution (adaptive vs. maladaptive) is a strong, though by no means perfect, predictor to outcomes of future developmental challenges. As such, this perspective may make predictions about developmental change and continuity both at a normative and individual difference level.

A related facet of this theoretical approach is that developmental status (with respect to the particular "crisis" of a given life stage) must be seen (or inferred) from the organization of behaviors or behavioral systems governing the coordination of behavior, affect, and cognition at a given point in the life course. Thus, single measures of behavior are not of primary concern. It is the interpretation of multiple measures, guided by organizing principles, that is the core of this approach; the meaning of any specific pattern or constellation of behavior is not of primary concern. Finally, the meaning of specific patterns or constellations of behavioral complexes may change with increasing age.

This emphasis on multiple measures has two distinct implications. The first is that one cannot interpret an observed behavior in isolation. Any observation must be placed in the context of other developmental achievements, social interactions, cultural contexts, and physical environments to be fully understood. This is the heart of the theoretical approach we are taking here with respect to competence in general and (later) to mastery motivation in particular. The second implication pertains to measurement. Since single observations of behavior are inadequate to evaluate aspects of competence, research must be designated to include multiple measures of each construct, and preferably include multiple constructs measured in any particular context. This follows the reasoning of research based on multitrait–multimethod designs.

An important offshoot is that individual behavior may be interpreted as having an underlying strategy. Such strategies are obviously not at the conscious level, but reflect organized representations of the world held by infants and young children. This strategic interpretation of behavior is useful when attempting to understand how behavioral systems will be organized across changes in social and physical context. For constructs like mastery motivation, which are relatively content and context independent, a strategic interpretation is useful in organizing a diverse set of behaviors in different circumstances.

In order to understand a behavioral strategy, it is important, as noted above, to make multiple measurements of behavior. This may be manifest in many ways. For example, different behavioral systems of an individual may be measured concurrently, similar behaviors may be examined in different situations, or repeated observations of similar behaviors may be examined. This multiple measurement approach is important so that questions about strategy may be addressed: Do multiple behaviors appear directed toward the same end? Does the child attempt to achieve similar ends in different contexts? Is the child consistent in constructing similar goals when presented with similar situations?

Attachment as an Organizational Construct

One developmental crisis that all infants encounter is the establishment of independent, yet secure, relationships with primary caregivers. Sroufe himself (Sroufe, 1979b; Waters & Sroufe, 1983) has most carefully described and elaborated his organizational perspective with respect to the infant–mother attachment relationship (Ainsworth, 1973; Ainsworth, Blehar, Waters, & Wall, 1978; Bretherton, 1985). The classification of attachment quality is based on patterns of proximity seeking, contact maintenance, avoidance, and resistance to interaction in a procedure that is psychologically stressful to most infants and toddlers. Though individual behavioral units (e.g., reaching, smiling, turning away, stamping feet) may have only small relationships with each other and low moment-to-moment (or month-to-month) stabilities (Coates, Anderson, & Hartup, 1972a, 1972b; Waters, 1978), the nature or quality of the attachment relationship reflected in the organized patterns among the multiple behavioral dimensions is quite stable over periods as long as six months (e.g., Main & Weston, 1981; Vaughn et al., 1979; Waters, 1978).

Sroufe emphasized another aspect of the organizational perspective (also derived from Erikson's (1950) epigenetic schematic of psychosocial development) that seemingly disparate arenas of activity may be grouped with reference to higher-order constructs (Waters & Sroufe, 1983). Thus, the construct of security within the infant–mother relationship is assessed between 12 and 21 months with reference to proximity and contact in the face of stress caused by separation from the caregiver. In contrast, during the third year (24 to 36 months) security within the child–mother relationship is assessed with reference to stresses associated with the child's motivations to explore independently and autonomously from the mother (Gove, 1982; Matas, Arend, & Sroufe, 1978), although separation is still important in activating attachment systems (Greenberg, Cicchetti, & Cummings, 1990).

Beyond the third year, Sroufe and associates (e.g., Arend, Gove, & Sroufe, 1979; Sroufe, 1983; Waters, Wippman, & Sroufe, 1979) have evaluated behavior and personality characteristics in the context of peer interactions as outcomes predictable from the early resolutions of attachment relationships. As such, peer relations are thought to reflect (indirectly) the security derived from the child–mother relationship.

To summarize, distinct strategies in attachment behaviors of infants and young children have been identified. These strategies are derived from organizational aspects of many specific attachment behaviors, and reflect the degree to which the child can effectively strike a balance between proximity/contact with an attachment figure and engage in exploration or independent play away from that person. For example, during reunions with parents, two children may both greet their parent, spend equal amounts of time in solitary play during the reunions with parents, and equal amounts of time oriented so they are facing away from the parent. However, one child who turns away from the parent at the moment of reunion and greets the parent only after a substantial lapse of time would be characterized as having an insecure strategy. A second child who greets his or her parent immediately on reunion and turns away only in the context of play after contact has been clearly reestablished with the parent would be said to have a secure strategy. It is the temporal organization of similar behaviors that leads to different inferences about their attachment strategy. In another example, one child may reestablish contact by crying, running to the parent, and sitting in the parent's lap for 30 seconds while regaining composure, all followed by independent play. A second child may smile, talk to the parent, and bring a toy to the parent to engage in joint play for 30 seconds, again followed by independent play. These very different sets of behavior would both be seen as secure reunion strategies. Thus, from the organizational perspective, similar behaviors may have different meaning in different contexts, and different behaviors may have similar meanings when organized in particular ways.

Mastery Motivation Viewed From the Organizational Perspective

Like attachment relationships, mastery motivation may be expressed in diverse individual behaviors. It is thus reasonable to interpret mastery motivation behavior in an organizational framework. For example, behaviors such as attending to task, persisting toward a solution, or expressing positive affect are all indicators of mastery motivation. The measurement question then becomes how to discern the strategy apparent in the child's behavior with respect to the construct of mastery motivation.

The initial question posed by the organizational approach is: What is the goal of the system in question? Recall that in the case of attachment, the goal of the system was to achieve a balance between secure base behavior and exploratory behavior. Further, under changes of context, the relative balance of these competing interests shifts (e.g., when danger is perceived, there is more emphasis on secure base behavior). In a similar way, one may define a goal for the mastery motivation system (MacTurk, McCarthy, Vietze, & Yarrow, 1987). Following the definition of Morgan et al. (1990), such a goal would be to engage in goal-directed exploration of the environment. By goal-directed exploration, we mean interaction with the physical and social world that is not simply exploratory, but interaction that also has a specific purpose. Conversely, it is not the specific pragmatic goal of the behavior that is of most interest. That is, task success is not the crucial feature of mastery motivation. Instead, it is the attention and persistence toward some goal, typically constructed by the child and not supported by social partners, that is the core of the mastery motivation construct. Empirical evidence from sequential analyses of 6- and 12-month-olds that such goal-directed behavior precedes positive affect displays is provided in MacTurk et al. (1987).

Once the goal of the behavioral system is identified, the next step is to identify the individual behaviors whose organization provides evidence about the strategy employed by the child with respect to the identified system goals. In the case of mastery motivation, such behaviors have been identified at a relatively macroscopic level—as in attention or persistence. In reality, the behaviors that are indicators of attention or persistence are more microscopic. For example, direction of gaze, motor patterns associated with individual objects, social patterns associated with individual people, productive repetition of motor or social schemes, body orientation toward objects or people, or affect expression contingent on some form of success are all examples of specific behaviors used to evaluate mastery motivation. Many different schemes have been presented to organize these types of behaviors to evaluate an individual's mastery motivation (Maslin-Cole, Bretherton, & Morgan, in press; Seifer, Schiller, Hayden, & Geerher, 1993; Yarrow, McQuiston, Mac-Turk, McCarthy, Klein, & Vietze, 1983)

In addition to evaluating many discreet behaviors with respect to systemic goals, organizational constructs have other properties. For example, specific strategies should be apparent under different contextual conditions, and organizations of behavior should have some continuity across development (even though these organized patterns might be vastly different at different ages). There is some evidence that these conditions are met. Children appear to exhibit more mastery behavior in some contexts compared with others. When task difficulty is systematically varied, moderately difficult tasks are associated with the most mastery motivation behavior (Redding, Morgan, & Harmon, 1988). With respect to continuity across development, mastery motivation appears to have moderate correlations (about .30 to .50) across 6 months to one year (Maslin-Cole et al., in press; Seifer & Vaughn, unpublished data).

The final aspect to consider when thinking of mastery motivation as an organizational construct is its relation to other systems of behavior. For example, there may be common roots of competence that have implications for multiple domains of behavior (i.e., similar contexts may support multiple types of behavioral organization). Sensitive parenting (contingently responding to children's cues) is theoretically related to both mastery motivation and attachment relationships. In the case of mastery motivation, Harter (1981) and others have described how praise or assistance contingent on expression of mastery behaviors serves to promote a strategy of mastery and self-efficacy (see also Maslin-Cole et al., 1993). In the domain of attachment, contingent responses to hunger, distress, and other needs promotes the strategy of using the caregiver as a secure base for exploration (Ainsworth et al., 1978).

Independent of context, individual patterns of behavior in one domain may help to promote organizations of behavior in other domains, sometimes in complex ways. Maslin-Cole et al. (1993) described how mastery and attachment might be theoretically related. Infants who have secure relationship strategies should be those who are comfortable and flexible in their mastery strategies. That is, they have a good balance between social and object mastery motivation, and they can flexibly adapt their mastery motivation behavior when context pulls for more proximity to a primary caregiver.

Mastery as Individual and Social Behavior

One of the hallmarks of the organizational construct perspective is that it attempts to integrate individual and person-in-context perspectives. In the case of mastery motivation, this raises two related issues concerning the degree to which mastery motivation should be considered as an individual or a social construct. The first of these issues has to do with the empirical focus of studies—should stimulus materials be object oriented (thereby emphasizing the individual character of children's mastery behavior) or social in nature (emphasizing mastery as a social construct). The second issue is more theoretical—whether mastery motivation is best viewed as a within-the-individual variation in motivation or whether it should be viewed as a reflection of the development of an individual in social context.

On the empirical side, most studies have focused on children interacting with the object world (e.g., Yarrow et al., 1983). In fact, these approaches attempt to minimize any influence that parents or other social partners might have in the assessment of mastery motivation. In contrast, there have been some recent efforts to examine social mastery motivation (Morgan et al., 1993; Wachs, 1987), where persistence and exploration of social partners have been the focus of attention.

These empirical studies of social factors do not, however, address the issue of how social factors should (or should not) be conceived in the context of mastery motivation. Simply manipulating whether materials presented to children are physical or social in nature does not speak to the issue of how social and contextual influences support mastery motivation behavior. Studies that systematically investigate developmental relations among different organizational constructs—including those that are more or less social in nature—are required to address these questions. Some examples are Maslin-Cole et al.'s (in press) study of mastery motivation, attachment, parental teaching style, and family climate, and Seifer et al.'s (1993) examination of mastery motivation, attachment, maternal sensitivity, and infant temperament.

Related Competence Domains in Early Childhood

In many places we have noted that mastery motivation may best be viewed in the context of other domains of competence during the first years of life. In this section we outline some of those domains, and in the next section we will indicate theoretical links between mastery motivation and those domains. Different aspect of competence during these early years of development span a wide range of functions, and represent an interrelated network of individual and social behaviors. This section will not cover every construct related to individual competence or social context that promotes such competence, but does cover a broad range of function, much of it important to consider in the context of mastery motivation.

Attachment.   During the first year of life, infants negotiate a transition from total dependence on primary caregiver(s) to a more independent relationship with those individuals. Many competing interests must be balanced: the need for safety when there is perceived danger, the need for independent exploration, the need for comfort when distressed, and the need for provision of basic resources. As noted above, when attachment is evaluated, the child's strategy with respect to a particular caregiver is assessed in terms of its security (versus anxious–insecure nature), and whether that strategy minimizes or maximizes attachment behaviors. Secure children have strategies that allow them to express distress when the attachment system is stressed, reestablish contact with attachment figures when available, and modulate their arousal and return to normal play and exploration in the presence of the attachment figure. Insecure children may have problems in any or all of these areas. Expression of emotion may be overly constricted or totally unmodulated. There may be avoidance or ambivalence when contact is available with attachment figures, or stresses to the attachment system may inhibit the child's ability to engage in fluid, productive play and exploration.

Affect Regulation.   All individuals express and modulate their arousal and affects. What distinguishes individuals from one another is the range of affects they express, the freedom with which they express those affects, and their ability to self-regulate their expressions and return to baseline function when desired, which some have characterized as individual differences in temperament (Rothbart & Derryberry, 1982). One may look at the proportions of more positive (e.g., happiness, joy, delight, enthusiasm) versus more negative (e.g., sadness, withdrawal, anger, frustration) affects that are expressed (Goldsmith

& Rothbart, 1990). Alternatively, one can examine how the expression of these affects influences the stream of ongoing behavior in other domains—does it enhance or detract from other productive behaviors (Kagan, 1989). Although most often conceived as an individual variable, affect regulation may also have strong social components (Tronick, Cohn, & Shea, 1986), especially during the first year of life.

Affect regulation is clearly related to attachment strategies. Those children who can self-regulate the affect and arousal associated with stress are more likely to be able to successfully deal with moment-to-moment perturbations in their attachment systems. Viewed from the other direction, those relationships that promote successful mutual regulation of affect and arousal may promote the development of individuals who, when social supports are temporarily absent, are able to negotiate the changes in availability of their attachment figures.

Peer Relations.   One of the important accomplishments of young children is to negotiate the transition from a small number of relationships with primary caregiver(s) to participating in a larger social network that includes same-age peers. As our culture rapidly moves toward near-universal preschool or daycare experience for infants and toddlers, the importance of these relationship experiences increases. Among the different ways that children may be competent in these relationships are communication, social acceptance, appropriate play, and variety of social partners.

Again, attachment and affect regulation may be strongly related to peer relations. Those children who can regulate affect and arousal well may minimize the number and intensity of conflictual interactions with peers—aggression, out-of-control crying, or anger related to blocked goals that normally arise in peer interaction would all be less likely when individuals quickly return to baseline after being aroused. Similarly, secure attachment relationships with primary caregivers may provide useful working models or strategies of relationships (Bretherton, 1985) that are generalized to the peer setting.

Task Success–Developmental Milestones.   Although we have emphasized the need for moving beyond examination of cognitive growth and development when discussing competence during the first years of life, this should not be interpreted as minimizing the importance of such factors in the overall development of competence in young children. As described above, there are obvious relations between task success and the previously identified competence domains. Well-modulated affect allows for more frequent and higher quality interactions with the physical world, which are thought to promote cognitive growth. In a similar manner, secure attachment strategies also promote high-quality interaction with the larger physical and social context. More successful peer interactions also provide important learning experiences for young children. Conversely, more competence in the cognitive and motor areas should result in less frustration when engaged in age-appropriate play (promoting better affect modulation), the ability to comprehend the moment-to-moment changes in pressures on the attachment system perhaps allowing for more measured responses to those changes, and higher functioning children are routinely viewed as more desirable interaction partners among peers.

Ego Functioning. Perhaps the broadest conception of competence during the preschool years has been developed by Block and Block (1980). Their constructs of ego-control and ego-resiliency encompass many areas of function, and describe two broad dimensions on which young children vary. Ego-control is the degree to which individuals are able to modulate and control their affect and behavior across a wide range of circumstances. Low ego-control is characterized by impulsive, overactive, labile, and uninhibited behavior. High ego-control is reflected in behavior that is constricted, inhibited, and rigid. Those individuals who strike a good balance between over- and undercontrol are viewed as most competent. Ego-resiliency is characterized by the ability to flexibly adapt one's behavior to changing contexts and circumstances. In contrast, ego-brittle individuals have great difficulty in adapting to changing conditions. Behavior might be quite good in some settings, but when circumstances change such individuals are less able to use their personal resources to flexibly adapt to those changes.

Theoretical Links Among Mastery Motivation and Other Competence Domains

Of most interest when discussing mastery motivation is the degree to which mastery motivation is related to other domains of competence during infancy and early childhood. For the most part, these links are theoretical in nature—there is little empirical work that has examined mastery motivation in the context of other competence domains. The most empirical work is available with respect to mastery motivation and general cognitive development as measured by standard developmental exams. Most of this work, which typically has been done with mastery motivation measured with respect to physical objects, points to a moderate relation between developmental quotient (DQ) and mastery motivation assessment (e.g., Yarrow, Morgan, Jennings, Harmon, & Gaiter, 1982). This should not be surprising for two reasons. The first is a measurement issue—the means of assessing mastery motivation (with objects) and DQ shares some method variance. Children's positive and varied responses to objects will result in higher scores in both types of assessments. The second, theoretical, link is that high levels of mastery motivation, through focused and persistent exploration, should increase the types of experiences that are thought to promote cognitive growth during the first years of life. Conversely, better cognitive and motor skills should provide prerequisite abilities for engaging in the types of focused, persistent object and social interactions characterized as high on mastery motivation.

There is also some research that has examined concurrently mastery motivation and attachment, and the results have been less consistent than for those studies looking at cognitive growth. Theoretically, mastery motivation should be related to the type of behavior associated with secure base strategies— fluid exploration of the environment in a calm, focused way. However, some studies have failed to find such relations (e.g., Maslin-Cole et al., 1993) while others have found a small relation between the two constructs (e.g., Frodi, Bridges, & Grolnick, 1985).

Unfortunately, much less is known about relations among mastery motivation and other constructs like peer relations, affect regulation, or ego functioning. However, there are theoretical relations that are important to consider. For example, mastery motivation behaviors are characterized by persistent interaction with objects and people that are neutral or positive in nature. Thus, an abundance of negative affect expression, or an inability to self-regulate affects (i.e., return quickly to baseline) would be interpreted as low mastery motivation. Further, inability to achieve a goal, either because a particular situation is beyond the developmental capabilities of a child or because there are no age-relevant problems in that situation, should result in less obvious emotional distress if arousal is well regulated. This in turn would again be interpreted as higher level mastery motivation behavior. Preliminary findings from our own work (Seifer et al., 1993) indicate that (directly observed) infant temperament is moderately related to mastery motivation (with objects) at a level comparable to that found for cognitive growth (DQ).

To the extent that ego-control and ego-resiliency are higher order constructs that encompass many of the qualities already noted for attachment and affect arousal, the same types of relations between mastery motivation and ego functioning should be apparent. Moderate levels of ego-control should have bidirectional relations with mastery motivation behavior. From a developmental perspective, children with higher levels of mastery motivation should more consistently have the types of experience that would promote flexibility and adaptation to changing circumstances. Persistent attention to one's physical and social context, accompanied by positive or neutral affect, should increase the frequency and duration of such interactions that are both rewarding to the child (and thus increase their frequency of occurrence) and provide relevant experience so that relevant schemes for interacting with more varied contexts are available and well practiced.

With respect to peer relationships, the relation with mastery motivation is probably more indirect. The most direct link would be that those children with more predisposition toward persistent attention to social partners would be more likely to establish initial contact with peers. More indirect links would be that the degree to which both mastery motivation and peer relations are related to constructs like attachment, affect regulation, task success, and ego functioning, then these domains of competence should mediate relations between mastery motivation and peer relationships.

SUMMARY AND CONCLUSIONS

Mastery motivation is a construct that has attracted a consistent level of attention for the past 15 to 20 years. It has a special appeal because it represents a context-based examination of individual functioning in relation to physical and social environments. For the most part, mastery motivation has been treated as a within-the-individual construct, primarily from a motivational perspective. However, as we have attempted to illustrate, mastery motivation may be more richly examined within the framework of organizational constructs, as outlined by Sroufe and Waters (1977) in their analysis of attachment.

The advantages of this perspective are twofold. First, a method of analysis that has worked well in the field of attachment research may be more or less directly applied to the area of mastery motivation, which presents many of the same types of theoretical problems. Many different behaviors are used to index the construct; these behaviors may have different meanings in different contexts; different constellations of behavior may indicate high mastery motivation, so that a strategy interpretation may be appropriate; and organization of these behavioral indices of mastery motivation may change with development.

The second advantage of this organizational approach is that it encourages thinking about the relations among mastery motivation constructs and other related social competence constructs. Further, emphasis on the social–contextual supports for mastery motivation behavior and the effects of mastery motivation on other domains of functioning may be highlighted. Finally, examination of normative and nonnormative populations is important from this perspective, which may broaden the area of inquiry for mastery motivation researchers.

The empirical evidence for examining these theoretical issues is not large. However, the available evidence is mostly consistent with this organizational view of mastery behavior, as well as its relation to other important organizational constructs relevant to development in infants and young children. The areas that appear to be interesting from a theoretical perspective, but that have little empirical base, are obvious directions for future research. Some examples would be the relations among mastery motivation, affect regulation/temperament, peer relations, and ego functioning.

We have attempted to outline some important theoretical relations among domains of competence supported by our most current understanding of existing developmental theories. Many of these theoretical relations described may not ultimately be supported by empirical findings. However, it is important to understand how these theories of different domains of development come together to predict certain types of empirical results. When such results are not found, we are then guided back to the theories with specific areas where they might require modification of clarification. Conversely, full appreciation of diverse theoretical perspectives should help to guide research towards addressing crucial issues within a larger developmental perspective.

REFERENCES

Ainsworth, M. D. S. (1973). The development of infant–mother attachment. In B. Caldwell & H. Ricciuti (Eds.), *Review of child development research* (Vol. 3, pp. 1–94). Chicago: University of Chicago Press.

Ainsworth, M. D. S., Blehar, M. C., Waters, E., & Wall, S. (1978). *Patterns of attachment: a psychological study of the strange situation.* Hillsdale, NJ: Erlbaum.

Arend, R., Gove, F., & Sroufe, L. A. (1979). Continuity of early adaptation from infancy to kindergarten: A predictive study of ego-resiliency and curiosity in preschoolers. *Child Development, 50,* 950–959.

Bayley, N. (1969). *Bayley scales of infant development.* New York: Psychological Corporation.

Bell, R. Q., & Harper, L. V. (1977). *Child effects on adults.* Hillsdale, NJ: Erlbaum.

Block, J. H., & Block, J. (1980). The role of ego-control and ego-resiliency in the organization of behavior. In W. A. Collins (Ed.), *Minnesota symposium on child psychology* (Vol. 13, pp. 39–101). Hillsdale, NJ: Erlbaum.

Bretherton, I. (1985). Attachment theory: Retrospect and prospect. In I. Bretherton & E. Waters (Eds.), *Growing points of attachment theory and research* (pp. 3–35). Monographs of the Society for Research In Child Development, 50, (Serial No. 209).

Cicchetti, D., & Sroufe, L. A. (1976). The relationship between affective and cognitive development in Down's syndrome infants. *Child Development, 47,* 920–929.

Coates, B., Anderson, E., & Hartup, W. W. (1972a). Interrelations in the attachment behavior of human infants. *Developmental Psychology, 6,* 218–230.

Coates, B., Anderson, E., & Hartup, W. W. (1972b). The stability of attachment behaviors in the human infant. *Developmental Psychology, 6,* 231–237.

Erikson, E. H. (1950). *Childhood and society.* New York: Norton.

Frodi, A., Bridges, L., & Grolnick, W. (1985). Correlates of mastery-related behavior: A short-term longitudinal study of infants in their second year. *Child Development, 56,* 1291–1298.

Goldsmith, H. H., & Rothbart, M. (1990). *The laboratory temperament assessment battery* (Version 1.3; Locomotor Version). Unpublished manuscript, University of Oregon.

Gove, F. L. (1982). *Continuity of attachment relationships from 12 to 24 months of age in an economically disadvantaged population.* Unpublished doctoral dissertation, University of Minnesota, Minneapolis.

Greenberg, M. T., Cicchetti, D., & Cummings, E. M. (1990). *Attachment in the preschool years: Theory, research, and intervention.* Chicago: University of Chicago Press.

Harter, S. (1981). A model of intrinsic motivation in children: Individual differences and developmental change. In W. A. Collins (Ed.), *Minnesota symposium on child psychology,* (Vol 14, pp. 215–255). Hillsdale, NJ: Erlbaum.

Kagan, J. (1989). Temperamental contributions to social behavior. *American Psychologist, 44,* 668–674.

Knobloch, H., Stevens, F., & Malone, A. F. (1980). *Manual of developmental diagnosis: The administration and interpretation of the Revised Gesell and Amatruda Developmental and Neurologic Examination.* Philadelphia: Harper & Row.

Lerner, R. M., & Busch-Rossnagel, N. (1981). (Eds.), *Individuals as producers of their development: A life-span perspective.* New York: Academic.

Lewis, M., & Rosenblum, L. A. (1974). *The effect of the infant on its caretaker.* New York: Wiley.

MacTurk, R. H., McCarthy, M. E., Vietze, P. M., & Yarrow, L. J. (1987). Sequential analysis of mastery behavior In 6- and 12-month-old infants. *Developmental Psychology, 23,* 199–203.

Main, M., & Weston, D. R. (1981). The quality of the toddler's relationship to mother and to father: Related to conflict behavior and the readiness to establish new relationships. *Child Development, 52,* 932–940.

Maslin-Cole, C., Bretherton, I., & Morgan, G. A. (1993). Toddler mastery motivation and competence: Links with attachment security, maternal scaffolding, and family climate. In D. J. Messer (Ed.), *Mastery motivation in early childhood: Development, measurement and social processes* (pp. 205–229). London: Routledge.

Matas, L., Arend, R. A., & Sroufe, L. A. (1978). Continuity of adaptation in the second year: The relationship between quality of attachment and later competence. *Child Development, 49,* 547–556.

Morgan, G. A., Harmon, R. J., & Maslin-Cole, C. A. (1990). Mastery motivation: Definition and measurement. *Early Education and Development, 1,* 318–339.

Morgan, G. A., Harmon, R. J., Maslin-Cole, C. A., Busch-Rossnagel, N. A., Jennings, K. D., Hauser-Cram, P., & Brockman, L. M. (1993). Parent and teacher perceptions of young children's mastery motivation: Assessment and review of research. In D. J. Messer (Ed.), *Mastery motivation in early childhood: Development, measurement, and social processes.* (pp. 109–131). London: Routledge.

Moss, H. (1967). Sex, age, and state as determinants of mother–infant interaction. *Merrill–Palmer Quarterly, 13,* 19–36.

Patterson, G. R. (1986). Performance models for antisocial boys. *American Psychologist, 41,* 432–444.

Redding, R. E., Morgan, G. A., & Harmon, R. J. (1988). Mastery motivation in infants and toddlers: Is it greatest when tasks are moderately challenging? *Infant Behavior and Development, 11,* 419–430.

Rothbart, M. K., & Derryberry, D. (1982). Theoretical issues in temperament. In M. Lewis & L. T. Taft (Eds.), *Developmental disabilities: Theory, assessment, and intervention* (pp. 383–400). New York: Spectrum.

Sameroff, A. J. (1975). Early influences on development: Fact or fancy? *Merrill–Palmer Quarterly, 21,* 267–294.

Sameroff, A. J. (1983). Developmental systems: contexts and evolution. In W. Kessen (Ed.), & P. H. Mussen (Series Ed.), *Handbook of Child Psychology, Vol. 4: History, theories and methods* (pp. 237–294). New York: Wiley.

Sameroff, A. J., & Chandler, M. (1975). Reproductive risk and the continuum of caretaking casualty. In F. D. Horowitz (Ed.), *Review of Child Development Research* (Vol. 4, pp. 187–244). Chicago: University of Chicago Press.

Sameroff, A. J., & Seifer, R. (1983). Familial risk and child competence. *Child Development, 54,* 1254–1268.

Seifer, R., Schiller, M., Hayden, L., & Geerher, C. (1993). Mastery motivation, temperament, attachment, and maternal interaction. In R. Seifer (Chair), *Mastery motivation in high- and low-risk samples during the first four years of life.* Symposium presented at the Society for Research In Child Development meeting, New Orleans, LA.

Sroufe, L. A. (1979a). Socioemotional development. In J. Osofsky (Ed.), *Handbook of infant development.* New York: Wiley.

Sroufe, L. A. (1979b). The coherence of individual development: Early care, attachment, and subsequent developmental issues. *American Psychologist, 34,* 834–841.

Sroufe, L. A. (1983). Infant–caregiver attachment and patterns of adaptation in preschool: The roots of maladaptation and competence. In M. Perlmutter (Ed.), *Minnesota symposium on child psychology* (Vol. 16, pp. 41–83). Hillsdale, NJ: Erlbaum.

Sroufe, L. A., & Rutter, M. (1984). The domain of developmental psychopathology. *Child Development, 55,* 17–29.

Sroufe, L. A., & Waters, E. (1977). Attachment as an organizational construct. *Child Development, 48,* 1184–1199.

Tronick, E. Z., Cohn, J., & Shea, E. (1986). The transfer of affect between mothers and infants. In T. B. Brazelton & M. Yogman (Eds.), *Affective development in infancy* (pp. 11–25). Norwood, NJ: Ablex Publishing Corp.

Vaughn, B. E., Deane, K., & Waters, E. (1985). Attachment quality and out-of-home care: Another look at some enduring questions. In I. Bretherton & E. Waters (Eds.), New directions in attachment research (pp. 110–135). *Monographs of the Society for Research In Child Development, 50* (Serial No. 209).

Vaughn, B. E., Egeland, B., Sroufe, L. A., & Waters, E. (1979). Individual differences in infant–mother attachment at twelve and eighteen months: Stability and change in families under stress. *Child Development, 50,* 971–975.

Wachs, T. D. (1987). Specificity of environmental action as manifest in environmental correlates of infants' mastery motivation. *Developmental Psychology, 23,* 782–790.

Waters, E., & Sroufe, L. A. (1983). Social competence as a developmental construct. *Developmental Review, 3,* 79–97.

Waters, E. (1978). The reliability and stability of individual differences in infant–mother attachment. *Child Development, 49,* 483–494.

Waters, E., Wippman, J., & Sroufe, L. A. (1979). Attachment, positive affect, and competence in the peer group: Two studies in construct validation. *Child Development, 50,* 821–829.

Werner, E. E., & Smith, R. S. (1982). *Vulnerable but invincible: A longitudinal study of resilient children and youth.* New York: McGraw-Hill.

Yarrow, L. J., McQuiston, S., MacTurk, R. H. McCarthy, M. E., Klein, R. P., & Vietze, P. M. (1983). The assessment of mastery motivation during the first year of life: Contemporaneous and cross-age relationships. *Developmental Psychology, 19,* 159–171.

Yarrow, L. J., Morgan, G. A., Jennings, K. D., Harmon, R. J., & Gaiter, J. L. (1982). Infants' persistence at tasks: Relationships to cognitive functioning and early experience. *Infant Behavior and Development, 5,* 131–141.

Yarrow, L. J., & Pedersen, F. A. (1976). The interplay between cognition and motivation in infancy. In M. Lewis (Ed.), *Origins of intelligence: Infancy and early childhood* (pp. 379–399). New York: Plenum.

5

MOTHERS AND OTHERS: THE ROLE OF THE SOCIALIZING ENVIRONMENT IN THE DEVELOPMENT OF MASTERY MOTIVATION*

Nancy A. Busch-Rossnagel
Diana E. Knauf-Jensen
Fabiana S. DesRosiers

Department of Psychology
Fordham University

Although the concept of development has strong biological roots (Harris, 1957), humans are by nature social, and thus even biological processes occur in a milieu of interaction with others (Lerner & Busch-Rossnagel, 1981). An example of the importance of experiences with others may be found in research on mastery motivation. While White (1959) stressed that effectance motivation was an innate drive, he did suggest that later experiences influenced its development. Research designed to operationalize his construct has focused on individual differences in mastery motivation (Morgan, Harmon, & Maslin-Cole, 1990), and many studies have demonstrated that the social environment is an influence on the development of mastery motivation. This chapter reviews the key studies to explore the relationship between the interactions of caregivers

*Work on this chapter was supported by NICHD grant HD 30590 to the first author.

and their young children and the development of mastery motivation in those children.

We use the three premises of mastery motivation proposed by Barrett and Morgan (this volume). First, mastery motivation is multifaceted in that at least two aspects of mastery motivation may be observed, expressive and instrumental. In the studies reviewed in this chapter, the expressive aspect of mastery motivation has usually been indexed by pleasure during work on tasks and by pride. The instrumental aspect of mastery motivation has been operationalized most frequently by some index of the child's persistence at tasks that are moderately challenging. This instrumental aspect of mastery motivation has been seen as oriented toward objects, but more recent work has suggested that instrumental aspects may also be directed towards people (Morgan, Maslin-Cole, Harmon, Busch-Rossnagel, Jennings, Hauser-Cram, & Brockman, 1993; Riksen-Walraven, Meij, van Roozendaal, & Koks, 1993).

The second premise we accept is that there are transformations in the nature of mastery motivation during the early years. Again, we have followed Barrett and Morgan by using the phases they propose as the framework for the organization of this chapter. We suggest that these changes in mastery motivation are influenced by the activities of the significant others in the young child's social environment. Furthermore, consistent with developmental contextualism (Lerner & Busch-Rossnagel, 1981), we propose that the changes in the child's developmental level will, in turn, create changes in the significant other's behaviors.

Finally, the most basic assumption we accept is that "the development of mastery motivation can be and is affected by socialization" (Barrett & Morgan, this volume). As noted previously, the process of socialization is a critical link between biological processes and the development of individual differences, and we propose to explore this link in the development of mastery motivation.

DEFINITION OF THE SOCIALIZING ENVIRONMENT

We define the socializing environment to include both mothers and other caregivers. These individuals have been described as "socializing agents" who affect the "maintaining, enhancing, or attenuating of the components related to effectance motivation"

(Harter, 1978, p. 37). The mother is seen as the primary social-izing agent in the child's early years, so most of the research in this chapter is concerned with mother–child interaction. However, the socializing environment can include other care-givers, such as fathers, older siblings, grandparents and day-care providers.

We propose that three aspects of the socializing environment be studied (see Table 5.1). First, there is the caregivers' provi-sion of inanimate toys and objects. Rather than focusing on specific toys or objects, the emphasis of the research has been on the general characteristics of toys such as variety or feed-back potential. Second, there is the emotional communication (or the affective nature of exchanges) between caregiver and child, which is seen as social stimulation or exchange of affect. Finally, there is the instrumental caregiver–child interaction that focuses on didactic interchanges (in Table 5.1 these are referred to as ZPD behaviors as will be explained later). These three aspects of the socializing environment stem from two the-oretical traditions: social constructivism (Vygotsky, 1986) and developmental contextualism (Lerner & Busch-Rossnagel, 1981).

Social Constructivism

Vygotsky believed that humans are active constructors of their environment, thus a primary focus for developmental stud-ies is how the natural and social forces of development interact (Wertsch, 1985). An arena where this interaction can be seen is in the transmission of knowledge from one person to another. This exchange occurs on the interpsychological plane, which is the intersection of two individuals' psychological processes. It is not, however, reducible to those individuals' psychological processes. In other words, the whole is greater than the sum of the parts. Vygotsky felt that the key to understanding individ-ual psychological functioning is to understand its precursor, the exchanges that occur on the interpsychological plane (Wertsch, 1985).

When these interactions are with more knowledgeable part-ners, children are more likely to acquire knowledge (Cole, 1985; Vygotsky, 1986). Because Vygotsky conceptualized the individ-ual as embedded in a variety of interpersonal and institutional contexts, any person might take the role of more knowledgeable partner (Rogoff & Morelli, 1989). Although many view Vygot-

TABLE 5.1. SOCIALIZING BEHAVIORS RELATED TO MASTERY MOTIVATION AT DIFFERENT PHASES OF DEVELOPMENT

Phase & Aspect of Mastery Motivation	Dimension of the Socializing Environment			
	Inanimate Objects	Emotional Communication	ZPD Behaviors	
Phase 1 (0–9 mos.)				
Instrumental	• stimulating toys (responsiveness, variety, & complexity)	• positive affect (i.e. smiles, positive vocalizations)	• contingent responses • social, kinesthetic & sensory stimulation	
Expressive		• social referencing	• social referencing	
Phase 2 (9–17/22 mos.)				
Instrumental	• provision of moderately difficult toys	• social mediation • positive affect (vocalizations & smiles) • reaction to success declines	• not directive • "step ahead" model • cognitively oriented activities • specific feedback after failure	
Expressive		• positive affect	• refusal to give help when asked	
Phase 3 (17/22–32/36 mos.)				
Instrumental	• previous experience with challenging toys	• positive affect exchanges • scaffolding behaviors • encouragement • praise	• not directive • scaffolding behaviors (focusing, marking critical features) • demonstrations	
Expressive		• emotional support • positive affect exchange	• emotional support	

sky's theories as focused primarily on the academic arena, he felt that instruction and development are connected from the very first day of a child's life (Wertsch, 1985). Thus, the mother or primary caregiver is the most likely and frequent knowledgeable partner in the young child's life.

Children who interact with a more knowledgeable partner are able to bridge the zone of proximal development. This zone of proximal development (ZPD) can be defined as the distance between a child's developmental level, as determined by individual performance, and the level of potential development, as determined by the child's performance with help (Vygotsky, 1986; Wertsch, 1991). The ZPD is a "dynamic region of sensitivity in which the transition from interpsychological to intrapsychological functioning can be made" (Wertsch, 1985, p. 67). Vygotsky (1986) originally introduced the concept of the ZPD in order to explain functions that were in the process of developing rather than those already developed, and he argued that it is important to measure both individual cognitive functioning and the level of potential development. When knowledgeable partners guide children in learning activities just beyond the children's skill level or when they provide help in joint problem solving, they can give children enough information to cross the zone of proximal development and learn more than the children would have on their own. Bruner (1986) described the task of an adult tutor as taking the work needed to be done and turning it into play, thus coaxing a child beyond the limits of individual performance.

This kind of support has also been called *scaffolding*. Scaffolding involves strategies that support learning by providing the child with task-related information that changes in structure over time. To be consistent with Vygotsky's notions, the amount or type of structure used must be based on the child's current level of functioning (Pratt, Kerig, Cowan, & Cowan, 1988). Vandell and Wilson (1987) described the game of peek-a-boo to explain how scaffolding works for the mother–infant dyad. When first introducing the game, the mother covers the baby's face. She then uncovers the baby and registers surprise when the baby's face reappears. At this point, the amount of support provided from the mother is high, while the infant's participation is minimal. When the child begins to uncover his or her self, the mother's support decreases to covering the face and registering surprise. Eventually, the child learns both to cover and uncover the self. The more skilled the infant becomes at playing the game, the more involved he or she becomes, and the amount of support provided by the mother decreases.

Researchers have also used the term "apprenticeship" interactions to describe the support the adult gives the child to cross the ZPD (Heckhausen, 1987a). In an apprenticeship, the master or more knowledgeable partner guides apprentices in the acquisition of skills by compensating for weaknesses while challenging their potential for development. The "contingent shift" described by Pratt et al. (1988) is an example of this support. When a child has developed independent capabilities to complete the task, the caregiver should be able to recognize this new found ability and provide less technical support; this change in caregiver behavior is thus contingent on the child's development.

In this chapter we use the term "ZPD behaviors" to denote that a number of caregiver behaviors can be conceived of as helping the child to bridge this zone. In the ZPD there are two realities based in a concrete situation. Although both the adult and child are in the same location with the same objects and events, they do not share common definitions for the location, objects or events. By interacting, the two individuals create a shared social reality (Wertsch, 1985). While a socializing environment creates the zone of proximal development, it is limited by the individuals' intellectual abilities and current state of development (Vygotsky, 1986). In other words, it is jointly determined by child variables and environmental variables.

Developmental Contextualism

The joint influence of child and environmental variables is consistent with the second influence on our conceptualization of the socializing environment, that of developmental contextualism (Lerner & Busch-Rossnagel, 1981). Similar to Vygotsky's ideas, developmental contextualism assumes that development is multiply determined. Contextualism focuses on the multiple levels of functioning, such as the biological, the psychological, the sociocultural, and the physical (Riegel, 1976) and proposes that influences on development may be found at all of these levels. By heeding the call to examine possible physical influences on mastery motivation, we note that the young child's exposure to the physical environment is primarily mediated by the actions of the caregiver, and thus have included the objects in the inanimate environment as part of the socializing environment.

Developmental contextualism also stresses the notion of reciprocity in its proposition that changes in one level of the environment cause changes in other levels (Lerner & Busch-Rossnagel, 1981). We thus need to examine the literature for examples of the way in which changes in the young child's mastery motivation may result in changes in caregiver influences. Reciprocity is inherent in examinations of synchrony in microsequential examinations of mother–child interactions (Heckhausen, 1987a, 1987b), as well as in longitudinal examinations of scaffolding (Maslin-Cole, Bretherton, & Morgan, 1993).

Traditional definitions of validity are also challenged by developmental contextualism. If the assumption that development is multiply determined is accepted, then interactions among causal influences, rather than main effects, are likely to be the key to understanding human behaviors (Hultsch & Hickey, 1978). Thus, variables that are implicitly included in a research design may be influencing outcomes along with the variables explicitly acknowledged in the design. Thus, the adequate conceptualization of influences, rather than laboratory control, becomes the key to validity. In mastery motivation research, this means that conclusions based on nonrepresentative samples (e.g., middle-class, Euro-American families with nonworking mothers who have the time to participate in longitudinal research studies) may not generalize to other populations (e.g., lower class families in cultures with less of an individual work ethic).

The theoretical approaches of social constructivism and developmental contextualism complement each other. Vygotsky (1986) helped to define the instrumental aspects of adult–child interaction, here called ZPD behaviors, while Lerner and Busch-Rossnagel (1981) noted the need to consider other levels of the interaction, here, namely, the provision of inanimate objects and emotional communication. Both emphasized the importance of social interactions in influencing development and noted reciprocities as a key feature in those interactions. With this theoretical background, we turn now to an examination of the literature on caregiving influences at different phases of mastery motivation development.

Phase 1: 0 to 9 Months

There are several behaviors, in-cluding a preference for novel stimuli, awareness of contingencies involving the infant's own actions, and persistence at events that the infant controls, that are early indications of instrumental aspects of mastery motivation (Barrett & Morgan, this volume). The review by Barrett and Morgan shows the existence of individual differences in these behaviors, while Heckhausen (1993) suggested that the caregiver's sensitivity to and use of contingencies is the primary source of these individual differences in contingency awareness and exploration. Contingently responsive caregivers are those who correctly assess children's cues and respond appropriately to the needs ex-pressed (Hauser-Cram & Shonkoff, this volume).

Heckhausen's model of the importance of contingencies is supported by the results of a study by Yarrow, Rubenstein, Pedersen, and Jankowski (1972), involving 41 6-month-old infants and their caregivers from a predominantly lower income black sample. Three indications of the instrumental aspect of mastery motivation at phase 1 were measured: preference for novel stimuli, awareness of contingencies, and goal directedness or persistence in attempting to attain objects. Each of the three aspects of the socializing environment provided by the mother were assessed. First, the stimulation of the inanimate environment was assessed through three ratings of the objects available to the infants: variety (number of different objects), responsiveness (feedback potential), and complexity (amount of information provided). Second, the emotional communication of mother–child interaction was indexed by a rating of expression of positive affect and a time sampling of level of social stimulation. Third, maternal behaviors related to the ZPD included contingent maternal responses to both positive infant vocalization and distress and kinesthetic stimulation.

Correlational analyses supported the premise that all three aspects of the socializing environment were related to instrumental aspects of mastery motivation. Seven of the nine correlations between the measures of the inanimate environment and the measures of instrumental mastery motivation were significant, highlighting the importance of the provision of stimulating play materials by the caregiver. The mother's expression of positive affect and level of social stimulation were related to contingency awareness and persistence, while expression of positive affect was also related to preference for novelty. For the variables related to the ZPD, contingent response to distress, and kinesthetic stimulation were related to contingency awareness and persistence, while contingent response to vocalization was related to preference for novelty. This early study found relationships among all three aspects of the socializing environment and three indications of the instrumental aspect of phase 1 mastery motivation. This set the foundation for further exploration of the relationship between caregiver behaviors and instrumental mastery motivation.

The Yarrow et al. (1972) study related individual differences in instrumental aspects of mastery motivation to the socializing environment, but did not explore the affective aspects of mastery motivation. However, many studies of early emotional development emphasize social referencing to caregivers as an influence on infants' affective reactions to objects and events (Klinnert, Emde, Butterfield, & Campos, 1986). The concept of social referencing can be traced to social comparison theory, which was proposed by Festinger in 1954. When we are in a new or ambiguous situation, we turn to those around us for information about appropriate reactions. Thus, when an infant is presented with an unfamiliar toy, for example, he or she may turn to the mother to determine an appropriate response.

One study suggests that social referencing influences an infant's understanding of contingencies. Barrett and Morgan (study 1 in Barrett, Morgan, & Maslin-Cole, 1993) studied 24 6-month-olds and 24 12-month-olds and their caregivers. Half of the infants were assigned to a contingent condition and controlled the emergence of a jack-in-the-box by their manipulations. The infants in the noncontingent condition did not control the emergence of the jack-in-the-box. The results showed that infant smiling was clearly related to the contingency between the infant actions and the effect of the jack-in-the-box. Furthermore, infants in the noncontingent condition looked to the mothers, as if to understand the lack of effect of their actions. This reference to the mother is consistent with research showing social referencing to caregivers in order to interpret ambiguous situations (Gunnar & Stone, 1984). The Barrett and Morgan study provides information about infant behaviors, but does not tell us what the mother's response was.

Another pilot study suggests that mothers are protecting their children from the effects of failure across the transition from phase 1 to phase 2. In research designed to explore the interface between emotional development and self-regulation in the early years, Barrett, MacPhee, and Sullivan (1992) observed 2 8-month-old and 8 11-month-old children in a free play situation with their mothers. The goal-directed behaviors or mastery attempts of the infants were coded as being successful or unsuccessful; the performance of prohibited behavior (violations of standards) was also coded. The facial and vocal emotional responses of the mothers and infants and mothers' verbal responses to the mastery attempts and standard violations were categorized as positive (e.g., smiles, or positive vocalization) or negative (e.g., angry facial pattern or distress vocalization).

Barrett et al. (1992) found that the mothers showed uniformly positive responses to children's mastery attempts and did not differentiate between successful and unsuccessful attempts. Nevertheless, the children did show more positive responses to successful mastery attempts. However, mothers do differentiate between standard violations and mastery attempts (whether successful or unsuccessful), suggesting that caregiver behaviors might be one influence on the acquisition of standards that Barrett and Morgan (this volume) outline as beginning during the second phase of the development of mastery motivation.

In this first developmental phase of mastery motivation, the socializing environment appears to be of importance. The role of caregivers in establishing early play patterns involving contingencies is important. The provision of toys, caregiver responsiveness, and the display of positive maternal emotional affect are all related to early child mastery behaviors. Social referencing also appears to occur before 9 months of age. Future research with children in this age group will allow us to more fully describe the nature of the relationship between caregiver and child in the early development of mastery motivation.

Phase 2: 9 to 17–22 Months

In phase 2, instrumental mastery motivation continues to be indexed by a preference for control (e.g., playing with objects that produce effects such as a surprise or busy box) and by task-directed persistence, now particularly at moderately difficult tasks. The affective aspects of mastery motivation are now more observable; these include pleasure at completing a task and the beginnings of pride and shame (Barrett & Morgan, this volume). Do the individual differences observed in instrumental and expressive mastery motivation at this phase continue to be related to aspects of the caregiving environment? Support for this relationship comes both from contemporaneous and longitudinal studies of mother–toddler interaction.

Following up on the earlier study of low-income, black infants,

Yarrow and his colleagues (Gaiter, Morgan, Jennings, Harmon, & Yarrow, 1982; Jennings, Harmon, Morgan, Gaiter, & Yarrow, 1979; Yarrow, Morgan, Jennings, Harmon, & Gaiter, 1982) studied the socializing environment of 1-year-old infants and their mothers; approximately half of these dyads had participated in home observations when the infants were 6 months old. The sample was upper-middle class and predominantly white. Both free-play and structured-task measures of instrumental mastery motivation were included. Ratings of the variety and responsiveness or feedback potential of toys tapped the inanimate socializing environment. Behaviors related to bridging the ZPD included time spent in mother–infant play, contingent responding to infant vocalization and distress, and kinesthetic and auditory stimulation. Social mediation of play, defined as mediation of play with smiles and vocalizations, was an index of the emotional communication in the socializing environment, as was social stimulation.

Infants' mastery behavior at 12 months could be predicted from maternal behavior at 6 months but in some ways contrary to expectations. Two ZPD behaviors, maternal play with infants and vocal responsivity at 6 months were negatively correlated with infants' mastery motivation, namely production of effects during free play at 12 months. However, 12-month free play mastery motivation was positively related to responsiveness of toys at 6 months (Jennings et al., 1979). All three aspects of the socializing environment at 6 months—responsiveness of toys (tapping the inanimate environment), kinesthetic and auditory stimulation (ZPD behaviors), and social mediation of play (emotional communication)—were related to persistence at structured mastery tasks at 12 months (Yarrow et al. 1982). The contemporaneous relationships at 12 months were similar to the longitudinal relationships between 6 and 12 months. Mothers who played more with their infants had infants who showed less mastery motivation, again measured by effect production in free play (Jennings et al., 1979), while the variety of cognitively oriented caregiver activities was contemporaneously related to overall persistence at mastery tasks at one year (Gaiter et al., 1982).

The findings of negative relationships between maternal play and responsivity and instrumental mastery motivation in infants may surprise some. These findings may be interpreted or examined in two ways. First, the negative relationships were with the production of effects in free play. Morgan, Culp, Busch-Rossnagel, and Redding (Study 2 in Barrett et al., 1993) suggest that by 12 months effect production may not be a valid indicator of mastery motivation. Jennings et al. (1979) suggested a second explanation: Infants of very involved and responsive mothers may learn to expect social play when the mother is around. Because of the increased feedback from the social environment, they seek less feedback from the inanimate environment. Morgan, Maslin-Cole, Biringen, & Harmon (1991) agreed that a child may become "an efficient responder rather than an effective initiator" (p. 81) if the adult is too directive. This is consistent with the notion of caregiver behaviors related to bridging the ZPD: If the caregiver takes charge in interacting with the environment without being sensitive to the child's developmental level, the child may learn to respond to the environment rather than to initiate interactions with it. This supposition agrees with Morgan, Busch-Rossnagel, Culp, Vance, and Fritz (1982) who found that quality of infant play at 12 months was positively related to maternal responsivity to infant signals and variety of caregiver play. These findings suggest that it is not stimulation alone, but rather the nature of the stimulation as tied to the infant's cues, that is important.

Likewise, Harmon, Morgan, and Glicken (1984) found that while preterm infants made fewer bids for attention than fullterm infants, their mothers were more likely to initiate interaction with their infants during free play. The preterm infants were also less persistent, showed less self-initiation, and were less aware of their environment. Harmon et al., (1984) suggested that the increased maternal initiation is associated with the preterm infant's deficits in instrumental and expressive mastery motivation. However, an intervention program, designed in part to help mothers develop appropriate reciprocity, was effective in ameliorating the differences between preterm and fullterm infants (Butterfield & Miller, 1984). Hauser-Cram and Shonkoff (this volume) also characterized the caregivers of children with delayed development as directive, but suggested that changes in the nature of early intervention from child to family focused can lead to interventions based on contingent responding.

Another interpretation of the results of the studies by Yarrow and colleagues involves the transition from phase 1 to phase 2 mastery behaviors proposed by Barrett and Morgan (this volume). The change in the behaviors from simple exploration and practicing of acts in an infant's repertoire to the persistence toward a goal manifested by toddlers may be facilitated by—or even require—a change in maternal behaviors related to infant behavior. This notion that a change in one level of functioning would be related to change at another level is consistent with developmental contextualism. Vygotsky's (1986) notion of optimal caregiver–child interaction also requires caregiver sensitivity to both the child's current level of development and the child's potential for new behaviors. These theoretical notions of change in caregiver behaviors analogous to the mastery motivation transition are supported by several bodies of empirical work: (a) studies documenting changes in caregiving behaviors across time, (b) studies exploring the reciprocity of maternal behaviors and infant mastery motivation across time, and (c) studies examining the relationship between mother and toddler behaviors in microsequential analyses. We will examine each of these.

Changes in Caregiving Behaviors.   In a study of 68 middle-income families, Yarrow, MacTurk, Vietze, McCarthy, Klein, and McQuiston (1984) found that parents change the type of stimulation they provide to children between 6 and 12 months. At 6 months, sensory stimulation (e.g., prompting a motor act, tickling, etc.) predominated over attention focusing (e.g., demonstrating a toy, creating a problem), but the reverse was true at 12 months. Consistent with the notion of a transition in the relationship of socializing behaviors and child mastery motivation, sensory stimulation was predictive of problem solving, but there were few significant relationships between either sensory stimulation or attention focusing and children's mastery at 12 months. We suggest that these results are consistent with the studies by Yarrow and colleagues on maternal play and responding. At 6 months, the developmental level of the infant requires that caregivers initiate most interactions, probably through sensory stimulation. However, by 12 months infants should have progressed toward initiation of some activities. There needs to be a related shift in the nature of optimal maternal behavior from stimulation toward scaffolding types of interaction. Although attention focusing may be the first step in such scaffolding, it is likely that the nature of subsequent parental responses to child behaviors will determine the effectiveness of the scaffolding and thus be a better predictor of individual differences in mastery behavior than attention focusing alone.

Other findings suggest that changes in maternal stimulation continue until 18 months. The pattern found by Belsky, Goode, and Most (1980) involved both quantitative (increase in amount) and qualitative (difference in type) changes. Physical strategies, such as pointing, demonstrating, and moving motions, increased between 9 and 12 months, while verbal strategies, such as instructing, questioning, or naming an object, increased throughout this period and predominated by 18 months. At 12 months, physical strategies level off and eventually decline in some cases. This seems to be an appropriate change in caregiver behavior, given that most children are developing language during this time period.

Reciprocity Between Mother and Infant. The reciprocity inherent in ZPD behaviors was examined by Morgan, Culp, Busch-Rossnagel, Barrett, and Redding (1993; Morgan, Redding, Culp, Busch-Rossnagel, 1993) in a longitudinal study of relationships between mother–infant interaction and infant mastery motivation at 9 and 12 months. Twenty-three white, middle-class infants were tested at both ages with structured mastery tasks and observed in free play to assess both expressive and instrumental aspects of mastery motivation. A structured social interaction with the mother was used to obtain a score of response to mother. Although this score is based on the child's response, we assume that it is an index of the nature of the dyadic relationship and based on the mother's past affective behavior. Thus, we saw it as an index of the affective nature of the socializing environment. The mother was also interviewed to determine the hours she spent playing with her child and the variety of cognitively enriching play. Because the varieties of play assessed involved interaction with an adult, rather than with inanimate objects, we see both of these measures as tapping ZPD behaviors.

Infant persistence and task pleasure at 9 months were related contemporaneously to all three socializing variables: the hours a mother spent playing with her child, the variety of play, and positive affective response. Variety of play at 12 months also predicted 12-month task pleasure. Infant persistence at 9 months also predicted variety of caregiver play at 12 months, while 12-month persistence was related to the hours a mother spent playing with her child at 9 months. These findings suggest a reciprocal relationship between infant mastery motivation and maternal behaviors in the following way: Maternal variables at 9 months may have influenced infant mastery motivation at 12 months, and infant mastery motivation at 9 months predicted at least one maternal behavior at 12 months.

Microsequential Analysis. In a study directly examining apprenticeship interactions, Heckhausen (1987a, 1987b, 1993) found that maternal behavior continued to change during phase 2 and across the transition to phase 3. Using 12 lower-middle class, mother–toddler dyads in Scotland, she examined their interaction when mastering tasks of increasing difficulty. The dyads were observed at five bimonthly intervals when the children were between 14 and 22 months of age. The coding of maternal and infant behaviors in alternating turns allowed microsequential analysis of the maternal assistance along with analysis of longitudinal developments in both maternal and children behaviors. We classify the maternal actions she observed mostly as ZPD behaviors, while the child behaviors included both instrumental and expressive aspects of mastery motivation (e.g., task attempts and pride, respectively).

In longitudinal examinations of maternal instruction, Heckhausen (1987a) found that maternal assistance decreased over this time period and also changed in nature. The instruction became less explicit, less concrete, less nonverbal, and more verbal. Children also increased their per minute rate of task attempts across age. However, mothers' motivation attempts as operationalized by requests for task actions, while frequent (about 25% of the maternal turns), did not change across age, suggesting that children's gains in task attempts were associated with development of intentional action rather than maternal motivation attempts.

In the microsequential analysis, Heckhausen (1987a) found support for the "one-step ahead" model that tied maternal assistance to child performance. The mothers provided assistance at the level of performance that the child failed to complete in the previous action turn. This one-step ahead instruction was successful in helping the child attain the next level of performance, and shows again the reciprocity of influence between mother and child.

Heckhausen (1987b) found that the changes in maternal assistance at both the microsequential and macro levels were not tied to the child's age but to the child's performance. In a log-linear analysis of the data, a development-centered model was contrasted with an age-centered one. The results suggested that mothers use performance or developmental status of their children to modify their interactions. Although age was related to changes in maternal behaviors, its effects can be attributed to its influence on the child's performance.

In further exploration of mothers' emotional communication, Heckhausen (1993) found that mothers preceded children in expressing positive affect after the child's success at both 14 and 16 months. Up to 16 months the children merely noticed the success and continued with the task. After 16 months, pleasure was shown by increasing numbers of children either as enjoyment of success or pride. The affective expression of pride became common at 20 months. As the children were developing affective reactions to success, the mothers' positive reactions to success declined over the same period from 14 to 22 months.

The results of Heckhausen (1993) also showed that self-evaluative reactions to failure occur substantially later than pride reactions to success. Children started actively seeking help at 16 months, and by 22 months, some children started reacting to failure by asking for help. However, it was common for mothers to refuse to give help by about 20 to 22 months. Stipek, Recchia, and McClintic (1992) showed that failure reactions could be experimentally induced at a younger age, so Heckhausen (1993) suggested that caregivers are primarily responsible for the delay in failure reactions. At first glance this suggestion may seem to contradict Barrett et al. (1992), who found that mothers did not differentiate between success and failure with younger children. However, Heckhausen (1993) found that the mothers' reactions to failure were not negative evaluations of the child's competence, but were restricted to providing informational feedback. Such informational feedback would be developmentally inappropriate (i.e., outside the ZPD) for the younger children. These findings are consistent with the work of Kopp (1991), who reported that mothers replace "hands-on" strategies with verbal strategies to structure tasks for children between the ages of 30 and 42 months. Overall, Heckhausen's (1993) results suggest that the adult balanced for the child's weaknesses when the child's skills were insufficient. However, the mothers avoided superfluous help and challenged the child's developmental potential whenever possible.

The studies highlighted here emphasize the continuing importance of the socializing environment during phase 2. If caregivers are directive during mutual play, children tend to become good responders to the environment, but are less likely to initiate interactions. This same response was seen with preterm infants, and infants experiencing delayed development. It is important that the change in infant behaviors from phase 1 to phase 2 be mirrored by a change in maternal behaviors as has been noted in this section. Since infants are more capable of being initiators in phase 2, caregivers must shift to scaffolding-type interactions. Such interactions involve an early increase in physical helping strategies and a later increase in verbal helping strategies. Near the end of this phase, we can see mothers utilize the one-step ahead model by challenging their children's potential. These changes reflect developmental changes in the child, and indicate that there is a reciprocal relationship between a child's development and maternal behaviors.

Phase 3: 17–22 to 32–36 Months

According to Barrett and Morgan (this volume), the primary characteristics of phase 3 mastery motivation are the acquisition of behavior standards, self-evaluation, and the ability to undertake sequential steps towards a goal. These changes can be seen most vividly in toddlers' pride reactions, their desire for control or to "do it themselves" and their involvement with tasks on the basis of competence. Just as the transition from phase 1 to phase 2 mastery motivation behaviors was associated with a change in caregiver behaviors, phase 3 behaviors are also associated with changes in the socializing environment. These changes do seem to exist in the inanimate aspect of the social environment and in the integration of the aspects of ZPD behaviors and emotional communication. There is continuity across the transition as well, particularly in the negative relationship between caregiver behaviors, which are insensitive to the child's developmental level and mastery motivation.

ZPD Behaviors.   As illustrated by Heckhausen's work, the development of self-awareness across the transition from phase 2 to phase 3 allows children to select tasks that they can do— and maternal interference while mastering such tasks continues to be negatively related to mastery motivation. This maternal behavior might be considered behavior that impedes the child's performance in the ZPD. For example, Fung (1984) found that mothers who were overly directive by wanting to interact when the children were working on a task had children who showed lower task persistence at 18 months. Similarly, Jennings and Connors (1989) found a negative relationship between maternal perceptions of mastery motivation and maternal directiveness in 3-year-old children.

This relationship holds across the preschool years, with children of different cognitive abilities, and from different cultural/ethnic groups as well. Busch-Rossnagel, Vargas, Knauf, and Planos (1993) observed the interactions of 29 Hispanic mothers and preschool-age children during the teaching of cognitive–perceptual tasks. Using the Maternal Teaching Observation Technique (MTOT; Laosa, 1980), Busch-Rossnagel et al. (1993) found that the maternal behavior of modeling was negatively related to maternal ratings of object-oriented, social/symbolic, and gross motor persistence and mastery pleasure, while maternal inquiries showed a positive relationship with object-oriented persistence. Similarly, Sarimski (1992) found a negative relationship between task persistence and a directive maternal style in mentally retarded preschool German children.

Inanimate Environment. Interestingly, although maternal behaviors that are intrusive or directive are negatively related to the instrumental aspect of mastery motivation, provision of demanding materials in the inanimate environment may enhance the instrumental aspects of mastery motivation. Morgan and Maslin-Cole (Study 3 in Barrett et al., 1993) observed 48 children between the ages of 15 and 30 months on structured mastery motivation tasks of varying difficulty. Maternal reports provided information about experience at home with similar toys during the previous week. Experience at home with similar cause–effect toys (e.g., busy box, tape recorder) was positively related to persistence on difficult, but not easy or moderate cause–effect toys, and this relationship held for puzzles as well.

Emotional Communication. In addition to maternal behaviors helping the child to bridge the ZPD and aspects of the inanimate environment, researchers have examined the emotional communication in mother–child interaction and related it to mastery motivation during phase 3. Morgan, Maslin-Cole, Ridgeway, and Kang-Park (1988) observed 76 18-month-old children and their mothers in naturalistic play and scored children's mastery motivation and affective exchanges between mother and child. The mothers also rated their perceptions of their child's persistence and mastery pleasure. The results showed that positive mother–child affect exchanges were positively associated with the child's task directedness during semistructured tasks, their pride in their mastery attempts, and maternal ratings of mastery pleasure. Exchanges that were not reciprocated were related to low levels of task directedness and task pleasure. The lack of affect exchange was also negatively related to overall persistence (the composite score from both the tasks and maternal ratings), while low levels of mastery pleasure were related to mixed affective exchanges.

In a longitudinal follow up, Morgan, Maslin-Cole, Downing, and Harmon (1990; Morgan, Maslin-Cole, & Harmon, 1991) obtained maternal ratings of the child's mastery motivation at 39 months. Negative mother–child affect exchanges at 18 months were related to maternal ratings of low persistence at 39 months, while positive exchanges at 18 months predicted ratings of high persistence at 39 months. Positive exchanges at 18 months also predicted ratings of greater independence at 39 months, while mixed affect exchanges at 18 months predicted ratings of lower persistence at 39 months. These findings are consistent with the positive relationship between maternal praise and ratings of object-oriented persistence found in Hispanic preschool children by Busch-Rossnagel et al. (1993).

ZPD Behaviors and Emotional Communication. Finally, there is a body of research that examines the interchange between ZPD behaviors and emotional communication. Maternal–infant attachment represents such an intersection because ZPD behaviors, such as responsivity, and emotional communication, such as sensitivity and warmth, are hypothesized to be primary influences on the development of secure vs. insecure attachment (Ainsworth, Blehar, Waters, & Wall, 1978).

Riksen-Walraven et al. (1993) used Strange Situation assessments of attachment at 12 months and ratings of mastery motivation during exploration at 30 months to explore this relationship. Seventy-seven lower-class children and their primary caregivers participated in the longitudinal study. The results showed a significant interaction between sex and attachment security. Securely attached girls were significantly higher in mastery motivation at 30 months than insecurely attached girls. For boys the reverse pattern was obtained, with insecurely attached boys being insignificantly higher than securely attached boys. While the interaction was not significant using attachment security at 18 months, the trend was in the same direction. Riksen-Walraven et al. (1993) suggested that gender differences "in susceptibility of mastery motivation to social experience might be due to differential rearing of boys and

girls" (p. 201). This finding of sex differences in the relationships between mastery motivation and other variables is consistent with the work of Jennings, Yarrow, and Martin (1984)
and Vondra (1987) and highlights the need for consideration of
the differential influence of the socializing environment in
future research.

Maslin-Cole et al. (1993) also explored the relationship
between mastery motivation and attachment security, but added
the variable of maternal scaffolding in a longitudinal study of 41
toddler–mother dyads between the ages of 18 and 25 months.
Mastery motivation was assessed through observations of persistence at structured tasks and of engrossment during free
play, by experimenter ratings of goal directedness and attention
span, and from maternal ratings of persistence and mastery
pleasure. Attachment security at 18 months was observed using
the Strange Situation (Ainsworth et al., 1978); at 25 months the
Attachment Q-sort (Waters & Deane, 1985) was used.

Three aspects of maternal scaffolding—motivation, technical,
and emotional support—were rated during free play (Maslin,
Bretherton, & Morgan, 1986). Motivation support included behaviors such as encouragement, or calling the child's attention to
the toy, while technical support included modeling, or breaking
the problem into steps; both types of support are considered here
as ZPD behaviors. Discrete scaffolding behaviors (e.g., simplifica-
tions, interferences and demonstrations) were coded as well. An
example of emotional support is sensitivity to the child's emotional state and ability to reduce frustration; these represent an
overlap between emotional communication and ZPD behaviors.

In exploration of the concurrent relationships, ratings of
motivational and technical support during mother–child free
play were related to persistence at structured mastery tasks at
18 months (Maslin et al., 1986). Frequencies of the discrete
behaviors of focusing, encouragement, praise, and marking critical features were also predictors of persistence. At 25 months
the frequencies of demonstrations were positively related to
persistence, while frequencies of interference were negatively
related to persistence. Attachment security was not related to
persistence at 25 months.

After factor analysis to reduce the measures of mastery motivation, Maslin-Cole et al. (1993) used regressions to examine
the predictors of overall task directedness (which included persistence at structured tasks and maternal ratings of persis-

tence) and mastery pleasure. Maternal technical support, security of attachment, and child shyness predicted task directedness in same-age analyses at 18 months. No aspect of scaffolding or attachment security was a significant predictor of task directedness in same-age analyses at 25 months or in cross-age analyses from 18 to 25 months. Mastery pleasure at 18 months was predicted by less technical support, more emotional support, and child's activity level. In the cross-age analyses, task pleasure at 25 months was positively predicted by 18-month motivational and emotional support, and negatively by technical support. At 25 months, pleasure in free play was related to motivational support, but attachment security was not related to mastery pleasure.

These results are consistent with the work of Riksen-Walraven et al. (1993) in providing little support for a relationship between attachment security and mastery motivation. Instead, the studies support the premise that scaffolding and attachment security are separate aspects of the socializing environment. The relationship of the caregiver behaviors underlying the security of attachment with the caregiver actions we call ZPD behaviors and with emotional communication needs further examination. As a first step, Maslin-Cole et al. (1993) suggested that emotional attunement of the secure attachment relationship is a necessary but not sufficient condition for the most effective scaffolding. Maternal sensitivity may be what promotes expressiveness in the child, and expressive children give clearer feedback about their emotional state while working on moderately difficult tasks than nonexpressive toddlers.

Phase 3 also shows that changes in mastery motivation behaviors are related to changes in the socializing environment. Early in phase 3, children develop a self-awareness that allows them to select appropriate tasks on their own. This may be a difficult adjustment for caregivers who have shown more directive actions in the past. However, maternal scaffolding behaviors remain important in helping children to learn the sequential steps necessary for more complicated tasks. The provision of appropriately challenging toys is positively related to persistence, and so we can see that providing specifically appropriate inanimate objects in the environment becomes important. In phase 3, positive mother–child affect exchanges are also important for a child's task directedness, while negative exchanges appear to relate to low persistence. Attachment security, however, does not appear to predict mastery pleasure, but may be important in an indirect manner. There may also be some early indication of sex differences at this stage, but this will require further research.

CONCLUSIONS

To review the research on socializing influences on the development of mastery motivation, we proposed that the socializing environment contains three dimensions: (a) the provision of inanimate objects, (b) emotional communication, and (c) behaviors related to helping the child cross the zone of proximal development. As shown in Table 5.1, there is research evidence that each of these three aspects of the socializing environment is related to mastery motivation. Yarrow and his colleagues showed that aspects of toys provided to children, such as variety, responsiveness, and complexity, are related to instrumental aspects of mastery motivation in the early phases, while exposure to specific toys seems to be important at later phases (Barrett et al., 1993).

The dimension of emotional communication is most often tapped by the construct of positive affect. The positive relationship between this expression of caregiver warmth and mastery motivation echoes the findings regarding parental warmth and affectional ties in other child development literature (Maccoby & Martin, 1983). In the dimension of ZPD behaviors, the research shows the importance of a balance between maternal direction and child initiation. Several studies show that mothers who are overly directive or controlling of the interaction have children lower in mastery motivation (Busch-Rossnagel et al., 1993; Fung, 1984; Harmon et al., 1984; Sarimski, 1992). This balance is best exemplified by studies of scaffolding or apprenticeship interactions in which the mother is shown to be knowledgeable about her child's developmental level and provides help and support just above that level (Heckhausen, 1987a, b; Maslin-Cole et al., 1993)

Inspection of Table 5.1 also reveals that although the three dimensions are related to mastery motivation across the three phases of development, the specific effective behavioral expression of each aspect changes over time. For example, this means that the general provision of toys is associated with mastery motivation during phase 1 and early phase 2 (Yarrow et al.,

1972, 1982). However, by phase 3, it is repeated exposure to the same toy that facilitates persistence on moderately difficult tasks (Barrett et al., 1993). Perhaps this change is tied to the child's acquisition of standards along with learning. When children are familiar with a specific object, they are more likely to know what successful completion involves and be more persistent on the task to complete it in accordance with their standard of completing tasks (Barrett & Morgan, this volume).

In the area of emotional communication, the global aspect of positive affect is related to mastery motivation at the younger ages. In studies with older children, emotional communication becomes more refined into types of affective exchanges and emotional support. This differentiation is paralleled by the changes in ZPD behaviors. Contingent responding is related to mastery motivation at 6 months (Yarrow et al., 1972) while Heckhausen (1987a, 1993) and Maslin-Cole et al. (1993) show that mothers provide specific feedback to and use specific scaffolding behaviors with older children.

The timing of changes in maternal behavior seem to coincide with or just precede the transitions in mastery motivation development proposed by Barrett and Morgan (this volume). This relationship is fundamental if we are to continue to assume the importance of the socializing environment in influencing the development of mastery motivation. Further research is needed to examine more carefully the causal linkages between the socializing environment and mastery motivation. This research should also explore potential reciprocities between caregiving behaviors and mastery motivation. Two longitudinal studies noted the reciprocities between mother and child (Heckhausen, 1987b; Morgan et al., 1992), but many studies do not include possible bidirectional effects in their analyses.

Table 5.1 also highlights the relative dearth of literature on socializing influences on expressive mastery motivation. The early work on mastery motivation focused on instrumental aspects, particularly persistence, with expressive aspects getting little attention. Only recently have authors proposed potential relationships between the two aspects of mastery motivation. Barrett and Morgan (this volume) see them as separate aspects of mastery motivation, while Jennings (1993) suggested that emotion is the outcome of the action associated with motivation. Both suggested that advances in other areas of child development research, particularly socioemotional development and the sense of self, may be helpful in clarifying the relationship between instrumental and expressive mastery motivation. This body of literature may also provide clues about possible socializing influences.

In addition to further research on expressive aspects, there is a need for research on the universality of the relationship between mastery motivation and the socializing environment. The samples of the studies reviewed in this chapter are all from Western countries and involve primarily middle-class samples. Other relationships may appear if we explore groups with different traditions of childrearing or cultures with different values regarding individual effort and achievement.

In sum, mothers and other primary caregivers are an important influence on the development of mastery motivation. At its best, the socializing environment provides the young child with stimulating inanimate objects, positive emotional communication, and support for behaviors just above the child's current developmental level. These actions on the part of caregivers foster the child's persistence and have potential ramifications for the child's sense of self.

REFERENCES

Ainsworth, M. D. S., Blehar, M. C., Waters, E., & Wall, S. (1978). *Patterns of attachment*. Hillsdale, NJ: Erlbaum.

Barrett, K. C., MacPhee, D., & Sullivan, S. (May, 1992). *Development of social emotions and self-regulation*. Poster Presentation, International Conference on Infant Studies, Miami, FL.

Barrett, K. C., & Morgan, G. A., & Maslin-Cole, C. (1993). Three studies on the development of mastery motivation in infancy and toddlerhood. In D. J. Messer (Ed.), *Mastery motivation in early childhood: Development, measurement, and social processes*. (pp. 83–108). London: Routledge.

Belsky, J., Goode, M. K., & Most, R. K. (1980). Maternal stimulation and infant exploratory competence: Cross-sectional, correlational, and experimental analyses. *Child Development, 51*, 1163–1178.

Bruner, J. (1986). *Actual minds, possible worlds*. Cambridge, MA: Harvard University Press.

Busch-Rossnagel, N. A., Vargas, M., Knauf, D. E., & Planos, R. (1993). Mastery motivation in ethnic minority groups: The sample case of Hispanics. In D. J. Messer (Ed.), *Mastery motivation in early childhood: Development, measurement and social processes* (pp. 132–148). London: Routledge.

Butterfield, P. M., & Miller, L. (1984). Read your baby: A follow-up intervention program for parents with NICU infants. *Infant Mental Health Journal, 5,* 107–116.

Cole, M. (1985). The zone of proximal development: Where culture and cognition create each other. In J. V. Wertsch (Ed.), *Culture, communication and cognition: Vygotskian perspectives* (pp. 146–161). New York: Cambridge University Press.

Festinger, L. (1954). A theory of social comparison processes. *Human Relations, 7,* 117–140.

Fung, A. Y. (1984). *The relationship of mother's perception to the child's competence and mastery motivation.* Unpublished master's thesis, Department of Family Studies, University of Manitoba, Winnipeg, Canada.

Gaiter, J. L., Morgan, G. A., Jennings, K. D., Harmon, R. J., & Yarrow, L. J. (1982). Variety of cognitively oriented caregiver activities: Relationships to cognitive and motivational functioning at 1 and 3½ years of age. *Journal of Genetic Psychology, 141,* 49–56.

Grolnick, W., Frodi, A., & Bridges, L. (1984). Maternal control style and mastery motivation of one-year-olds. *Infant Mental Health Journal, 5,* 72–82.

Gunnar, M. E., & Stone, C. (1984). The effects of positive maternal affect on infant responses to pleasant, ambiguous, and fear-provoking toys. *Child Development, 55,* 1231–1236.

Harmon, R. J., Morgan, G. A., & Glicken, A. D. (1984). Continuities and discontinuities in affective and cognitive-motivational development. *Child Abuse and Neglect, 8,* 157–167.

Harris, D. B. (1957). Problems in formulating a scientific concept of development. In D. B. Harris (Ed.), *The concept of development: An issue in the study of human behavior* (pp. 3–14). Minneapolis: University of Minnesota Press.

Harter, S. (1978). Effectance motivation reconsidered: Toward a developmental model. *Human Development, 21,* 34–64.

Heckhausen, J. (1987a). Balancing for weaknesses and challenging developmental potential: A longitudinal study of mother–infant dyads in apprenticeship interactions. *Developmental Psychology, 23* (6), 762–770.

Heckhausen, J. (1987b). How do mothers know? Infants' chronological age or infants' performance as determinants of adaptation in maternal instruction? *Journal of Experimental Child Psychology, 43,* 212–226.

Heckhausen, J. (1993). The development of mastery and its perception within caretaker–child dyads. In D. J. Messer (Ed.), *Mastery motivation in early childhood: Development, measurement and social processes* (pp. 55–79). London: Routledge.

Hultsch, D. F., & Hickey, T. (1978). External validity in the study of human development: Theoretical and methodological issues. *Human Development, 21,* 76–91.

Jennings, K. D. (1993). Mastery motivation and the formation of self-concept from infancy through early childhood. In D. J. Messer (Ed.), *Mastery motivation in early childhood: Development, measurement and social processes* (pp. 36–54). London: Routledge.

Jennings, K. D., & Connors, R. E. (1989). Mothers' interactional style and children's competence at 3 years. *International Journal of Behavioral Development, 12,* 155–175.

Jennings, K., Harmon, R. J., Morgan, G. A., Gaiter, J., & Yarrow, L. (1979). Exploratory play as an index of mastery motivation: Relationships to persistence, cognitive functioning, and environmental measures. *Developmental Psychology, 15* (4), 386–394.

Jennings, K. D., Yarrow, L. J., & Martin, P. P. (1984). Mastery motivation and cognitive development: A longitudinal study from infancy to 3½ years of age. *International Journal of Behavioral Development, 7,* 441–461.

Klinnert, M. D., Emde, R. N., Butterfield, P., & Campos, J. J. (1986). Social referencing: The infant's use of emotional signals from a friendly adult with mother present. *Developmental Psychology, 22,* 427–432.

Kopp, C. B. (1991). Young children's progression to self-regulation. In D. Kuhn & M. Bullock (Eds.), *Contributions to human development: The development of intentional action* (pp. 38–54). Basel, Switzerland: Karger.

Laosa, L. M. (1980). Maternal teaching strategies in Chicano and Anglo-American families: The influence of culture and education on maternal behavior. *Child Development, 51,* 759–765.

Lerner, R., & Busch-Rossnagel, N. A. (1981). Individuals as producers of their development: Conceptual and empirical bases. In R. M. Lerner & N. A. Busch-Rossnagel (Eds.), *Individuals as producers of their development: A life-span perspective* (pp. 1–36). New York: Academic Press.

Maccoby, E. E., & Martin, J. A. (1983). Socialization in the context of the family: Parent–child interaction. In P. H. Mussen (Ed.), *Handbook of child psychology, Vol. IV: Socialization, personality, and social development* (pp. 1–101). New York: John Wiley and Sons.

Maslin, C. A., Bretherton, I., Morgan, G. A. (1986, April). *The influence of attachment security and maternal scaffolding on toddler mastery motivation.* Paper presented at the Biennial International Conference on Infant Studies, Beverly Hills, CA.

Maslin, C., Bretherton, I., & Morgan, G. A. (1987). *Toddler's independent mastery motivation as related to attachment security and quality of maternal scaffolding.* Poster presented at the MacArthur Foundation Research Network Summer Institute, Durango, CO.

Maslin-Cole, C., Bretherton, I., Morgan, G. A. (1993). Toddler mastery motivation and Competence: Links with attachment security, maternal scaffolding and family climate. In D. J. Messer (Ed.),

Mastery motivation in early childhood: Development, measurement and social processes (pp. 205–229). London: Routledge.

Morgan, G. A., Busch-Rossnagel, N. A., Culp, R. E., Vance, A. K., & Fritz, J. J. (1982). Infants' differential social response to mother and experimenter: Relationships to maternal characteristics and quality of infant play. In R. N. Emde & R. J. Harmon (Eds.), *Attachment and affiliative systems: Neurobiological and psychological aspects* (pp. 245–261). New York: Plenum Press.

Morgan, G. A., Culp, R. E., Busch-Rossnagel, N. A., Barrett, K. C., & Redding, R. E. (1993). A longitudinal study of mastery motivation in infants 9- to 25-months of age (abstract). In J. E. Jacobs (Ed.), *Developmental perspectives on motivation, Nebraska symposium on motivation: Vol. 40* (p. 273). Lincoln: University of Nebraska Press. Also presented as a poster at the Nebraska Symposium, Lincoln (1992, March).

Morgan, G. A., Harmon, R. J., Maslin-Cole, C. A. (1990). Mastery motivation: Definition and measurement. *Early education and development, 1,* 318–339.

Morgan, G., Maslin, C., Ridgeway, D., & Kang-Park, J. (1988, June). *Toddler mastery motivation and aspects of mother–child affect communication.* Poster presentation, Developmental Psychobiology Research Group Conference.

Morgan, G. A., Maslin-Cole, C. A., Biringen, Z., Harmon, R. J. (1991). Play assessment of mastery motivation in infants and young children. In C. E. Schaefer, K. Gitlin, & A. Sandgrund (Eds.), *Play diagnosis and assessment* (pp. 65–86). New York: John Wiley and Sons.

Morgan, G. A., Maslin-Cole, C. A., Downing, K., & Harmon, R. J. (1990). Antecedents of mastery and prediction of behavior problems (summary). *Program and Proceedings of the Developmental Psychobiology Research Group Fifth Biennial Retreat, 5,* 15–16.

Morgan, G. A., Maslin-Cole, C. A., & Harmon, R. J. (1991, July). *Antecedents of mastery behaviors.* Paper presented at the biennial meeting of the International Society for the Study of Behavioral Development, Minneapolis, MN.

Morgan, G. A., Maslin-Cole, C. A., Harmon, R. J., Busch-Rossnagel, N. A., Jennings, K. D., Hauser-Cram, P., & Brockman, L. M. (1993). Parent and teacher perceptions of young children's mastery motivation: Assessment and review of research. In D. J. Messer (Ed.), *Mastery motivation in early childhood: Development, measurement, and social processes* (pp. 109–131). London: Routledge.

Morgan, G. A., Redding, R. E., Culp, R. E., & Busch-Rossnagel, N. A. (1993). *A longitudinal study of relationships of mastery motivation with mother–infant and infant free play.* Submitted for publication.

Pratt, M. W., Kerig, P., Cowan, P. A., & Cowan, C. P. (1988). Mothers and fathers teaching 3-year-olds: Authoritative parenting and adult scaffolding of young children's learning. *Developmental Psychology, 24* (6), 832–839.

Riegel, K. F. (1976). The dialectics of human development. *American Psychologist, 31,* 689–700.

Riksen-Walraven, J. M., Meij, H. T., van Roozendaal, J., & Koks, J. (1993). Mastery motivation in toddlers as related to quality of attachment. In D. J. Messer (Ed.), *Mastery motivation in early childhood: Development, measurement and social processes* (pp. 189–204). London: Routledge.

Rogoff, B., & Morelli, G. (1989). Perspectives on children's development from cultural psychology. *American Psychologist, 44,* 343–348.

Sarimski, K. (1992). Ausdauer bei zielgerichteten tötigkeiten und mutterliche strategien in der interaktion mit behinderten kindern [Persistence of intentional actions and maternal interaction style in mentally retarded children]. *Psychologie in Erziehung und Unterricht, 39,* 170–178.

Stipek, D., Recchia, S., & McClintic, S. (1992). Self-evaluation in young children. *Monographs of the Society for Research in Child Development, 57* (8, Serial No. 236).

Vandell, D. L., & Wilson, K. S. (1987). Infant's interactions with mother, sibling, and peer: Contrasts and relationships between interaction systems. *Child Development, 58*(1), 176–186.

Vondra, J. I. (1987, April). *Early mastery motivation: How can we measure it and what does it mean?* Paper presented at the biennial meeting of the Society for Research in Child Development, Baltimore, MD.

Vygotsky, L. (1986). *Thought and language.* Cambridge, MA: MIT Press.

Waters, E., & Deane, K. E. (1985). Defining and assessing individual differences in attachment relationships: Q-methodology and the organization of behavior in infancy and early childhood. *Monographs of the Society for Research in Child Development, 50,* 41–65.

Wertsch, J. V. (1985). *Vygotsky and the social formation of mind.* Cambridge, MA: Harvard University Press.

Wertsch, J. V. (1991). Voices of the mind: A sociocultural approach to mediated action. Cambridge, MA: Harvard University Press.

White, R. W. (1959). Motivation reconsidered: The concept of competence. *Psychological Review, 66,* 297–333.

Yarrow, L. J., Klein, R., Lomonaco, S., & Morgan, G. (1975). Cognitive and motivational development in early childhood. In B. Z. Friedlander, G. M. Sterritt, & G. E. Kirk, (Eds.), *Exceptional infant: Assessment and intervention* (pp. 491–502). New York: Bruner/Mazel.

Yarrow, L. J., MacTurk, R. H., Vietze, P. M., McCarthy, M. E., Klein, R. P., & McQuiston, S. (1984). Development course of parental stimulation and its relationship to mastery motivation during infancy. *Developmental Psychology, 20*(3), 492–503.

Yarrow, L. J., Morgan, G. A., Jennings, K. D., Harmon, R. J., & Gaiter, J. L. (1982). Infant's persistence at tasks: Relationships to cognitive functioning and early experience. *Infant Behavior and Development, 5,* 131–142.

Yarrow, L. J., Rubenstein, J. L., Pedersen, F. A., & Jankowski, J. J. (1972). Dimensions of early stimulation and their differential effects on infant development. *Merrill–Palmer Quarterly, 18,* 205–218.

6

THE DOMAINS OF INFANT MASTERY MOTIVATION*

Theodore D. Wachs
Terri Tarr Combs
Department of Psychological Sciences
Purdue University

MASTERY MOTIVATION AS A POTENTIAL INDIVIDUAL DIFFERENCES PARAMETER

Historically, the recent work on mastery motivation has stemmed from White's (1959) seminal paper on competence, as well as Hunt's (1965) extension of this concept into the infancy period. In his original paper, White defined competence as "the organism's capacity to interact effectively with its environment" (p. 297). In understanding the nature of competence motivation it is critical to ask the question: What aspects of the environment can the organism effectively interact with? Much of the mastery motivation literature has focused almost exclusively on the child's ability to affect the inanimate environment. This emphasis on mastery of the inanimate environment is not necessarily inherent in the original conceptualization of the mastery motivation construct. As White noted in his 1959 paper:

*The authors wish to thank Iris Comer, Dianne Dranitto, Deierdre Elliott, Susan Friedhofer, Helen Hughes, Jennifer Metro, Karen Nunning, Rhonda Pritchard and Regina Wright, for their help as research assistants during the course of this project. Portions of the research reported were supported by a grant to Theodore D. Wachs from the Spencer Foundation.

The concept of competence can be most easily discussed by choosing as we have done, examples of interaction with the inanimate environment. It applies equally as well however, to transactions with other animals and with other human beings, where the child has the same problem of finding out what effect he can have upon the environment and what effect it can have upon him. (p. 32)

We believe there are three reasons why mastery over the inanimate environment has been a major focus. First, a careful reading of the papers by White and by Hunt indicates that the concept of competence motivation was derived from earlier research on learning, play, exploration, and Piagetian cognitive performance. In this earlier research, objects rather than people were the predominant focus of investigation. Second, a good deal of research has attempted to tie competence motivation to cognitive development (Jennings, Yarrow, & Martin, 1984; Messer, McCarthy, McQuiston, MacTurk, Yarrow, & Vietze, 1986; Ulvund, 1980; Yarrow & Messer, 1983 Yarrow, Morgan, Jennings, Harmon, & Gaiter, 1982;) and school performance (Harter, 1981). The aspects of cognitive development studied typically involved object manipulation or object problem solving rather than the social aspects of cognitive performance, as seen both in developmental research (McCall, 1976) and in developmental theory (Rogoff & Lave, 1984).

Finally, in earlier theoretical statements about the nature of mastery motivation it was hypothesized that different domains of mastery were not well differentiated in infancy (Dweck & Elliot, 1983; White, 1959). While different types of mastery tasks were utilized in initial studies of infant mastery (e.g., effect production, practicing emerging skills—Jennings, Harmon, Morgan, Gaiter, & Yarrow 1979), for the most part the tasks all focused on different aspects of object mastery. In general, specific domains of mastery were delineated only after the child entered the preschool period (Harter, 1981). This shift in the nature of mastery motivation after infancy was seen as a function of experience with extrinsic reward (Deci, 1975), exposure to different mastery goals of socialization agents, or observation of others (Harter, 1981).

The Empirical Basis for Infant Social Mastery Motivation

In contrast to this traditional view, more recent research has suggested that a broader view of the nature of mastery motivation in the infancy period may well be warranted. Specifically, a number of researchers have suggested that, in addition to the traditional domain of object mastery, infants and toddlers may also display what might be called *social mastery motivation* (MacTurk, Hunter, McCarthy, Vietze, & McQuiston, 1985; Morgan, Harmon, & Maslin-Cole, 1990; Wachs, 1987). For the present, social mastery motivation will be defined as the infant's "motivation to generate, maintain and influence the course of social interactions" (MacTurk et al., 1985, p. 94).

Evidence supporting the validity of a distinction between social and object mastery in infancy appears in a number of sources. Different *developmental courses* for object and social mastery are suggested by the finding that the frequency of object-directed behaviors decreases from 6 to 12 months of age, while the frequency of socially directed behaviors increases over the same age period (MacTurk, McCarthy, Vietze, & Yarrow, 1987). Evidence for different *developmental correlates* emerges in two areas. First, while developmentally disabled and normal infants do not differ in object motivation, both Down syndrome infants (MacTurk, Vietze, McCarthy, McQuiston, & Yarrow, 1985) and deaf infants (MacTurk & Trimm, 1989) show different social interaction patterns with adults than do normal infants. Secondly, Wachs (1987) has reported different environmental correlates for measures of social and object mastery motivation. Finally, Wenar (1976), Maslin and Morgan (1985), and Hupp, Abbeduto, and Jaeger (1995) all have reported nonsignificant relations between measures of social competence and the child's attempts at object mastery. It is important to note that all of these three studies utilized small samples of infants; as such, this lack of significance could be due to low power rather than an actual lack of a relation. However, using a larger sample (85 toddlers), Combs & Wachs (1993) reported either nonsignificant or negative relations between measures of social and object mastery.

**The Theoretical Basis for Infant
Social Mastery Motivation**

For the most part, available research on social mastery motivation during the infancy period has been atheoretical in nature. That is, this research has suggested that mastery motivation in infancy may be differentiated into the social and object domains, but has not dealt with the question of why there is this type of differentiation. We will argue that this differentiation between social and object mastery motivation in infancy is part of a broader individual differences parameter that has the potential to mediate relations between environment and infant development. We refer here to the concept of *organismic specificity*, which refers to nonuniform responding to similar environmental stimuli by different individuals (Wachs, 1992). A fundamental question for researchers in this area has been which classes of individual characteristics have the potential to mediate environment–development relations. Available evidence suggests that one potential individual difference domain involves children who are primarily oriented either toward objects in their environment or toward persons in their environment (Wachs, 1992).

The social–object distinction has appeared in a variety of areas, including the study of early *language* development (Nelson, 1981), *classroom behavior* (Nakamura & Finck, 1980), *reactivity* to institutional environments (Langmeier & Matejcek, 1975), infant *attentional patterns* (Escalona, 1968; Parrinello & Ruff, 1988), *temperament* (Balleyguier, 1991), *attachment* classification (Braungart & Stifter, 1991; Lewis & Feiring, 1989) and children's *play behavior* (Shotwell, Wolf, & Gardner, 1980). Results from all of these diverse areas center around a common theme, namely that there is a distinct cluster of children whose behavior is characterized primarily by interest in and interaction with objects, as well as another distinct cluster of children whose development is characterized primarily by interest in and interaction with persons. It could be argued that most dichotomies rarely prove to be adequate conceptual models. We are certainly willing to consider the possibility suggested by Morgan, Maslin-Cole, Biringen, & Harmon (1991), that there may be children who are interested in coordinating their mastery of both objects and persons. This group would be congruent with one of the clusters described by Nakamura and Finck (1980). There may also be children who are not interested in mastering either objects or people; these children may be at particular risk for developmental problems (Morgan et al., 1991). However, we feel that our dichotomy is currently necessary, if only to correct the historical emphasis on object mastery motivation, particularly in the infancy period.

Generalizing the specificity framework to infant mastery, we hypothesize that there may be at least two different clusters of infants, *differing primarily on which aspects of the environ-*

ment they are oriented to master. We propose that one cluster of infants would be primarily oriented toward objects, and would devote their attempts at mastery primarily toward objects (object mastery orientation). A second cluster of infants would be oriented primarily toward the social environment, and would devote their attempts at mastery primarily toward influencing and obtaining reactions from others in the environment (social mastery orientation). To test the construct validity of our generalization of the social–object distinction to infant mastery three questions will be addressed: (a) Are individual differences in social and object mastery stable across time—if social and object orientation are individual traits they should be stable across time, (b) Can we replicate the lack of relation between measures of social and object mastery motivation shown in earlier studies—if social and object orientation are distinct traits they should be unrelated to each other; and (c) Can infants be characterized as predominantly socially or object oriented in terms of their motivational style—if our generalization is valid, then we should be able to identify clusters of infants with these characteristics. Prior to considering these three questions it is important to discuss how we measure the construct of social mastery motivation.

The persistence of infant attempts to obtain adult attention was our definition of social mastery motivation. This usage follows the definition originally utilized by White (1959), as well as the definition of social mastery motivation noted earlier by MacTurk et al. (1985). While a common definition exists, there is less agreement on the operations used to measure social mastery motivation. Different patterns of results have emerged as a function of whether affect is included in the assessment of mastery, whether mastery is measured using social versus object games, whether structured versus free play situations are used, or whether measures involve observations versus parent ratings. In a detailed review of this question, Combs and Wachs (1993) have noted major problems in assuming functional equivalence of different measures of social mastery. Given ambiguities in measurement it is essential that mastery researchers define exactly how they operationalize this construct.

In the research to be described in this Chapter, we have revised the codes originally developed by Yarrow and his colleagues as follows: Our codes 0 to 4 are congruent with the original Yarrow object mastery codes. Code 0 refers to situations when the child is not involved with objects or people.

Code 1 reflects looking at or touching objects without attempting to manipulate objects. Code 2 refers to active object exploration. Code 3 describes task-related behaviors that are precursors of mastery. Code 4 is scored when the child demonstrates goal directed behaviors that enable the child to produce an effect or solve a problem. Our code 5 reflects the infant's attempts to involve the adult in joint interaction with objects. Code 6 reflects the infant's attempts to interact with the adult *independent of objects,* even though objects are available to the infant. Code 7 is best viewed as infant passive social orientation, which, unlike code 6, does not involve attempts at generating, maintaining, or influencing social interactions. Code 9 refers to acute infant distress (Code 8 records interference by the mother or inability of the observer to record infant behaviors). Codes 3, 4, and 6 are the reference points for the object–social dichotomy. In all of the research to be reported in this chapter children's behaviors were coded directly onto an Apple 2+ microcomputer especially programmed for this purpose, with coding being done by an observer seated in a second room watching the infant's behavior through a two-way mirror. Scores reflect the amount of time (in seconds) that the child was engaged in each of the activities defined by the nine codes described above. A description of the codes and the coding procedures can be found in Wachs (1987).

Are Measures of Social Mastery Stable Across Time?

To assess short-term stability 83 18-month-old toddlers were seen two times in a structured play situation in sessions approximately two weeks apart. The eight mastery tasks were presented for three minutes each in a fixed sequence with alternating object and social tasks. The nine codes described previously were used for both social and object tasks, and slightly different toys were used in the second session than in the first session. The four object tasks consisted of two toys that required problem solving and two toys that involved practicing emerging skills. The four social tasks consisted of games that made use of mutual involvement in social interactions. Two of the games involved turntaking and two were based on imitation (for details see Combs & Wachs, 1993). Given the level of intercorrelation between mastery code scores on the social and objects tasks (mean $r = .40$), plus the fact that our factor analy-

TABLE 6.1.   STABILITY CORRELATIONS
OF NONMASTERY, OBJECT AND SOCIAL
MASTERY CODES

Codes	r
0 - Off-task	.47**
1 - Passive object	.40**
2 - Active object	.30**
3 - Object premastery	.11
4 - Object mastery	.42**
5 - Social object mastery	.51**
6 - Active social mastery	.26*
7 - Passive social	.44**
9 - Distress	-.03

$* = p < .05$ $** = p < .01$

sis did not support a differentiation between social and object tasks (Combs & Wachs, 1993), comparable scores on the two tasks were combined for all analyses.

Inspection of the stability correlations, shown in Table 6.1 indicates that, with the exception of two codes (code 3: object premastery; code 9: distress), there is modest but significant stability for measures of both social and object mastery motivation.

Are Measures of Social and Object Mastery Independent of Each Other?

To test this second question we looked at the correlation between object and social mastery performance in both a structured and a free-play situation. A positive and significant correlation between our measures of social and object mastery would support the assumption of functional equivalence: A zero order or negative correlation would replicate previous research on this question. Subjects were 88 12-month-old infants, who were seen twice in the Developmental Psychology laboratories at Purdue University. One session was devoted to the infant's performance in a standard structured mastery motivation assessment situation, similar to that developed by Yarrow and his colleagues (e.g., Yarrow, McQuiston, MacTurk, McCarthy, Klein, & Vietze, 1983; specific procedural details are found in Wachs, 1987). The other session assessed infant mastery using a free-play procedure, which took place in the same room. A chair for

TABLE 6.2.   INTERCORRELATIONS BETWEEN SOCIAL AND OBJECT
MASTERY MOTIVATION CODES FREE PLAY (ABOVE DIAGONAL)
AND STRUCTURED PLAY (BELOW DIAGONAL) INTERCORRELATIONS

Codes	3	4	5	6
3	—	.49**	.19	−.24*
4	.26*	—	−.03	−.21*
5	.04	.13	—	.25*
6	−.24*	.02	.10	—

Cross Play Intercorrelations (FP = free play; SP = structured play)

Codes	FP3	FP4	FP5	FP6
SP3	.15	.29**	.03	−.16
SP4	.39**	.32**	.28*	−.13
SP5	−.07	−.02	.11	.15
SP6	−.06	.02	−.14	.22*

$* = p < .05$ $** = p < .01$
Code 3 = object premastery
Code 4 = object mastery
Code 5 = social–object mastery
Code 6 = social mastery

the parent was placed against the center of one end wall, with
a pile of 30 toys placed 6 feet away from the parent's chair. A
research assistant sat across the room from the parent, who
placed the child on the floor, halfway between the parent's chair
and the toys. For a 30-minute period, the child was free to do
what it wished. Parents were instructed not to initiate activities
with the child, but were allowed to respond briefly as they normally would if the child initiated activities with the parents.
Again, observers coded all child behaviors, using the 10 code
system described earlier.

The intercorrelation of our social (code 6) and object mastery
codes (code 3 and 4), as measured in the structured and free-
play situations, are shown in Table 6.2. The results shown in
Table 2 indicate a moderate and significant correlation between
codes 3 and code 4. The relation between the social and object
mastery codes were either zero-order or significant and negative
in direction.

It could be argued that the negative or zero-order correlations
between our object and social mastery codes are artifactual,
being based on the fact that these codes are measured within
the same session. To test this possibility we computed the
cross-situation correlations between our object and social mastery codes (see Table 6.2). Even going across situations the cor-

relations between structured-object premastery and free-play object mastery or free-play object premastery and structured-play object mastery are significant and positive. The cross-situation object–social correlations are all zero order. Besides yielding evidence for construct validity, the last set of results shown in Table 6.2 also confirm the stability data shown in Table 6.1.

Can Individual Children be Characterized as Socially or Object Mastery Oriented?

While the previous analyses indicate that there is a relative independence of object and social mastery motivation *behaviors*, this analysis does not us allow us to determine whether *individuals* who are high on object mastery motivation are also low in social mastery motivation, and vice versa. To assess whether our extension of the social–object distinction can be generalized to individual infant's motivational orientation we utilized cluster analyses procedures on the sample of 88 infants described previously. Cluster analysis was used as a means of determining whether relatively homogeneous, distinct groups of infants could be identified and whether these groups would differ on the object and social mastery motivation behaviors we were measuring. Specifically, we utilized the Fastclus casewise clustering procedures contained in the Statistical Analysis System statistical package (SAS, 1985). Given that cluster constitution may vary as a function of the specific type of cluster analysis utilized, we analyzed our data utilizing two different procedures. The *complete linkage method* defines clusters as a function of the maximum distance between observations across clusters. *Ward's minimum variance method* defines clusters on the bases of minimizing the within cluster sum of squares (SAS, 1985). Reviews indicate that either of these procedures are more likely to recover existing clusters than are other alternative clustering procedures (Green, 1990). Since there is no commonly accepted procedure for determining the number of clusters that should be recovered, available evidence suggests the need to use a variety of alternative statistical criteria. As suggested by Green (1990), specification of the number of clusters obtained was based on congruence among our visual inspection of the cluster pattern, plus changes in the pseudo-f, pseudo-T^2, and cubic clustering criterion statistics. Specifically, where the three clustering statistical methods differed in the number of clusters obtained we utilized visual inspection of the cluster pattern, as a means of determining which statistical method had the highest level of fit with our visual inspection. Generation of mean scores for individuals within a cluster were obtained only *after* we had decided on the number of clusters. To minimize clusters unique to a particular measurement technique the analyses were based on summing scores across the free and structured play situations. The means defining clusters for both approaches are shown in Table 6.3.

For Ward's procedure, the cubic clustering criterion suggested the existence of three clusters, while the pseudo-T^2 indicated a two cluster solution. The pseudo-f statistic was inconclusive. Visual inspection of the cluster distribution suggested that a third cluster was, at best, poorly defined. As a result we choose the two cluster solution, with the clusters of approximately equal size. For the complete linkage method, both the pseudo-f and pseudo-T^2 statistics supported a three cluster solution while the cubic clustering criterion suggested a four cluster result. Visual inspection indicated that a three cluster solution was a better fit.

In terms of cluster interpretation, Ward's cluster two was characterized by relatively high levels of active object interaction (code 2), object premastery behavior (code 3), and object mastery behavior (code 4), as well as by relatively low levels of active social mastery (code 6) and passive social orientation (code 7). Given this pattern, we tentatively labeled Ward's cluster 2 as *object mastery.* A similar pattern, which we also labeled as object mastery, appears for Complete Linkage cluster two.

Ward's cluster one was characterized by relatively low levels of object mastery behavior (code 4), relatively high levels of passive object orientation (code 2), social–object mastery (code 5), active social mastery (code 6), passive social orientation (code 7) and a moderate level of distress (code 9). Given this pattern we tentatively labeled cluster one as *social orientation–social mastery.* No clearly comparable cluster appears in the Complete Linkage analysis. However, Complete Linkage cluster one (which we labeled as *non-object involvement*), encompassing a high level of passive object orientation (code 2), moderate levels of social mastery (code 6) and distress (code 9) and low levels of object premastery (code 3) and object mastery (code 4), bears some similarity to Ward's cluster one.

Unique to the Complete Linkage analysis is the small cluster three, which was characterized by relatively low levels of active

TABLE 6.3. NONMASTERY AND MASTERY MOTIVATION BEHAVIOR CATEGORY MEANS FOR INDIVIDUAL CLUSTERS

Mean Scores (in Seconds) for Toddlers in Specific Clusters

Complete Linkage Method

Codes	Cluster 1 (n = 11) (Non-object Involvement)	Cluster 2 (n = 43) (Object Mastery)	Cluster 3 (n = 10) (Anxious-Clinging)
0 Noninvolvement	181.50	139.97	139.70
1 Passive object	333.86	150.84	143.35
2 Active object	684.45	764.94	528.15
3 Object premastery	184.82	251.00	216.80
4 Object mastery	118.55	248.10	213.70
5 Social–object mastery	8.00	15.17	12.30
6 Active social mastery	62.77	48.02	94.80
7 Passive social	118.50	84.99	285.05
9 Distress	20.32	9.05	73.35

Wards' Minimum Variance Method

Codes	Cluster 1 (n = 29) (Social-Orientation Mastery)	Cluster 2 (n = 35) (Object-Orientation Mastery)
0 Noninvolvement	166.79	128.25
1 Passive object	217.60	150.90
2 Active object	612.37	798.40
3 Object premastery	211.03	253.54
4 Object mastery	180.70	253.40
5 Social–object mastery	17.94	9.80
6 Active social mastery	84.72	35.61
7 Passive social	182.00	72.30
9 Distress	37.32	7.52

object interaction (code 2), moderate levels of object mastery (code 4), high levels of active social mastery (code 6), passive social orientation (code 7), and a high level of distress (code 9). Given this pattern we felt that a label of *anxious–clinging child* was the most appropriate label for this cluster.

Summing across our cluster analyses we feel that the results are not inconsistent with our hypothesis, in that none of the clusters was defined primarily by high levels of *both* social and object mastery behavior. In both analyses we can observe clusters of children whose behavior is characterized by an emphasis on object mastery. While less clear cut, in both analyses we also find clusters of children who avoid active object mastery in favor of social orientation/social mastery. Finally, there appears to be a small minority of children who use social mastery behaviors as a means of dealing with distress in a new situation.

IMPLICATIONS

The major findings of the studies described above indicate that infant behaviors indicative of object mastery motivation (code 4) and active social mastery motivation (code 6) are moderately stable across different testing intervals and different testing situations. Our results also indicate that the correlations between our measures of object and social mastery are either zero order or negative. These results are congruent with previous research (Combs & Wachs, 1993; Maslin & Morgan, 1985; Wenar, 1976). Finally, our results extend previous research findings in terms of showing that social and object mastery motivation are independent, not only at a trait level, but at an *individual level.* Individual children who are motivated to master objects are less likely to show behaviors indicative of a desire to master persons. Similarly, children who are motivated to get reactions and attention from adults are less likely to spend time attempting to master objects.

All of the results discussed support our extension of the organismic specificity hypotheses to the domain of infant mastery. Congruent with previously cited research in other domains, such as language (Nelson, 1981), attentional patterns (Parrinello & Ruff, 1988), and children's play interactions (Shotwell et al., 1980), our present findings, plus those of other researchers (MacTurk et al., 1987; Morgan et al., 1993), suggest that object and social mastery motivations are distinct, individual styles of dealing with one's environment. This conceptualization of the nature of infant mastery stands in sharp contrast to the original developmental conceptualization of mastery, as noted by White (1959) and elaborated by later researchers (Dweck & Elliot, 1983), which suggested a lack of differentiation in mastery motivation during infancy. Our results are congruent with Harter's (1981) differentiation of social and object mastery after infancy, as well as with evidence indicating different developmental *courses* (e.g., MacTurk et al., 1987; Wenar, 1976), *correlates* (Combs & Wachs, 1993, MacTurk et al., 1985) and *etiologies* (e.g., Wachs, 1987; Wenar, 1976) for measures of infant social and object mastery motivation.

The association between high levels of active social mastery and distress found in the *anxious–clinging* cluster, in conjunction with the significant relation between positive affect and the number of social interactions found by Combs and Wachs (1993), also suggests that we may want to modify our definition of social mastery motivation. Conceptually, positive affect shown during mastery behavior is thought to be an indication of the pleasure derived from the behavior (Morgan et al., 1993), and should be included in the definition in order to help distinguish social mastery from pseudomastery brought on by distress. Additionally, Combs and Wachs (1993) have found indications that active social interactions may be better than passive social interactions as indicators of social mastery motivation. Accordingly, we would now define social mastery motivation as an interest in competently interacting with other people, as shown primarily by persistence of attempts to initiate social interactions and secondarily by attempts to maintain social interactions and by displays of positive affect during interactions.

Mastery Motivation as an Individual Differences Parameter

If we accept the hypothesis that there may be stylistic differences in what infants are motivated to master, it then becomes legitimate to consider the implications of these different motivational styles for subsequent development. One framework within which to consider these implications is the "goodness of fit" concept developed by Chess and Thomas (1991). Goodness of fit is similar to organismic specificity, in terms of hypothesizing that similar environments do not necessarily lead to similar developmental outcomes. The goodness of fit approach assumes that optimal development occurs when the child's individual characteristics mesh with those of the parents. Up to the present, most research on the goodness of fit concept has involved the fit between child and parent temperament, as this fit mediates developmental outcomes. To the extent that infant motivation is a stylistic, individual dimension, it may be equally valid to also look at differences in motivational orientation as a mediator of outcomes, again using the goodness of fit model. For example, a number of studies (Fagot, 1978; Vibbert & Bornstein, 1989) have reported that caregivers differ in the extent to which they emphasize object or social play with their young children. Within the fit model, positive developmental outcomes would be more likely to occur when object-oriented caregivers have children who are object motivated, or when socially oriented caregivers have children who are socially motivated; negative developmental outcomes should more likely result when object-oriented caregivers have socially motivated children, or when socially motivated caregivers have object-oriented children.

What is most likely to cause these differences in developmental outcomes is the degree to which the child's own attempts at structuring its environment are supported by its caregivers. If a socially motivated child attempts to create its own social niche, through repeated interactions with parents, the child's attempts are more likely to be supported if the parents are themselves socially motivated; the child's attempts are more likely to be frustrated if the parents are object-oriented. This type of process need not be restricted to the home. Another example would occur in situations where a basically object-oriented child is placed in a caregiving environment, such as a nursery school, which stresses play with toys or puzzles (a positive fit), as opposed to an environment that stresses high levels of adult–child interaction (a negative fit). In the former situation, the positive fit would be expected to promote growth, whereas in the latter, the negative fit would be expected to retard growth. The basic point is that our ability to understand why different outcomes occur for children in the same environment (organismic specificity) may be considerably enhanced, if we can assess the degree of fit between the infant's motivational orientation and the characteristics of the environment or the caregiver.

While considering infant motivation as a mediator of environment–development relations may seem highly speculative, it is speculation that is congruent with our research on the nature of infant mastery motivation. Further, our reconceptualization of mastery motivation as a stylistic variable is not as radical as it may seem. As noted in the introduction, White (1959) considered mastery motivation to be relevant for either people or objects. We do not deny the potential relevance of object mastery motivation for infant development. However, our research suggests that understanding mastery motivation in infancy is not simply a matter of viewing babies as "engineers" (object mastery); rather, we must also consider that some babies would rather be "politicians" (social mastery).

Viewing infant motivation in this way not only opens up interesting new research possibilities, as in the relation between different motivational components and different environmental components, but also allows us to tie the study of infant mastery motivation to ongoing theoretical models of environmental action, such as goodness of fit and organismic specificity. This allows us to increase our understanding of the correlates and consequences of individual differences in mastery motivation much more than if we simply viewed mastery motivation in infancy as an undifferentiated, unidimensional construct.

REFERENCES

Balleyguier, G. (June, 1991). *The structure of infant personality and its comparison with the big 5 model.* Paper presented to the Conference on the Development of the Structure of Temperament and Personality from Infancy to Adulthood, Wassenaar, The Netherlands.
Braungart, J., & Stifter, C. (1991). Regulation of negative reactivity during the strange situation. *Infant Behavior and Development, 14,* 349–364.
Chess, S., & Thomas, A. (1991). Temperament and the concept of goodness of fit. In J. Strelau & A. Angleitner (Eds.), *Explorations in temperament* (pp. 15–28). New York: Plenum.
Combs, T., & Wachs, T. D. (1993). The construct validity of measures of social mastery motivation. In D. J. Messer, (Ed.), *Mastery motivation in early childhood: Development, measurement and social processes* (pp. 168–188). London: Routledge.
Deci, E. (1975). *Intrinsic motivation.* New York: Plenum.
Dweck, C., & Elliot, E. (1983). Achievement motivation. In P. Mussen (Ed.), *Handbook of child psychology, Vol. 4* (pp. 643–692). New York: Wiley.

Escalona, S. (1968). *The roots of individuality.* Chicago: Aldine.

Fagot, B. (1978). The influence of sex of child on parental reactions to toddlers. *Child Development, 49,* 459–465.

Green, J. (1990). Analyzing individual differences in development: Correlations and cluster analysis. In J. Colombo & J. Fagen (Eds.), *Individual differences in infancy* (pp. 77–111). Hillsdale, NJ: Erlbaum.

Harter, S. (1981). A model of intrinsic mastery motivation in children: Individual differences and developmental change. In A. Collins (Ed.), *Minnesota symposium on child psychology, Vol. 14* (pp. 215–258). Hillsdale, NJ: Erlbaum.

Hunt, J. McV. (1965). Intrinsic motivation and its role in psychological development. In M. Levine (Ed.), *Nebraska symposium on motivation* (pp. 189–282). Lincoln,: University of Nebraska Press.

Hupp, S., Abbeduto, L., & Jaeger, J. (1995). *Comparative analysis of motivational correlates of play by nondelayed children and children with moderate and severe developmental delays.* Manuscript submitted for publication.

Jennings, K. D., Harmon, R. J., Morgan, G. A., Gaiter, J. P., & Yarrow, L. (1979). Exploratory play as an index of mastery motivation: Relationships to persistence, cognitive functioning and environmental measures. *Developmental Psychology, 15,* 386–394.

Jennings, K. D., Yarrow, L. J., & Martin, P. P. (1984). Mastery motivation and cognitive development: A longitudinal study from infancy to 3½ years of age. *International Journal of Behavioral Development, 7,* 441–461.

Langmeier, J., & Matejcek, Z. (1975). *Psychological deprivation in childhood.* New York: Wiley.

Lewis, M., & Feiring, C. (1989). Infant, mother and mother–infant interaction behavior and subsequent attachment. *Child Development, 60,* 831–837.

McCall, R. (1976). Toward an epigenetic conception of mental development in the first three years of life. In M. Lewis (Ed.), *Origins of intelligence* (pp. 97–112). New York: Plenum.

MacTurk, R. H., Hunter, F. T., McCarthy, M. E., Vietze, P. M., & McQuiston, S. (1985). Social mastery motivation in Down syndrome and nondelayed infants. *Topics in Early Childhood Special Education, 4,* 93–109.

MacTurk, R. H., McCarthy, M. E., Vietze, P. M., & Yarrow, L. J. (1987). A sequential analysis of mastery behavior in six- and twelve-month-old infants. *Developmental Psychology, 23,* 199–203.

MacTurk, R. H., & Trimm, V. M. (1989). Mastery motivation in deaf and hearing infants. *Early Education and Development, 1,* 19–34.

MacTurk, R. H., Vietze, P. M., McCarthy, M. E., McQuiston, S., & Yarrow, L. J. (1985). The organization of exploration behavior in Down syndrome and nondelayed infants. *Child Development, 56,* 573–581.

Maslin, C., & Morgan, G. A. (April, 1985). *Measures of social compe-tence: Toddlers' social and object orientation during mastery tasks.* Paper presented to the Society for Research in Child Development, Toronto, Canada.

Messer, D. J., McCarthy, M. E., McQuiston, S., MacTurk, R. H., Yarrow, L. J., & Vietze, P. M. (1986). Relation between mastery behavior in infancy and competence in early childhood. *Developmental Psychology, 22,* 366–372.

Morgan, G. A., Harmon, R. J., & Maslin-Cole, C. (1990). Mastery motivation: Definition and assessment. *Early Education and Development, 1,* 318–339.

Morgan, G. A., Maslin-Cole, C. A., Harmon, R. J., Busch-Rossnagel, N. A., Jennings, K. D., Hauser-Cram, P., & Brockman, L. M. (1993). Parent and teacher perceptions of young children's mastery motivation: Assessment and review of research. In D. J. Messer (Ed.), *Mastery motivation in early childhood: Development, measurement, and social processes.* (pp. 109–131). London: Routledge.

Morgan, G. A., Maslin-Cole, C., Biringen, Z., & Harmon, R. J. (1991). Play assessment of mastery motivation in infants and young children. In C. Schaefer, K. Gitlin, & A. Sandgrund (Eds.), *Play diagnosis and assessment* (pp. 65–86). New York: Wiley.

Nakamura, C., & Finck, D. (1980). Relative effectiveness of socially oriented and task oriented children and predictability of their behaviors. *Monographs for the Society for Research in Child Development, 45* (3–4, Serial No. 185).

Nelson, K. (1981). Individual differences in language development. *Developmental Psychology, 17,* 170–187.

Parrinello, R., & Ruff, H. (1988). The influence of adult intervention on infant's level of attention. *Child Development, 59,* 1125–1135.

Rogoff, B., & Lave, J. (1984). *Everyday cognition.* Cambridge: Harvard University Press.

SAS (1985). *SAS users guide—statistics.* Cory, NC: SAS Institute.

Shotwell, J., Wolf, D., & Gardner, H. (1980). Styles of achievement in early symbol use. In M. Foster & S. Brandes (Eds.), *Symbol as sense* (pp. 175–199). New York: Academic Press.

Ulvund, S. (1980). Cognition and motivation in early infancy. *Human Development, 23,* 17–32.

Vibbert, M., & Bornstein, M. (1989). Specific associations between domains of mother–child interaction and toddler referential language and pretense play. *Infant Behavior and Development, 12,* 163–184.

Wachs, T. D. (1987). Specificity of environmental action as manifest in environmental correlates of infant's mastery motivation. *Developmental Psychology, 23,* 782–790.

Wachs, T. D. (1992). *The nature of nurture.* Newbury Park: Sage.

Wenar, C. (1976). Executive competence in toddlers. *Genetic Psychology Monographs, 93,* 189–285.

White, R. (1959). Motivation reconsidered: The concept of competence. *Psychological Review, 66,* 297–333.

Yarrow, L. J., McQuiston, S., MacTurk, R. H., McCarthy, M. E., Klein, R. P., & Vietze, P. M. (1983). The assessment of mastery motivation during the first year of life. *Developmental Psychology, 19,* 159–171.

Yarrow, L. J., & Messer, D. J. (1983). Motivation and cognition in infancy. In M. Lewis (Ed.), *Origins of intelligence* (2nd Ed.) (pp. 451–478). New York: Plenum.

Yarrow, L. J., Morgan, G. A., Jennings, K. D., Harmon, R. J., & Gaiter, J. (1982). Infants persistence at tasks: Relationships to cognitive functioning and early experience. *Infant Behavior and Development, 5,* 131–141.

7

CONTRIBUTIONS AND CONFOUNDS FROM BIOLOGY AND GENETICS

Joan I. Vondra

University of Pittsburgh

INTRODUCTION

There is enough broad consensus in research findings relating to infant mastery motivation to support in general terms the two scenarios described below. Each reflects a small but growing body of correlational research on the expression of mastery motivation in infants. Each also provides a reasonably representative example of the data on which current understanding of mastery motivation is typically based.

Case 1 Scenario

Jenny, a 15-month-old infant from a middle-class family, is a competent explorer. She manipulates objects in a way that is thorough and deliberate and that generates critical knowledge about how they function. When left to her own devices, she spends time with objects that allow her to discover and produce interesting effects, create functional combinations, and act out some of the symbolic schemes that are emerging in her pretend play. When tested by a female examiner, she is generally responsive to requests, imitates readily, and stays with a challenging task for relatively long periods of time. She also tends to succeed at the tasks more often than is common for her age, particularly those that are moderately challenging for her. Jenny's mother loves to encourage her daughter's early learning and provides her with the freedom and play materials to do so. Their home is not large, but is safe for Jenny to move around in independently and offers a variety of interesting toy and non-toy objects to experiment with. Jenny spends time playing with her mother on most days and is accustomed to having adults respond positively to her curiosity and desire to learn.

From this scenario we could conclude that Jenny is an infant who tends to score well on measures of mastery motivation. Her mother would also tend to score well on measures of behavioral responsiveness to her daughter and of encouraging Jenny's developmental advance. Are the correlations these data illustrate sufficient information to support a model of environmental effects on the early development of competence?

Case 2 Scenario

Eric is from a family currently on welfare and living in a housing project. At eight months, Eric was much interested by the simple objects given to him and spent time holding, looking at, and mouthing them. He did not, however, manipulate any objects very actively and only occasionally discovered what even the simplest could do. When tested by a female examiner, Eric seemed more interested in watching the woman's unfamiliar face than in following her directives. He seemed to enjoy the test materials, but showed little positive affect and did not complete many of the tasks that were age-appropriate. He grew fussy about halfway through the testing period and was difficult to engage thereafter.

By 14 months, Eric had advanced much in his manipulation and could move all the different parts on many toys. He enjoyed combining objects in simple ways to produce noise and movement, although sometimes seemed to become disorganized due to the stimulation. His play covered a wide variety of toys, but he spent only short bouts with any one toy and did not often exploit the functional ways in which two toys could be used together. Only once did Eric's play move briefly to the symbolic level, when he pushed a plastic bus toward the examiner's feet with sputtering motor noises. During testing, Eric spent more time with the individual toys he was presented and imitated some of the activities the examiner had demonstrated, but grew restless when the toy seemed to challenge his skills or the examiner was less actively involved.

This scenario suggests that Eric would tend to score poorly on measures of mastery motivation at both ages, although his performance would depend to some extent on the context and nature of the measures used. Consistency in his performance over time would require looking at the quality and persistence of his exploration at newly emerging skills at each age. Are the correlations Eric's data illustrate sufficient information to support a model of developmental continuity in mastery motivation?

In each case, as this chapter will argue, key causal influences that may help account for relations found among the variables are not considered. Consequently, developmental models derived solely from these correlations may fail to capture accurately the nature and evolution of mastery motivation. Missing from the scenarios are such critical influences on behavior and development as parental genes for intelligence and psychological well-being, infant (and parent) temperament, cognitive processing abilities, and gender. Consider, for example, how the interpretation of these scenarios can change when the following information is also available.

Case 1 Scenario

Jenny's mother considers her daughter an "easy" baby. In comparison to her older sister, Jenny has been less fussy throughout infancy and, though initially shy with strangers, warms up quickly. Like her father, Jenny is sociable and "person-oriented," responsive to social overtures and ready to imitate. She separates from her mother more easily than did her sister at this age and explores for fairly long periods without needing to return to her mother's side.

Jenny's mother is bright and describes herself as well-adjusted and symptom free. These are, to a measurable degree, partly heritable traits. Her responsiveness to and encouragement of her daughter's curiosity and exploration are, in part, products of these traits as well as responses to Jenny's behavior—so is her perception of Jenny as "easy." In other words, then, aspects of both Jenny's behavior and her mother's (and father's) are genetically related.

Case 2 Scenario

Eric's mother was delighted that after two girls she finally had her "little man." She was not surprised that Eric slept less and squirmed and fussed more than his sisters, since this fit her understanding of what makes boys different. She remembers the tantrums her brothers used to have (although she has forgotten her own). Eric is, in fact, more active than his sisters, although all three children tend to be restless and distractible. These traits, shared by their mother, are most tolerated in Eric.

Unfortunately, when Eric was still a young infant, his mother experienced one of her recurrent bouts of depression, a partly heritable disorder. Eric's father, who is unlike the girls' father in being neither verbal nor bright, broke up with her just after the baby's birth. One year after Eric's birth, his mother continues to appear low in affect and responsivity and does not appear successful in regulating her son's attention and emotionality.

Eric differed from his sisters in a number of developmental milestones. He had a surge of motor development beginning around 8½ months and was walking by 10 months, but did not start using any words until about two months after his first birthday. His symbolic play is also limited for his age. If tested, Eric would score very modestly on tests of visual habituation and preference for novelty (i.e., information processing) at both ages. If measured, his mother's quality of caregiving would also tend to be scored similarly at each age. Both are, however, partly products of genetic differences with developmental pathways that evoke certain reinforcing experiences over time.

The descriptions provided here suggest some of the ways in which biological factors, inherited traits, and genetically influenced developmental pathways can confound the interpretation of motivational processes and environmental influences. Shared genes between parents and child (for intelligence, cognitive processes, emotionality, sociability, etc.) account for some of the variance not only in relations between parental behavior (and report) and child functioning, but also between characteristics of the home environment and child functioning. Biological and/or genetic components of temperament, affectivity, attention, effortful behavior, cognitive processing, and gender—which, themselves, surely contribute to differences in mastery motivation scores—can be responsible, to some extent, for correlations between parent and child behavior and, perhaps, even for continuity and change in individual differences over time. Figure 7.1 illustrates the complex interplay of environment and inheritance that may give rise to the individual differences that are observed in behaviors relevant to measures of mastery motivation. Characteristics that presumably contribute to motivated behavior probably reflect a dynamic interaction of biology, genes, and socialization like that depicted in this figure.

The aforementioned characteristics are some of the more obvious expressions of biological and genetic factors that tend to be ignored as potential confounds in many psychological models and research. Until very recently, psychologists have chosen to focus almost exclusively on that proportion of developmental variance which covaries with environmental context and/or is predictable over time. Data from twins and adoptees, however, demonstrate that a proportion of this variance is actually the result of genetic differences shared between parents and child. Increasingly, the work of behavioral geneticists is calling for a reconsideration not only of the psychological models we have developed but also of the nature of the research we conduct to evaluate them (Plomin, DeFries, & Fulker, 1988; Scarr & McCartney, 1983).

This chapter considers in greater depth the role that factors relating to temperament, cognitive processing, and gender may play in behavioral differences and developmental change observed in infant mastery motivation. It should be noted that although some data exist on biological and genetic contributions to early behavior and functioning, few data have been collected that speak directly to early mastery motivation. Research on mastery motivation has not addressed questions about biological or genetic influences. However, a number of behaviors and tasks similar to those used to measure mastery motivation have been included in research on biological and genetic differences. Thus, the evidence reviewed in this chapter can only

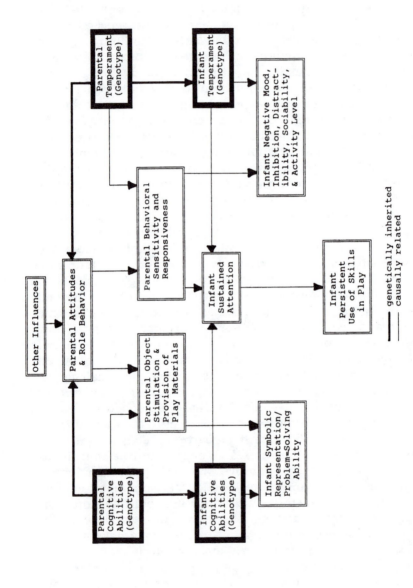

FIGURE 7.1. A MODEL OF PARENTAL GENETIC AND ENVIRONMENT EFFECTS ON EARLY MASTERY MOTIVATION.

suggest, through inference, the possible role that biology and genetics play in the individual differences observed on indices of mastery motivation during early childhood.

The discussion opens with a brief summary of the strategies that have been used to assess infant mastery motivation and the behavioral constructs that are central to each measure. Evidence for biological and/or genetic contributions to behavior relevant to such assessments is then reviewed and their potential significance for measuring mastery motivation considered. This is followed by speculation about genetic mechanisms underlying developmental change in and environmental correlates of mastery motivation. Finally, implications from these data for future studies of mastery motivation in infancy and early childhood are presented and examined in an effort to reframe our understanding and investigation of this construct.

Biological and Genetic Contributions to Effortful Behavior

White (1959) proposed that effectance motivation is an *innate* drive to be competent that becomes differentiated over time as a result of experience. In much of the research conducted to date on mastery motivation, however, attention accorded the role of experience has overshadowed consideration of biogenetic factors. In turn, the failure to consider possible biological contributions to the behaviors assessed in measures of mastery motivation has led to measurement and design issues that weaken the integrity and validity of the construct. Accurate causal interpretation of correlational and/or longitudinal data on mastery motivation requires close attention to relevant, biologically based processes and mechanisms. Otherwise, the opportunities for misinterpreting statistical associations threaten our accurate understanding of development. The brief review of current measurement strategies that follows sets the stage for considering the role of biology and genetics in models of mastery motivation.

Mastery Motivation: What Are We Measuring?

Investigations of mastery motivation in infancy typically utilize one of two basic measurement paradigms with multiple variations. Either a female examiner briefly demonstrates play and problem-solving activities that the infant may imitate and/or expand on, or the infant is provided with a set of toys to explore and play with independently for a given period of time. Occasionally variations on the two strategies are combined in a single design (Belsky, Garduque, & Hrncir, 1984; Vondra & Belsky, 1991). Although both paradigms share a number of common conceptual and measurement features, unique skills are also called on in each instance. In either case, the possible role of a variety of biological and/or genetic factors is worth noting (Vondra & Jennings, 1990).

For both paradigms, the emphasis in measurement is on frequent and/or sustained bouts of object manipulation that are relatively sophisticated for that infant or for infants of that age (i.e., recently emerging skills for the developmental period). There are underlying skills required for both tasks. These include curiosity, sustained attention and resistance to distractions, active involvement with objects, moderate to high cognitive understanding (e.g., means–end problem solving and concept formation among infants around 12 to 18 months old), and ability to overcome behavioral inhibitions. There are also skills required that are more specific to the particular measurement paradigm. These include social responsiveness (for interacting with and playing near an unfamiliar female adult), ability to separate from one's caregiver (for independent exploration), and responsiveness to the physical properties of objects (for continuing to focus on individual objects and their functions more than a minute or so). Data suggest the existence of biological and/or genetic contributions to all of these skills that may affect scores on measures of mastery motivation. Any biogenetic contributions would then inflate relations between measures of mastery motivation and measures of (genetically related) maternal behavior, maternal report, and/or quality of the home environment. Without recognizing these possible contributions, causal models of the origins and development of mastery motivation risk inaccuracy and misrepresentation of causal effects.

The Role of Temperament

In this section, the possible effects of temperamental differences on play and problem-solving activities are considered. Select studies are summarized that illustrate the role biology and genes may play in early behavioral inhibition, activity level, and sociability. At the same time, the potential relevance of these temperamental factors to measures of early mastery motivation is discussed.

Behavioral Inhibition. The readiness with which an infant or young child relinquishes contact with his or her parent to interact with an unfamiliar adult or separate to explore unfamiliar objects has been termed "behavioral inhibition" by Kagan, and represents the cornerstone of a major program of research he has undertaken (Kagan, Reznick, Clarke, Snidman, & Garcia-Coll, 1984; Kagan, Reznick, & Gibbons, 1989; Reznick, Kagan, Snidman, Gersten, Baak, & Rosenberg, 1986). Kagan and his colleagues have documented both biological and genetic bases for behavioral inhibition during infancy and early childhood. Specific indices of inhibition in his longitudinal study of 400 children—all of which have special significance for measurement of mastery motivation—included long latency to play with unfamiliar objects, long latencies to speak or interact with an unfamiliar woman in the laboratory, and maintenance of proximity to mother (Kagan, Reznick, & Snidman, 1987, 1988). Consistent behavioral inhibition, noted in about 15–20% of healthy one- to two-year-old children, was associated with physiological evidence of greater reactivity of the sympathetic nervous system and with maternal report of greater irritability and sleeplessness during the infant's first year, evidence for biological mechanisms.

More importantly, an aggregate index of behavioral inhibition and wariness collected on 178 twin pairs has showed evidence of heritability (Robinson, Kagan, Reznick, & Corley, 1992). Estimated heritability coefficients were .53 at 14 months and .42 at 20 months. In addition, correlational analysis revealed likely genetic contributions to stability and change in behavioral inhibition from 14 to 24 months (estimated heritability coefficient for change of .52). Genetic foundations for anxious, inhibited behavior have also been indicated in primate studies conducted by Suomi and his colleagues (Suomi, Kraemer, Baysinger, & DeLizio, 1981). In the latter case, the computed heritability index for the measure of inhibition (a heart rate change score) was .73 for half-sib monkeys raised in controlled environments.

Data on the expression of inhibition suggests that individual variation in mastery motivation may be a product, in part, of inherited, biologically based differences in behavioral inhibition. Children who are more inhibited will tend to react less positively when introduced to an unfamiliar laboratory setting and asked either to observe and play by an unfamiliar adult or separate and explore an unfamiliar set of toys. Thus, measuring their persistence in initiating or imitating age-appropriate exploration and problem solving may also assess the degree to which they experience behavioral inhibition.

Obviously, individual differences in behavioral inhibition span a broad continuum of severity. However, even moderate levels of wariness and inhibition may affect object exploration—if not in terms of latency to explore, then perhaps in the frequency of interruptions to look at or show objects to mother, the readiness to abandon exploration (at least temporarily) to interact with mother, or the latency to use an object in one of the ways demonstrated by an unfamiliar examiner. As Goldsmith, Bradshaw, and Rieser-Danner (1986) pointed out:

> Temperamental variation in fearfulness . . . could influence the chronic levels of the set goal of the attachment, such that temperamentally fearful infants would tend to have lower thresholds for activation of attachment behaviors . . . An infant whose fear system is chronically easily activated tends to experience correspondingly quick deactivation of the exploratory system. (p. 10)

Jones (1985) demonstrated that when attachment needs are heightened—as when an infant is introduced to a new setting or when a stranger undertakes interaction with an infant—infants are less likely to undertake independent and/or extended exploration. Any of these effects on exploration may reflect individual differences in behavioral inhibition. If that is the case, mastery motivation scores may be showing biogenetic influences.

Activity Level. Another dimension of temperament with relevance to infant mastery motivation is activity level or behavioral tempo. There are often marked individual and gender differences in motor activity and physical energy level—apparent early in life—that are partly attributable to genetic inheritance (Emde et al., 1992; Goldsmith & Campos, 1986; Matheny, 1980, 1983). In one investigation, for example, motion recorders attached to 60 two-year-old twins for periods of 48 hours indicated significantly more similarity in daily activity level for monozygotic than for dizygotic twins (Saudino & Eaton, 1991). Differences were also observed between the high correspondences of physical development scores on the Bayley Scales for twins of greater and lesser genetic similarity. In her discussion of the development of self-regulatory skills, Kopp (1982) concluded that, "In all probability, the ability to modulate sensorimotor acts [in the first year] reflects individual differences related to biological predispositions (e.g., tempo and activity level) as well as to conditions external to the child" (p. 203).

Such individual differences may be especially likely to influence measures of mastery motivation in infancy, given the sensorimotor demands and constraints inherent in the measures. On the one hand, infants are scored essentially on their ability to remain in one area, to relinquish large motor activities like exploring the room, and to persist in a variety of fine motor tasks. Indeed, it seems somewhat ironic that "mastery" motivation for an infant or toddler making enormous strides in mastering gross motor skills and exploring the boundaries of his or her environment is typically assessed in this sedentary fashion. The constraints are perhaps more obvious in the structured measures that involve presentation of toys one at a time, but they are also present in free-play measures. In each case, time away from functional manipulation of toys, whether to give a toy to mother or walk/crawl around the room, lowers persistence scores. On the other hand, infants with faster behavioral tempos may perform a greater variety of sensorimotor acts in more rapid succession (i.e., higher total number and/or variety of manipulations) than infants who are slower and more deliberate in their activities. One infant may quickly and repeatedly work levers on an activity box, slam down the covers, and try again, whereas another may pause to manipulate the figure that pops up, to push it back in, and to try to pry open the door that covers it, in the same amount of time. Although each is persisting in his or her activity, their scores are likely to differ since the level of play in each case differs. These differences may, in part, reflect behavioral tempo. Possible effects of behavioral tempo are a particular concern when individual toys are presented for relatively brief periods of time (e.g., two or three minutes) and when such toys possess a number of movable parts. In each case, total amount of time manipulating toys in a cognitively sophisticated manner (e.g., "problem solving") may be at least partly a function of biological and genetic differences in behavioral tempo and motor activity level.

Sociability. Sociability, or orientation toward people, and object or task orientation also appear to be temperamental traits with origins, in part, in genetic predispositions (Goldsmith & Gottesman, 1981). In an extensive program of research employing over 300 pairs of monozygotic and dizygotic twins studied from three months to over three years of age, Matheny, Wilson, and their colleagues have documented substantial heritability in infant developmental test-taking behavior and (to a lesser degree) mental performance (Matheny, 1980, 1983, 1990; Wilson, 1983; Wilson & Matheny, 1986). Concordance on behavioral clusters of Bayley's Infant Behavior Record representing task orientation and test affect/extraversion—at any one point in time and across development—was greater for twins who shared more genes (for example, r's of .20–.25 for dizygotic twins, r's of .50–.55 for monozygotic twins). Composite measures including persistence in imitation and problem-solving activities, interest in toys, cooperation with a female examiner, and social orientation to examiner and mother during developmental testing showed evidence of genetic influence. Results have been replicated using adoptive and nonadoptive infant siblings, with genetic effects accounting for between 40% and 50% of the variation in ratings on the Infant Behavior Record at 12 and at 24 months (Braungart, Plomin, DeFries, & Fulker, 1992). The implications of such data for genetic variation in measures of mastery motivation, which can often resemble the Bayley Scales' procedure (i.e., an examiner provides a toy and a brief demonstration and/or verbal instruction), are significant, if indirect. Some proportion of the variance observed in mastery motivation measures may reflect inherited differences in social and object orientation.

Interestingly, there is also evidence for temperamental and/or coping differences in patterns of secure and insecure attachment relationships that may account for inconsistencies in results relating infant–mother attachment security to mastery motivation and play. Some researchers find that securely attached infants or toddlers score higher on mastery motivation or other play measures. Others find no differences for children with secure versus insecure attachments, whereas still others find higher scores for infants with one pattern of insecure attachment (see Maslin & Spieker, 1990). Data indicate that infant physiological and emotional reactivity play a role in how relationship security is expressed when caregiving is attuned to infant psychological needs, and how insecurity is expressed when caregiving is unresponsive and insensitive (Belsky & Rovine, 1987; Frodi & Thompson, 1985).

Infants demonstrating less negative reactivity (i.e., "easy" temperaments) appear more likely to exhibit the secure patterns that involve less separation distress and proximity seeking (attachment subtypes B1 and B2), or the insecure pattern that involves social gaze and contact avoidance (the avoidant, or "A," classification). These infants may be especially likely to persist in higher level object exploration, given their tendency in attachment assessments to spend less time distressed and seeking proximity to mother and more time separating to explore.

Infants demonstrating greater negative reactivity (i.e., "difficult" temperaments), on the other hand, appear more likely to exhibit secure patterns that involve more separation distress, proximity-seeking, and contact-maintenance (attachment subtypes B3 and B4), or the insecure pattern that involves contact resistance (the resistant, or "C," classification). These infants may be less likely to persist in higher level object exploration, given their frequent distress and their focus on proximity to and interaction with mother. Preliminary data support the links between distress–proneness in attachment patterns and quality of free play (Vondra, 1993).

Not surprisingly, then, studies are as likely to report equal or greater object exploration and mastery motivation for infants having avoidant attachments as they are for infants having secure attachments (e.g., Frodi, Bridges, & Grolnick, 1985; Harmon, Suwalsky, & Klein, 1979; Lyons-Ruth, Connell, Zoll, & Stahl, 1987; Maslin & Spieker, 1990; Popper, Cohn, Campbell, & Ross, 1992). These mastery motivation results may reflect temperamental variation or strategies of coping with temperamental reactivity as much as or more than they reflect differences in infant–mother attachment security.

The Role of Cognition

Sensorimotor activities in infancy and symbolic representation in early childhood have long been used as indices of a child's cognitive ability and development (Bayley, 1955; Nicolich, 1977; Uzgiris, 1976). Less sophisticated forms of object exploration (such as mouthing and simple manipulation of objects) decline as children get older, whereas more advanced forms of exploration (activities tailored to object functions, pretense play) increase (see Vondra & Belsky, 1991). Cognitively sophisticated play, particularly symbolic representation, correlates with other cognitive achievements, including problem-solving and information-processing abilities, linguistic competence, and developmental test scores (Clarke-Stewart, 1973; Rosenblatt, 1977; Tamis-LeMonda & Bornstein, 1989; Ungerer & Sigman, 1984). Importantly, all of these indices of cognitive functioning can be attributed in part to inherited intelligence, based on a growing body of literature.

Symbolic Representation. Despite the dearth of studies reporting data on *both* maternal and paternal intelligence, there is evidence that parental intelligence contributes to mental functioning (as assessed by standard developmental or intelligence tests) in early childhood, especially after the first year or two, when variability in functioning increases (Wilson, 1983). For example, DiLalla and her colleagues (DiLalla et al., 1990) reported that, at one year, there was essentially no association between performance on the Bayley Scales and parental IQ, but by two years, the correlation was significant ($r[114] = .25$, $p < .01$). Without data from twin or adoption studies, however, one cannot distinguish between genetic and environmental pathways of influence for parental intelligence. Bright parents provide the genetic foundation for bright children, but also tend to provide more enriched environments.

With the availability of data from twin and adoption research on the heritability of global cognitive assessment scores (from measures of "sensorimotor intelligence") across infancy and early childhood, Plomin, DeFries, and Fulker (1988) have concluded that although there is little evidence of genetic variance in the first year of life, there appears to be "considerable" genetic influence between one and two years. More recently, in a series of investigations studying the development of symbolic representation in infancy, Tamis-LeMonda and Bornstein (1989, 1992) have documented associations ranging from .26 to .63 (using samples of about 38 infants) among maternal intelligence, infant visual habituation and/or novelty preference in the *first* six months, and attention span and symbolic representation in the second year. Importantly, maternal intelligence predicted toddler exploratory competence, a latent variable representing attention span and cognitive sophistication in play (partial $r = .63$, $p < .001$) even after controlling for level of maternal stimulation (i.e., environmental quality), suggesting that a nonenvironmental pathway such as inheritance plays a role in the relation.

There is, in fact, some evidence for stronger, though modest, genetic effects on early information processing (visual habituation/preference for novelty) and symbolic functioning (language competence and pretend play) than on sensorimotor intelligence in infancy. Estimated heritability indexes in DiLalla et al.'s (1990) twin study (sample size of approximately 200) were .24 for a seven- and nine-month composite score on infant preference for novelty, but only .13 for a composite of Bayley Scale sensorimotor items at seven months and .06 at nine months. There is also better prediction to stable childhood intellectual functioning from early habituation or preference for novelty and symbolic functioning in language and play than from sensorimotor competence (see Bornstein & Sigman, 1986).

Thus, there is documented continuity in cognitive functioning across infancy—using measures of early information processing and symbolic representation—that is associated with later intelligence and also with maternal (and, presumably, paternal) intelligence. This association appears to be mediated, at least in part, by genetic inheritance. To the extent that infant exploration and play reflect the kinds of information processing and symbolic representational skills measured in these studies, individual differences in play may represent genetic as well as experiential differences between infants. Consequently, measures of mastery motivation could be assessing genetically inherited intellectual ability in addition to motivational differences if they include pretend play or if they are susceptible to differences in information processing (e.g., speed of habituation during single toy presentations)

Sensorimotor Intelligence. Only a subset of measures of mastery motivation include symbolic representation (pretend play) in the assessment. All measures, however, include sensorimotor tasks such as functionally combining objects (e.g., placing rings on a pole, shapes in a shape sorter), producing effects (e.g., turning a dial to make a phone ring), and engaging in simple problem solving (e.g., moving an object in some way to get at something inside). These types of sensorimotor activities are well represented on traditional infant developmental assessments (e.g., the Bayley Scales, the Gesell Scale). As pointed out in the previous section, there is less evidence for genetic effects on these measures of "sensorimotor intelligence." Rather, data indicate that the sensorimotor skills tapped by traditional infant developmental assessments may be more reflective of overall organismic intactness and integrity of basic mental functioning than of intellectual/information processing ability (McCall, Eichorn, & Hogarty, 1977). In other words, an infant's ability to perform means–end problem solving, demonstrate functional relations between objects, and explore the functional aspect of objects reflects his or her global developmental status. These are all skills tapped not only on tests of developmental status (which assess *whether* an infant can do them), but also on measures of mastery motivation (which assess how *often* an infant does, or at least attempts, them). Note, however, that there is some distinction here between, for example, working (unsuccessfully) to push a shape block into a shape sorter and successfully matching the correct shape with its hole. Only the latter would raise a developmental test score, but both activities would raise a mastery motivation persistence score. Product is emphasized in developmental assessments, whereas process is emphasized in mastery motivation paradigms.

Wilson's (1983) twin data are consistent with other data (see Plomin et al., 1988) in demonstrating a small but consistent degree of genetic relatedness, a significant influence of (shared) prenatal environment, and relatively little effect of normal (shared) post-birth rearing environment on sensorimotor functioning in the first year of life. Thus, measures of mastery motivation that are based on the absolute frequency, amount, or duration of more sophisticated exploration and play—particularly nonsymbolic manipulation—appear to be partly confounded with overall sensorimotor developmental status, influenced in the first year more by prenatal environment than by genes. At the same time, an infant's persistence in engaging in any of these sensorimotor behaviors as well as in symbolic play may tap important individual differences in another aspect of what may be partially inherited cognitive functioning—the ability to focus and sustain attention.

Sustained Attention. Information-processing ability involves specific components of cognitive functioning that would seem to play a critical role in early measures of mastery motivation. One aspect of information processing in particular, sustained attention (the ability to focus attention and ignore distractions), may help to illustrate possible genetic effects of information processing on mastery motivation. Sustained attention has been linked both empirically and theoretically to infant intellectual functioning and, as noted earlier, also shows at least some evidence of genetic inheritance.

The ability to maintain attention to a physical object/stimulus, presented either alone or with other objects/stimuli significantly increases from 1 to 2 years and from 2 to 3½ years. Sustained attention increases during nonsymbolic play across the first year of life and increases during symbolic play across the second year (Tamis-LeMonda & Bornstein, in press). Among one-year-olds, but not two- or three-year-olds, there is a decrement in focused attention even from the first minute after presentation of a novel object to the second, which has been attributed to the possible effects of habituation, that is, decreased interest following some form of mental assimilation of stimulus properties (Ruff & Lawson, 1990). Attention in the first year appears to be especially sensitive to the physical properties of objects, whereas attention after the first year is apparently controlled to a significantly greater extent by the complexity of activities that can be generated by the object. Although the transition in focus from "What is this object?" to "What can I do with it?" may typically occur around 8 months (McCall et al., 1977), infants at the end of the first year are still likely to be more susceptible to physical familiarity effects than are children in toddlerhood and in the preschool period. Greater decrement in attention to a single object (i.e., less persistence) during the first year, therefore, may be indicative of more rapid habituation to physical (and perhaps simple functional) properties, and thus more efficient information processing.

McCall and Carriger (1993), in fact, argued that the components of infant habituation that may reflect stable individual differences in (partly inherited) intelligence are the ability to focus swiftly on the novel stimulus in a field; inhibit attention to more familiar, less prominent "noise" stimuli (e.g., characteristics of the testing room and other potential distractions); and maintain primary attention to the novel stimulus until assimilation has occurred. Thus, more intelligent infants would process new information in a more "efficient" and "businesslike" manner. With respect to development, the researchers suggested "the simplest possibility is that the disposition to inhibit attention to "noise" remains continuous in form over development, although the ability . . . to do so in progressively more complex situations improves with age." By adulthood, they pointed out, the "successful problem solvers and intelligent adults are ones who can separate information that is relevant to the solution of a problem from that which is irrelevant" (McCall & Carriger, 1993 p. 50). Within mastery motivation paradigms, this implies more rapid, focused attention among brighter infants to novel toys or objects, sustained attention by these infants to functional aspects that produce new information (to the extent that the mental age of the child and the object's properties permit this), and greater readiness to move on to other objects following more rapid assimilation of the information to be gained from the initial toy. Consequently, infants who perform better in play—strictly from an attentional standpoint—turn out to be the brighter individuals.

Data by Ruff and Lawson (1991) support the association between sustained attention and later intelligence. In their study of object exploration at 7 and 9 months, infants who spent more of the brief presentation period engaged in visually guided manipulation and less time dropping, banging, or throwing objects looked no different from infants scoring lower on attentive manipulation in terms of sensorimotor competence (Bayley MDI) at 1 and 2 years, but scored significantly higher on a Stanford–Binet intelligence test at 3½ years.

Similarly, Tamis-LeMonda and Bornstein (1992) suggested that "shorter visual fixation [habituation] in laboratory procedures might index more efficient or faster processing in young infants; in contrast, in situations which permit older infants to explore actively (as during free play), sustained interest, particularly when coupled with more sophisticated play activity, appears to index greater competence" (p. 19). In their own investigation (Tamis-LeMonda & Bornstein, 1992, in press), more sophisticated free play (nonsymbolic prior to 9 months, both nonsymbolic and symbolic beginning around 9 months, and symbolic only by 17 months) was associated with more sustained attention during that play. Sustained attention during free play, was, in turn, associated with both speed of habituation and maternal intelligence.

In summary, rapid focusing on and exploration of individual objects, followed by a decrement of attention to the same objects (particularly to their physical appearance and perhaps their simpler functional features), and more sustained attention to functional and symbolic properties of an array of objects, appear to be products of individual differences in information processing (sustained attention). Whether one considers the potential role of genetics in attentional skills per se (DiLalla et al., 1990) or its role in stable intelligence—which attentional skills in infancy predict (McCall & Carriger, 1993)—there is reason to hypothesize that sustained attention during the first two years reflects some genetic influence. To the degree that individual differences in attention-focusing abilities set constraints on persistence of "goal-directed" exploratory activities, inherited cognitive differences may play a role in performance on measures of infant mastery motivation. From an information-processing perspective, infants who become disinterested more quickly with a particular object may (a) have less desire or interest in "mastering" the physical environment, (b) have prior familiarity with the object that prevents them from demonstrating their actual level of general mastery motivation, or (c) assimilate the physical (and even simple functional aspects) more rapidly and thus end their exploration more quickly, regardless of their level of mastery motivation. Only in the first case is performance presumably indicative of individual differences in mastery motivation. The third possibility, in contrast, again draws attention to the influence of what may be partly inherited cognitive (versus motivational) differences on "mastery motivation" measures.

The Role of Gender

Mean differences between males and females in a number of the characteristics described previously, as well as in the nature and effect of socialization experiences, suggest that gender differences may exist, to some extent, in the *expression* of infant mastery motivation, and to a greater extent, in the *correlates* of infant mastery motivation. Many of these expected differences, however, appear likely to depend on infant age, measurement context, and interactive experiences.

In general, empirical evidence indicates that, during infancy, girls are less willing to separate from their caregiver to explore, seek assistance from the mothers more often during free play, take longer to interact with relatively unfamiliar adults, are less interested in solitary object manipulation and, conversely, are more interested in social interaction with familiar peers and adults (Aydlett, West, & Leung, 1992; Brooks & Lewis, 1974; Fagot, 1978; Goldberg & Lewis, 1969; Sorce & Emde, 1981; Wasserman & Lewis, 1985). Boys have a higher activity level and play tempo (DiLalla et al., 1990; Eaton & Enns, 1986;

McCall, 1974), are less inhibited (Robinson et al., 1992), show more object-mediated play with their caregiver, and are more likely during free play to show a pattern of decreasing (versus increasing for girls) involvement with their caregiver over time (Olesker, 1990). Presumably, these differences reflect the influence of both biology and socialization, a conclusion reached in the vast majority of research on behavioral differences between the sexes across childhood.

Data on gender-specific behavior patterns across interactive contexts suggest that some early gender differences can be explained by the notion that boys devote more instrumental attention to their caregiver, whereas girls' attention in relation to their caregiver is more focused on social and expressive goals. Weinberg (1992) observed that, at six months, boys make more negative and positive bids for attention to their mother during the "still-face" paradigm (a period of sudden adult unresponsiveness during face-to-face interaction), whereas girls spend more time self-comforting and turning away to look at objects. At 14 months, boys seek attention from their mother after dropping toys from a high chair, in an apparent attempt to retrieve the toys, whereas girls seek more attention from their mother *before* dropping toys and then seem to use toy dropping as a means to gain further attention (Roggman, Jennings, & Hart, 1992). Such differences are consistent with gender-related patterns of parental care, including more verbal and social interaction with girls and both more encouragement of autonomy and more prohibitions directed to boys (Belsky, Lerner, & Spanier, 1984).

Exploration and Social Interaction. Responsive and sensitive maternal behavior (e.g., responding to infant bids for attention, not intruding when infants are engaged in play) and infant–mother attachment security are both differentially correlated with exploratory behavior of girls versus boys. Martin (1981; Martin, Maccoby, & Jacklin, 1981) found that responsive maternal behavior during free play was associated with proximity to mothers among female toddlers but with distance to mothers among male toddlers. Lollis (1990) observed that the greatest amount of toy play and least amount of unoccupied time for toddlers during a separation episode from mother differed systematically by sex and experience. Increased exploration for girls occurred when mothers had been minimally interactive prior to separation, but occurred for boys when mothers had been extensively interactive prior to separation. During an interactive task with their mothers, two- to three-year-old boys showed greater attention, exploration, persistence, and positive affect when mothers gave hints earlier in the task, but girls performed *less* well when mothers started out by giving high-level hints (Hron-Stewart, Lefever, & Weintraub, 1990). Finally, Roggman and her colleagues (Roggman et al., 1992) found the greatest difference in toy exploration associated with infant–mother attachment security among 14-month-old girls. Attachment security was associated with relatively more attention given to mother and less to toys in a high chair task for all children (see also Malatesta, Culver, Fesman, & Shepard, 1989), but especially among girls at this age. A similar finding was reported by Popper and her colleagues (Popper et al., 1992). Differential correlations by sex have also been found for maternal behaviors and sensorimotor competence on the Bayley Scales (Bayley & Schaefer, 1964).

Exploration and Cognitive Functioning.   Prediction from task behavior and toy exploration to subsequent cognitive functioning differs by child gender as well. In one study, time spent exploring simple toys at eight months improved prediction of sensorimotor competence at two years for boys only (Kopp & Vaughn, 1982). In another, concurrent measures of motivation (attentiveness, persistence, affect) during structured play and sensorimotor competence at two years were correlated for girls only (Hron-Stewart, Lefever, & Weintraub, 1990). Task orientation and affective reactions during developmental testing in toddlerhood have also predicted parental IQ (a proxy used for child IQ in adulthood) for girls only (DiLalla et al., 1990). Finally, persistence during structured play (as well as sensorimotor competence) at one year predicted effortful behavior at 3½ years for boys, but predicted intellectual performance for girls (Jennings, Yarrow, & Martin, 1984; see also Messer et al., 1986; Vondra, 1987). In other words, measures of motivation during exploration/testing in infancy may be more predictive of effortful, sensorimotor behavior among boys and of intellectual functioning among girls.

These different correlational patterns across sexes suggest that there is value in testing for them more systematically in research on mastery motivation. The significance of engaging in persistent, effortful exploration in infancy may be different for boys versus girls, given differential patterns of socialization. For example, this kind of behavior could reflect an emerging style of physically engaging the environment among boys, whereas for girls, its presence might signify a home environment that offers more encouragement of autonomy and intellectual achievement. The data summarized here suggest that there is justification for expecting gender differences in correlates of play behavior (including mastery motivation) during early childhood.

Gender Differences and Mastery Motivation.   The pattern of gender differences in preferences for object or object-mediated play versus social interaction and in latency to explore and behavioral tempo during exploration suggests that measures of mastery motivation may be affected by infant gender. For example, familiarity of the examiner during structured play assessments of mastery motivation and physical distance of the toys from the caregiver as well as psychological availability of the caregiver during free play assessments of mastery motivation should tend either to accentuate or diminish differences in male and female performance. Published studies of infant mastery motivation have not yet explored methodological variations that might highlight or obscure gender differences, but the research just summarized indicates that this could prove to be valuable.

Instead, the various indices of exploration used to assess motivation have traditionally been examined for mean differences and/or differences in correlational patterns by gender. Most studies reporting no gender differences focus on mean differences (e.g., Belsky et al., 1984; Frodi, Bridges, & Grolnick, 1985). The absence of such differences does not, however, ensure the comparability of data on males and females. This is most apparent in studies that explore possible pattern differences; that is, sex differences in correlational patterns between measures of motivation and other measures of infant functioning or environmental context. An informal survey of published studies that report testing for such pattern differences indicates that some three quarters find significant differences (e.g., Messer et al., 1986; Wachs, 1987; Yarrow et al., 1984; but see Caruso, 1990, for an exception).

Conclusion

Recognizing the potential biogenetic basis for behaviors thought to reflect early mastery motivation—defined in terms of persistent problem-solving behavior, sophisticated sensorimotor activities, and/or symbolic representation during play—provides researchers with an opportunity to reinterpret the study of motivational differences to some degree, in terms of genetic variation in temperamental, cognitive, and gender-related functioning across individuals. Suggestive evidence for biogenetic contributions to behaviors thought to represent mastery motivation also supports the argument that these behaviors be evaluated and interpreted in context rather than globally, because different contexts or strategies of measurement (i.e., independent free play, structured play in imitation of an adult model) may highlight different genetic (and experiential) influences, only some of which are relevant to a more general construct of mastery motivation.

What does this mean for studies of mastery motivation in infancy and early childhood? Inasmuch as both motivational behavior itself and context-specific behavior captured in measurement paradigms reflect biogenetic factors, caution is required in drawing conclusions about relations (particularly causal relations) between measures of motivation and measures of such constructs as competence. Any relations between the two—either contemporaneous or longitudinal—may represent consistency in gene-driven differences in temperament or socialization that have little relevance to either construct but are captured in measures of both. In addition, since partly inherited cognitive abilities could influence performance on measures of mastery motivation as well as measures of cognitive competence, the issue of causal priority cannot be addressed even indirectly using correlational data unless common biological bases for behavior can, to some degree, be identified and isolated. Otherwise, biogenetic "third variables" represent alternative hypotheses for the associations observed between motivation and competence. Without raising such hypotheses in studies of infant mastery motivation and cognitive competence, it is intuitively appealing to conjecture about a significant facilitative effect of motivation on competence that is not yet warranted by the data. Indeed, Harter and Connell (1984) presented (correlational) data to support their argument that, during the school years, causal influence occurs in the *opposite* direction; that is, from competent performance to enhanced motivation. When data collection includes measures of parental intelligence and relevant temperamental or any other partly inherited traits, we will be a step closer to making causal inferences from correlational data on motivation and competence in infancy and childhood.

Additionally, reliance on single measures or paradigms (which often differ across studies) to capture a global construct like mastery motivation accentuates the validity issues always inherent in the early stages of construct development. Since measures of early exploration presumably differ in their susceptibility to cognitive, temperamental, and gender influences, not only is it unclear from single measure studies to what extent a unitary construct of mastery motivation exists, but it is also difficult to pull apart variance that can be considered motivational in nature from variance that is attributable to other sources. Identifying variance that is common across mastery measures and paradigms but is distinct from that captured on cognitive and temperamental measures requires multiple measures of multiple constructs. Thus, factor-analytic studies, including several measures of "mastery motivation" as well as measures of cognitive ability and temperamental variation, are critical to the empirical and conceptual advancement of the field.

The significance of genetic contributions to performance on mastery motivation measures is not limited to problems of construct (convergent *and* discriminant) validity. Important data regarding genetic influences on development and genetic mediation of environment–competence correlations suggest the need to take genetic factors into account in all models of developmental process, including models of the development of mastery motivation. These data are summarized in the next two sections, and their implications for theory and research on mastery motivation are subsequently discussed.

BIOGENETIC CONTRIBUTIONS TO DEVELOPMENTAL STABILITY AND CHANGE

The twin studies described earlier have been valuable not only in identifying genetic components to motivated behavior and cognitive performance, but also in documenting genetic influences on stability and change in each over time Matheny (1990), Matheny, Wilson, Dolan, & Kranz (1993), and Wilson (1983) published data indicating some genetic synchronization of changes in test behavior and in sensorimotor performance across the first two years of life. Identical twins were significantly more alike than fraternal twins in how their behavior and performance *changed* over time, and this concordance increased across childhood. Based on their own and others' data, Plomin and his colleagues (Plomin et al., 1988) concluded that "nearly all [the] modest phenotypic stability [in cognitive performance across infancy and early childhood] appears to be mediated genetically" (p. 156).

Measures of infant mastery motivation, it has been argued here, may be influenced by some of the same biogenetic factors that contribute to infant test behavior and sensorimotor performance, as well as by actual (partly inherited) intellectual ability. It is possible, though not probable, that when modest stability is found in motivational scores across periods of up to a year, this stability is, itself, partly a product of genetic inheritance. In fact, the relatively greater degree of *change* documented in mastery motivation scores across periods of up to a year (e.g., Messer et al., 1986; Yarrow et al., 1983) could even be a product of inheritance. Twin and adoption data demonstrate that sudden surges or decrements in relative standing on, say, task orientation ratings from 12 to 18 months are not simply the result of measurement error or of random developmental spurts, but also reflect genetically influenced periods of rapid developmental change. These changes are not consistent across individuals at any particular time, but vary from individual to individual partly in response to genetic "blueprints" for development (McClearn, 1970).

Evidence for some limited degree of genetic control over both behavioral stability and patterns of change over time could even help explain some of the inconsistency of findings in longitudinal studies of mastery motivation where measures differ both across studies and over time. Discrepancies in the strength of correlations over time could actually reflect differences to the degree that individual measures are influenced by distinct inherited traits that follow different genetic/developmental pathways. In many studies, however, only very modest prediction is found in motivation scores gathered over periods of six months or more, and when such prediction is found, it is between measures that differ by age, probably as a result of being the most developmentally "appropriate" at that age (e.g., Jennings et al., 1984; Yarrow et al., 1983). From both the perspective of developmental change in early abilities and functioning (or at least in the measures used to assess them) and some genetic influence on change, this modesty of prediction is not surprising.

Substantial cognitive, social, and emotional change takes place within the first two years of life, and these changes (influenced partly by inheritance) should have an impact on expressions of motivation.

<hr>

BIOGENETIC CONTRIBUTIONS TO INFANT–ENVIRONMENT CORRELATIONS

The implications of possible biogenetic bases for performance on measures of motivation are of significance for studies correlating early care with motivation. Biogenetic contributions immediately confound the interpretation of relations to the quality of the home environment and/or of parent–child interaction because both home environment and parent–child interaction are substantially correlated with parental and child intelligence and other heritable traits. Plomin (Plomin, DeFries, & Loehlin, 1977; see also Scarr & McCartney, 1983) has described this phenomenon as "passive" genotype–environment correlations, and behavioral genetics studies have indicated that such associations are most widespread in the first year or two of life (Plomin et al., 1988). After this, the role of the child in actively eliciting different kinds of care/interactions and selecting particular kinds of contexts and experiences increases. Note, however, that even in the latter instances, parent–child genetic inheritance should be correlated with (because it is indirectly responsible for) evoked differences in care and experience.

Numerous studies have documented the association between quality of home environment/child care and parental education (a proxy for IQ), and results from the smaller number of studies that directly measure parental IQ concur with this finding (e.g., Gottfried & Gottfried, 1984; Longstreth et al., 1981). One of the more thorough and rigorous of these latter investigations is the large adoption study conducted by Plomin and his colleagues (Plomin et al., 1988). In their research, differences in correlations between child sensorimotor competence (Bayley Mental Development Index) and adoptive versus nonadoptive home environment provided evidence that associations between home environment and child competence have some genetic mediation (see also Wilson, 1983). In particular, provision of play materials (and other indices of encouraging developmental advancement) and maternal affection/support both showed some genetic influence, especially during the second year of life. Play materials, in fact, were apparently influenced in adoptive homes by child cognitive functioning, because there were significant correlations between play materials provided for adopted children and the IQ of the children's biological mother, despite little evidence of selective placement of adoptive children. On the other hand, genetic mediation of home environment–child competence correlations could not be restricted to parental intelligence that is passed down to children (Plomin, Loehlin, & DeFries, 1985), since statistical control for parental IQ (or SES or major personality factors) did not alter results. It seems likely, then, that inheritable parent temperamental factors (not captured on self-report personality instruments) that affect both their caregiving *and* their infant's performance on the Bayley Scales must be taken into consideration.

As one example, a mother who is active, curious, and interested in making things happen (or some other adult version of the partly inherited infant "task-orientation" factor) may be likely to have a child who shows comparable traits early in development that will influence his or her exploratory and testing behavior and, ultimately, performance (Bathurst & Gottfried, 1987; DiLalla et al., 1990). At the same time, such a mother may be especially likely to provide a rich array of stimulating opportunities for her child in and around the home environment. Does the resulting infant–environment correlation mean that home environment *fosters* motivation and competence? Not necessarily. However, causal influences of the environment cannot be ruled out. (In fact, if anything, adoption studies have provided compelling evidence for environmental facilitation of cognitive performance). Rather, the correlation can be presumed to reflect both genetically shared functioning in mother and child *as well as* facilitative environmental effects on child development.

Clearly, there are critical conceptual problems related to the interpretation of child care–child motivation correlations, and these conceptual problems stem from possible genetic influences on measures of motivation. Failure to take biogenetic factors into account undermines the validity of evolving developmental models in all fields, including that of early mastery motivation. If a model or theory of the role of mastery motivation in child development is to be developed, it would be worthwhile to flesh out relations between and among different but related aspects of behavior, all of which could be influenced to some extent by genetic inheritance. It seems premature to make data-driven inferences about either the meaning of motivation for subsequent development or the significance of experience (versus biology) for the development of motivation.

STUDYING EARLY MASTERY MOTIVATION IN THE FUTURE

The data summarized in this chapter have been used heuristically to argue that parental genetic and socialization differences, parental behavior, and infant cognitive, temperamental, and motivational functioning may all be intertwined. A sense of these complex linkages is suggested in Figure 7.1, which offers one possible model of genetic and environmental influences on infant mastery motivation. From this figure it is apparent that one cannot interpret correlations between parental behavior/home environment and child functioning without first taking into account genetic correlations. Similarly, one cannot interpret developmental correlations without first taking into account genetic factors in the child and parents that contribute to both stability and change in child functioning and in the environment. Previous research on mastery motivation suggests a causal role of environmental experience and motivational behavior that may be disproportionately large because genetic factors are not measured and autoregressive correlations (i.e., stability of functioning regardless of context) are not statistically controlled. These design flaws in developmental studies, it should be noted, are in no way unique to the field of mastery motivation (Biddle & Marlin, 1987; Gollob & Reichardt, 1987), but future correlational research on the topic will prove to be more informative regarding nature and development of early mastery motivation when these methodological limitations are addressed.

Several methodological suggestions have been raised in this chapter for future studies of mastery motivation. In addition, many specific recommendations for altering measurement and/or design parameters have already been recommended by Vondra and Jennings (1990). In both cases, emphasis was placed on including multiple measures of motivation in single studies and/or systematically varying measurement strategies, assessing cognitive ability and temperamental variation in addition to mastery motivation, and using sample sizes large enough to permit examination of gender differences with sufficient power to detect them when they exist.

The field of mastery motivation remains in its infancy as the need continues for studies that (a) explore effective ways to capture effortful or "motivated" behavior that are distinct from biologically based constructs such as sociability, emotionality, and cognitive ability, and (b) study patterns of stability within and associations between effortful behavior and aspects of competence that take genetic influences on development into account. Even then, these descriptive approaches represent only the first in a series of steps to prove the theoretical usefulness of mastery motivation. Such studies, however, would provide a promising start.

REFERENCES

Aydlett, L. A., West, M., & Leung, E. (1992, May). *Gender differences in social behavior.* Research presented at the International Conference on Infant Studies, Miami, FL.

Bathurst, K., & Gottfried, A. W. (1987). Untestable subjects in child development research: Developmental implications. *Child Development, 58,* 1135–1144.

Bayley, N. (1955). On the growth of intelligence. *American Psychologist, 10,* 805–818.

Bayley, N., & Schaefer, E. S. (1964). Correlates of maternal and child behaviors with the development of mental abilities: Data from the Berkeley Growth Study. *Monographs of the Society for Research in Child Development, 29* (6, Serial No. 97).

Belsky, J., Garduque, L., & Hrncir, E. (1984). Assessing performance, competence, and executive capacity in infant play: Relations to home environment and security of attachment. *Developmental Psychology, 20,* 406–417.

Belsky, J., Lerner, R. M., & Spanier, G. B. (1984). *The child in the family.* Reading, MA: Addison-Wesley.

Belsky, J., & Rovine, M. (1987). Temperament and attachment security in the Strange Situation: An empirical rapprochement. *Child Development, 58,* 787–795.

Biddle, B. J., & Marlin, M. M. (1987). Causality, confirmation, credulity, and structural equation modeling. *Child Development, 58,* 4–17.

Bornstein, M. H., & Sigman, M. D. (1986). Continuity in mental development from infancy. *Child Development, 57,* 251–274.

Braungart, J. M., Plomin, R., DeFries, J. C., & Fulker, D. W. (1992). *Developmental Psychology, 28,* 40–47.

Brooks, J., & Lewis, M. (1974). Attachment behavior in 13-month-old opposite sex twins. *Child Development, 45,* 243–247.

Caruso, D. (1990). Exploratory behavior, task persistence, and problem-solving ability across the second year of life. *Early Education and Development, 1,* 354–370.

Clarke-Stewart, K. A. (1973). Interactions between mothers and their young children: Characteristics and consequences. *Monographs of the Society for Research in Child Development, 38,* (6–7, Serial No. 153).

DiLalla, L. F., Thompson, L. A., Plomin, R., Phillips, K., Fagan, J. F., Haith, M. M., Cyphers, L. H., & Fulker, D. W. (1990). Infant predictors of preschool and adult IQ: A study of infant twins and their parents. *Developmental Psychology, 26,* 759–769.

Eaton, W. O., & Enns, L. R. (1986). Instrumented motor activity measurement of the young infant in the home: Validity and reliability. *Psychological Bulletin, 100,* 19–28.

Emde, R. N., Plomin, R., Robinson, J., Corley, R., DeFries, J., Fulker, D. W., Reznick, J. S., Campos, J., Kagan, J., & Zahn-Waxler, C. (1992). Temperament, emotion, and cognition at fourteen months: The MacArthur Longitudinal Twin Study. *Child Development, 63,* 1437–1455.

Fagot, B. I. (1978). The influence of sex of child on parental reactions to toddler children. *Child Development, 49,* 459–465.

Frodi, A., Bridges, L., & Grolnick, W. (1985). Correlates of mastery behavior: A short-term longitudinal study of infants in their second year. *Child Development, 56,* 1291–1298.

Frodi, A., & Thompson, R. (1985). Infants' affective responses in the Strange Situation: Effects of prematurity and of quality of attachment. *Child Development, 56,* 1280–1290.

Goldberg, S., & Lewis, M. (1969). Play behavior in the year-old infant: Early sex differences. *Child Development, 40,* 21–31.

Goldsmith, H. H., Bradshaw, D. L., & Rieser-Danner, L. A. (1986). Temperamental dimensions as potential developmental influences on attachment. In J. V. Lerner & R. M. Lerner (Eds.), *New directions for child development: Temperament and psychosocial interactions in infancy and childhood* (pp. 5–34). San Francisco: Jossey-Bass.

Goldsmith, H. H., & Campos, J. J. (1986). Fundamental issues in the study of early temperament: The Denver Twin Temperament Study. In M. E. Lamb, A. L. Brown, & B. Rogoff (Eds.), *Advances in developmental psychology* (Vol. 4, pp. 231–283). Hillsdale, NJ: Erlbaum.

Goldsmith, H. H., & Gottesman, I. I. (1981). Origins of variation in behavioral style: A longitudinal study of temperament in young twins. *Child Development, 52,* 91–103.

Gollob, H. F., & Reichardt, C. S. (1987). Taking account of time lags in causal models. *Child Development, 58,* 80–92.

Gottfried, A. W., & Gottfried, A. E. (1984). Home environment and mental development in young children. In A. W. Gottfried (Ed.), *Home environment and early cognitive development: Longitudinal research* (pp. 57–115). New York: Academic Press.

Harmon, R. J., Suwalsky, J. D., & Klein, R. P. (1979). Infants' preferential response for mother versus an unfamiliar adult. *Journal of the American Academy of Child Psychiatry, 18,* 437–444.

Harter, S., & Connell, J. P. (1984). A model of children's achievement and related self-perceptions of competence, control, and motivational orientation. In J. G. Nicholls (Ed.), *Advances in motivation and achievement: The development of achievement motivation* (pp. 219–250). Greenwich, CT: JAI Press.

Hron-Stewart, K. M., Lefever, G. B., & Weintraub, D. (1990, April). *Correlates and predictors of mastery motivation: Relations to mother–child problem-solving, temperament, attachment, and home environment.* Research presented at the International Conference on Infant Studies, Montreal, Canada.

Jennings, K. D., Yarrow, L. J., & Martin, P. P. (1984). Mastery motivation and cognitive development: A longitudinal study from infancy to 3½ years of age. *International Journal of Behavioral Development, 7,* 441–461.

Jones, S. S. (1985). On the motivational bases for attachment behavior. *Developmental Psychology, 21,* 848–857.

Kagan, J., Reznick, J. S., Clarke, C., Snidman, N., & Garcia-Coll, C. (1984). Behavioral inhibition to the unfamiliar. *Child Development, 55,* 2212–2225.

Kagan, J., Reznick, J. S., & Gibbons, J. (1989). Inhibited and uninhibited types of children. *Child Development, 60,* 838–845.

Kagan, J., Reznick, J. S., & Snidman, N. (1987). Physiology and psychology of behavioral inhibition. *Child Development, 58,* 1459–1473.

Kagan, J., Reznick, J. S., & Snidman, N. (1988). Biological bases of childhood shyness. *Science, 240,* 167–171.

Kopp, C. B. (1982). Antecedents of self-regulation: A developmental perspective. *Developmental Psychology, 18,* 199–214.

Kopp, C. B., & Vaughn, B. E. (1982). Sustained attention during exploratory manipulation as a predictor of cognitive competence in preterm infants. *Child Development, 53,* 174–182.

Lollis, S. P. (1990). Effects of maternal behavior on toddler behavior during separation. *Child Development, 61,* 99–103.

Longstreth, L. E., Davis, B., Carter, L., Flint, D., Owen, J., Rickert, M., & Taylor, E. (1981). Separation of home intellectual environment and maternal IQ as determinants of child IQ *Developmental Psychology, 17,* 532–541.

Lyons-Ruth, K., Connell, D. B., Zoll, D., & Stahl, J. (1987). Infants at social risk: Relations among infant maltreatment, maternal behavior, and infant attachment behavior. *Developmental Psychology, 23,* 223–232.

Malatesta, C. Z., Culver, C., Tesman, J. R., & Shepard, B. (1989). The development of emotional expression during the first two years of life. *Monographs of the Society for Research in Child Development, 54* (1–2, Serial No. 219).

Martin, J. A. (1981). A longitudinal study of the consequences of early mother–infant interaction: A microanalytic approach. *Monographs of the Society for Research in Child Development, 46* (3, Serial No. 190).

Martin, J. A., Maccoby, E. E., & Jacklin, C. N. (1981). Mothers' responsiveness to interactive bidding and nonbidding in boys and girls. *Child Development, 52,* 1064–1067.

Maslin, C. A., & Spieker, S. J. (1990). Attachment as a basis for independent motivation: A view from risk and non-risk samples. In M. T. Greenberg, D. Cicchetti, & E. M. Cummings (Eds.), *Attachment in the preschool years: Theory, research, and intervention* (pp. 245–272). Chicago: University of Chicago Press.

Matheny, A. P., Jr. (1980). Bayley's Infant Behavior Record: Behavioral components and twin analyses. *Child Development, 51,* 1157–1167.

Matheny, A. P., Jr. (1983). A longitudinal twin study of stability of components from Bayley's Infant Behavior Record. *Child Development, 54,* 356–360.

Matheny, A. P., Jr. (1990). Developmental behavior genetics: Contributions from the Louisville Twin Study. In M. E. Hahn, J. K., Hewitt, N. D. Henderson, & R. H. Benno (Eds.), *Developmental behavior genetics: Neural, biometrical, and evolutionary approaches* (pp. 342–362). New York: Oxford University Press.

Matheny, A. P., Jr., Wilson, R. S., Dolan, A. B., & Krantz, J. Z. (1981). Behavioral contrasts in twinships: Stability and patterns of differences in childhood. *Child Development, 52,* 579–588.

McCall, R. B. (1974). Exploratory manipulation and play in the human infant. *Monographs of the Society for Research in Child Development, 39* (2, Serial No. 155).

McCall, R. B., & Carriger, M. S. (1993). Infant habituation and recognition memory performance as predictors of later IQ: A review and conceptual analysis. *Child Development, 64,* 57–79.

McCall, R. B., Eichorn, D., & Hogarty, P. (1977). Transitions in early mental development. *Monographs of the Society for Research in Child Development, 42* (3, Serial No. 171).

McClearn, G. E. (1970). Genetic influences on behavior and development. In P. H. Mussen (Ed.), *Carmichael's manual of child psychology* (Vol. 1, pp. 39–76). New York: John Wiley.

Messer, D. J., McCarthy, M. E., McQuiston, S., MacTurk, R. H., Yarrow, L. J., & Vietze, P. M. (1986). Relation between mastery behavior in infancy and competence in early childhood. *Developmental Psychology, 22,* 366–372.

Nicolich, L. M. (1977). Beyond sensorimotor intelligence: Assessment of symbolic maturity through analysis of pretend play. *Merrill–Palmer Quarterly, 2,* 88–99.

Olesker, W. (1990). Sex differences during the early separation–individuation process: Implications for gender identity formation. *Journal of the American Psychoanalytic Association, 38,* 325–346.

Plomin, R., DeFries, J. C., & Loehlin, J. C. (1977). Genotype–environment interaction and correlation in the analysis of human behavior. *Psychological Bulletin, 84,* 309–322.

Plomin, R., DeFries, J. C., & Fulker, D. W. (1988). *Nature and nurture during infancy and early childhood.* New York: Cambridge University Press.

Plomin, R., Loehlin, J. C., & DeFries, J. C. (1985). Genetic and environmental components of "environmental" influences. *Developmental Psychology, 21,* 391–402.

Popper, S. D., Cohn, J. F., Campbell, S. B., & Ross, S. (1992, May). *Do securely attached infants show higher mastery motivation?* Research presented at the International Conference on Infant Studies, Miami Beach, FL.

Reznick, J. S., Kagan, J., Snidman, N., Gersten, M., Baak, K., & Rosenberg, A. (1986). Inhibited and uninhibited behavior: A follow-up study. *Child Development, 57,* 660–680.

Robinson, J. L., Kagan, J., Reznick, J. S., & Corley, R. (1992). The heritability of inhibited and uninhibited behavior: A twin study. *Developmental Psychology, 28,* 1030–1037.

Roggman, L. A., Jennings, M. L., & Hart, A. D. (1992, May). *Play, attention, and attachment in one year olds.* Research presented at the International Conference on Infant Studies, Miami, FL.

Rosenblatt, D. (1977). Developmental trends in infant play. In B. Tizard & D. Harvey (Eds.), *Biology of play* (pp. 33–44). Philadelphia: J.B. Lippincott Co.

Ruff, H. A., & Lawson, K. R. (1991). Development of sustained, focused attention in young children during free play. *Developmental Psychology, 26,* 85–93.

Ruff, H. A., & Lawson, K. R. (1991). Assessment of infants' attention during play with objects. In C. E. Schaefer, K. Gitlin, & A. Sandgrund (Eds.), *Play diagnosis and assessment* (pp. 115–129). New York: John Wiley and Sons.

Saudino, K. J., & Eaton, W. O. (1991). Infant temperament and genetics: An objective twin study of motor activity level. *Child Development, 62,* 1167–1174.

Scarr, A., & McCartney, K. (1983). How people make their own environments: A theory of genotype → environment effects. *Child Development, 54,* 424–435.

Sorce, J. F., & Emde, R. (1981). Mother's presence is not enough: Effect of emotional availability on infant exploration. *Developmental Psychology, 17,* 737–745.

Suomi, S. J., Kraemer, G. W., Baysinger, C. M., & DeLizio, R. D. (1981). Inherited and experiential factors associated with individual differences in anxious behavior displayed by rhesus monkeys. In D. F. Kline & J. G. Rabkin (Eds.), *Anxiety: New research and changing concepts* (pp. 179–199). New York: Raven Press.

Tamis-LeMonda, C. S., & Bornstein, M. H. (1989). Habituation and maternal encouragement of attention in infancy as predictors of toddler language, play, and representational competence. *Child Development, 60*, 738–751.

Tamis-LeMonda, C. S., & Bornstein, M. H. (1992, May). *Antecedents of exploratory competence at one year.* Paper presented at the Biennial Meeting of the International Conference on Infant Studies, Miami Beach, FL.

Tamis-LeMonda, C. S., & Bornstein, M. H. (in press). Two components of play: Questions about their interrelations and relations to other mental functions in the child. In M. H. Bornstein (Ed.), *Play in the development of thought*, W. Damon (Series Ed.), *New Directions for Child Development.* San Francisco: Jossey-Bass.

Ungerer, J. A., & Sigman, M. (1984). The relation of play and sensorimotor behavior to language in the second year. *Child Development, 55*, 1448–1455.

Uzgiris, I. C. (1976). Organization of sensorimotor intelligence. In M. Lewis (Ed.), *Origins of intelligence* (pp. 123–164). New York: Plenum Press.

Vondra, J. I. (1987, April). *Early mastery motivation: How can we measure it and what does it mean?* Research presented at the Biennial Meeting of the Society for Research in Child Development, Baltimore, MD.

Vondra, J. I. (1993, March). *Maternal and toddler correlates of behavior during free play at 12 and 18 months.* Paper presented at the Biennial Meeting of the Society for Research in Child Development, New Orleans, LA.

Vondra, J., & Belsky, J. (1991). Infant play as a window on competence and motivation. In C. E. Schaefer, K. Gitlin, & A. Sandgrund (Eds.), *Play diagnosis and assessment* (pp. 13–33). New York: John Wiley and Sons.

Vondra, J. I., & Jennings, K. D. (1990). Infant mastery motivation: The issue of discriminant validity. *Early Education and Development, 1*, 340–353.

Wachs, T. D. (1987). Specificity of environmental action as manifest in environmental correlates of infant's mastery motivation. *Developmental Psychology, 23*, 782–790.

Wasserman, G. A., & Lewis, M. (1985). Infant sex differences: Ecological effects. *Sex Roles, 12*, 665–675.

Weinberg, M. K. (1992, May). *Boys and girls: Sex differences in emotional expressivity and self-regulation during early infancy.*

Paper presented at the International Conference on Infant Studies, Miami, FL.

White, R. W. (1959). Motivation reconsidered: The concept of competence. *Psychological Review, 66,* 297–333.

Wilson, R. S. (1983). The Louisville Twin Study: Developmental synchronies in behavior. *Child Development, 54,* 298–316.

Wilson, R. S., & Matheny, A. P. (1986). Behavior–genetics research in infant temperament: The Louisville Twin Study. In R. Plomin & J. Dunn (Eds.), *The study of temperament: Changes, continuities, and challenges* (pp. 236–295). Hillsdale, NJ: Erlbaum.

Yarrow, L., MacTurk, R., Vietze, P., McCarthy, M., Klein, R., & McQuiston, S. (1984). The developmental course of parental stimulation and its relationship to mastery motivation during infancy. *Developmental Psychology, 20,* 492–503.

Yarrow, L., McQuiston, S., MacTurk, R., McCarthy, M., Klein, R., & Vietze, P. (1983). Assessment of mastery motivation during the first year of life: Contemporaneous and cross-age relationships. *Developmental Psychology, 19,* 159–171.

8

THE MOTIVATIONAL CHARACTERISTICS OF INFANTS AND CHILDREN WITH PHYSICAL AND SENSORY IMPAIRMENTS

Kay Donahue Jennings

University of Pittsburgh

Robert H. MacTurk

Gallaudet University Research Institute Center for Studies in Education and Human Development

Access to environmental information is provided by three main channels: visual, auditory, and tactile/motor systems. Thus, physical and sensory impairments provide special challenges to the development of mastery motivation. In this chapter we will explore the effects of such channels being partially or fully blocked from birth. We will focus on the early development of motivation to explore and master the inanimate environment, but will include important social influences on behavior with objects.

When children are deprived of one of the three main channels of obtaining information about the environment, they experience some deprivation of environmental stimulation. They also receive less contingent feedback from the environment. Children with physical disabilities experience difficulties in retrieving and manipulating objects. Deaf children cannot hear auditory feedback from objects nor can they hear parents' comments and suggestions about objects. Blind children may not be aware of the availability of objects and cannot receive visual feedback from objects. While some deprivation of environmental stimulation is probably inevitable for these children, they can develop compensatory coping strategies. For example, a blind child may be able to obtain information through the auditory and tactile channels that sighted children are able to obtain only through the visual channel.

From studies of children without disabilities, we know that a responsive environment is essential to the development of motivated behavior and competence. In the first six months of life, contingent responses from the social environment are especially important because all infants have very limited abilities to interact with the inanimate environment on their own. Responsive caretakers help the infant to build up expectations that he or she can affect the environment. Another source of early contingency experiences for children without disabilities is hand-regard and, later, hand-and-foot play. Spontaneous arm movements visually alert the infant; over time, the infant associates the visual feedback with movement cues from his or her arm (Sonksen, Levitt, & Kitsinger, 1984). Thus, the infant can provide some contingency experiences by moving his or her body. A general expectation of being able to affect the environment is already present when the nondisabled infant becomes capable of interacting with the physical environment on their own.

Infants born with a disability generally experience a less responsive environment. Hand-regard and hand-and-foot play are impaired for blind and physically disabled infants. In addition, parents and other caretakers face special challenges in providing a warm, responsive environment for their disabled infant. Because a disability impairs either sending or receiving information, such infant's cues are often difficult to read. Parents may also misread or miss their infant's cues and, consequently, fail to respond appropriately. They may then begin to perceive their infant as being unresponsive and dull, further undermining the quality of interaction. In addition, when the infant's disability is first identified, parents must make a major adjustment in their expectations for their infant and for themselves as parents. They need to grieve the loss of the "perfect" infant they expected while simultaneously caring for their infant with a disability. During this adjustment period, not all parents will be able to provide a warm responsive environment for their infant.

As disabled and nondisabled infants begin the second half of the first year of life, parents play additional roles in facilitating mastery motivation. One important role is to provide safe access for exploring the physical environment—both disabled and nondisabled infants can only explore that to which they have access. A second role played by parents is reinforcing their child's independent exploration and mastery attempts. Parents' attention to and praise of these behaviors enhance the development of mastery motivation. Unobtrusive help that enables children to succeed in their mastery attempts also bolsters the development of motivation. In contrast, parental behaviors that impede the development of mastery motivation include rewarding dependency behaviors and being intrusive or overly helpful (Lutkenhaus, 1984).

The "vulnerable child syndrome" has been described in children who have recovered from life-threatening illnesses and in children with disabilities (Green & Solnit, 1964; Wasserman, Allen, & Solomon, 1986). This syndrome involves mothers becoming overprotective and children becoming more dependent and demanding, leading to mothers eventually becoming angry and hostile. Thus, parents of children with a disability may become overprotective—providing less support for their child's independent mastery attempts and, instead, reinforcing dependency behavior. Research and clinical observations have typically described mothers of handicapped children as more directive and intrusive as well as less responsive. These behaviors are characteristic of mothers of children with a variety of handicapping conditions (Barsch, 1968; Field, 1987; Wasserman, Allen, & Soloman, 1985; Wedell-Monnig & Lumley, 1980). In addition, teachers have been found to give more unrequested help to disabled children than to their nondisabled peers (Stipek & Sanborn, 1985).

In this chapter, we will examine the impact of a motor or sensory disability in isolation—that is, with other systems intact. Although children with a single disability are not representative of disabled children, studying children with a single disability allows us to better understand the effect of a particular disability. It is important to remember, however, that the majority of physically handicapped and fully blind children experience other handicaps, including mental retardation (Batshaw, Perret, & Harryman, 1986; Wachs & Sheehan, 1988).

The development of mastery motivation has been explicitly studied only in physically handicapped and deaf children, with which we will begin. We will then conclude with the little that is known about motivational development in blind children.

CHILDREN WITH PHYSICAL DISABILITIES

Children with physical disabilities have impairments in mobility and/or manipulation skills. This is a very heterogeneous group. Some children have mild impairment in only one or two limbs, whereas others lack control over almost all muscle groups. Cerebral palsy and spina bifida are the most common physical disabilities, both being associated with central nervous system damage. Not surprisingly, the majority of children with physical disabilities have cognitive impairments as well (Batshaw, Perret, & Harryman, 1986, Wachs & Sheehan, 1988; Wills, Holmbeck, Dillon, & McLone, 1990;). In order to assess the effects of a physical disability alone, this chapter will focus on children with IQs in the normal range. Furthermore, since mastery motivation has traditionally been inferred from interactions with objects, only children with some manipulative skills have been included. Consequently, our knowledge of the effect of a physical disability on the development of mastery motivation is limited to the least disabled children.

Early in life, a physical disability reduces contingency experiences. Inability to control movement can diminish experiences of contingency from both one's own body and from caretakers. Parents may view their infant as passive and dull. Later, a physical disability can limit access to inanimate objects and interfere with manipulating objects; thus, opportunities for exploring and receiving contingent feedback from the environment are decreased. In addition, failure is more likely to occur following mastery attempts. Parents can help compensate for their child's difficulties in interacting with the physical environment by positioning the child to maximize their motor abilities thus freeing their hands for manipulating objects, placing objects so that they are accessible, and changing them frequently to maintain interest.

Only a few studies have specifically addressed parenting styles among parents of physically disabled children, but they concur in indicating greater directiveness on the part of mothers of physically disabled infants and preschoolers even when mental age or IQ is controlled. Jennings, Stagg, Connors, and Ross (in press) observed mothers playing with their disabled and nondisabled 4-year-old children; 24 children had a physical disability and 44 did not. They were given a series of toys that varied in structure and level of difficulty. Mothers of physically disabled children were found to give more commands to their children and were rated as more controlling, even when IQ and SES were partialled out. No difference was found in the number of praises given by the two groups of mothers. Barrera and Vella (1987) studied mothers and infants during free play and obtained similar results. Interactions of 11 mothers of infants with physical disabilities were compared to a group of mothers with nondisabled infants. Mothers of the physically disabled children engaged in more verbal and commanding behavior.

Thus, mothers of physically disabled children appear to be more controlling and directive with their children than mothers of nondisabled children, but this directiveness cannot be fully accounted for by IQ or SES differences. Studies of mothers of children with other disabilities suggest that, at least in part, mothers become more directive to compensate for their child's greater passivity (Brooks-Gunn & Lewis, 1984; Wasserman, Allen & Solomon, 1985). Mothers of physically disabled children have been found to perceive their children as less motivated, as preferring easier and more familiar tasks, and as seeking more adult help and approval (Jennings, Connors, Stegman, Sankaranaryan, & Mendelsohn, 1985).

Observations of physically disabled children indicate that they show less mastery motivation in a variety of situations. In a longitudinal study of 25 physically disabled preschoolers, Jennings (Jennings, Conners, & Stegman, 1988; Jennings, Connors, Stegman, Sankaranarayan, & Mendelsohn, 1985) found evidence of lower mastery motivation in physically disabled preschoolers compared to nondisabled preschoolers (n = 44) while engaged in a series of tasks. At 3 years of age, disabled preschoolers were less persistent at tasks but showed equivalent levels of curiosity. One year later, these disabled preschoolers continued to be less persistent at tasks but again showed equivalent levels of curiosity. In addition, physically disabled children at 4 years showed a greater preference for easy tasks over challenging tasks when asked to choose between tasks of differing difficulty than did their nondisabled peers. These differences in motivation were found even when groups matched on intellectual level and socioeconomic level were compared. In addition, individual differences were stable over the one year period; thus, individual children who were less motivated continued to be less motivated one year later.

Consistent with findings using structured tasks, Jennings et al. (1985; 1988) also found that physically disabled preschoolers displayed less mastery motivation during their free play. The duration of their play activities was shorter, their play activities were less complex and less cognitively mature, and they spent more time unengaged in any play activity. When groups matched on IQ and SES were compared, the differences in play remained except for time spent unengaged.

A study by Landry, Copeland, Lee, and Robinson (1990) suggests that the decreased mastery motivation of physically disabled children continues into the early school years. Landry et al. observed children between the ages of 6 and 12 with spina bifida and compared them with an age- and IQ-matched control group. The children were given three independent play tasks. The children with spina bifida engaged in less goal-directed activities and more simple manipulation than did the nondisabled children. Landry et al. identified three components of the mastery motivation process: initiation of activities with objects, persistence in activity toward a particular goal, and carrying out activities independently. Their findings indicated a deficit only in persistence in goal-directed activity for the physically disabled children.

Taken together, research to date suggests that the presence of a physical disability impedes the development of children's motivation to persist in mastery attempts even though their curiosity for exploring the world remains high. Having a physical disability decreases early contingency experiences, impairs exploration of the environment, and interferes with controlling the environment through manipulation. It is not clear, however, that children's physical limitations are the main obstacles to developing mastery motivation. Severity of physical disability does not relate to level of mastery motivation (Jennings et al., 1988). This lack of relationship suggests that other life experiences, including parental styles of interaction, perhaps, play an important role. Hopefully, future research can begin to untangle this complex transactional process to determine ways in which parents can best support the motivational development of their physically disabled child.

DEAF CHILDREN

Studies of the early development of deaf infants provide the opportunity to address the range of adaptive responses available to human infants and examine the implicit assumption that verbal/vocal communication is crucial for the infant's social, emotional, and cognitive development. The majority of reports on the influence of parental behavior on infant development have focused on measures that come under the general heading of "responsiveness" or "sensitivity to infant cues." These measures typically include physical behaviors, such as touching, holding, smiling, and game playing in combination with a variety of vocal responses, such as "babytalk," cooing, and laughing (Belsky, Taylor & Rovine, 1984; Clarke-Stewart, 1973; McCarthy & McQuiston, 1983). The reasons for this are clear—in hearing families these sets of behaviors usually occur simultaneously, thereby masking possible separate influences of auditory and physical contact. Thus, investigations of normally developing deaf infants and children provide a window through which it is possible to examine what, if any, developmental differences emerge when auditory contact with the environment is absent or attenuated.

Our understanding of normative developmental patterns in young deaf infants has been, until recently, limited by several problems. The most important surrounds the general lack of early identification of early hearing loss. This problem of late diagnosis accounts for the generally older subjects in most studies involving deaf children. While 10 years ago the average age for a firm diagnosis of a hearing loss was 24 months, the situation has improved only moderately in the ensuing years but is still estimated to be between 15 to 16 months, on average (Bess, 1993; Meadow, 1980). The bulk of the existing literature reflects this problem of late diagnosis (Lederberg, 1984; Schlesinger, 1985; Schlesinger & Meadow, 1972; Wedell-Monnig & Lumley, 1980).

The few investigations of very young infants are hampered by very small sample sizes and cross-sectional research designs, two factors that further impede the accumulation of a systematic body of literature about this population. An additional problem is introduced when the hearing status of the parents is taken into consideration. As several chapters in this volume have outlined, parents' emotional resources have a significant impact on their atypical infant's development. Studies of deaf infants and children present a unique problem because the parents' reactions to the diagnosis of deafness is strongly dependent on the hearing status of the parents.

A high degree of assortative mating is a unique characteristic of the contemporary deaf community in the United States. For example, approximately 95% of the married deaf individuals surveyed by Ranier, Altshuler, and Kallman (1969) had deaf spouses. More recent population-based studies reveal significant increases in the rate of marriages in which both couples are deaf, a rate that has almost tripled in the past 100 years (Fay, 1898; Hothkiss, 1989; Marazita, Ploughman, & Rawlings, 1993). Though the attitudes of deaf couples toward having a deaf child displays wide variability, it is not unusual for many deaf adults to express positive feelings toward the possibility of having a deaf child. This is illustrated by the following excerpt of an interview of a young deaf man:

> We will become parents in June. I am very excited about becoming a father. I hope to have a deaf child. The doctor told us we will never have a deaf son because my deafness is X-linked, through my mother. But maybe we could have a daughter. (Orlansky & Hewett, 1981, p. 24)

Deaf infants with deaf parents experience a social environment in which their caregivers may have an advantage over hearing parents with deaf infants. The small body of existing literature suggests that deaf parents are as effective in their parenting roles as are their hearing peers (Rienzi, 1990). In addition, they have practiced coping tactics and adaptive strategies and have the experience to deal successfully with many of the situations their deaf child will face (Schein, 1989). Deaf parents' existing skills are buttressed by the existence of a well-bounded deaf community in many larger urban areas that may be characterized by its common language and experience and a nonpathological view of deafness (Padden, 1980). The existence of the deaf community also serves to provide an extended social support network to deaf families that can provide deaf role models and adult and peer social experiences with other deaf individuals. While reactions to the birth of a deaf child among deaf couples may range from the joy of met expectations to some degree of equanimity, the reactions of hearing parents to the diagnosis of deafness uniformly is characterized by shock, anger, and mourning (Meadow-Orlans, in press).

As the previous discussion suggests, the view of deafness from within the deaf community is very different from the perspective of hearing couples. Deafness is seen as a nonpathological condition, which, while it presents the developing child with its own special problems, is not seen as a major handicap, nor one which presents insurmountable problems, either for the parents or the child. Thus, the presence of a deaf child for deaf couples is not seen as an atypical event in their lives and does not result in the same perturbations in parent–child interactions seen with hearing parents with a deaf infant. This is in sharp contrast to the typical reactions of hearing parents when they are presented with the diagnosis of deafness. Though it is not possible to establish causal links between the parents' reactions and any later behavioral disturbances, the existing data, which parallels that of Harmon and Morrow (this volume) consistently suggests a broad range of subsequent problems.

Because most parents of deaf children have never had experience with deafness prior to the birth of their child, strong emotions are evoked with the initial diagnosis of the child's deafness that make the interactional system between mother and infant anxious, awkward, and full of uncertainty (Nienhuys & Tikotin, 1983). It is also believed that these initial parental feelings can be reactivated frequently during the maturation of the deaf child (Mindel & Feldman, 1987). Hearing mothers with deaf infants appear to "lead" rather than to "follow," have interactions that are less rich, and focus on objects rather than on social play (Nienhuys & Tikotin, 1983; Spencer & Gutfreund, 1990). The interactions between parents and handicapped infants in general and deaf infants in particular are typically characterized as being less rich and more directive or intrusive (Field, 1987; Lederberg, 1984; Schlesinger, 1985; Wedell-Monnig & Lumley, 1980). Not only is the range of interactive variation restricted, but the opportunities to control, direct, and otherwise effect the environment is restricted by the external controls imposed by an overly intrusive parent. Both of these characteristics may serve to undermine the infants' motivation to learn from their interactions with the environment.

For the past several years, the second author and his colleagues have been involved in a series of comparatively large-scale investigations of the early development of deaf and hearing infants from deaf and hearing families. The available results, based primarily on comparisons of deaf and hearing infants from middle-class hearing families, have produced mixed findings when compared to earlier reports.

In a study of face-to-face (FTF) interaction at 9 months of age, Koester (1990) found that deaf infants appeared to respond to episodes of maternal still face by resorting more frequently to self-comfort than to the other-directed behaviors observed in the hearing infants. Koester and MacTurk (1991) also found that

18-month-old hearing infants in the Strange Situation seek contact and attempt to maintain proximity to their mothers more than deaf infants when reunited after a brief separation. This involves such actions as greeting, approaching, gesturing to be picked up, or reaching toward the mother; they may therefore be thought of as parallel to the socially directed signaling behaviors observed during the infants' earlier FTF interactions with their caregivers.

In contrast, the deaf infants displayed greater avoidance of the mother on her return during the Strange Situation procedure, suggesting that their efforts to cope with the stress of separation are more internalized than for the hearing infants. The conclusions derived from these cross-sectional analyses were confirmed by the strong predictive relations between the ability of 9-month-old deaf infants to manage the stress associated with the maternal still-face episode and the quality of mother–child interactions at 18 months of age (MacTurk, Meadow-Orlans, Koester, & Spencer, 1993).

In a preliminary report based on a time series analysis of the interaction patterns of 6-month-old infant–mother dyads, MacTurk, Day, and Meadow-Orlans (1986) found that mothers of deaf infants tended to lead their infants' interaction in a FTF situation. This was in contrast to the mothers of hearing infants; in these dyads, the behavior of the mothers and infants tended to be independent of each other. Subsequent analyses of the FTF data with a larger sample failed to find a strong and consistent impact of infant deafness on maternal behavior. We can only surmise why this may be. The mostly likely explanation centers on the fact the this was a middle-class sample with comparatively direct access to services for their deaf child and the resources to take advantage of existing diagnostic and rehabilitation technologies. In addition, as MacTurk et al. (1993) found, the size of the support network represented a significant contributor to a positive mother–child relationship at 18 months of age.

With regard to deaf children's motivational characteristics, there is some evidence from a few early studies that suggests that deaf children of hearing parents score significantly lower in assessments of achievement motivation when compared to hearing children of hearing parents (Stinson, 1978b). Furthermore, these decrements are positively related to the overprotectiveness of the parents (Stinson, 1974, 1978a), findings strikingly similar to those for physically handicapped children as discussed earlier. Direct investigations of deaf infants' motivation have been conducted only recently. In a preliminary report of deaf infants' motivational characteristics, MacTurk and Trimm (1989) found that while 12-month-old deaf and hearing infants spent equivalent amounts of time engaged with objects, the deaf infants spent a longer time looking at the mother or examiner, had shorter latencies to show positive affect and to engage in a social behavior than the hearing infants. This suggests that, for the deaf infants, socially directed behaviors may serve as an adaptive response to the lack of auditory feedback from the environment. The two samples were very small and the group of deaf infants included children of both deaf and hearing parents, thus severely limiting our confidence in these findings.

In a longitudinal analysis of 20 hearing infants and 20 deaf infants from hearing families that examines the relationships between object-oriented and socially directed behaviors, Mac-Turk and colleagues (MacTurk, 1993; MacTurk, Trimm, & Platt, 1990) found that, for hearing infants, mastery motivation at 9 months was significantly correlated with mastery motivation at 12 months. For the deaf infants, it was social smiling at 9 months that predicted mastery motivation at 12 months. The within-age correlations suggest that their object-related and socially directed activities were less differentiated than for the hearing infants. This comingling of social and mastery behaviors suggests that social smiling may serve a different psychological function for the deaf infants. Social smiling for the hearing infants may represent an invitation to participate in the child's exploration of the object. The deaf infants may be seeking visual feedback concerning their performance in an effort to reduce greater perceived situational ambiguity. We are unsure of why this might be. It may be that the deaf infants are showing a delay in their ability to process two competing sources of information about their environment. Though this developmental delay argument may have some merit, we feel that these results support a conclusion that the deaf infants have developed a unique set of compensatory behaviors. Hearing infants have access to environmental information through three main channels (visual, tactile, and auditory), all of which may be processed simultaneously. The deaf infants must develop skills that enable them to acquire information in a sequential manner.

As Wood (1982) has suggested, deafness prevents the child from simultaneously exploring the world visually and receiving the vocal narrative that often accompanies such activity. Thus, for the deaf infant, visual attention to an object or person, and communication about that object or person, must typically occur in a sequential rather than parallel fashion. This places an increased strain on the infants' developing attention, memory, and integrative capacities, possibly diminishing their early interactions with both the animate and inanimate environment. However, as may be seen from the results presented here, those deaf infants who are better able to integrate the social–object sequences appear to have a relative advantage over their deaf peers who were not as adept with this sequencing skill. It remains unclear if these differences are a function of deafness or of differences in parental styles of interaction.

Gregory's (1976, 1985, 1988) investigations of deaf mother–deaf infant dyads suggests that there is a relative advantage when both members are deaf in terms of their mutual attunement. This mutuality hypothesis may also be observed in several studies which provide evidence that deaf mothers engage in the sign language analogue of "motherese" when communicating with their infants and engage in styles of interaction that are temporally connected to their infant's focus of visual attention (Erting, Prezioso, & Hynes, 1990; Masataka, 1992). Perhaps deaf parents are also better at structuring interactions that support their deaf infant's feelings of control by providing appropriate levels of parental scaffolding of their activities, in contrast to the uncertain and less well-structured activities of hearing parents with a deaf infant. In an effort to address this question, data are currently being collected on comparable samples of deaf and hearing infants with deaf parents.

BLIND CHILDREN

Blind children are probably the most disadvantaged group in early infancy because the visual channel carries the most information about the environment. The blind infant lives in a relative void because it is difficult to make sense out of information received from the auditory and tactile channels without information from the visual channel. In addition, information received from the auditory and tactile channels can be overwhelming and frightening for the blind infant. Sudden touches, movement, or noises can be startling without the forewarning provided by vision.

Blind infants show initial delays in motor and cognitive development. Sighted infants learn early that the floor is a concrete base and continuous surface. Because the blind infant cannot see that the floor is there, saving reactions such as propping oneself up while sitting emerge slowly; crawling and walking are delayed (Sonksen, Levitt, & Kitsinger, 1984). Reaching for objects is also delayed; some understanding of object permanence and accurate sound-localizing skills are prerequisites for reaching. Localization of sound is difficult without verification through vision; the development of object permanence is also made much easier by vision. Despite initial delays, there is some evidence that blind children can eventually reach the cognitive and motor level of sighted children (Teplin, 1983; Wachs & Sheehan, 1988).

Blind infants must rely on the auditory and tactile channels for information about the environment. As the infant becomes aware that information comes from the auditory channel, the infant learns that concentration on sounds is enhanced by immobility; this further decreases motor experiences. In addition, this immobility is easily misinterpreted by parents as passivity and disinterest. Parents who are already deprived of eye contact with their blind infant also experience failure when they attempt to stimulate their infant into activity (in typical games of infancy) (Burlington, 1979). Parents can thus easily feel they do not matter to the child and become discouraged and perceive the child as slow. Poor quality of attachment to parents is a frequent result of these obstacles (Fraiberg, 1977).

Because of all these obstacles, the outside world initially holds little interest for the young infant. Eventually, sound becomes a motivator of behavior. As the infant develops object permanence, he or she begins to understand that there is an outside world that can be explored. For an extended period of time (perhaps the entire first year of life), however, the infant has very little incentive to reach out and explore the world as well as limited contingency experiences. Consequently, blind infants tend to sit immobile with the arms hanging limply from their shoulders (Fraiberg, 1977). Thus, the blind infant has very little opportunity to develop mastery motivation in the first year of life. Clinically, the blind infant has been described as having "diminished drive" (Sonksen et al., 1984).

Although mastery motivation and goal-directed behavior have not been explicitly studied in the blind child, the development of exploratory behavior and spatial relations has received attention. In general, these studies indicate that by preschool age, blind children have equivalent skills to sighted children. Olson

(1983) compared 15 legally blind preschoolers with a matched group of sighted preschoolers and found no differences in the children's exploration of two novel toys. Landau (1991) compared three totally blind and three sighted children in a short term longitudinal study from 18 to 36 months. She examined haptic (motoric) exploration and understanding of spacial object relations. She found that the blind children showed specific patterns of exploration that were generally similar to those of sighted children. However, the blind children fingered and handled objects more than the sighted children, thus taking longer to habituate. Understanding of spatial relations as shown by rotation of objects was equivalent in the two groups. In a case study of a blind 2½ year old, Landau, Gleitman, and Spelke (1981) found that the child had an understanding of three-dimensional space as indicated by locomotion. After taking the child along several paths connecting four objects in a room, she was able to move directly between the objects along paths she had never taken.

These few studies on a small number of children suggest that exploration may be similar for blind and sighted children by preschool age. These studies contrast with the frequent description of blind preschoolers as passive (Burlingham, 1979; Fraiberg, 1977). Further studies of blind children, including studies of persistence, are needed; they can help determine whether later experience can help the child compensate for the lack of opportunities for motivated behaviors in the first year of life.

SUMMARY AND CONCLUSIONS

Research on motivation in young children with disabilities is limited, particularly for blind children. Blind and physically disabled children appear to be more at risk than deaf children for diminished motivation. If confirmed, it may indicate that visual and motoric experiences are more important than auditory experiences in the development of mastery motivation. Parents can play an important role in providing experiences that help compensate for the disability. Unfortunately, much evidence suggests that the parent–child relationship may be compromised by the disability. The parent may misunderstand the child's cues, especially in infancy. In addition, parents may have a difficult time adjusting to having a child with a disability and become overly protective and directive in part as a response to their perception of their child as passive and poorly motivated. Despite these obstacles, children with disabilities develop adaptive strategies over time in an effort to master their surroundings.

REFERENCES

Barrera, M. E., & Vella, D. M. (1987). Disabled and nondisabled infants' interactions with their mother. *American Journal of Occupational Therapy, 41,* 168–172.

Barsch, R. H. (1968). *The parent of the handicapped child: Study of childbearing practices.* Springfield, IL: Charles C. Thomas.

Batshaw, M. L., Perret, Y. M., & Harryman, S. E. (1986). Cerebral Palsy. In M. L. Batshaw & Y. M. Perret, (Eds.), *Children with handicaps: A medical primer* (2nd ed.). Baltimore, MD: Brookes.

Belsky, J., Taylor, D. G., & Rovine, M. (1984). The Pennsylvania Infant and Family Development Project II: The development of reciprocal interaction in the mother–infant dyad. *Child Development, 55,* 706–717.

Bess, F. (1993). Early identification of hearing loss: A review of the whys, hows, and whens. *The Hearing Journal, 46,* 22–28.

Brooks-Gunn, J., & Lewis, M. (1984). Maternal responsivity in interactions with handicapped infants. *Child Development, 55,* 782–793.

Burlingham, D. (1979). To be blind in a sighted world. *Psychoanalytic Study of the Child, 34,* 5–30.

Clarke-Stewart, K. A. (1973). Interactions between mothers and their young children: Characteristics and consequences. *Monographs of the Society for Research in Child Development, 38,* (6–7, Serial No. 153).

Erting, C. J., Prezioso, C., & Hynes, M. O. (1990). Mother signs in baby talk. In W. Edmondson & F. Karlson (Eds.), *SLR '87: Papers from the Fourth International Symposium on Sign Language Research* (pp. 190–199). Hamburg, Federal Republic of Germany: Signum Press.

Fay, E. (1898). *Marriages of deaf in America.* Washington, DC: Volta Bureau.

Field, T. M. (1987). Interaction and attachment in normal and atypical infants. *Journal of Consulting and Clinical Psychology, 55,* 853–859.

Fraiberg, S. (1977). *Insights from the blind: Comparative studies of blind and sighted infants.* New York: Basic Books.

Green, M., & Solnit, A. (1964). Reactions to the threatened loss of a child: A vulnerable child syndrome. *Pediatrics, 34,* 58–66.

Gregory, S. (1976). *The deaf child and his family.* London: George Allen and Unwin.

Gregory, S. (1985). *The relationship between language development and symbolic play in deaf children.* Paper presented in IRSA Conference, Brussels, Belgium.

Gregory, S. (1988, September). *Parent–child communication: The implications of deafness.* Paper presented at the Conference of the Developmental Section of the British Psychological Society, Harlech, Wales, United Kingdom.

Hothkiss, D. (1989). *Demographic aspects of hearing impairment: Questions and answers.* Washington, DC: Center for Assessment and Demographic Studies, Gallaudet University Press.

Jennings, K. D., Connors, R. E., & Stegman, C. E. (1988). Does a physical handicap alter the development of mastery motivation during the preschool years? *Journal of the American Academy of Child and Adolescent Psychiatry, 27,* 312–317.

Jennings, K. D., Connors, R. E., Stegman, C. E., Sankaranarayan, P., & Mendelsohn, S. (1985). Mastery motivation in young preschoolers: Effect of a physical handicap and implications for educational programming. *Journal of the Division for Early Childhood, 9,* 162–169.

Jennings, K. D., Stagg, V., Connors, R. E., & Ross, S. (in press). Social networks of mothers of physically handicapped and nonhandicapped preschoolers: Group differences and relations to mother–child interaction. *Journal of Applied Developmental Psychology.*

Koester, L. S. (1990, July). *Mothers and infants in face-to-face interaction: Does infant hearing status make a difference?* International Congress on Education of the Deaf, Rochester, NY.

Koester, L. S., & MacTurk, R. H. (1991, July). *Predictors of attachment relationships in deaf and hearing infants.* Poster presented at the Eleventh Biennial Meetings, International Conference on Infant Studies, Montreal, Canada.

Landau, B. (1991). Spatial representation of objects in the young–blind child. *Cognition, 38,* 145–178.

Landau, B., Gleitman, H., & Spelke, E. (1981). Spatial knowledge and geometric representation in a child blind from birth. *Science, 213,* 1275–1278.

Landry, S. H., Copeland, D., Lee, A., & Robinson, S. (1990). Goal-directed behavior in children with spina bifida. *Journal of Developmental and Behavioral Pediatrics, 11,* 306–311.

Lederberg, A. R. (1984). Interaction between deaf preschoolers and unfamiliar hearing adults. *Child Development, 55,* 598–606.

Lutkenhaus, P. (1984). Pleasure derived from mastery in three year olds: Its function for persistence and the influence of maternal behavior. *International Journal of Behavioral Development, 7,* 343–358.

MacTurk, R. H. (1993). Social and motivational development in deaf and hearing infants. In D. J. Messer (Ed.), *Mastery motivation: Chil-*

dren's investigation, persistence and development (pp. 149–167). London: Routledge.

MacTurk, R. H., Day, P. S., & Meadow-Orlans, K. P. (1986, November). *Coping strategies in a stressful situation: Six-month-old deaf and hearing infants.* Poster presented at the 20th Annual Meeting of the International Society for Developmental Psychobiology, Annapolis, MD.

MacTurk, R. H., Meadow-Orlans, K. P., Koester, L. S., & Spencer, P. S. (1993). Social support, motivation, language, and interaction: A longitudinal study of mothers and deaf infants. *American Annals of the Deaf, 138,* 19–25.

MacTurk, R. H., & Trimm, V. M. (1989). Mastery motivation in deaf and hearing infants. *Early Education and Development, 1,* 19–34.

MacTurk, R. H., Trimm, V. M., & Platt, D. (1990, April). *Development of mastery motivation in deaf and hearing infants.* Poster presented at the International Conference on Infant Studies, Montreal, Canada.

Marazita, M., Ploughman, L., & Rawlings, B. (1993). Genetic epidemiological studies of early-onset deafness in the U.S. school-age population. *American Journal of Medical Genetics, 46,* 486–491.

Masataka, N. (1992). Motherese in a signed language. *Infant Behavior and Development, 15,* 453–460.

McCarthy, M. E., & McQuiston, S. (1983, April). *The relationship of contingent parental behaviors to infant motivation and competence.* Paper presented at the Biennial Meeting of the Society for Research in Child Development, Detroit, MI.

Meadow, K. P. (1980). *Deafness and child development.* Berkeley: University of California Press.

Meadow-Orlans, K. P. (in press). Parenting by deaf, blind, and physically disabled adults. In M. H. Bornstein (Ed.), *The handbook of parenting, volume IV: Applied and practical considerations.* Norwood, NJ: Erlbaum.

Mindel, E. D., & Feldman, V. (1987). The impact of deaf children on the families. In E. D. Mindel & M. Vernon (Eds.), *They grow in silence: Understanding deaf children and adults* (pp. 1–29). Boston, MA: College Hill Press.

Nienhuys, T. G., & Tikotin, J. A. (1983). Pre-speech communication in hearing and hearing-impaired children. *Journal of the British Association of Teachers of the Deaf, 7,* 182–194.

Olson, M. R. (1983). A study of the exploratory behavior of legally blind and sighted preschoolers. *Exceptional Children, 50,* 130–138.

Orlansky, M., & Hewett, W. (1981). *Voices: Interviews with handicapped people.* Columbus, OH: Charles E. Merrill.

Padden, C. (1980). The deaf community and the culture of deaf people. In C. Baker & R. Battison (Eds.), *Sign Language and the deaf community.* Silver Spring, MD: National Association of the Deaf.

Rainer, J., Altshuler, K., & Kallmann, F. (Eds.). (1969). *Family and mental health problems in a deaf population* (2nd ed.) Springfield, IL: Charles C. Thomas.

Rienzi, B. (1990). Influence and adaptability in families with deaf parents and hearing children. *American Annals of the Deaf, 138,* 402–408.

Schein, J. D. (1989). *At home among strangers: Exploring the Deaf community in the United States.* Washington, DC: Gallaudet University Press.

Schlesinger, H. S. (1985). Deafness, mental health, and language. In F. Powell, T. Finitzo-Hieber, S. Friel-Patti, & D. Henderson (Eds.), *Education of the hearing impaired child* (pp. 103–116). San Diego: College-Hill.

Schlesinger, H. S., & Meadow, K. P. (1972). *Sound and sign: Childhood deafness and mental health.* Berkeley: University of California Press.

Sonksen, P. M., Levitt, S., & Kitsinger, M. (1984). Identification of constraints acting on motor development in young visually disabled children and principles of remediation. *Child Care, Health, and Development, 10,* 273–286.

Spencer, P. E., & Gutfreund, M. K. (1990). Directiveness in mother–infant interactions. In D. F. Moores & K. P. Meadow-Orlans (Eds.), *Educational and developmental aspects of deafness* (pp. 350–365). Washington, DC: Gallaudet University Press.

Stinson, M. S. (1974). Relations between maternal reinforcement and help and the achievement motive in normal-hearing and hearing-impaired sons. *Developmental Psychology, 10,* 348–353.

Stinson, M. S. (1978a). Deafness and motivation for achievement: Research with implications for parent counseling. *The Volta Review, 80,* 140–148.

Stinson, M. S. (1978b). Effects of deafness on maternal expectations about child development. *Journal of Special Education, 12,* 75–81.

Stipek, D. J., & Sanborn, M. E. (1985). Teachers' task-related interactions with handicapped and nonhandicapped preschool children. *Merrill–Palmer Quarterly, 31,* 285–300.

Teplin, S. W. (1983). Development of blind infants and children with retrolental fibroplasia: Implications for physicians. *Pediatrics, 71,* 6–12.

Wachs, T. D., & Sheehan, R. (1988). Developmental patterns in disabled infants and preschoolers. In T. D. Wachs & R. Sheehan, (Eds.), *Assessment of young developmentally disabled children* (pp. 3–23). New York: Plenum.

Wasserman, G., Allen R., & Solomon, C. R. (1986). Limit setting in mothers of toddlers with physical anomalies. *Rehabilitation Literature, 47,* 290–294.

Wasserman, G. A., Allen, R., & Solomon, C. R. (1985). At-risk toddlers and their mothers: The special case of physical handicap. *Child Development, 56,* 73–83.

Wedell-Monnig, J., & Lumley, J. M. (1980). Child deafness and mother–child interaction. *Child Development, 51,* 766–774.

Wills, K. E., Holmbeck, G. N., Dillon, K., & McLone, D. G. (1990). Intelligence and achievement in children with myelomeningocele. *Journal of Pediatric Psychology, 15,* 161–176.

Wood, D. J. (1982). The linguistic experiences of the pre-lingually hearing-impaired child. *Journal of the British Association of Teachers of the Deaf, 6,* 86–93.

9

THE IMPACT OF MENTAL RETARDATION ON MOTIVATED BEHAVIOR

Susan C. Hupp

University of Minnesota
Department of Educational Psychology
Special Education Programs

The study of mastery motivation provides a critical perspective regarding the mechanisms of cognition, the causes of mental retardation, and the development of strategies to facilitate effective learning by persons exhibiting cognitive disabilities. The special education literature abounds with suggestions that children and adults with mental retardation are often passive and depend on others to provide direction in learning new tasks (Certo, 1983; Floor & Rosen, 1975; Sailor & Guess, 1983). Two concerns are of interest. First is the issue of the degree to which diminished use of mastery behaviors defines the concept of mental retardation. As a corollary, what percentage of persons with mental retardation exhibit a reduction in the expression of mastery motivation? Also, does observed passivity arise as a function of interactions experienced by children with mental retardation following birth? Second, to what degree may children with mental retardation profit from educational procedures designed to enhance persistent and goal-directed exploration of their environment, whether or not they demonstrate performance that is below average on tasks designed to measure mastery motivation? This chapter will focus on research and theoretical conceptualizations that may lead to answers to these questions, and guide the design of appropriate early and mid-childhood experiences to maximize learning.

VALIDITY OF MEASURES OF MASTERY MOTIVATION

A question that must be answered prior to delving into comparisons of the use of mastery behaviors and interventions to enhance performance is the validity of the concept of mastery motivation, as measured within extant studies, for children with mental retardation. Validation studies of mastery motivation have largely been conducted with nondelayed children (Mac-Turk, McCarthy, Vietze, & Yarrow, 1987; Messer et al., 1986; Yarrow et al., 1984; Yarrow & Messer, 1983).

One may posit that children with mental retardation are different, and that the expression of mastery motivation is different. Differences might relate to the nature of stimuli that elicit goal-oriented exploratory behavior, including factors such as familiarity, level of difficulty, and type of feedback. Schwethelm and Mahoney (1986), for example, reported that children with mental retardation persisted more when playing with easy toys, or toys whose demands closely matched their cognitive level, than with difficult toys. Based on an expectation that mastery motivation is reflected by persistent exploration with challenging toys, they concluded that goal-directed persistence might not be a good measure of motivation for the participants in their study. Subsequently, Hupp and Abbeduto (1991) questioned this interpretation, noting three procedural issues that may have affected the results: the sessions were very short, and may have precluded detection of waning interest with the easiest toys; there was an apparent ceiling for five of the six toys for the most competent children; and the definition of moderate challenge, as applied to toy selection, may have resulted in inclusion of rather difficult toys in the moderately difficult category.

To further explore the validity of the concept of mastery motivation for application with young children with moderate and severe cognitive delays, Hupp and Abbeduto (1991) designed three analyses to determine if behaviors coded as goal-directed persistence (reflecting mastery motivation) during children's play with toys were, alternatively, occurrences of perseveration. First, they reasoned that nongoal-directed exploration and goal-directed exploration would be distinguished if the children were applying mastery behaviors and would not be distinguished if the children were perseverating, given that, by definition (Wolman, 1989), perseverative behaviors do not relate to the characteristics of the stimuli presented. Analyses indicated that the children used significantly more goal-directed exploration, supporting the interpretation that the children were exhibiting mastery behaviors.

Second, the relationship between goal-directed persistence and success was examined for a subset of toys for which success was not readily achieved as a function of goal-directed persistence. These toys required combining parts, such as putting a peg into the hole on a pegboat. While merely relating the peg to the top of the boat would be considered goal-directed persistence, exact placement was required for success to occur. There was a significant relationship between the use of mastery behaviors and the attainment of success, indicating that the children had the goal in mind.

Finally, it was determined that success followed occurrences of goal-directed persistence at levels significantly above chance, again underscoring the interpretation that these behaviors were related to the goal. Thus, it appears that typical procedures for assessing mastery motivation with young, nondelayed children are valid measures of the concept when employed with young children with mental retardation.

This position has also been supported by Vietze, McCarthy, McQuiston, MacTurk, and Yarrow (1983). In their study of infants with Down syndrome at 6, 8, and 12 months of age, they found that the use of mastery behaviors at 12 months related in a significant and positive direction to Bayley mental scores, and that off-task behaviors related in a significant, yet negative direction.

COMPARISONS BETWEEN CHILDREN WITH AND WITHOUT MENTAL RETARDATION

Comparisons of performance between children with and without mental retardation may provide evidence regarding the degree to which performance reflecting mastery motivation characterizes mental retardation. An exceptionally strong design would be provided by a longitudinal, comparative analysis, controlling for confounding factors related to etiology and experience. Unfortunately, this type of study has not been done. Rather, studies are available to describe differences that occur at various times across childhood, based on studies of children with varying etiologies. This approach to the investigation has the potential of providing insight regarding the range of patterns that may exist, in lieu of a definitive conclusion.

Before reviewing comparative studies, it is important to consider methodological issues that affect interpretation of results. The long-term debate over deficit versus difference explanations for cognitive development and mental retardation may serve as a lesson to us all, given how such perspectives affect the design of studies (Baumeister, 1984). Interpreting group similarities and differences is an exacting task. For example, consider a situation in which no differences were found between two comparison groups regarding the use of mastery behaviors. One would want to consider the potential confound of the presence or absence of supportive adults in the daily lives of the children in each group. If the groups differed significantly on this variable, then the apparent similarity of performance between the groups might actually signify a difference.

Alternatively, when comparisons reveal differences, caution must be exercised in the event that other group differences account for the differential behavior (Baumeister, 1984). As stated by Zigler (1969), in reference to understanding motivational differences, "you cannot safely attribute a difference in performance on a dependent variable to a known difference in subject characteristics . . . if the populations also differ on other factors which could reasonably affect . . . performance on the dependent measure" (pp. 544–545).

With these concerns in mind, a review of the literature comparing performance of children with and without mental retardation must be undertaken cautiously. If one could make the assumption that development in this area is continuous, studies including infants and toddlers may provide the best source of information regarding the relationship between defining characteristics of mental retardation and the expression of mastery motivation. Clearly, across the lifespan, the effect of personal experience (nurture) on development increases, by the sheer number of events. With each passing month, it becomes more and more difficult to control for the impact of new experiences. Statistical controls, while helpful, tend to be artifactual.

Early Childhood

Comparative studies of young children with cognitive delays have been based on both chronological and mental age matches. In addition, a few studies have examined children with retardation in the absence of a comparison group. Each strategy addresses different research questions. Goodman (1981) examined the organization of exploratory play with preschool-aged children both with and without retardation. She used a cross-sectional design across four successive age groups for the non-delayed children and three successive age groups for the children with delays. Her procedure entailed having children play with a lock box: a toy constructed with ten locked doors, with a toy hidden behind each. While this procedure is different from that typically used to assess mastery motivation, it entails similar abilities in that children must explore the mechanism to unlock a door to retrieve a toy. Goodman (1981) found increases in both competence and organization of exploration as nondelayed children increased in age. Performance increases did not correlate with a child's intelligence quotient, leading Goodman to suggest that this task measured more than mental ability.

For the children with mental retardation, competence also increased with chronological age. Competence included successful attempts, unsuccessful attempts, and adaptive moves among the ten locked doors—behaviors that are reflective of mastery motivation. Correlations between intelligence quotients and these measures yielded significant relationships, with adaptive moves related positively to level of intelligence.

Recall that Goodman (1981) concluded that the experimental procedures measured more than mental ability based on analyses of the performance of children without delay. Thus, it is interesting to speculate on the relationship between mental ability and mastery motivation for children with cognitive delays. Alternatively, Goodman compared performance between groups matched for the number of locked doors opened successfully. The children with retardation exhibited fewer adaptive moves between doors and less orderly exploration than did the nondelayed children. Of particular interest, the children with retardation exhibited significantly more aimless behavior. Thus, even with similar levels of success, the children with retardation were more disorganized and purposeless in their play.

Goodman draws on Zigler's (1966) explanation for the tendency of children with retardation to perform repetitive tasks. Zigler has asserted that past experience with failure and accompanying social disapproval lead children to engage in simple and monotonous behaviors that often result in success and yield social approval. If this assertion is correct, the environments of young children with retardation will inhibit the very learning that they need. Goodman (1981) cautioned that her sampling procedures may have tended to exclude children with retardation who had good exploratory behaviors, because they may not have been identified as needing special education, from which she drew her sample.

To get a broader picture of the exploratory abilities of young children, it may be necessary to study children who are even younger than those represented in Goodman's (1981) study, who may not yet have met with equivalent failure, social approval, and social disapproval. MacTurk et al. (1985) conducted such a study. Comparing 11 infants with Down syndrome with 11 non-delayed infants, matched for mental age based on Bayley (1969) mental raw scores, they found that the infants with Down syndrome looked more at toys and exhibited less general exploration (not reflective of mastery motivation) and less social response. Interestingly, there were no differences detected for goal-directed exploration (termed "persist," reflective of mastery motivation), success, or off-task behaviors. There was also a high degree of similarity in behavioral organization between groups, determined by mapping the probability that specific behaviors would be followed by the other behaviors.

The findings of MacTurk and his colleagues differ from those of Goodman (1981), who witnessed less intense and sophisticated exploration with children with retardation whose success was equivalent to that of nondelayed children. There may be several reasons. MacTurk et al.'s (1985) subjects were much younger; thus, their experience with failure was more limited in time. More importantly, the imperative to succeed probably was different for the children in the two studies. The toys used in the study by MacTurk and his colleagues, such as a chime ball or three men that can be placed in or removed from a wobbly tub, do not entail a single-minded function in the same way that Goodman's lock box did. Certainly, success adds an element of interest to the play situation, when chimes ring and parts move, but other behaviors may also lead to compelling outcomes, like looking at mom. By the time a child is 3 or 4 years of age, she knows that success is a desired outcome, and "failure" may be more consequential.

In a related vein, Hupp and Abbeduto (1992) compared the performance of two groups of young children, moderately and severely cognitively delayed, each functioning at a 12-month mental age, with nondelayed children of both 12 and 18 months of age. Thus, the 12-month nondelayed group was a mental age match. The 18-month age group was included to determine a continuum of performance by nondelayed children for whom the toys were "just right" (12 months) or too easy (18 months). One could suggest that the similarity in performance between delayed and nondelayed infants documented by MacTurk and his colleagues was a function of subject selection, given that children with Down syndrome often exhibit only mild delays, which may not be significantly discrepant for children less than a year of age.

Hupp and Abbeduto (1992) found a high degree of similarity in performance between groups of delayed and nondelayed children matched for cognitive ability. With respect to the types of play exhibited, the two groups of children with delays never differed significantly from each other and always functioned at a level between that exhibited by the 12- and 18-month nondelayed groups. However, the children with moderate delays used significantly less general exploration (not reflective of mastery motivation) and experienced more success than did the 12-month nondelayed children, behaving more like the 18-month-old nondelayed group. A similar pattern occurred when analyzing group differences for the latency to the first experience of success with the toys. The latency to success of the group with moderate delays was significantly shorter than that of the 12-month nondelayed group. These results are similar to those documented by MacTurk et al. (1985), suggesting that young children with cognitive delays do not necessarily demonstrate deficient exploratory strategies in relation to children with similar mental age. The results of Hupp and Abbeduto further suggest that the increased chronological age of children with delays, in comparison to nondelayed children of the same mental age, may afford some children an "edge," perhaps due to increased experience.

While mastery motivation is often assessed within the context of playing with toys, the concept also may be applied to exploring the "functions" of people, trying to figure how to make them work. Social mastery motivation was the subject of study by MacTurk, Hunter, McCarthy, Vietze, and McQuiston (1985), based on the same study of children with and without Down syndrome reported previously. Both toy play and social sessions were administered, and object mastery and social mastery were coded. The social situations were based on games often played by babies and their parents. Behaviors reflective of social mastery motivation included attending, gesturing, and vocalizing, among other behaviors directed toward the child's mother or the experimenter. While the nondelayed children exhibited more social behavior during object play sessions ($p < .01$), this difference did not occur with the social situation ($p = .06$).

Middle Childhood

As children with mental retardation grow older, differences in the use of mastery behaviors become marked. In a comparison of children with and without mental retardation, Harter and Zigler (1974) studied three groups at each of two different mental ages (i.e., 6.6 and 7.7 years). Children in two of the three groups at each age had mental retardation, one being institutionalized and one noninstitutionalized. They were matched for mental age with a nondelayed group. This design is fascinating because it enables speculation regarding the effects of two different environments on children with retardation.

Harter and Zigler (1974) monitored three measures. For response variations, each group differed significantly from each other, in the following order from highest to lowest: nondelayed, noninstitutionalized, and institutionalized. With respect to curiosity, the nondelayed children preferred challenging tasks significantly more than did either group of children with retardation. For the low mental age group only (6.6 years), the nondelayed children demonstrated less mastery. Given the converging measures, the differences documented for effectance motivation can be considered robust.

Harter and Zigler suggested that mental age may mediate the degree to which children succeed and fail. A child's intelligence quotient, which factors in age, may have an impact due to the discrepancy between a child's actual performance and the level of performance one might expect to observe if the child were not mentally retarded. The living context, within a family or an institution, may further contribute to performance.

For example, with the competence task of placing pegs in a pegboat, the noninstitutionalized children with mental retardation who had a high mental age appeared to act impulsively. Harter and Zigler (1974) proposed that they may have been trying to finish the task quickly to avoid failure anxiety that might arise from their being compared to nondelayed children in everyday life. Institutionalization may protect children from developing failure anxiety. Also consider, however, that the institutionalized children demonstrated less response variation and curiosity. Harter and Zigler speculated that institutionalized environments may attenuate variations in response given their highly structured routines.

Subsequently, Vandenberg (1985) contrasted the exploratory performance of children with mild mental retardation, 7 to 12 years of age, with two groups of nondelayed children, one matched for chronological age and one matched for mental age. Exploration was measured according to duration and systematic search. While these measures are different from those used in the study of mastery motivation, systematic search reflects goal seeking. For this measure, nondelayed children of the same chronological age scored more highly than did the children with mental retardation. No differences emerged with the mental age comparison. Duration of exploration varied inversely with search strategy, and a direct group comparison was not made. Vandenberg concluded by suggesting that the delays in exploratory behavior of the children with retardation (when compared with the chronologically matched children) reflected appropriate developmental functioning, and should not be attributed to retardation per se.

Abe (1981) also found no difference between elementary-aged children with and without mental retardation, matched for mental age (mean of 7 to 8 years). Mastery motivation was inferred from the amount of time that the children spent engaged in a block design test considered to be very difficult. Abe interpreted the results as being consistent with Zigler's motivation theory; however, Abe did not indicate the lifestyle (e.g., institutionalized vs. noninstitutionalized) of the children with mental retardation.

Thus, comparative studies support the notion that mental retardation is not necessarily caused by deficits in motivational deficits. Differences in the use of mastery behaviors by chronologically matched children with and without mental retardation is symptomatic of differing cognitive levels (mental age). This does not mean to suggest that all children with mental retardation will function at the same level as that exhibited in nondelayed children. The impact of the environment has been shown to be significant. Situations that heighten stress may lead to impulsiveness, which may in turn interfere with the expression of mastery motivation. Similarly, situations that impose high levels of structure, which are often controlled by adults, may reduce the expression of mastery motivation.

The mechanisms by which the environment actually affects exploratory behavior in general, the use of mastery behaviors in particular, and the development of a need or preference for social reinforcement are not well understood. Individual components have been analyzed, but the weight that each carries when factored within a multivariate model has not been determined. Nonetheless, it is helpful to consider mechanisms individually as a basis for considering intervention. Implicated are events related to the development of attachment, maltreatment, and the availability of varied and responsive persons and objects, which may affect children with mental retardation.

For example, in the study of preschool-aged children with Down syndrome of a similar chronological age, Serafica and Cicchetti (1976) documented differences in attachment and exploration using fine motor manipulation. Within-group comparisons between attachment and exploration were not conducted. Either this type of analysis, or a comparison incorporating children with and without mental retardation based on a mental age match, might have highlighted further mechanisms by which attachment affects exploration.

Toy responsivity is related to exploration in general by young children with mental retardation. Bambara, Spiegel-McGill, Shores, and Fox (1984) documented children with moderate and severe retardation as playing for substantially longer periods of time with reactive than nonreactive toys.

It is difficult to determine how individual life events and environmental differences may ultimately impact on a single child's expression of mastery motivation. It is unknown which factors contribute most to the variance of performance, particularly given the multivariate nature of the problem.

Intervention Strategies

An alternative approach to understanding how a particular child's expression of mastery motivation is determined is to review the intervention literature. Specifically, can the use of mastery behaviors be modified and result in improved learning? One would hope one could reverse a deficit in the use of mastery behaviors caused by a less-than-optimal environment, although this is not a sure proposition. While intervention is discussed elsewhere in this text (Hauser-Cram & Shonkoff, this volume), it may be useful to consider how malleable the use of mastery behaviors may be.

Three approaches may guide intervention, including teaching teachers to attend to motivation and its relationship to child learning, matching a child's motivation style to the type of direction and reinforcement given by teachers, and increasing a child's use of mastery behaviors through manipulation of the physical and social environment. While these approaches are overlapping and may lead to similar action by teachers, they are categorized as such to highlight different perspectives for intervention.

Switzky and Schultz (1988, 1990) have discussed the need for teachers to increase their awareness of motivation of children enrolled in special education. They noted that much special instruction is dominated by externally controlled teaching strategies, which may be contrary to practices supported by motivational theory. They suggested that teachers need practical guidelines for identifying children's motivational orientation and designing educational demands that support the expression of intrinsic motivation.

Switzky and Haywood (1974) demonstrated the value of matching reinforcement strategies with children's motivation orientation, whether that be extrinsic or intrinsic. Children in grades two through five were exposed to either a self-monitoring reinforcement condition or an externally imposed reinforcement condition. Children performed for longer periods when the reinforcement strategy matched their motivation orientation.

Several strategies for enhancing intrinsic motivation have been proven to be successful. For example, in a study of institutionalized adolescents with mental retardation, Lee, Syrnyk, and Hallschmid (1976) contrasted providing low, as opposed to high, levels of incentive for task engagement with intrinsically interesting and noninteresting tasks. High and low incentive rewards were determined individually for each participant through a paired-choice paradigm. Their results provided evidence that, with an intrinsically interesting task, task persistence was actually higher under the low incentive reward condition than under the high incentive reward condition, suggesting that intrinsic interest may be undermined by highly prized external rewards.

Harter, Brown, and Zigler (1971a) compared successful task completion of institutionalized and noninstitutionalized children with retardation with task completion of nondelayed children. The tasks entailed an oddity problem and a three-choice discrimination. The measures can be considered reflective of, but more restricted than those typically used to assess, mastery motivation, because the use of mastery behaviors is a necessary but not sufficient condition for attainment of success. Of particular interest for this discussion is the comparison between the two groups of children with retardation living in different environments. The use of social reinforcement throughout the session, contingent on success, resulted in superior performance for the noninstitutionalized children in comparison to the nonsocial condition, in which social interaction was absent during the session and reinforcement consisted of a prize at the end of the session. The opposite pattern was found with the institutionalized children. Observations of the children during the tasks indicated that social reinforcement interfered with the performance of the institutionalized children, who increased attentiveness with the experimenter at the expense of task-related performance.

Directly to the point, Zigler and Balla (1972) compared social responsiveness of nondelayed children to institutionalized children with retardation, matched for mental age. The children with retardation were more highly motivated by social reinforcement, which was provided when a child interacted with an adult (a necessary act to proceed through components of the game) and on a ratio basis when children successfully manipulated the game materials, than were the nondelayed children. Within the group of children with retardation, the authors were able to correlate early social deprivation and the children's inclinations to engage an adult socially during the experimental task, documenting that the more deprived children were the most likely to be motivated by social reinforcement. These data suggest a mechanism whereby motivation can be affected by environmental conditions that covary with group (i.e., nondelayed, delayed and institutionalized, delayed and noninstitutionalized).

The impact of penalties for incorrect performance was investigated by Harter, Brown, and Zigler (1971b), who contrasted a reward-only condition with a reward-and-penalty condition. Nondelayed first- and second-grade children were matched by mental age with children living in an institution who had either organic or familial retardation. The nondelayed children and the children with familial retardation performed best in the reward-plus-penalty condition, while the children with organic retardation did not. These findings indicate that it is important to clearly document the exact nature of contingencies for performance and to consider differences among children with retardation, rather than presume that children with retardation constitute a homogeneous group.

Reactions to successful problem solving were further studied by Harter (1977) by presenting tasks of different levels of difficulty. The participants were two groups of children, one being nondelayed of first grade age and the other being retarded, attending a special education class, matched for mental age with the first graders. While problem-solving ability did not differ, supporting the mental age match, the nondelayed children exhibited more pleasure when their problem-solving attempts met with success than did the children with retardation. Harter (1977) noted, "The retarded children seemed more concerned about failure, appeared to have more doubts about their ability, particularly on the more difficult puzzles, and were more dependent on the adult experimenter for feedback, praise, or direction" (p. 489).

Critical to analyzing the effectiveness of intervention is the degree to which subsequent cognitive performance of children is enhanced. While most intervention studies have not analyzed long-term impact, Messer and his colleagues (1986) have provided supportive evidence from the study of young, nondelayed children that early use of mastery behaviors is related significantly to subsequent cognitive abilities. In examining the prediction of 30-month McCarthy general cognitive and memory scores, from 6-month Bayley and 6-month mastery motivation scores, they found that neither 6-month score individually predicted the 30-month cognitive indicators. However, the 6-month mastery scores significantly added to the predictive power of the Bayley scores, while the 6-month Bayley scores did not improve the predictions derived from the 6-month mastery motivation scores.

SUMMARY

Mastery motivation is a complex phenomenon of great importance for the developing child—when developmental trajectory is compromised, mastery motivation may be considered even more critical. Deficits in mastery motivation do not appear to define mental retardation, but may characterize performance of children with retardation. The evidence suggests that very young children with cognitive deficits perform at levels equivalent to those of nondelayed children who have been matched for mental age. Over the course of time, the children with cognitive deficits may, however, lose ground. Speculation abounds concerning the reasons why. The children may not be expected to be independent, they may experience excessive anxiety when they meet with failure, or they may not receive adequate social praise for independent exploration, with the focus of adults placed alternatively on success. That the use of mastery behaviors may be diminished by circumstance is clear, thus, a necessary agenda is to preserve the use of mastery behaviors by young children with disabilities. For children who do not express a high level of intrinsic motivation, the options are twofold. Matching of instructional strategies to child characteristics appears warranted. More germane to those committed to the importance of mastery motivation as a mechanism for learning is the design of research to discover strategies for enhancing the use of mastery behaviors, both through environmental management and direct instructional opportunities.

References

Abe, K. (1981). Mastery motivation and problem solving behavior in normal and retarded children on a three choice problem. *Journal of Child Development (Japan)*, 17, 1–5.

Bambara, L. M., Spiegel-McGill, P., Shores, R. E., & Fox, J. J. (1984). A comparison of reactive and nonreactive toys on severely handicapped children's manipulative play. *Journal of the Association for Persons with Severe Handicaps*, 9, 142–149.

Baumeister, A. A. (1984). Some conceptual and methodological issues in the study of cognitive processes. In P. Brooks, R. Sperber, & C. McCauly (Eds.), *Learning and cognition in the mentally retarded* (pp. 1–38). Hillsdale, NJ: Erlbaum.

Bayley, N. (1969). *Bayley scales of infant development*. New York: Psychological Corporation.

Certo, N. (1983). Characteristics of educational services. In M. E. Snell (Ed.), *Systematic instruction of the moderately and severely handicapped* (pp. 2–15). Columbus: Charles E. Merrill.

Floor, L., & Rosen, M. (1975). Investigating the phenomenon of helplessness in mentally retarded adults. *American Journal of Mental Deficiency*, 79, 565–572.

Goodman, J. F. (1981). The lock box: A measure of psychomotor competence and organized behavior in retarded and normal preschoolers. *Journal of Consulting and Clinical Psychology,* 49(3), 369–378.

Harter, S. (1977). The effects of social reinforcement and task difficulty level on the pleasure derived by normal and retarded children from cognitive challenge and mastery. *Journal of Experimental Child Psychology,* 24, 476–494.

Harter, S., Brown, L., & Zigler, E. (1971a). Discrimination learning in retarded and nonretarded children as a function of task difficulty and social reinforcement. *American Journal of Mental Deficiency,* 76(3), 275–283.

Harter, S., Brown, L., & Zigler, E. (1971b). The discrimination learning of normal and retarded children as a function of penalty conditions and etiology of the retarded. *Child Development,* 42, 517–536.

Harter, S., & Zigler, E. (1974). The assessment of effectance motivation in normal and retarded children. *Developmental Psychology,* 10, 169–180.

Hupp, S. C., & Abbeduto, L. (1991). Persistence as an indicator of mastery motivation in young children with cognitive delays. *Journal of Early Intervention,* 15(3), 219–225.

Hupp, S. C., & Abbeduto, L. (1992). *Comparison of the use of mastery behaviors by eight-, twelve-, and eighteen-month-old children.* Manuscript submitted for publication.

Lee, D. Y., Syrnyk, R., & Hallschmid, C. (1976). Self-perception of intrinsic and extrinsic motivation: Effects on institutionalized mentally retarded adolescents. *American Journal of Mental Deficiency,* 81(4), 331–337.

MacTurk, R. H., Hunter, F., McCarthy, M., Vietze, P., & McQuiston, S. (1985). Social mastery motivation in Down syndrome and nondelayed infants. *Topics in Early Childhood Special Education,* 4, 93–109.

MacTurk, R. H., McCarthy, M. E., Vietze, P. M., & Yarrow, L. J. (1987). Sequential analysis of mastery behavior in 6- and 12-month-old infants. *Developmental Psychology,* 23(2), 199–203.

MacTurk, R. H., Vietze, P. M., McCarthy, M. E., McQuiston, S., & Yarrow, L. J. (1985). The organization of exploratory behavior in Down syndrome and nondelayed infants. *Child Development,* 56, 573–581.

Messer, D. J., McCarthy, M. E., McQuiston, S., MacTurk, R. H., Yarrow, L. J., & Vietze, P. M. (1986). Relation between mastery behavior in infancy and competence in early childhood. *Developmental Psychology,* 22, 336–372.

Sailor, W., & Guess, D. (1983). *Severely handicapped students: An instructional design.* Boston: Houghton-Mifflin.

Schwethelm, B., & Mahoney G. (1986). Task persistence among organically impaired mentally retarded children. *American Journal of Mental Deficiency,* 90(4), 432–439.

Serafica, F. C., & Cicchetti, D. (1976). Down's syndrome children in a strange situation: Attachment and exploration behaviors. *Merrill–Palmer Quarterly, 22*(2), 137–150.

Switzky, H. N., & Haywood, H. C. (1974). Motivational orientation and the relative efficacy of self-monitored and externally imposed reinforcement systems in children. *Journal of Personality and Social Psychology, 30*(3), 360–366.

Switzky, H. N., & Schultz, G. F. (1988). Intrinsic motivation and learning performance: Implications for individual educational programming for learners with mild handicaps. *Remedial and Special Education, 9*(4), 7–14.

Switzky, H. N., & Schultz, G. F. (1990). The development of intrinsic motivation in students with learning problems: Suggestions for more effective instructional practice. *Preventing School Failure, 34*(2), 14–20.

Vandenberg, B. R., (1985). The effects of retardation on exploration. *Merrill–Palmer Quarterly, 31*(4), 397–409.

Vietze, P. M., McCarthy, M., McQuiston, S., MacTurk, R., & Yarrow, L. J. (1983). Attention and exploratory behavior in infants with Down's syndrome. In T. Field & A. Sostek (Eds.), *Infants born at risk: Physiological, perceptual, and cognitive processes* (pp. 251–268). New York: Grune & Stratton.

Wolman, B. B. (1989). *Dictionary of behavioral science* (2nd ed.). New York: Academic Press.

Yarrow, L. J., MacTurk, R. H., Vietze, P. M., McCarthy, M. E., Klein, R. P., & McQuiston, S. (1984). Development course of parental stimulation and its relationship to mastery motivation during infancy. *Developmental Psychology, 20*(3), 492–503.

Yarrow, L. J., & Messer, D. J. (1983). Motivation and cognition in infancy. In M. Lewis (Ed.), *Origins of intelligence (2nd ed.,* pp. 451–477). Hillsdale, NJ: Erlbaum.

Zigler, E. (1966). Mental retardation: Current issues and approaches. In L. W. Hoffman & M. L. Hoffman (Eds.), *Review of child development research, 2.* Newbury Park, CA: Sage.

Zigler, E. (1969). Developmental versus difference theories of mental retardation and the problem of motivation. *American Journal of Mental Deficiency, 73,* 536–556.

Zigler, E., & Balla, D. (1972). Developmental course of responsiveness to social reinforcement in normal children and institutionalized retarded children. *Development Psychology, 6*(1), 66–73.

10

THE EFFECTS OF PREMATURITY AND OTHER PERINATAL FACTORS ON INFANTS' MASTERY MOTIVATION*

Robert J. Harmon
Nancy S. Murrow
University of Colorado School of Medicine

The impact of prematurity and other perinatal risk factors on an infant has been a popular research area over the past two decades. It is clear that these factors affect more than one aspect of an infant's development, as their effects go beyond the infant to include the family system. For instance, some of the possible complications of premature infants are a very low birth weight (< 1500 gm), intraventricular hemorrhage (IVH), respira-

*Portions of the studies discussed were supported by the W. T. Grant Foundation Endowment Fund of the Developmental Psychobiology Research Group, a NIMH Research Scientist Development Award 5 K01 MH00281 and a Research Project Grant 5 RO1 MH34005 to Dr. Harmon, and a grant from the John D. and Catherine T. MacArthur Foundation. The authors wish to express their appreciation to a number of colleagues for their involvement: George Morgan and Rob MacTurk for the editorial assistance and support; Anne Culp for her help in the data collection and scoring; Leola Schultz for statistical consultation; David Messer for his comments on the manuscript; and the members of the Developmental Psychobiology Research Group for their helpful advice while the research was being conducted.

tory distress syndrome (RDS), hypoxia, and underdeveloped internal systems (Cohen, Parmelee, Beckwith, & Sigman, 1986). As a result, these infants have longer hospital stays, have many caretakers, and have less physical contact with their mothers (Harmon, Glicken, & Good, 1982; Klaus & Kennel, 1982).

In comparison to a term birth, the family system is disrupted more by a preterm birth, because it affects the mother–child relationship as well as the marital relationship (see review in Macey, Harmon, & Easterbrooks, 1987). In particular, the mother's caretaking practices tend to be overprotective and her interactional style is typically overstimulating, less positive, and less sensitive to her infant's cues. The infant is characteristically fussy, restless, and less engaged to the point of avoiding the mother. Although ethnicity, parents' education, and socioeconomic status are factors that can mediate the effect on the family (Cohen et al., 1986; Macey et al., 1987), a premature birth poses a more stressful and less optimal situation than that experienced by full-term infants and their families.

Other high risk infants, such as drug-exposed and chronically ill infants, and their families face a comparable situation. Drug-exposed infants, though, are more at risk because of their medical and neurodevelopmental problems, the inadequate and/or inconsistent parenting abilities of their substance-abusing mothers, and their unstable and often dangerous home environment (Howard, Beckwith, Rodning, & Kropenske, 1989; Kieckhefer & Dinno, 1992; Weston, Ivins, Zuckerman, Jones, & Lopez, 1989).

A particular interest of past studies has been how these risk factors affect an infant's cognitive development. This chapter will review the results of some of these recent studies, the assessments used, and expand the discussion to include the mastery motivation of perinatal risk infants, primarily focusing on premature infants. There is some correlation between mastery motivation and cognitive development in infancy (Yarrow et al., 1983; Yarrow, Morgan, Jennings, Harmon, & Gaiter, 1982), but the correlation diminishes as children become older (Redding, Morgan, & Harmon, 1988). Despite this early relationship, we think that mastery motivation and cognitive level, or competence, should be viewed as two distinct concepts: The former refers to a child's "efforts to master the environment," or attempts to increase competence, whereas the latter refers to the level of ability/skill already achieved by the child (Morgan, Maslin-Cole, Biringen, & Harmon, 1991).

It has been our belief, supported by some empirical studies, that early mastery motivation may be a better predictor of outcome in perinatal risk infants than early cognitive measures. Since there are not many studies assessing mastery motivation in perinatal risk infants, we will review studies of both competence and mastery motivation in this population. A majority of these studies used the Bayley Scales of Infant Development (Bayley, 1969) to assess cognitive and developmental level, while a few studies also included a measure of object play or mastery motivation as part of their assessment. It will become apparent in this review that the Bayley scales alone do not adequately assess the developmental level of perinatal risk infants.

REVIEW OF COGNITIVE DEVELOPMENT STUDIES

Recent studies typically have found that infants born prematurely have lower scores on developmental assessments in comparison to full term infants, with a tendency also to perform less well on motor skills. Crnic, Ragozin, Greenberg, Robinson, and Basham (1983) found that preterm infants scored significantly lower than a term comparison group on the Bayley Mental Developmental Index (MDI) and Psychomotor Developmental Index (PDI) scales over the first 12 months, although the scores of both groups were within the normal range. Harmon and Culp (1981) described similar results in a study of 29 low birth weight preterm infants and 30 full-term infants, with the former scoring significantly lower than the latter on the MDI (106 vs. 118 respectively, $p < .001$) and on the PDI (91 vs. 103 respectively, $p < .01$). Another study (Ross, 1985), which had similar results to the above mentioned studies, found that there were significant differences on both the MDI and PDI scores between the preterm and term samples. In addition, the within group difference between the MDI and the PDI was much larger in the preterm sample.

However, the results have varied as to whether mental or motor ability was compromised more depending on such factors as medical complications, birth weight, ethnicity, parents' education, and whether the family received additional support as part of an intervention program. Ludman, Halperin, Driscoll, Driscoll, and Belmont (1987) studied the effect of very low birth weight and/or respiratory distress syndrome (RDS) in 30 preterm infants of middle-class families at the ages of 1, 3, and

4 years. The scores were within or near the normal range (except for the PDI of the Bayley Scales of Infant Development), yet there was a large difference between the scores of the very low birth weight (VLBW) preterm group and the high birth weight (HBW) preterm group. The VLBW preterm infants, who had the lowest scores of the sample, improved their scores over time, but not dramatically, when compared to the rest of the group. The presence of RDS was not a differentiating factor among the preterm subgroups, although preterm infants without RDS tended to have higher scores. One of the conclusions for why no differences were found over time is that the instruments administered at the ages of 3 and 4 years (the Merrill–Palmer and Stanford–Binet scales respectively) assess verbal ability, whereas the Bayley Scales, administered at 1 year, evaluate sensorimotor skills. It is possible that developmental delays would have been apparent in this sample of preterm infants at the older ages if their motor skills had been tested.

Depending on the severity of intraventricular hemorrhage (IVH), preterm infants have been found to be delayed in both the cognitive and motor functioning areas (Sostek, Smith, Katz, & Grant, 1987). A sample of 113 preterm infants, divided into five subgroups based on IVH grade, were evaluated and followed up during the their first two years. Although mental delay increased with severity of hemorrhage, only the infants in the Grade 4 group, who were diagnosed with the severest IVH symptoms, had significantly lower Bayley mental scores than the other subgroups at 1 year of age. The motor skills of the infants with more bleeding (Grades 3 and 4) were significantly lower than those of the infants who had less bleeding (Grades 1 and 2) as well. At age 2, the mental and motor scores of the Grade 4 infants had improved and were comparable to the other bleed groups, but continued to be the lowest of the sample. Clearly, mental and motor delays were found to be related to severity of IVH at 1 year, but differences were less prominent by the next year with a majority of the most severely affected infants scoring within normal range.

Another study examined the interaction between ethnic group, medical complications, and socioeconomic level and later cognitive level (Cohen et al., 1986). Using a sample of preterm infants from English-speaking and Spanish-speaking families (70% vs. 30%), assessments of prenatal and perinatal complications, neurological problems, cognitive and motor functioning, and overall developmental level were made as the infants were followed up to 8 years old. Both groups were functioning within normal range at 8 years. The IQ scores varied between the two groups but not significantly, with the children from the Spanish-speaking families scoring lower on language items despite being presumably "fluent" in English. When the sample was divided based on birth weight, no differences were found on the 8-year assessments within the English-speaking sample. However, within the Spanish-speaking sample, the very low birth weight children had significantly lower IQ scores. The IQ scores of all of the Spanish-speaking children seem to be affected by birth weight, length of hospitalization, and medical complications, whereas only mother's education appeared to influence IQ scores of the English-speaking children.

The developmental outcomes of other perinatal risk infants has also been studied. Fischer-Fay, Goldberg, Simmons, and Levinson (1988) found that a sample of 23 infants diagnosed with cystic fibrosis had significantly lower Bayley MDI scores than the control sample of healthy infants. However, this discrepancy between Bayley scores could be explained by the difference between the parents' level of education, with the parents of the control sample being more educated. Howard et al. (1989) found that drug-exposed infants had significantly lower developmental scores in comparison to a control sample of high risk preterm infants, but the scores were within the low average range. Similarly, in a sample of 19 drug-exposed infants, 6 of the infants demonstrated either a developmental delay or borderline evidence for a delay (Kieckhefer & Dinno, 1992). In addition, infants with dysmorphologic features were more likely to have developmental delays.

It is clear from the above studies that these risk populations typically function at a lower cognitive level during their first years of life than term or healthy infants, with significance dependent on severity of medical condition and age at time of assessment. In general, however, this difference tends to decrease with age. Many of these studies utilized the Bayley Scales of Infant Development to measure cognitive functioning.

However, the Bayley scales are problematic when used as the only assessment of developmental level. First, there has been a controversy concerning whether to use corrected or uncorrected gestation ages when testing premature infants. Barrera, Rosenbaum, and Cunningham (1987) concluded that very low birth weight preterm infants (VLBW) (< 1500 gm) do not reach the same developmental level as high birth weight (HBW) preterm and full-term (FT) infants at the age of 16 months. Their results indicated that when using uncorrected gestational ages, VLBW infants scored significantly lower than the HBW and FT infants on both the mental and motor scales, whereas there was only a trend when corrected gestational ages were used. Most researchers and clinicians now agree that corrected gestational age should be used up to approximately age two for VLBW infants (Krall & Feinstein, 1991; Parmelee, 1975). HBW infants, on the other hand, were found to be comparable to the FT infants, using either corrected or uncorrected ages.

Second, it has been suggested that premature infants attain poor motor scores when evaluated using the Bayley scales because the items do not adequately measure gross and fine motor skills (Ross, 1985), since the Bayley scales primarily measure sensorimotor skills (Barrera et al., 1987).

Hence, the Bayley outcome for perinatal risk infants can be misleading, depending on whether the age correction was made, and is considered by some researchers as giving an incomplete appraisal of developmental level, as noted earlier. An assessment of mastery motivation, in addition to developmental level, may expand our understanding of the perinatal risk infant and give a more realistic view of the child's developmental status.

REVIEW OF STUDIES OF OBJECT PLAY

Other researchers, interested in the behaviors that correlate with later cognitive level, have utilized measures of behavioral states and object play to predict Bayley score outcomes. Di-Pietro and Porges (1991) examined the relationship between the neonatal state behaviors of 16 preterm infants and their developmental outcome at 8 months of age. They found that newborn infants with a higher gestational age and fewer perinatal complications were more fussy, irritable, and demonstrated a broader range of state behaviors. These behaviors were positively related to higher 8-month Bayley scores, particularly the MDI, as well as a relational play variable, which coded the level of exploration of toys' characteristics during object play. Conversely, infants who had lower gestational ages and/or more perinatal risks were found to be more alert, but have a restricted range of state behaviors, which were associated with poorer developmental outcome at 8 months.

In considering how infants organize their behaviors, Als and Brazelton (1981) illustrated, using two case examples, how a preterm infant and term infant differed in their behaviors over the first 12 months. The behavioral organization of both infants was assessed at approximately 1 month postterm using the Assessment of Preterm Infants Behavior, based on the Brazelton Neonatal Behavioral Assessment Scale (Brazelton, 1973). The full-term infant was found to be quite stable in the physiological motor areas and could be engaged by the examiner, while the preterm infant was lacking organization, particularly in the attentional interactive area and regulatory system, and required facilitation and support from the examiner.

The Als and Brazelton infants were followed up at 3 and 5 months and observed during a face-to-face interaction with their mothers. At both ages, the preterm infant appeared to avoid the mother, was unresponsive as she increasingly tried to engage the infant, and was restricted in play behaviors. In comparison, the full term infant's behavior was similar, but exhibited different levels of involvement in the interaction by 3 months, and had reached a higher level of interaction by 5 months.

At 12 months, the Als and Brazelton infants were evaluated with a problem-solving task. Each dyad played with a clear, plastic box containing an attractive toy retrievable through a latched door for 6 minutes, after which the mother withdrew from play and sat away from the child with a neutral facial expression. Overall, the preterm infant played at a low level with the toy, had difficulty balancing sustained attention on both the toy and mother, rarely attempted to engage the mother during the still-face episode, and exhibited minimal affect. The full-term infant was more active and engaged with the mother, and demonstrated more affective involvement and interest in the toy and the mother than the preterm infant. Even though the preterm infant had reached the same developmental level as the full term infant at 5 months of age as assessed by the Bayley scales, clearly the behavioral organization of the preterm infant is quite different from that of the full term infant. It appears that assessments measuring the process or approach used by an infant when faced with a problem task provide a better appraisal of preterm infants' developmental level than those measuring the product/result, such as the Bayley scales.

Similar results were reported by Howard et al. (1989), using a sample of 18 drug-exposed infants at 18 months of age. As previously mentioned, these infants had significantly lower developmental outcomes, but scored within the low average range. However, when assessed using an unstructured play situation, deficits in representational play were more apparent in the drug-exposed sample in comparison with a high-risk preterm sample. The play of the drug-exposed toddlers consisted of "scattering, batting, and picking up and putting down the toys" instead of demonstrating a higher level of play by exploring the toys' properties, using the toys in pretend play, or combining the toys in play. This is another example supporting the view that the Bayley scales are not an adequate assessment of developmental level when used alone.

Ruff (1986) found that high-risk infants differed from full-term infants in how they react to and examine a new toy. A sample of 17 preterm infants and 24 full-term infants at 7 months of age were given six toy objects to examine for a period of one minute per object. Behaviors such as examining (e.g., looking, manipulating, focusing on the toy), mouthing, and banging as well as latency to respond to the object were coded for each object. The preterm infants spent significantly less time examining and exhibited fewer object-related behaviors. The full-term infants tended to follow an organized behavioral pattern when responding to a new object, while the preterm infants did not demonstrate any pattern or organization. In addition, there was a significant difference in latency to examine, with the full term infants having shorter latencies. These results are consistent with the Als and Brazelton case examples described previously, in that preterm infants are not very active and are less organized in their reaction to a novel object.

Another study assessed task persistence of premature infants and found continuity in this characteristic during the preschool period (Sigman, Cohen, Beckwith, & Topinka, 1987). A sample of 43 two-year-old preterm infants was given two separate toy tasks: a clear, plastic box containing a toy accessible by unfastening the wooden peg latch and a wooden puzzle with various geometric shapes that could be removed using the attached handles except for one, which required reaching for a handle that was out of view. Task persistence was measured as the total time focused on the task prior to the examiner demonstrating the solution of the task and the total time focused on the task after the demonstration. The children were also coded for the number of times they requested help from the examiner and their mothers.

The children who were more focused on the tasks before and after the demonstrations had fewer requests for help from the examiner, had longer latencies before requesting help from their mothers, and were rated by their mothers, using the Conners rating scale (Conners, 1989), at 3 and 5 years of age, as being more likely to finish their work. In addition, task persistence on the box task was significantly related to developmental level as measured by the Gesell Scale (Knobloch & Pasamanick, 1974) at 2 years of age ($r = .32$, $p < .05$), and a strong correlation was found between task persistence after demonstration of the solution of the puzzle to the Stanford–Binet IQ scores at age 3 years ($r = .67$, $p < .05$) and at age 5 years ($r = .37$, $p < .05$). It was concluded that task persistence is stable between 2 to 5 years of age and may be an important factor as children learn more skills and become more competent as they advance developmentally.

Significant group differences on "task involvement" were found between two chronically ill samples and a healthy comparison sample (Goldberg, Washington, Morris, Fischer-Fay, & Simmons, 1990). At 12 months of age, infants diagnosed with cystic fibrosis (CF) or with congenital heart disease (CHD) were less persistent, less compliant, and less positive when provided with a puzzle task to complete with their mothers. The outcomes of the CF group were the most discrepant from those of the healthy sample, while the CHD outcomes fell in the middle. When the mother's age and education were covaried, some of the differences remained, but to a lesser extent. However, the above differences did not appear when the Bayley MDI score was used as a covariate, implying that there was a correlation between the infant's developmental level and the dyad's interactive style. This is consistent with the result that mothers of the CHD infants provided more structure during the puzzle task than the mothers of the other two groups.

Many of these studies assessing object play measured behaviors similar to those that compose mastery motivation, such as object-related behaviors, affective involvement, and interest in and persistence at a task. It is apparent that perinatal risk infants tend to be at a lower level or delayed in these areas, despite being at a comparable developmental level when matched to full-term or normally developing infants. Since this population seems to have a different behavioral organization that cannot be detected by the Bayley scales, it would be important to use an assessment that measures an infant's approach to play and problem tasks, such as mastery motivation, in conjunction with cognitive measures to better evaluate perinatal risk infants.

REVIEW OF MASTERY MOTIVATION STUDIES

The concept of mastery motivation has been refined over the past decade (see Morgan & Harmon, 1984; Morgan, Harmon, & Maslin-Cole, 1990; Morgan et al., MacTurk et al., Barrett & Morgan, chapters 1, 2, 3, this volume). Our research group has defined mastery motivation as "a psychological force that stimulates an individual to attempt independently, in a focused and persistent manner, to solve a problem or master a skill or task which is at least moderately challenging for him or her" (Morgan et al., 1990, p. 319). Barrett and Morgan (this volume) describe mastery motivation as comprised of "instrumental and expressive" components. The instrumental component, in part, refers to an individual's persistence at a difficult task, preference for physical and/or mental control of the events in his/her environment, and interest in moderately challenging and/or novel tasks or situations. Using ratings of persistence during several types of play, the instrumental component has been divided into three domains: persistence at object-oriented, social/symbolic, and gross-motor tasks (Morgan et al., 1993). The expressive component refers to the emotional aspects and attentiveness as expressed in "facial, vocal, postural, and behavioral communication of pleasure, interest, pride, and/or frustration/anger, sadness, and shame" (Barrett & Morgan, this volume). As children develop, these two components (instrumental and expressive) are ongoing characteristics of mastery motivation, but the specific behavioral indicators associated with them change to incorporate recently acquired abilities.

Various assessment methods of mastery motivation have been developed and utilized (see review by MacTurk, Morgan, & Jennings, this volume). The senior author of this chapter has been involved in the development and implementation of three types of assessments, which will be described below. Despite the growing use of these assessments in research studies, there are few published results that evaluate mastery motivation in perinatal risk infants. The findings of these studies indicate that perinatal risk infants tend to demonstrate less mastery motivation, even when they are functioning at a comparable developmental level. The specific research studies are described by the type of assessment in the following sections.

FREE PLAY ASSESSMENT

One of the assessments—free play—requires having the infant play with toys independently in an unstructured setting while the mother is occupied with an examiner and instructed not to interact with her infant unless the infant initiates the interaction. The infant's sustained, high-level play (similar to task persistence) as well as the infant's affective and social behavior are coded (Jennings, Harmon, Morgan, Gaiter, & Yarrow, 1979; Morgan et al., 1991). In a study by the senior author (Harmon & Culp, 1981; Harmon, Morgan, & Glicken, 1984) of 30 full term and 29 low birth weight infants evaluated at 12 months of age, it was concluded that the preterm infants were less active and explored the room less than the full term infants as indicated by staying close to their mothers (see Table 10.1).

The preterm infants were not significantly different in the amount of active play from the full term infants, although there

TABLE 10.1. COMPARISON OF THE FREE PLAY OF FULL TERM AND PRETERM (< 1500 GM) INFANTS AT ONE YEAR GESTATIONAL AGE

| | Means | | | |
	Preterm N = 29	Full term N = 30	t-test	ANCOVA[a]
Activity Level & Play				
Activity Level	7.07	14.79	-3.48***	7.01**
Active Play	39.69	38.82	.60	.37
High Level Play	13.10	17.15	-1.64*	.08
Mother–Child Relationship				
Proximity and contact with mother	18.76	11.44	2.25**	5.95**
Interest in mother	10.03	15.15	-4.38***	11.14***
Mother initiation	4.10	1.72	2.31**	3.54

* $p \leq .10$
** $p \leq .05$
*** $p \leq .001$
[a] Analysis of Covariance with Bayley MDI as covariate

was a trend for them to show less "high level" or quality play. The preterm infants also exhibited less interest in their mothers, even though they were more likely to remain near or in contact with them, perhaps because the mothers tended to initiate interaction with their infants and hence keep them nearby.

Similar to the Goldberg et al. (1990) study, this pattern of mother–child interaction remained after controlling for the differences in the Bayley MDI outcomes with ANCOVA, implying that the interactive style of high risk dyads is affected more by perinatal risk status than by infants' cognitive level. These results support the findings of the case examples described previously (Als & Brazelton, 1981) that preterm infants tend not to engage or show as much interest in their mothers as full-term infants and are minimally active in their play behaviors. It should be noted that the trend toward difference in the quality of play disappeared when using the Bayley MDI scores as a covariate.

Morgan, Maslin, Ridgeway, and Kang-Park (1988) found that affective interchanges between a mother and child seem to affect the child's task-directed play. Children who demonstrated more task-directed behavior and pleasure in their play experienced more positive dyadic interactions with their mothers. On the other hand, if the mother–child interaction was negative or had mixed affect, the child exhibited less motivation and pleasure.

STRUCTURED TASKS ASSESSMENT

The second mastery motivation assessment involves a series of mastery tasks. The infant is allowed to explore and attempt to master specific problem-posing, challenging toys for 3–5 minutes each, with limited help or encouragement from the examiner, after a demonstration of some properties of each toy. The mother is instructed not to encourage or initiate interaction and to respond minimally, even if the infant bids for her attention. Of particular interest is the infant's affect and task-directed behavior, or persistence, toward the toys. The concern is not whether the infant is successful, but rather to what extent there is sustained effort by the infant to complete a portion of the task. Morgan, Busch-Rossnagel, Maslin-Cole, and Harmon (1992) developed an individualized procedure for administering tasks that were moderately difficult to each child. These tasks were be classified into three categories that: (a) produce auditory and/or visual effects; (b) require parts of a toy to be combined or disassembled appropriately; and (c) entail bypassing an obstacle or barrier in order to obtain a goal. Chapter 2 of this volume describes several similar structured methods used in studies of mastery motivation.

In the previously mentioned study (Harmon & Culp, 1981; Harmon et al., 1984), preterm infants demonstrated less task-directed behavior (persistence), tended to do relatively more exploration of the tasks, exhibited less positive affect, and were slower and not as effective in solving the tasks as the full-term infants (see Table 10.2). These results are consistent with the findings that preterm infants show less affective expression/reactivity, have longer latencies before acting on tasks, and exhibit less relational play behaviors (Als & Brazelton, 1981; DiPietro & Porges, 1991; Ruff, 1986).

When the data was reanalyzed using the Bayley MDI scores as covariates, the difference in task pleasure, particularly the amount of smiling on achieving the solution of a task, remained significant (latency to solution remained a trend difference). However, the persistence and, as expected, the competence differences were no longer significant. These results are consistent with Hauser-Cram (1992), who found differences in positive affect but not task persistence when using the individualized mastery task method, which equates for competence level, with developmentally delayed toddlers.

TABLE 10.2.   COMPARISON OF MASTERY TASKS OF PRETERM (< 1500 GM) AND FULL TERM INFANTS AT ONE YEAR GESTATIONAL AGE

	Preterms N = 29	Full terms N = 30	ANOVA	ANCOVA[a]
General Exploration	30.34	22.16	18.40***	3.56*
Mastery Motivation				
Persistence	75.00	82.20	13.85***	.07
Ratio of Persistence				
to Exploration	3.12	5.59	3.30*	1.25
Mastery Pleasure	.51	2.76	8.86***	4.98**
Competence				
Latency to Solution	59.00	46.13	4.55**	2.96*
Intervals with Solution	46.72	58.50	18.37***	1.10

* $p \leq .10$
** $p \leq .05$
*** $p \leq .01$
[a] Analysis of Covariance with Bayley MDI as covariate

The performance on mastery tasks by preterm infants has been shown to improve when they have been part of an intervention program. In a study by Butterfield and Miller (1984), 12 out of 24 families of medium-risk preterm infants received intervention services through monthly visits during the first year by a psychologist and/or a neonatal nurse. The purpose of the visits was to help the families relate to and interact with their infants, to realistically anticipate their infant's developmental stages, and to address their concerns. At 12 months of age, the intervention infants were more persistent with the tasks, showed more mastery pleasure, reacted to the task quicker, and demonstrated a variety of task-directed behaviors.

A similar intervention program, which provided educational and family services, was also found to improve the cognitive level of high-risk infants younger than 36 months in age (Brooks-Gunn, Liaw, & Klebanov, 1992). One-third of a large sample of low birth weight infants (LBW) (N = 985) received intervention services, which included pediatric follow-up care, home visits, child care, and parent group meetings; the rest of the sample only received the pediatric follow-up care. The sample was also subdivided into groups based on birth weight: lighter LBW and heavier LBW infants. At 24 months, intervention infants had significantly higher Bayley MDI scores, with the largest difference being in visual–motor and spatial skills. In relation to birth weight, the heavier LBW infants benefited more from the intervention program than the lighter LBW infants. The effects of the intervention program continued when the infants were evaluated at 36 months, with the heavier LBW being more developmentally advanced than the lighter LBW infants. The ethnic minority children in the sample (blacks and Hispanics) benefited more from the intervention program than the children in the white/other group at 36 months. If the infants in this study had been evaluated for mastery motivation, we predict that these group differences (birth weight and ethnicity) would have also been found.

ADULT REPORT QUESTIONNAIRE

The third assessment tool for assessing mastery motivation is the Dimensions of Mastery Questionnaire (DMQ), which obtains an adult's (i.e., a parent or teacher) perception of the mastery behavior of an infant or preschool-aged child. The current version of the questionnaire is comprised of 31 items and assesses five dimensions of mastery motivation: object, social/symbolic, and gross motor persistence; mastery pleasure; and general competence. Earlier versions of the appropriate DMQ scales have proven to be modest predictors of task persistence and pleasure and relatively good predictors of the Bayley MDI scale (see review in Morgan et al., 1993; MacTurk, Morgan, & Jennings, this volume).

One of the reasons for the development of the DMQ is that Harmon and Culp (1981) found that mothers of premature infants talked about their children differently than mothers of low-risk infants. Thus, it seemed desirable to have an instrument that could assess differences in mothers' perceptions of their child's mastery behavior. Harmon and Culp (1981) predicted that high-risk mothers would perceive their children as being less motivated, even though behavioral observations of the children resulted in small differences.

Using an earlier version of the DMQ, this prediction was confirmed when the results of three samples of infants as reported in Harmon et al. (1984) were compared. The groups were: (a) low-risk or normally developing infants; (b) premature infants who received intervention; and (c) nonintervention premature infants (Butterfield & Miller, 1984) (see Table 10.3). The nonintervention infants were reported by their mothers as being less persistent than the low-risk and intervention infants. The low-risk infants received higher ratings for preference of challenge and novelty. These findings are consistent with those just described for very low birth weight premature infants.

SUMMARY

Recent studies of cognitive development and mastery motivation of perinatal risk infants, particularly premature infants, have been reviewed. It is apparent that using a cognitive assessment alone does not sufficiently describe and evaluate the developmental level and behavioral organization of this population. Although perinatal risk infants seem to be functioning at a similar cognitive level in comparison to full term/low risk infants, these infants have been found to be less likely to explore and actively play with toys, have fewer object-related behaviors, to be unfocused, and have fewer affective expres-

TABLE 10.3. COMPARISON OF MOTHERS' PERCEPTIONS OF MASTERY BEHAVIOR OF LOW- AND MEDIUM-RISK 12-MONTH-OLD INFANTS WITH AND WITHOUT INTERVENTION

	Means				t-Tests		
	GI $N = 17$	GII $N = 12$	GIII $N = 12$	F	GI vs. GIII	GI vs. GIII	GII vs. GIII
MOMM Cluster							
Persistence	11.0	11.2	9.6	*	NS	*	*
Prefers Challenge	18.9	16.3	15.9	*	*	**	*
Self-Produced Interest	11.4	10.5	10.6	NS	NS	NS	NS
Independent Mastery	19.6	18.3	17.8	NS	NS	NS	NS
Independent Judgment	11.3	10.4	10.6	NS	NS	NS	NS
Exploration	11.6	12.1	11.8	NS	**	NS	NS
Prefers Novel	12.3	9.9	10.3	*	**	**	NS

GI—Low risk full term infants
GII—Medium risk (mostly preterm) infants with intervention
GIII—Medium risk (mostly preterm) infants without intervention
* $p \leq .05$
** $p \leq .01$
Note: This table is adapted from Morgan, Harmon, Pipp, & Jennings (1983).

sions. They also demonstrate disinterest in their mothers despite remaining in close proximity to them. In addition, mothers of these infants reported their children as being less persistent with problem-solving tasks. We believe that in order to adequately describe an infant's development, it is important to utilize an assessment that measures multiple aspects of an infant's behavior, including the mastery motivation instruments described in this chapter (and volume), to better predict developmental outcome of these perinatal risk infants.

REFERENCES

Als, H., & Brazelton, T. B. (1981). A new model of assessing the behavioral organization in preterm and fullterm infants. *Journal of the American Academy of Child Psychiatry, 20*, 239–263.

Barrera, M. E., Rosenbaum, P. L., & Cunningham, C. E. (1987). Corrected and uncorrected Bayley scores: Longitudinal developmental patterns in low and high birth weight preterm infants. *Infant Behavior and Development, 10*, 337–346.

Bayley, N. (1969). *The Bayley Scales of Infant Development*. New York: Psychological Corporation.

Brazelton, T. B. (1973). *Neonatal Behavioral Assessment Scale*. London: Heinemann.

Brooks-Gunn, J., Liaw, F., & Klebanov, P. K. (1992). Effects of early intervention on cognitive function of low birth weight preterm infants. *Journal of Pediatrics, 120*, 350–359.

Butterfield, P. M., & Miller, L. (1984). Read your baby: A follow-up intervention program for parents with NICU infants. *Infant Mental Health Journal, 5*(2), 107–116.

Cohen, S. E., Parmelee, A. H., Beckwith, L., & Sigman, M. (1986). Cognitive development in preterm infants: Birth to 8 years. *Developmental and Behavioral Pediatrics, 7*(2), 102–110.

Conners, C. K. (1989). *Manual for Conner's Rating Scales*. New York: Multi-Health Systems.

Crnic, K. A., Ragozin, A. S., Greenberg, M. T., Robinson, N. M., & Basham, R. B. (1983). Social interaction and developmental competence of preterm and full-term infants during the first year of life. *Child Development, 54*, 1199–1210.

DiPietro, J. A., & Porges, S. W. (1991). Relations between neonatal states and 8-month developmental outcome in preterm infants. *Infant Behavior and Development, 14*, 441–450.

Fischer-Fay, A., Goldberg, S., Simmons, R., & Levinson, H. (1988). Chronic illness and infant–mother attachment: Cystic fibrosis. *Journal of Developmental and Behavioral Pediatrics, 9*(5), 266–270

Goldberg, S., Washington, J., Morris, P., Fischer-Fay, A., & Simmons, R. J. (1990). Early diagnosed chronic illness and mother–child relationships in the first two years. *Canadian Journal of Psychiatry, 35*(9), 726–733.

Harmon, R. J., & Culp, A. M. (1981). The effects of premature birth on family functioning and infant development. In I. Berlin (Ed.), *Children and our future* (pp. 1–9). Albuquerque: University of New Mexico Press.

Harmon, R. J., Glicken, A. D., & Good, W. V. (1982). A new look at maternal–infant bonding: Implications for perinatal practice. *Perinatalogy–Neonatology, 5*, 27–31.

Harmon, R. J., Morgan, G. A., & Glicken, A. D. (1984). Continuities and discontinuities in affective and cognitive–motivational development. *Child Abuse and Neglect, 8*, 157–167.

Hauser-Cram, P. (1992). *Mastery motivation in toddlers with developmental disabilities.* Manuscript submitted for publication.

Howard, J., Beckwith, L., Rodning, C., & Kropenske, V. (1989). The development of young children of substance-abusing parents: Insights from seven years of intervention and research. *Zero to Three, 9*(5), 8–12.

Jennings, K., Harmon, R., Morgan, G., Gaiter, J., & Yarrow, L. (1979). Exploratory play as an index of mastery motivation: Relationships of persistence, cognitive functioning and environmental measures. *Developmental Psychology, 15*, 386–394.

Kieckhefer, G. M., & Dinno, N. (1992). Neurodevelopmental outcomes and family needs of infants born mothers with a history of substance abuse. *Newsletter of the Clearinghouse for Drug Exposed Children, 3*(4), 1–5.

Klaus, M. H., & Kennel, J. H. (1982). *Parent–infant bonding* (2nd ed.). St. Louis, MO: C. V. Mosby Co.

Knobloch, H., & Pasamanick, B. (Eds). (1974). *Gesell and Amatruda's developmental diagnosis* (3rd edition). Hagerstown, MD: Harper & Row.

Krall, V. & Feinstein, S. C. (1991). *Psychological development of high risk multiple birth children.* Chur, Switzerland: Harwood.

Ludman, W. L., Halperin, J. M., Driscoll, J. M., Driscoll, Y. T., & Belmont, I. (1987). Birth weight, respiratory distress syndrome, and cognitive development. *American Journal of Diseases of Children, 141*(1), 79–83.

Macey, T. J., Harmon, R. J., & Easterbrooks, M. A. (1987). Impact of premature birth on the development of the infant in the family. *Journal of Consulting and Clinical Psychology, 55*(6), 846–852.

Morgan, G. A., Busch-Rossnagel, N. A., Maslin-Cole, C. A., & Harmon, R. J. (1992). *Mastery motivation tasks: Manual for 15- to 36-month-old children.* New York: Fordham University.

Morgan, G. A., & Harmon, R. J. (1984). Developmental transformations in mastery motivation: Measurement and validation. In R. N.

Emde & R. J. Harmon (Eds.), *Continuities and discontinuities in development* (pp. 263–291). New York: Plenum.

Morgan, G. A., Harmon, R. J., & Maslin-Cole, C. A. (1990). Mastery motivation: Definition and measurement. *Early Education and Development, 1*(5), 318–339.

Morgan, G. A., Harmon, R. J., Pipp, S., & Jennings, K. D. (1983). *Assessing mother's perceptions of mastery motivation: The utility of the MOMM questionnaire.* Unpublished manuscript, Colorado State University, Fort Collins, CO.

Morgan, G. A., Maslin, C. A., Ridgeway, D., & Kang-Park, J. (1988). Toddler mastery motivation and aspects of mother–child affect communication (summary). *Program and proceedings of the Developmental Psychobiology Research Group Fifth Biennial Retreat, 5,* 15–16.

Morgan, G. A., Maslin-Cole, C. A., Biringen, A., & Harmon, R. J. (1991). Play assessment of mastery motivation in infants and young children. In C. E. Schaefer, K. Gitlin, & A. Sandgrund (Eds.), *Play diagnosis & assessment* (pp. 65–86). New York: Wiley.

Morgan, G. A., Maslin-Cole, C. A., Harmon, R. J., Busch-Rossnagel, N. A., Jennings, K. D., Hauser-Cram, P., & Brockman, L. (1993). Parent and teacher perceptions of young children's mastery motivation: Assessment and review of research. In D. Messer (Ed.), *Mastery motivation in early childhood: Development, measurement and social processes* (pp. 109–131). London: Routledge.

Parmelee, A. H. (1975). Neurophysiological and behavioral organization of premature infants in the first months of life. *Biological Psychiatry, 10,* 501–512.

Redding, R. E., Morgan, G. A., & Harmon, R. J. (1988). Mastery motivation in infants and toddlers: Is it greatest when tasks are moderately challenging? *Infant Behavior and Development, 11,* 419–430.

Ross, G. (1985). Use of the Bayley Scales to characterize abilities of premature infants. *Child Development, 56,* 835–842.

Ruff, H. A. (1986). Attention and organization of behavior in high-risk infants. *Developmental and Behavioral Pediatrics, 7*(5), 298–301

Sigman, M., Cohen, S. E., Beckwith, L., & Topinka, C. (1987). Task persistence in 2-year-old preterm infants in relation to subsequent attentiveness and intelligence. *Infant Behavior and Development, 10,* 295–305.

Sostek, A. M., Smith, Y. F., Katz, K. S., & Grant, E. G. (1987). Developmental outcome of preterm infants with intraventricular hemorrhage at one and two years of age. *Child Development, 58,* 779–786.

Weston, D. R., Ivins, B., Zuckerman, B., Jones, C., & Lopez, R. (1989). Drug exposed babies: Research and clinical issues. *Zero to Three, 9*(5), 1–7.

Yarrow, L. J., McQuiston, S., MacTurk, R. H., McCarthy, M. E., Klein, R. P., & Vietze, P. M. (1983). Assessment of mastery motivation during the first year of life: Contemporaneous and cross-age relationships. *Developmental Psychology, 19,* 159–171.

Yarrow, L. J., Morgan, G. A., Jennings, K. D., Harmon, R. J., & Gaiter, J. L. (1982). Infants' persistence at tasks: Relationships to cognitive functioning and early experience. *Infant Behavior and Development, 5,* 131–142.

11

MASTERY MOTIVATION: IMPLICATIONS FOR INTERVENTION*

Penny Hauser-Cram

Boston College, School of Education

Jack P. Shonkoff

Brandeis University, Florence Heller Graduate School

The concept of early childhood intervention has undergone a dramatic evolution over the past several decades. To a large extent, the most fundamental changes in the service delivery agenda have been guided by sociopolitical forces and the efforts of tireless advocates. Concurrently, scholars have broadened the available knowledge base by pushing both the theoretical and empirical boundaries of the study of children's development. This chapter will examine the extent to which our growing understanding of the construct of mastery motivation can contribute to the ongoing development of more sophisticated models of intervention for children with delayed or atypical development and their families.

―――――――――

*Support for the preparation of this chapter was provided by Grant No. MCJ–250583 from the Maternal and Child Health Bureau (Title V, Social Security Act), U.S. Department of Health and Human Services.

THE HISTORICAL ROOTS OF EARLY CHILDHOOD INTERVENTION

Traditional special education efforts typically trace their origins to the work of Edouard Seguin in the 19th century (Crissey, 1975). Beginning in Paris, and subsequently through the promotion of his techniques in the United States, Seguin developed a "physiological method of education" for individuals with disabilities that was based on the use of sensorimotor activities to treat specific developmental deficits in young children. For Seguin and his followers, treatment for children with disabilities was most effective when it was based on the promotion of specific skills and when it was initiated as early as possible.

The modern era of early childhood intervention in the United States began in the 1960s. Building on President Kennedy's commitment to expanded educational opportunities for individuals with mental retardation, the enactment of the Handicapped Children's Early Education Assistance Act in 1968 (Public Law 90–538) provided federal resources for the development, evaluation, and replication of programs for young children with disabilities. During this period of creative energy and heightened advocacy, the prototypical approach to the education of vulnerable children (e.g., the Portage Project) remained firmly focused on the facilitation of discrete skill development (Shearer & Shearer, 1976). Staffed by a variety of early childhood disciplines, and anchored to a range of educational and therapeutic orientations, the pioneering intervention programs of the 1960s were focused on teaching children specific sensorimotor and functional skills. Parental participation in service delivery was variable, and some therapeutic interventions were provided to young children in the absence of any active involvement by their parents.

ASSESSING CHILDREN'S DEVELOPMENT: THE CONSTRAINTS OF TRADITIONAL MEASURES

The assessment of competence in children with developmental vulnerabilities and the measurement of child change over time have been embedded within the context of a fundamental tension in the technology of early childhood assessment. This tension arises from the fact that traditional standardized measures do not always address the most salient aspects of child competence, and the features of development that are fundamental to learning (such as attentional processes) have been extremely difficult to assess. The unfortunate consequence has been a tendency to avoid measurement of constructs that often are deemed most important and to assign exaggerated importance (by default) to those domains that are relatively easy to measure (such as motor skill acquisition).

The legacy of this dilemma has been the predominance of standardized measures of intelligence and tests of specific skill acquisition. For example, we conducted a meta-analysis of efficacy studies of early intervention services for children with biologically based disabilities under 3 years of age and found that 51% of the measured effects were assessments of standardized developmental quotients or IQ, 15% were measures of motor skills, and 12% were assessments of specific language abilities (Shonkoff & Hauser-Cram, 1987). Less than 1% of the outcomes evaluated caregiver–child interaction, and none of the studied outcomes measured underlying developmental processes.

The limitations of standardized intelligence/developmental tests for atypical populations have been noted repeatedly for decades (Cicchetti & Wagner, 1990; Shonkoff, 1983). More fundamentally, such measures are typically normed on populations that exclude children with documented disabilities or known atypical performance. The validity of such instruments for assessing the "mental" abilities of young children with motor deficits or sensory impairments is particularly well known, yet these measures continue to be used despite their acknowledged inappropriateness.

In view of the limitations of traditional developmental tests for understanding the mechanisms of change in children, it is reasonable to ask why such measures continue to be used by investigators who are aware of this dilemma. Perhaps the strongest influences on this practice are the well documented psychometric properties and associated "respectability" of the standardized IQ. Although scholars have debated endlessly about the meaning of the construct of intelligence, policymakers and the lay public accept the general concept as having considerable face validity.

Until recently, standardized measures of intelligence, developmental level, or specific skill acquisition also received widespread acceptance in the early intervention community because they generally reflected the goals of service programs. That is to say, the objectives of traditional intervention programs for children with disabilities were embedded in a "curriculum" that typically focused on the development of many of the specific skills that are required to perform well on standardized developmental tests. However, as the goals of early intervention services have shifted from child-focused skill development to family-focused promotion of broad domains of child and parent competence, the relevance of many traditional measures has been increasingly questioned. It is within this context that the crisis in child assessment has become more acute and the demands for alternative assessment strategies have intensified.

A New Agenda for Intervention and Assessment

The recent transformation of early intervention services for young children with developmental disabilities represents a radical departure from traditional therapeutic models of care. For children, the concept of competence as a service objective now extends far beyond the development of skills for stacking blocks or completion of form boards. For the parents of children with special developmental needs, professional service providers are seen increasingly as potential partners in a collaborative effort rather than as authoritarian dispensers of specific treatment protocols. Perhaps of greatest importance, the development of children and the adaptation of their families are now viewed as dynamic processes that unfold within a series of interactive contexts that involve the intimate domains of primary caregiving and extended family relationships, as well as community-based dimensions that include formal services, informal support, and the cultural milieu (Bronfenbrenner, Moen, & Garbarino, 1984).

The essential elements of the new agenda for early intervention services for developmentally vulnerable children are reflected in the original provisions of the Education for All Handicapped Children Act Amendments of 1986 (Public Law 99–457), and the 1991 Amendments to the renamed Individuals with Disabilities Education Act (IDEA) (Public Law 102–119). Under current federal mandates, early intervention services must be highly individualized and guided by family-centered service plans (Hauser-Cram, Upshur, Krauss, & Shonkoff, 1988). Because child-oriented goals are now defined jointly by parents and professionals, service programs tend to focus more on promoting abilities that have functional significance in everyday life and less on arbitrary "splinter skills" that have relevance primarily in a structured testing situation. Consequently, the processes of development and the mediators of individual differences are of equal, if not greater, interest than specific skill acquisition. For example, *how* a child approaches a problem-posing task may be viewed with greater interest than *whether* he or she "passes" the test item.

Within this framework, the concept of mastery motivation has considerable salience. As a fundamental substrate for learning across multiple developmental domains, it represents a key focus for intervention efforts. Thus, the way in which a child approaches a challenging situation may serve as a highly sensitive measure of the learning process and as an important marker of his or her prognosis for future successful engagement in intellectual challenges. Indeed, one potential contribution afforded by the assessment of mastery motivation in children with developmental disabilities is a greater understanding of the extent to which this domain of competence reflects individual differences in the style and organization of behavior—what experienced clinicians often refer to as the "quality" of a child's performance. For many children with moderate to severe disabilities, such qualitative differences can be observed from one evaluation session to another and may serve as a more useful metric of change than simply recording whether the child is able to successfully "pass" specific test items. The need for a broader understanding of the influence of mastery motivation on the development of young children with delays or disabilities is implicated further by the well-documented literature on general passivity in children with mental retardation (Hupp, this volume).

Although it appears that they are not less motivated as infants (MacTurk, Hunter, McCarthy, Vietze, & McQuiston, 1985) or toddlers (Hauser-Cram, in press), older children with cognitive delays often appear to have increasing difficulties in maintaining high levels of motivation for challenging tasks (Harter & Zigler, 1974). At school age, such children typically exhibit high rates of "learned helplessness" and low rates of self-reliant problem-solving activity (Weisz, 1979). Thus, although supportive empirical data are unavailable, it would be reasonable to hypothesize that a targeted focus by service providers and caregivers on children's early motivation to master tasks might prevent later motivational decline in youngsters with cognitive impairments. The implications of such speculation fit well with current models of early intervention that concentrate on caregivers' facilitation of children's development and the social milieu in which motivation is reinforced (Krauss & Hauser-Cram, 1992). In this context, further study of mastery motivation in young children is likely to generate useful data that can inform the way in which intervention services might enhance the investment of vulnerable infants and toddlers in the process of mastering challenging developmental tasks.

RESEARCH ON THE RELATION BETWEEN CAREGIVER–CHILD INTERACTION AND MASTERY MOTIVATION

The theoretical basis for research on aspects of caregiver–child interaction that affect the early development of mastery motivation derives largely from the work of Vygotsky (1978, 1986). According to his model, children develop greater independence in mastering tasks through a gradual acquisition process that evolves with the support of adult guidance during problem-solving activity. Generally speaking, caregivers facilitate children's learning by regulating activity that involves a joint focus. Over time, and most typically during the second year of life, caregivers reduce the provision of direct assistance and prompt their children to take more independent responsibility (Heckhausen, 1987). During this process of supporting the child to take action that is increasingly self-reliant, caregivers also encourage the child to attain a level of performance just slightly above that which was demonstrated previously. Ideally, this is facilitated through the caregiver's ability to break down the task into various components that can be presented to the child in such a way as to maintain a balance of success and challenge (Wood, Bruner, & Ross, 1976). Heckhausen (1987) has termed this phenomenon the "one-step-ahead" approach. In recent years, a growing empirical data base focused on the way in which the guided participation of caregivers affects children's learning has emerged as a central theme in the study of child development (e.g., Diaz, Neal, & Amaya-Williams, 1990; Rogoff, Malkin, & Gilbride, 1984).

Based on Vygotsky's general view of the development of self-regulation in learning, Heckhausen (1993) suggested the following model for the emergence of mastery motivation within the caregiver–child dyad during the first few years of life: First, infants gradually develop an awareness of behavior–event contingencies through their initial recruitment into such activities by their primary caregivers. Heckhausen speculated that such awareness is a precursor of mastery motivation. Over time, the infant strives for action–contingent outcomes and achieves success with the guided assistance of his or her caregiver. The caregiver, in turn, provides an emotionally positive setting and attends to the child's goals so that such goals become mutual. Gradually, perhaps around nine months of age, the child shifts from enjoyment of action to competent problem solving (Barrett, Morgan, & Maslin-Cole, 1993). This shift is marked by the child's transition from reliance on exploratory activities (demarcated by the enjoyment of action) to more goal-oriented behavior. MacTurk and his colleagues (MacTurk, McCarthy, Vietze, & Yarrow, 1987) maintained that such persistent goal-directed behavior, which is often displayed by about 12 months of age, contributes to the infant's feeling of efficacy.

During the second year of life, children become aware of their own success, and anticipation of success eventually serves as a motivating source that frees them from complete reliance on adults (Heckhausen, 1993). According to Jennings (1991), children come to view themselves as independent agents through mastery-motivated actions. Thus, the "self as agent" is an important part of understanding oneself as an autonomous originator of action and is linked closely to the construction of positive self-regard. Consequently, by the end of the second year, children often protest against offers of help that might serve to diminish their own sense of competence on problem-posing tasks (Geppert & Kuster, 1983). Indeed, this emergence of "wanting to do it oneself" by 2 years of age may be a critical precursor of motivation to master intellectual challenges.

Empirical evidence on the relation between the characteristics of caregivers and the development of competence in their children has generally supported this theoretical model (Busch-Rossnagel, Knauf & DesRosiers, this volume). Within this framework, three critical aspects of caregiver behavior have been found to influence children's mastery motivation: the amount and type of stimulation provided, support of autonomy, and the demonstration of positive affect.

Amount and Type of Stimulation

During the first year of life, the amount and variety of stimulation provided by caregivers has been demonstrated to correlate with children's exploration and examination of the world of objects. For example, Yarrow and his colleagues (Yarrow et al., 1984) found sensory stimulation to be related to the persistence demonstrated by young children (especially boys) in attempting to master sensorimotor skills. In a prospective study, Yarrow, Morgan, Jennings, Harmon, and Gaiter (1982) found aspects of the social environment of infants at 6 months of age to predict persistence and competence at 13 months. With respect to mastery motivation, they also reported that mothers who provided more kinesthetic and auditory stimulation and engaged in more social mediation of their infants' play (with smiles and vocalizations) had children who were more persistent at mastery motivation tasks. In a longer term study, Gaiter, Morgan, Jennings, Harmon, and Yarrow (1982) found that the variety of cognitively oriented caregiver activities at 1 year of age predicted persistence at tasks at age 3½ years. Morgan et al. (1992) (in Barrett, Morgan, & Maslin-Cole, 1993) reported contemporaneous correlations between the amount and variety of mother–infant play and children's task persistence and mastery pleasure.

Tempering these findings, however, other studies have demonstrated that too much maternal stimulation may have negative consequences for children's later motivation to solve problems independently. For example, in an attempt to explain why preterm infants were found to have lower levels of mastery motivation in comparison to their 12-month-old full-term peers, Harmon, Morgan, and Glicken (1984) hypothesized that the preterm infants had been exposed to higher levels of maternal stimulation during the first year of life and that such levels of stimulation were associated with less self-initiation and less awareness of personal impact on the environment by the child. Similarly, Hauser-Cram (1993) found that 3-year-old children with Down syndrome living in homes with high levels of maternal involvement in structuring children's play had lower levels of mastery motivation on challenging tasks. Thus, the nature of the stimulation and involvement provided by caregivers, rather than the amount, may be more critical variables in understanding their influences on children's mastery motivation.

Support of Autonomy

Appreciating individual differences in the interactional styles displayed by caregivers when engaged in tasks with their children is essential to understanding the relation between children's social environment and their motivation to master tasks. A consistent finding that emerged in a study of infants at 12 months (Grolnick, Frodi, & Bridges, 1984) and 20 months of age (Frodi, Bridges, & Grolnick, 1985) is that children whose mothers supported their autonomous striving to master challenging tasks were more persistent than those whose mothers were controlling. The latter behaviors were characterized by attempts to change the child's ongoing activity, whereas autonomy-oriented behaviors were reflected in actions designed to help the child maintain his or her ongoing activity (Frodi, Bridges, & Grolnick, 1985).

Bullock and Lutkenhaus (1990) suggested that parents who interfere with a child's efforts to succeed in a task essentially remove responsibility for success from the child and thereby diminish his or her sense of autonomy. Multiple studies of children's motivation to master tasks have supported this assertion, with consistent documentation that parental interference has a negative relation to children's independent persistence. Wachs (1987), for example, found that parental interference in their children's interaction with objects was associated with lower levels of mastery motivation on problem-posing tasks at 12 months of age. Similarly, Lutkenhaus (1984) reported that parents who physically interfered with their child's attempts to work on a challenging task had children who persisted less at 3 years of age.

Positive Affect

Although relatively few in number, studies assessing the relation between caregiver affect and children's mastery motivation have demonstrated the importance of both general affective tone (e.g., maternal depression or maternal warmth) and affective behavioral responses during specific exchanges. The literature on depression in caregivers (most often in mothers) suggests that this aspect of maternal affect has wide-ranging impacts on children's development. For example, Lyons-Ruth and her colleagues (Lyons-Ruth, Zoll, Connell, & Grunebaum, 1986) found children of depressed mothers to score lower on tests of general cognition; Breznitz and Friedman (1988) reported that children of depressed mothers displayed poorer attention to objects during spontaneous play; and Redding, Harmon, and Morgan

(1990) demonstrated that children with depressed mothers, unlike other children, persisted more at easy rather than difficult tasks and demonstrated less task competence and pleasure in all problem-posing situations.

Research on caregivers' (usually mothers') affect during joint task engagement or play episodes also shows a consistent pattern. Specifically, two aspects of maternal interaction have been noted to have important associations with child behavior. First, the extent to which mothers display warmth when interacting with their children has been reported to be related significantly to children's competence during play with objects (Jennings & Connors, 1989). Second, maternal contingent responsiveness has been found to be associated with optimal child development. Caregivers are said to be contingently responsive to their children if they are able to read the child's cues and respond appropriately to his or her cognitive and emotional needs. Castaldi, Hrncir, and Caldwell (1990) found maternal responsiveness during interactive play to be significantly associated with the level of spontaneous solitary play displayed by their one-year-old infants. Mothers who were sensitive to their children's affective bids tended to have children who were more competent in exploring the inanimate world independently. In contrast, negative mother–child affective exchanges during interactive play were found to relate to subsequent low persistence and competence ratings on mastery-motivation (Morgan, Maslin-Cole, Downing, & Harmon, 1990).

RESEARCH ON CAREGIVERS' INTERACTION WITH CHILDREN WHO ARE DELAYED IN THEIR DEVELOPMENT

The results of a number of studies of interaction between caregivers and their children with delayed development have converged on a common conclusion that contrasts with conventional knowledge of the interactional patterns that appear to promote mastery motivation. Specifically, caregivers of young children with atypical development tend to be more highly directive and controlling in their interactions than parents of typically developing children (Barnard & Kelly, 1990; Schneider & Gearhart, 1988). For example, Stoneman and her colleagues (Stoneman, Brody, & Abbot, 1983) characterized the parents of children with Down syndrome as "manager," "teacher," and "helper," in contrast to more egalitarian maternal roles observed in interactions of parents with children of typical intelligence. Jones (1977) found that mothers of infants with Down syndrome tended to be highly directive in exchanges with their child. Wasserman, Allen, and Solomon (1985) found that mothers of both premature children and children with physical disabilities initiated more interaction and were less responsive to their child's behavior than were other mothers. Eheart (1982) reported that mothers of preschoolers with mental retardation dominated a play session with their child to a greater extent than did other mothers. Similarly, Hanzlik and Stevenson (1986) reported that mothers of infants and young children with developmental delays were more directive in their interactions during free-play sessions at home than mothers of children developing typically.

The common tendency for caregivers of children with delayed development to be controlling in their interactions may be a natural reaction to the apparently less responsive behaviors of their children. Additionally, some intervention programs may promote directive and didactic exchanges between caregivers and their children by emphasizing the caregivers' educational responsibility. Indeed, intervention programs in the past often encouraged parents to provide stimulation to their infant and more recently emphasize the importance of parents as educational partners in the parent-child relationship (Spiker, 1990). However, the full extent to which early intervention services prompt parents to become more directive with their children has not been investigated. In fact, the very nature of the intervention process itself has not been delineated or studied sufficiently at the present time to fully understand its effect on caregiver–child interaction (Shonkoff, Hauser-Cram, Krauss, & Upshur, 1992).

MASTERY MOTIVATION: A FOCUS FOR FUTURE INTERVENTION EFFORTS

As early childhood intervention programs continue to evolve from a largely child-focused "treatment" model to a more family-ly-centered facilitative model, both service providers and caregivers would benefit from a greater understanding of the value of supporting children's motivation to master challenging tasks. Only one study to date has assessed the extent to which intervention efforts can assist parents to communicate with infants in ways that facilitate their independent mastery-motivation efforts. Butterfield and Miller (1984) reported on a strategy used with parents of preterm infants to help them experience positive and contingently responsive interactions with their infants by helping them to become better "baby watchers" (i.e., better able to understand their child's cues and behaviors). They found that 12-month-old infants whose parents had participated in the intervention program, in comparison to those whose parents had not participated, were more competent on standard measures of cognition and displayed higher levels of mastery motivation by persisting at challenging tasks.

Vygotsky's developmental model, which underscores the importance of social interaction and the benefits accrued from joint effort by the child and caregiver, offers early intervention service providers a framework within which caregivers can be encouraged to support their child's autonomy. In contrast to traditional "hand-over-hand" problem solving, in which the adult shows the child how to solve a problem, service providers and caregivers can be encouraged to think of ways to adapt the "one-step-ahead" theory to a variety of tasks for children with a range of developmental patterns. Furthermore, service providers can be sensitized to the need to consider the importance of the general affective tone in the family environment and encouraged to assist parents in ways that will maximize positive affective interactional exchanges.

Contemporary state-of-the-art programs for young children with developmental vulnerabilities are interested ultimately in how children will function in the world outside of the assessment or therapeutic environment. Consequently, a child's responses to challenging situations and his or her motivation to succeed should be key mediators of learning and a central focus of intervention efforts. Thus, the development and availability of psychometrically sound measures for assessing mastery motivation offer great promise for this rapidly growing field.

REFERENCES

Barnard, K. E., & Kelly, J. F. (1990). Assessment of parent–child interaction. In S. J. Meisels & J. P. Shonkoff (Eds.), *Handbook of early childhood intervention* (pp. 278–302). New York: Cambridge University Press.

Barrett, K. C., Morgan, G. A., & Maslin-Cole, C. (1993). Three studies on the development of mastery motivation in infancy and toddlerhood. In D. J. Messer (Ed.), *Mastery motivation in early childhood: Development, measurement, and social processes* (pp. 83–108). London: Routledge.

Breznitz, Z., & Friedman, S. L. (1988). Toddlers' concentration: Does maternal depression make a difference? *Journal of Child Psychology and Psychiatry, 29,* 267–279.

Bronfenbrenner, U., Moen, P., & Garbarino, J. (1984). Child, family, and community. In R. D. Parke (Ed.), *Review of child development research* (pp. 283–328). Chicago: University of Chicago Press.

Bullock, M., & Lutkenhaus, P. (1990). Who am I? Self-understanding in toddlers. *Merrill–Palmer Quarterly, 36,* 217–238.

Butterfield, P. M., & Miller, L. (1984). Read your baby: A follow-up intervention program for parents with NICU infants. *Infant Mental Health Journal, 5,* 107–116.

Castaldi, J., Hrncir, E. J., & Caldwell, C. B. (1990). Future models for the study of individual differences in motivation during infancy. *Early Education and Development, 1,* 385–393.

Cicchetti, D., & Wagner, S. (1990). Alternative assessment strategies for the evaluation of infants and toddlers: An organizational perspective. In S. J. Meisels & J. P. Shonkoff (Eds.), *Handbook of early childhood intervention* (pp. 246–277). New York: Cambridge University Press.

Crissey, M. S. (1975). Mental retardation—past, present, and future. *American Psychologist, 30,* 800–808.

Diaz, R. M., Neal, C. J., & Amaya-Williams, M. (1990). The social origins of self-regulation. In L. C. Moll (Ed.), *Vygotsky and education* (pp. 127–154). New York: Cambridge University Press.

Eheart, B. K. (1982). Mother–child interactions with nonretarded and mentally retarded preschoolers. *American Journal of Mental Deficiency, 87,* 20–25.

Frodi, A., Bridges, L., & Grolnick, W. (1985). Correlates of mastery-related behavior: A short-term longitudinal study of infants in their second year. *Child Development, 56,* 1291–1298.

Gaiter, J. L., Morgan, G. A., Jennings, K. D., Harmon, R. J., & Yarrow, L. J. (1982). Variety of cognitively oriented caregiver activities: Relationships to cognitive and motivational functioning at 1 and 3½ years of age. *Journal of Genetic Psychology, 141,* 49–56.

Geppert, U., & Kuster, U. (1983). The emergence of "wanting to do it oneself": A precursor of achievement motivation. *International Journal of Behavioral Development, 6,* 355–369.

Grolnick, W., Frodi, A., & Bridges, L. (1984). Maternal control style and the mastery motivation of one year olds. *Infant Mental Health Journal, 5,* 72–82.

Hanzlik, J. R. & Stevenson, M. B. (1986). Interaction of mothers with their infants who are mentally retarded, retarded with cerebral palsy, or nonretarded. *American Journal of Mental Deficiency, 90,* 513–520.

Harmon, R. J., Morgan, G. A., & Glicken, A. D. (1984). Continuities and discontinuities in affective and cognitive–motivation development. *Child Abuse and Neglect, 8,* 157–167.

Harter, S., & Zigler, E. (1974). The assessment of effectance motivation in normal and retarded children. *Developmental Psychology, 10,* 169–180.

Hauser-Cram, P. (in press). Mastery motivation in toddlers with developmental disabilities. *Child Development.*

Hauser-Cram, P. (1993). Mastery motivation in three-year-old children with Down syndrome. In D. J. Messer (Ed.), *Mastery motivation in early childhood: Development, measurement and social processes* (pp. 230–250). London: Routledge.

Hauser-Cram, P., Upshur, C., Krauss, M. W., & Shonkoff, J. P., (1988). Implications of Public Law 99–457 for early intervention services for infants and toddlers with disabilities. *Society for Research in Child Development Social Policy Report, III* (3), autumn.

Heckhausen, J. (1987). Balancing for weaknesses and challenging developmental potential: A longitudinal study of mother–infant dyads in apprenticeship interactions. *Developmental Psychology, 23* (6), 762–770.

Heckhausen, J. (1993). The development of mastery and its perception within caretaker-child dyads. In D. J. Messer (Ed.), *Mastery motivation in early childhood: Development, measurement and social processes* (pp. 54–79). London: Routledge.

Jennings, K. D. (1991). Early development of mastery motivation and its relation to the self-concept. *Contributions to human development: Vol. 22. The development of intention action: Cognitive, motivational and interactive processes* (pp. 1–13). Basel, Switzerland: S. Karger.

Jennings, K. D., & Connors, R. E. (1989). Mothers' interactional style and children's competence at 3 years. *International Journal of Behavioral Development, 12,* 155–175.

Jones, O. H. M. (1977). Mother–child communication with prelinguistic Down's syndrome and normal infants. In H. R. Schaffer (Ed.), *Studies in mother–infant interaction* (pp. 379–401). San Francisco: Academic Press.

Krauss, M. W., & Hauser-Cram, P. (1992). Policy and program development for infants and toddlers with disabilities. In L. Rowtiz (Ed.), *Mental retardation in the year 2000* (pp. 184–196). New York: Springer-Verlag.

Lutkenhaus, P. (1984). Pleasure derived from mastery in three year olds: Its function for persistence and the influence of maternal behavior. *International Journal of Behavioral Development, 7,* 343–354.

Lyons-Ruth, K., Zoll, D., Connell, D., & Grunebaum, H. U. (1986). The depressed mother and her one-year-old infant: Environment, interaction, attachment, and infant development. In E. Z. Tronick & T. Fields (Eds.), *Maternal depression and infant disturbance. New directions for child development* (No. 34, pp. 61–82). San Francisco: Jossey-Bass.

MacTurk, R. H., Hunter, F., McCarthy, M. E., Vietze, P., & McQuiston, S. (1985). Social mastery motivation in Down syndrome and nonde-layed infants. *Topics in Early Childhood Special Education, 4*, 93–109.

MacTurk, R. H., McCarthy, M. E., Vietze, P., & Yarrow, L. J. (1987). Sequential analysis of mastery behavior in 6- and 12-month-old infants. *Developmental Psychology, 23*, 199–203.

Morgan, G. A., Maslin-Cole, C. A., Downing, K., & Harmon, R. J. (1990). Antecedents of mastery and prediction of behavior problems (summary). *Program and Proceedings of the Developmental Psychobiology Research Group Sixth Biennial Retreat, 6*, 31–32.

Redding, R. E., Harmon, R. J., & Morgan, G. A. (1990). Relationships between maternal depression and infants' mastery behaviors. *Infant Behavior and Development, 13*, 391–395.

Rogoff, B. (1990). *Apprenticeship in teaching: Cognitive development in social context*. New York: Oxford University Press.

Schneider, P., & Gearhart, M. (1988). The ecocultural niche of families with mentally retarded children: Evidence from mother–child interaction studies. *Journal of Applied Developmental Psychology, 9*, 85–106.

Shearer, D. E., & Shearer, M. S. (1976). The Portage Project: A model for early childhood intervention. In T. D. Tjossem (Ed.), *Intervention strategies for high-risk infants and young children* (pp. 335–350). Baltimore: University Park Press.

Shonkoff, J. (1983). The limitations of normative assessment of high-risk infants. *Topics in Early Childhood Special Education, 3*, 29–43.

Shonkoff, J. P. & Hauser-Cram, P. (1987). Early intervention for disabled infants and their families: A quantitative analysis. *Pediatrics, 80*, 650–658.

Shonkoff, J. P., Hauser-Cram, P., Krauss, M. W., & Upshur, C. C. (1992). Development of infants with disabilities and their families: Implications for theory and service delivery. *Monographs of the Society for Research in Child Development, 57* (6) (Serial No. 230).

Spiker, D. (1990). Early intervention from a developmental perspective. In D. Cicchetti & M. Beeghly (Eds.), *Children with Down syndrome: A developmental perspective* (pp. 424–448). New York: Cambridge University Press.

Stoneman, Z., Brody, C. H., & Abbott, D. (1983). In-home observations of young Down syndrome children with their mothers and fathers. *American Journal of Mental Deficiency, 87*, 591–600.

Vygotsky, L. S. (1978). *Mind in society: The development of higher psychological processes*. Cambridge, MA: Harvard University Press.

Vygotsky, L. S. (1986). *Thought and language.* Cambridge, MA: MIT Press.

Wachs, T. D. (1987). Specificity of environmental action as manifest in environmental correlates of infant's mastery motivation. *Developmental Psychology, 23,* 782–790.

Wasserman, G. A., Allen, R., & Solomon, C. R. (1985). At-risk toddlers and their mothers: The special case of physical handicap. *Child Development, 56,* 73–83.

Weisz, J. R. (1979). Perceived control and learned helplessness among mentally retarded and nonretarded children: A developmental analysis. *Developmental Psychology, 15,* 311–319.

Wood, D., Bruner, J. S., & Ross, G. (1976). The role of tutoring in problem solving. *Journal of Child Psychology and Psychiatry, 17,* 89–100.

Yarrow, L. J., MacTurk, R. H., Vietze, P. M., McCarthy, M. E., Klein, R. P., & McQuiston, S. (1984). Developmental course of parental stimulation and its relationship to mastery motivation during infancy. *Developmental Psychology, 20*(3), 492–503.

Yarrow, L. J., Morgan, G. A., Jennings, K. D., Harmon, R. J., & Gaiter, J. L. (1982). Infants' persistence at tasks: Relationships to cognitive functioning and early experience. *Infant Behavior and Development, 5,* 131–141.

12

On Definitions and Measures of Mastery Motivation

Robert B. McCall

University of Pittsburgh

As a general concept, mastery motivation is loaded with appeal and importance. No matter how smart or competent a child or an adult is, ultimately they need to *do* something for them and others to benefit from their competence. Further, the developmental process is one of tackling new tasks, solving new problems, striving for new standards, and overcoming frustrations and failures. The motivation to do these things—to attempt to conquer new challenges—is mastery motivation.

One way to assess the importance of mastery motivation is to consider its absence. At the worst extreme, children and adults would never tackle any new task without mastery motivation. Less extremely, the concepts of learned helplessness, external locus of control, and inability to cope—concepts that represent or are closely linked to the lack of mastery motivation—are widely implicated as explanations of school failure, chronic impoverishment, joblessness, and a variety of other social and economic problems. Specifically, a recent longitudinal study (McCall, Evahn, & Kratzer, 1992) of underachievers—youth who perform more poorly in school than would be predicted on the basis of their abilities—suggested that the common theme running through their lives was the inability to persist at a task in the face of challenge, which is nearly the operational definition of a lack of mastery motivation (see discussion later).

It can, however, be argued that while the concept of mastery motivation is pregnant with vital theoretical and practical implications, the empirical study of mastery motivation, after almost 20 years of effort performed mostly by the contributors to this volume, has itself under-achieved its importance and potential. It is appropriate to speculate about the factors that have limited the development of this topic of inquiry.

One reason may be that the field of mastery motivation started with Yarrow's search for motivational predictors during infancy of later competence to improve on the near-zero correlations from traditional developmental milestones. As a result, the field has been focused almost solely on infants and toddlers; only recently has it considered young children. Consequently, although 20 years is long enough to follow infants into childhood and adolescence, empirical links have not been studied between mastery motivation in infants and young children on the one hand and its analogous concepts of achievement motivation, internal locus of control, and status attainment in older children and adults on the other. Given the uncertain status of early measures of mastery motivation (to be discussed later), perhaps it was reasonable not to invest in longitudinal studies until these early measurement issues were resolved. Sooner or later, however, such longitudinal relationships must be studied, because they seem to me to be an obvious validity test for the study of precursors of mastery or achievement behavior. Perhaps, now that a childhood assessment of mastery motivation is available, such data will soon be forthcoming.

Instead of studying these relationships, students of mastery motivation have been wrestling for two decades with the definition and measurement of mastery motivation during the first five years of life. From my vantage point as a semi-outsider, it has been a tough struggle, and the conceptual and measurement problems are perhaps the main reason why the field is not yet in full bloom. For example, how can you isolate motivation from competence? This is a problem familiar to students of motivation, but it is made considerably more murky when dealing with infants and toddlers. More specifically, mastery motivation refers to the attempt to solve a problem, for example, and it is typically measured by the extent to which the child persists in the face of challenge. How, though, does one separate the motivation from the ability to complete a task or the desirability of the goal from the attempt to attain it? And how does one equate the difficulty of the problem—the challenge—across ages and individuals within an age? These are tough nuts to crack, and it is easy to understand why the scholarly squirrels are still chewing on them.

Sometimes it is easier and, one hopes, helpful, for an outsider to a field to examine its basic definitions and measurement strategies and even to suggest some sacrificial conceptual and strategic foils that might stimulate thought and empirical progress (e.g., for an example, see McCall, 1987). The editors of this volume have assigned me such a task (or, at least, I have accepted it). I discuss here two fundamental issues—the definition of mastery motivation and its measurement—basing these remarks largely on the first three chapters in this volume by Morgan, MacTurk, and Hrncir; MacTurk, Morgan, and Jennings; and Barrett and Morgan. The outsider's role has the advantage of being independent, the hope of contributing perspective, and the limitation of being substantially ignorant of the details of the written and unwritten literature and lore of this field. I ask the reader's forbearance of the latter circumstance; I invite the reader to debate, qualify, and dismantle what I offer in the service of furthering thought and directed research; and I pray that if I happen to offer a shoe that fits, someone will put it on.

The Concept and Definition of Mastery Motivation

The definition of mastery motivation has evolved from White's (1959) concept of effectance to several refinements presented in this book (see Morgan, MacTurk, & Hrncir, this volume). In the next sections, I offer a few selected observations on the context and early history of the concept of mastery motivation followed by a slight reorientation in the definition and its implications.

The Historical Context and Its Legacies

American experimental psychology in the 1940s and 1950s emphasized basic learning processes, primarily in subhuman species, that were reinforced (one did not talk about "motivation") by satisfying appetitive biological drives (e.g., hunger, thirst, sex) and avoiding pain. Although random operant behavior was acknowledged, the focus was on the organism's response to reinforcement by biological drive reduction. Behavior was governed primarily by factors "extrinsic" to the organism (i.e., food, water), and "higher order" behaviors were reinforced secondarily by stimuli associated with drive reduction. The organism was almost a victim of its experience, and no one thought much about why organisms, especially humans, engaged in a great deal of behavior apparently unrelated to drive reduction (e.g., the "random" operant behavior that experimenters relied on to produce the behavior targeted for reinforcement).

In this context, a "fringe element" of "spooky" researchers began to study behaviors in rats and other organisms that were seemingly motivated by "intrinsic" factors, which was called "curiosity" or "information seeking." These behaviors included *spontaneous alternation,* the tendency of rats to explore one and then the other arm of a T-maze in alternation if no reinforcement was offered (December & Fowler, 1958); *light contingent bar pressing,* in which rats would press a bar simply to turn on a light or to change the level of illumination in the cage (Lockard, 1963; McCall, 1965, 1966); and *exploratory behavior,* the tendency for animals simply to explore the novel objects in their environment (Berlyne, 1960). These behaviors were presumably motivated by "intrinsic" factors, and theorists postulated an "exploratory" or "curiosity" drive that was reduced or satisfied by such behaviors—still within a drive-reduction framework (Berlyne, 1960).

But "drive naming" provided little explanatory value and seemed like grabbing at withered straws, especially when applied to human beings, whose higher mental capabilities made intrinsic motivation intuitively plausible and less heretical. Developmental researchers studied the deployment of attention, exploration, and play in infants and young children, but the focus of interest was on what these activities revealed about cognition more than what they said about motivation (e.g., McCall, 1971). It was in this context that White (1959) postulated a competence motive—it was a reaction against extrinsic drive reduction as the only reinforcement or motivation.

While White is widely cited as the patriarch of mastery motivation and his 1959 paper was exceedingly influential, it did little more than call attention to such behaviors, give them succinct names, declare that they were not motivated by traditional drive-reduction principles, and urged colleagues to study them. White did not articulate a theory or a even a highly specific definition of these behaviors or motives—he proposed an agenda. The rationale for these concepts was fleshed out in detail two years later by Hunt (1961), who published *Intelligence and Experience,* which attempted to show the role of intrinsic motivation in the development of intelligence, and later (1963) a paper entitled "Motivation Inherent in Information Processing and Action," which was to be only a forerunner to a book on motivation and experience that he never wrote. It is for these reasons that Morgan et al. (this volume) state that mastery motivation is "sometimes referred to effectance motivation, intrinsic motivation, or competence motivation."

The legacies of this history are still with us. On the positive side, the field of motivation escaped from the bondage of an exclusive focus on biological drive reduction and the avoidance of pain. This opened the door to a vast collection of other motivational behaviors that arguably account for most of human existence. On the other hand, we—including myself—have not progressed much beyond drive naming. For example, 11 years after White, I (McCall, 1970) proposed that organisms had two basic "dispositions," one to *acquire information* (e.g., attend to novelty, explore, and remember the environment) and one to *influence or control the environment* (or know how to do so), and that these two dispositions were at the heart of adaptive and intelligent behavior. This constituted little more than a revisitation of White, replacing "drive" with "disposition," the latter term stripping the former of some of its excess conceptual baggage (e.g., the appetitive nature of drives) but offering little additional explanatory power and utterly no theory. This volume suggests that we have not advanced much beyond even this.

The Definition of Mastery Motivation

The definition of mastery motivation has narrowed over its 20-year history. What started as a broad concept nearly akin to intrinsic or effectance motivation, now (Morgan, Harmon, & Maslin-Cole, 1990) is defined as a "psychological force that stimulates an individual to attempt independently, in a focused and persistent manner, to solve a problem or master a skill or task that is moderately challenging to him or her" (p. 319).

Because I think it will be easier to discuss some of the implications of the definition, I offer the following rephrasing:

Mastery motivation is the disposition to persistently attempt to attain a goal in the face of moderate uncertainty about whether the goal can be achieved.

It is, in common parlance, the motivation to conquer challenges or, more colloquially, "stick-to-itiveness."

Major Terms.   This rephrasing consists of several important terms:

1. *Disposition.* Disposition replaces "drive" and "force" in an attempt to shed as much historical conceptual baggage associated with these terms as possible (e.g., it is not appetitive). The disposition, I believe, is inborn, but its degree and form of expression is influenced substantially by learning.

2. *Persistently attempt.* This implies that some sustained work or energy is involved, it emphasizes the *process* by which the goal is pursued rather than the goal itself, and it suggests that attaining the goal is uncertain.

3. *Attain a goal.* The goal is simply some unrestricted desired end-state, but typically this would involve completing a task, solving a problem, getting someplace, mastering knowledge about a topic, attaining a standard of performance, and so forth. Perhaps the most important implication is that mastery motivation is *goal-directed*, it is a *means to an end*, with the emphasis on the *means* rather than on the *end*.

This, I believe, is an element that has been underemphasized in some previous conceptualizations and some lines of research, and this represents my biggest departure from what has gone before. For example, in my view, attending to new stimuli in the environment, including action–consequence contingencies (e.g., shaking a rattle), is not mastery motivation, because it is typically not directed at a *separate* goal. The organism is disposed to attend to new information, even to encode and remember that information, and this contributes to adaptive behavior and survival (McCall, 1970). However, subhuman organisms and very young infants, in particular, do not perform these behaviors purposely to attain these or other goals distinct from the actions themselves. Since infants are said to develop means–ends differentiation between approximately 8 and 13 months (McCall, Eichorn, & Hogarty, 1977), mastery motivation presumably does not exist before this age period (see later discussion).

Determining whether a separate goal is involved when children and adults are the focus is more difficult and admittedly unclear in some situations. The separate goal may be intrinsic to the task (e.g., attaining a standard of performance, as in climbing Mt. Everest or setting a personal record time in the marathon) or extrinsic to it (e.g., attaining praise, recognition, influence, or money). For example, an adult may read voraciously in a topical area for the purpose of being an expert in that area. That individual is exercising mastery motivation, because he or she is attempting to attain a standard or acquire skills to attain a *separate* goal (e.g., being competent, avoiding embarrassment, writing and publishing papers, teaching the material, attaining tenure). In contrast, reading "for fun or entertainment" is not mastery motivation any more than is watching TV entertainment programs, because no separate goal is being pursued by these behaviors. Admittedly, we can think of numerous examples in which it might be very ambiguous to discern a separate goal. But, I submit, this is primarily academic quibbling. From a practical standpoint, the distinction is meaningful, it has a major implication that *no* mastery motivation per se exists during the first few months of life, and assessment techniques are likely to avoid ambiguities by using procedures in which a separate goal is clearly present (perhaps even one that is built into the procedure).

4. *Moderate uncertainty about whether the goal can be achieved.* This also is a crucial component to the definition, because it separates mastery motivation from competence and from goal attainment per se. Typically, if the child or adult perceives no uncertainty as to whether the goal can be attained, then there is nothing to master—it has already been mastered (if that were needed at all). Similarly, if there is no uncertainty because the organism believes that the goal cannot be attained, then the organism is not motivated to try to attain the goal. Viewed in different terms, competence consists of what the organism already knows how to do. If that competence is invoked to attain a goal with no uncertainty, the behavior is motivated only by the desire for the goal, not at all by the challenge of obtaining it.

The line between competence and mastery motivation can become fine. For example, wealthy and very accomplished financiers may continue to pursue the same goal (e.g., making money), but each new deal offers a challenge because of its unique circumstances. If however, it is the same old deal, just a new customer, this may not be mastery motivation if there is no uncertainty. It then simply consists of making money.

Is there, then, uncertainty about attaining a goal in infants and young children? Yes, I think so, at least by the end of the first year. For example, many students of infant and toddler behavior believe that even one-year-olds seem to make a decision about whether they can or cannot accomplish a task, and if they decide they cannot, they do not try. Specifically, if a behavioral sequence of two or more elements is modeled, 12-month-old infants either imitate the whole sequence or do not try at all, sweeping away the objects or looking elsewhere. They almost never execute the first step and stop in the middle of the sequence. This gives at least the impression that they decide initially *in the face of some uncertainty* whether they can perform the sequence or not, and if not, they do not try (McCall, Parke, & Kavanaugh, 1977).

The challenge and uncertainty in a situation also varies during the process of pursuing the goal. Uncertainty may be very high at the beginning but, as the individual solves parts of the problem, may decrease. At some point, the individual may realize the solution is in hand and little uncertainty remains, even though "mop-up" work remains before the task is completed. At this point, mastery motivation gives way to goal attainment, because the individual is no longer attempting to discover the means but rather to attain the end or goal. I speculate that this is why smiling often occurs before the actual goal is attained, because smiling occurs at the completion of "effortful assimilation" (McCall & McGhee, 1977), when the individual knows he or she has solved the problem even if there is more calculation or other work to be done to complete the task.

Implications.   There are several conceptual and measurement implications to this definition:

1. *Mastery motivation is not cognitive or behavioral competence.* Competence is knowing how to do X. Mastery motivation is the disposition to persistently attempt to obtain competence. Competence is what you know; mastery motivation is the disposition to work to acquire what you don't know.

2. *Similarly, mastery motivation is not general intellectual competence (e.g., IQ), although measures of the two concepts are likely to be correlated.* Mastery motivation, if successful, produces knowledge and competence (including IQ). Intelligence helps to define goals and what is moderately uncertain, which become the object of mastery motivation. Therefore, mastery motivation and competence are conceptually distinct but typically related.

3. *The issue of whether mastery motivation is intrinsic or extrinsic is moot.* Frankly, I don't see that it matters for mastery motivation whether the goal is intrinsic or extrinsic to the

task or to the individual. Take the case of a long distance runner who runs for health reasons alone: There is no uncertainty, so this is not mastery behavior. Alternatively, the runner may want to accomplish something about which uncertainty exists, such as winning a trophy (extrinsic) or setting a new personal record (intrinsic).

In either case, this is mastery behavior, because a separate goal exists with some uncertainty about attaining it. Therefore, the intrinsic or extrinsic nature of the goal seems less relevant to the definition than does the attempt to conquer a separate challenge of moderate uncertainty. This is why the procedure developed by Morgan and Harmon (see Morgan et al., 1990) to assess the level of difficulty of problem-solving tasks for subjects is a major advance in methodology; it seeks to determine tasks that present moderate levels of uncertainty (neither too easy nor too difficult) to the individual subject.

4. *No mastery motivation per se occurs before the infant is able to distinguish between means and ends, which typically occurs between 8 and 12 months.* Taking in information, as in exploratory behavior, investigating contingencies, and studying stimuli are not mastery motivation, because no goal exists separate from the information acquisition process and no uncertainty exists about whether the information can be acquired. In Piagetian terms, a primary circular response is simply exercising a behavioral pattern, and a secondary circular response is exercising a response–stimulus contingency with the awareness that the response has produced the contingency. These are not mastery motivation behaviors. In contrast, however, a tertiary circular response, in which the infant actively explores different manipulations of an object to observe different consequences to those manipulations, more clearly involves a means–ends differentiation and some degree of uncertainty. This may be mastery motivation, but tertiary circular responses typically do not occur much before the second year of life (McCall, 1974).

Obviously, this is a debatable proposition (e.g., see Barrett & Morgan, this volume), and some early behaviors at least look like persistent attempts to gain a goal. For example, some infants appear to make deliberate bids to engage a still-faced mother in reciprocal social interactions. Is this a persistent attempt to attain a separate goal, or is it the persistence of a learned behavior (i.e., resistance to extinction of social behavior) or a predisposed response to a unique stimulus? I'm inclined to believe that any apparent separation of means from ends during the first six months are ambiguous or very rudimentary at best, and so, too, must be the existence of mastery motivation, if either exists at all.

5. *Measures of persistence during free play are ambiguous indices of mastery motivation.* For decades, scholars have debated behind the scenes what it meant for an infant to sustain attention to individual objects or stimuli for a long time. Does the infant who spends a long time looking at stimuli or playing with a toy take in more information about these stimuli, or is the infant who spends relatively short amounts of time with a given stimulus processing the information in that stimulus faster? It now appears from a variety of research that the latter is the case, at least when infants are young and/or the stimuli are relatively simple and not very meaningful. Indeed, short looking and rapid habituation predict higher childhood IQs (e.g., Colombo, 1993; McCall & Carriger, 1993). In the face of this evidence, is it reasonable to assume that infants who persist in studying a given stimulus or object have more mastery motivation? Furthermore, as argued previously, what is the separate goal of exploration and curiosity behaviors beyond acquiring information (which is imbedded in the process itself), and what is the uncertainty involved in trying to attain that goal? In my view, these factors make spontaneous play and exploration very ambiguous measures of mastery motivation at best and not measures of mastery motivation at worst.

6. *A child who chooses a task that has a higher degree of difficulty may or may not have more mastery motivation.* Mastery motivation is the attempt to accomplish something, not the degree of difficulty (competence) or the individual's expectation or aspiration level. For example, underachieving adolescents, who do not show much mastery motivation, nevertheless voice very unrealistically high goals for themselves (McCall et al., 1992). Nevertheless, degree of difficulty or aspiration level relative to accomplishment may be correlated with mastery motivation, because the individual who is willing to tolerate greater levels of uncertainty associated with difficult tasks may well persist longer in attempting to gain a solution. Choosing a degree of difficulty may be more useful as a method to select a task of moderate uncertainty than as an actual measure of mastery motivation, although it may be a marker for it.

7. *"Executive capacity" is not a direct measure of mastery motivation.* Belsky, Garduque, and Hrncir (1984) proposed a measure of mastery motivation called "executive capacity,"

which is the disparity between the level of competence displayed in spontaneous play and the maximum level of competence that can be elicited by encouraging and modeling behavior for the infant to imitate. The assumption is that infants with high mastery motivation should spontaneously play at or near their maximum level of ability. As previously discussed, free or spontaneous play is an ambiguous situation in which to measure mastery motivation. Moreover, consider an analogous competence/performance disparity. Typically, a disparity exists between comprehension vocabulary (i.e., all the words one understands) and speaking vocabulary (i.e., all the words a person typically uses in their speech). Does someone who uses all or most of the words that he or she knows have more mastery motivation? What is the goal, and what is the uncertainty?

8. *Persistence can be different for different types of skills and tasks (e.g., academic, social, athletic), but it is not clear that mastery motivation per se is different.* Persistence at different tasks may vary in the same individual because uncertainty and desire for the goals are different. For example, some people have no self-confidence, low aspirations, and low expectations when it comes to mathematics, and consequently they do not persist in such tasks because they perceive them as too difficult. The same individuals, however, may be quite confident and skilled in social behavior and persist for long periods of time attaining social goals. This difference may exist because of different degrees of uncertainty or desire for the two goals, not differences in mastery motivation per se for different task domains. Since uncertainty and desire for the goal are inextricable parts of the definition of mastery motivation, it will be difficult to tease these elements apart from mastery motivation. Ideally, one would need to hold constant perceived uncertainty and desire for the goal on different types of tasks and performance domains before one could assert that mastery motivation per se is different for different skill areas. My point is that these components are likely to be confounded, and it will be difficult to conclude that mastery motivation per se varies across domains, although persistence is likely to vary with specific tasks and perhaps domains.

9. *The developmental transitions observed in the degree of persistence may reflect age changes in skills, competence, and desire for goals rather than qualitative changes in the nature of mastery motivation per se.* This is the same problem of confounding as described earlier. Essentially, persistence is contin-

uous—that is, it is the same concept and behavior at each age. It may or may not change in quantity across age. What certainly does change are the tasks, the uncertainty in attaining a given task, the skills employed by the individual, and the desirability of the goals. For example, the transitions in instrumental mastery behaviors given in Figure 3.1 of Barrett and Morgan (this volume) look very similar to the transitions in mental development (i.e., competence) described by McCall et al. (1977). The first 8 months of mentality can be characterized by attention to stimuli and the exercising of response–stimulus contingencies. Means–ends differentiation occurs between 8 and 12 or 13 months, and symbolic thought begins at approximately 21 months. The advent of means–ends differentiation allows the infant to have a separate goal and to vary the means to achieve it—it is necessary to produce some uncertainty between means and ends, which I have argued is crucial for the definition of mastery motivation. The advent of symbolic relations permits the child to have a separate symbolic standard of performance as a goal. In short, the transitions may be ones pertaining to skills, competence, and goals, not qualitative changes in mastery motivation per se. More generally, it will be difficult to tease these components apart across ages as well as tasks.

MEASURES OF MASTERY MOTIVATION

Measuring mastery motivation is messy. The biggest problems are separating means from ends and insuring that a moderate amount of uncertainty exists in the subject about attaining the goal. Unfortunately, there is not clear, direct assessment of the degree of uncertainty a subject, especially a non- or limited-verbal infant or toddler, feels about a given task. A first approximation is to select a moderately difficult task, but a task that is moderately difficult for one subject may be easier for another, and a given task that is moderately difficult at one age may not be at another age. Therefore, the most appropriate task may be different from one age to the next and even for one individual to the next within an age. This state of affairs is not a researcher's dream.

The achievement motivation literature with older children and adolescents handles this situation in part by having scaled tasks, asking subjects their aspirations (e.g., what would you like to achieve?) and their expectations (what you think you will be able to achieve?), and then selecting tasks that appear to be at some specified point in reference to these personal markers. Tasks are then rigged to be unsolvable (unbeknown to the subject), and the extent of persistence at the task in the face of this frustration is assessed. Clearly, this approach is easier with older children and adolescents who are mentally and verbally competent to make and communicate these judgments, but the strategy does seem to get closer to the concept than many attempts in the mastery motivation literature.

MacTurk et al. (this volume) have provided a systematic review of measurement procedures at different ages, and what follows are brief comments on their review in the light of the conceptual propositions made here earlier.

Free Play

One of three categories of measurements identified by Mac-Turk et al. (this volume) is free play. A great many measures of play behavior have been taken, including the extent of sustained behavior with individual objects, the maturity level of the actions performed, the length of time in which the child engages in manipulative exploration of an object, the length of time in which the infant explores the auditory and visual consequences of manipulating an object, the highest level of play activity demonstrated, and the disparity between the highest level of competence versus the highest level of spontaneous performance.

The problem with such measures is that it is difficult to know if they reflect mastery motivation or some other characteristic, especially competence. From the standpoint of the definition of mastery motivation above, it is difficult to specify that a goal exists other than the sheer intake of information (i.e., no separate means and ends), and whether the task is challenging or moderately uncertain. This is not simply theoretical, academic quibbling, because persistence in many free-play behaviors used as indices of mastery motivation are *inversely* related to subsequent measures of competence (i.e., IQ; see Colombo, 1993; McCall, 1994; McCall & Carriger, 1993). For example, habituation, response to novelty, and recognition memory are positive predictors of later IQ (e.g., McCall & Carriger, 1993), which makes it ambiguous as to whether they are measures of mastery motivation or competence and raises a question about the meaning of persistence in this context (since it predicts *lower* IQ).

In short, the construct validity of most measures derived from free-play assessments as indices of mastery motivation, in my opinion, is ambiguous at best and in serious doubt at worst. That correlations exist from these measures to later indices of competence or even mastery motivation is not surprising, especially if they reflect some stable thread in the fabric of a developing intelligence. Such correlations alone do not substantiate the validity of these measures as indices of mastery motivation per se.

Structured Tasks

Tasks have been structured to create a goal or problem to be solved and to observe how long infants, toddlers, and children persist in an attempt to solve the problem. Unfortunately, in most cases, the problem is potentially solvable. If the subject solves the problem quickly, then the raw amount of time persisting at the task may be inversely related to competence and such subjects get a low persistence score because they are skilled at the task. If the percent time on task is used, then the measure may reflect the propensity of the subject to disengage attention from or inhibit attention to low salient or irrelevant stimuli in the testing environment. Such behavior has recently been hypothesized to be a potential explanation for the ability of early assessments of recognition memory to predict later IQ (McCall, 1994), and therefore they may be measures of competence rather than mastery motivation. Also, a subject who solves the problem quickly has a smaller denominator in the calculation of the percentage. Consequently, even small amounts of off-task behavior will reduce the percentage disproportionately, again giving a "low mastery-motivation score" to subjects who are the most skilled at the task. If such children are allowed to repeat the task, as is sometimes permitted, what does it mean to repeat a task that was already solved? Is there still uncertainty? Is this mastery motivation?

Tasks for 6- and 12-Month-Old Infants These tasks were among the first indices of mastery motivation and among the first measures that presented a problem for the subject to solve, thereby presumably creating a separation of means and ends and producing some degree of uncertainty in the subject.

Some of these tasks were rather straightforward in this regard. A particular behavior might be modeled for the infant, who is then encouraged verbally by the examiner to "make it work" or "try it yourself." The primary measure of mastery motivation was task persistence, but the actual variable was often the percentage of time during each task that the child was engaged in task-directed behaviors, an index that potentially suffers from the limitations described above.

Another assessment consists of a barrier or detour-reaching task, and to make it continuously difficult, the end around which the object could be retrieved was changed if the subject solved the problem. In this case, the raw amount of persistence was a reasonable measure of mastery motivation. However, a serious question exists as to whether 6-month-old infants separate means from ends and whether their "persistent" behavior is simply frustration. The data seem to bear this ambiguity out, since reliabilities are low and similar types of items do not cluster on the same factors. Other kinds of items, especially effect-production tasks in which some manipulative action produces an auditory or visual consequence, are essentially exploratory behaviors and suffer from the same limitations described earlier.

Although MacTurk et al. (chapter 2, this volume) concluded that the data provide "evidence for the validity of the mastery assessment model" described previously for 8- to 12-month-old infants, some of the evidence could be debated. For example, it is argued that differences between Down-syndrome and nondisordered infants on such behaviors testify to their validity as measures of mastery motivation. At a minimum, to draw this conclusion it must be assumed that Down-syndrome infants have less mastery motivation than do nondisabled infants, but there is no independent, direct confirmation that this is assumption is true. Moreover, Down-syndrome infants are also much lower in competence, although tasks were adjusted to fit developmental levels. One of the problems in determining validity during the early years is selecting a criterion—no very certain index of mastery motivation exists against which to validate these measures, except perhaps longitudinal predictions to mastery behaviors at older ages, which has not been done.

Tasks for 15–36-Month-Old Subjects. Morgan and his colleagues have made the most direct assault on mastery motivation at these ages. They observed that children persisted much less at very difficult tasks and somewhat less at very easy tasks, relative to tasks that were moderately difficult. They then created a set of items that varied in difficulty level, pretested subjects to determine which task represented a moderate level of difficulty for the individual subject, and then permitted the subject to try to solve the problem. I believe this to be one of the most important measurement advances. If the task is unsolvable (which is often *not* the case) and the goal is highly desired, then raw persistence is a direct measure of mastery motivation.

Tasks for Preschoolers.   Tasks have been developed for this age group parallel to those used for younger subjects. The most direct assessment of mastery motivation consists of presenting 3½- and 4½-year-olds with certain tasks (e.g., fitting wooden cutouts of animals into a small wooden box, catching paper fish with a magnetized fishing pole). The tasks look solvable by all children, but they have been surreptitiously made difficult (e.g., some fish are too heavy to be picked up by the magnetized fishing pole). Persistence at the task was the measure of mastery motivation. Unfortunately, the compassionate researchers felt that it was necessary to permit off-task activity (e.g., fantasy play with the fish or animal cutouts to prevent undue frustration), and then take the proportion of the total possible time that was spent in goal-directed activity as the measure of persistence. As described above, this index may suffer from the confound of requiring children to inhibit or disengage attention from other stimuli and behaviors, which has less conceptual relevance to mastery motivation and perhaps some relevance to competence (McCall, 1994). It might be better to use raw accumulated persistence time.

Dimensions of Mastery Questionnaire

The third approach to assessing mastery motivation has been to ask parents and teachers to rate the child's mastery motivation with respect to objects, social or symbolic entities, and gross motor behaviors as well as their affective pleasure in pursuing such goals and the child's competence. While adults are capable of making intuitive judgments about mastery motivation, little attempt is made to define or standardize particular tasks or the size of the challenge they present to the individual child.

The ratings may be quite useful nonetheless. Not surprisingly, as is true for most adult-rated assessment instruments, reliability and stability are much higher than for direct assessments on the children. Analyses verify the five categories of items, and mothers of at-risk or delayed children rate them lower in instrumental mastery motivation and in competence. Finally, modest correlations exist between adult ratings and child persistence at difficult tasks and standardized assessments of competence.

Limited validity data exist, however, except for differences in the ratings of mothers of high- versus low-risk children. I would like to see correlations with locus of control, assessments of learned helplessness, achievement motivation, and school grades.

Measures of Affect

Numerous studies of mastery motivation measure children's smiling and other displays of positive affect during and following problem-solving activities. Presumably, such positive affect reflects pleasure in solving the problem, and therefore testifies to an effortful, perhaps somewhat challenging, activity. Smiling in the problem-solving tasks is analogous to the smiling at effortful assimilation observed many years ago when infants attempted to recognize stimuli that were partly discrepant from familiar ones (McCall & McGhee, 1977).

Unfortunately, such measures of affect are difficult to use as assessments of mastery motivation, because only a few infants and children display them. Further, when they occur in the process is crucial to their interpretation (if they occur early in the process they may not reflect accomplishment), and more than one smile may not be more meaningful than a single smile (e.g., the *number* of smiles may not be a measure of the *degree* of mastery motivation). The best use of affect, in my opinion, is as a confirmation of mastery behavior—one smile is sufficient to do this, but no smiles does not mean that mastery behavior has not occurred.

CONCLUSION

The authors of chapters in this volume have themselves displayed a great deal of mastery motivation—they have tackled a challenging task, many have persisted for nearly 20 years, and there are no signs of their quitting. I have focused my remarks on issues of definition and measurement, especially during the first year or two of life. This leaves unmentioned the vast knowledge accumulated about such behaviors that is reported in other chapters in this volume.

While it is easy to make prescriptions, I urge researchers in this field to use tasks that more specifically conform to the definition of mastery motivation, perhaps as defined here earlier. Some attempts must be made to select tasks that represent moderate difficulty and, therefore, moderate challenge for *individual* subjects, and progress has been made in this area. In addition, I feel that the task must not be solvable during the assessment, which may require the experimenter to rig the apparatus to prevent solution. Also, off-task opportunities should be minimized or discounted, since such behavior may tell us more about competence and style than about mastery motivation. I believe attempting to assess mastery motivation per se in infants younger than 12 months represents a conceptual anomaly and should be abandoned, because infants this young cannot separate means from ends. Of course, predictors of subsequent mastery may be found and could be conceptually meaningful and important, but I, for one, would be reticent to call such behaviors mastery motivation. Finally, attempts should be made to link assessments of mastery motivation to more traditional measures of achievement motivation, locus of control, learned helplessness, and instrumentality, since this would be a principal way in which serious construct validity can be achieved in the absence of a certain criterion against which to validate mastery-motivation assessments.

Mastery motivation is a crucial factor governing large segments of behavior that are important in the lives of children, adolescents, and adults. The pursuit is definitely worthwhile, which perhaps explains my impatience.

Rᴇꜰᴇʀᴇɴᴄᴇꜱ

Belsky, J., Garduque, L., & Hrncir, E. (1984). Assessing performance, competence, and executive capacity in infant play: Relations to home environment and security of attachment. *Developmental Psychology, 20,* 406–417.

Berlyne, D. E. (1960). *Conflict, arousal, and curiosity.* New York: McGraw Hill.

Colombo, J. (1993). *Infant cognition: Predicting later intellectual functioning.* Newbury Park, CA: Sage.

Dember, W. N., & Fowler, H. (1958). Spontaneous alternation behavior. *Psychological Bulletin, 55,* 412–428.

Hunt, J. McV. (1961). *Intelligence and experience.* New York: Ronald Press.

Hunt, J. McV. (1963). Motivation inherent in information processing and action. In O. J. Harvey (Ed.), *Motivation and social interaction* (pp. 35–94). New York: Ronald Press.

Lockard, R. B. (1963). Some effects of light upon the behavior of rodents. *Psychological Bulletin, 60,* 509–529.

McCall, R. B. (1965). Stimulus change in light-contingent bar pressing. *Journal of Comparative and Physiological Psychology, 59,* 258–262.

McCall, R. B., (1966). The initial-consequent-change surface in light-contingent bar pressing. *Journal of Comparative and Physiological Psychology, 62,* 35–42.

McCall, R. B. (1970). Qualitative transitions in behavioral development in the first three years. In M. H. Bornstein & W. Kessen (Eds.), *Psychological development from infancy* (pp. 183–224). Hillsdale, NJ: Erlbaum.

McCall, R. B. (1971). Attention in the infant: Avenue to the study of cognitive development. In D. Walcher and D. Peters (Eds.), *Early childhood: The development of self-regulatory mechanisms* (pp. 107–140). New York: Academic Press.

McCall R. B. (1974). Exploratory manipulation and play in the human infant. *Monographs of the Society for Research in Child Development, 39* (2, Serial No. 155).

McCall, R. B. (1987). Commentary. In H. H. Goldsmith (Convener), What is temperament? Four approaches. *Child Development, 58,* 524–529.

McCall, R. B. (1994). What process mediates predictions of childhood IQ from infant habituation and recognition memory? Speculations on the roles of inhibition and rate of information processing. *Intelligence, 18,* 107–125.

McCall, R. B., & Carriger, M. S. (1993). Infant habituation and recognition memory performance as predictors of later IQ. *Child Development, 64,* 57–79.

McCall, R. B., Eichorn, D. H., & Hogarty, P. S. (1977). Transitions in early mental development. *Monographs of the Society for Research in Child Development, 42* (3, Serial No. 171).

McCall, R. B., Evahn, C., & Kratzer, L. (1992). *High school underachievers: What do they achieve as adults?* Newbury Park, CA: Sage.

McCall, R. B., & McGhee, P. E. (1977). The discrepancy hypothesis of attention and affect in human infants. In I. C. Uzgiris & F. Weizmann (Eds.), *The structuring of experience* (pp. 179–210). New York: Plenum.

McCall, R. B., Parke, R. D., & Kavanaugh, R. D. (1977). Imitation of live and televised models in children 1–3 years of age. *Monographs of the Society for Research in Child Development, 42* (4, Serial No. 173).

Morgan, G. A., Harmon, R. J., & Maslin-Cole, C. A. (1990). Mastery motivation: Definition and measurement. *Early Education and Development, 1*(5), 318–339.

White, R. W. (1959). Motivation reconsidered: The concept of competence. *Psychological Review, 66,* 297–333.

13

MASTERY MOTIVATION: PAST, PRESENT AND FUTURE

David J. Messer

Psychology Division
University of Hertfordshire, England

This chapter begins with a brief review of the past work on mastery motivation and draws attention to themes that have not always been considered in other chapters of this volume. The next section considers more recent research with a focus on transitions in development, on new conceptualizations of mastery, and on the relation between attachment and mastery. The third section looks to the future in terms of issues that need to be addressed and ways to further develop research on this topic.

THE PAST: THE CLASSIC STUDIES OF MASTERY MOTIVATION

As we have already seen in this volume, interest in mastery motivation can be traced back to White's (1959) writings. His observations about activities that were not a result of physiological drives showed the limitations of previous conceptualization of play and exploratory behavior and demonstrated the need for new ways of thinking about such activities.

Slightly later, the work of Hunt (1965) considered links between motivational and cognitive processes. Hunt drew on Piagetian ideas about cognitive development and took them further by suggesting that motivation to explore and discover is the result of incongruity between the environment and children's understanding of the world. He distinguished between intrinsic and other forms of motivation, intrinsic motivation being believed to be the result of cognitive processes and not physiological deficits. In Hunt's words, "an optimal standard of incongruity supplies a motivation for behavior change and learning that is inherent within the organism's information interaction with its circumstances" (p. 227). It was also supposed that because the relationship between motivation and incongruity was curvilinear, the highest degree of motivation would be elicited by an optimal degree of incongruity.

This period of theoretical development was not accompanied by a corresponding growth in empirical research. It was not until the 1970s that investigations by Harter (1978, 1981) provided both a model and a set of studies concerning motivation in preschool children. Harter proposed a model in which three different components of effectance motivation were identified: cognitive, interpersonal, and motor competencies. She believed that effectance motivation had two sources—an instinctive desire to have an effect, and an acquired motivational drive. The latter was hypothesized to become internalized during development so that motivation could become less dependent on the praise and encouragement of others. This was more in accord with traditional learning theory than White's and Hunt's formulations. The internalization was believed to involve a self-reward system that provided self-praise for one's own attempts and successes, the system being based on the responses of others in rewarding or punishing early mastery attempts.

Later, the work of Yarrow and his colleagues provided the first program of research to examine mastery motivation during infancy and early childhood. (See chapters 1 and 2 of this volume.) Mastery was defined by Yarrow and his colleagues as a motive that leads infants to "explore and play with objects about them" (Jennings, Harmon, Morgan, Gaiter, & Yarrow, 1979, p. 386). Gaiter, Morgan, Jennings, Harmon, & Yarrow (1982) used persistence as their measure of mastery motivation; this was coded as the proportion of time spent in task directed activities. A second study at the National Institutes of Health involved further refinements of the measures with infants (Yarrow, McQuiston, MacTurk, McCarthy, Klein, & Vietze, 1983). In addition, an investigation of 30-month-old children examined a number of dimensions of behavior that could be influenced by mastery motivation, such as persistence, exploration, speech, and visual attention (Messer, Rachford, McCarthy, & Yarrow, 1987). Thus, the focal measure in these studies of mastery was persistence in attempts to solve tasks or, as it has sometimes been termed, task-directed behavior.

There has been a strong tradition in developmental psychology that views learning and motivation as two important dimensions of development. Given this, it is somewhat surprising that issues about learning have not figured more prominently in discussions about mastery motivation, particularly when there has been findings in existence for some time that show the importance of this interrelationship. For example, Papoušek (1969) reported that young infants produce actions when they generate an effect on their environment, even though there may be no reward except a successful contingent outcome. In a similar vein, Watson (1966, 1972) claimed that infants derived pleasure when they identified a relation between their action and some external result. Watson also suggested that experience of such relations lead to *contingency awareness*, this, in turn, increases motivation and facilitates learning.

The learning of contingent relations has also been stressed by Lewis and Goldberg, but they considered the contingencies in the social rather than physical environment (Goldberg, 1975; Lewis & Goldberg, 1969). Like Watson, they supposed that when infants learn contingencies they are also learning that they can influence the world around them. Lewis and Goldberg went so far as to suggest that failure to learn such relationships could effect development by reducing exploration and investigation so that a child has a more limited experience. In addition, it is suggested that such an environment may result in children failing to detect other contingencies because they only have a limited awareness of their own influence.

Thus, in the classic studies of motivation and learning, a number of different themes can be identified, including discussions about the intrinsic rewards of mastering a problem, the need to resolve cognitive conflict by investigation, and the way that contingent effects can provide the basis of feelings of control. This work has provided the foundation of current interest in mastery motivation by identifying important principles and continuing areas of controversy. However, as we will see in the next section, mastery motivation is now discussed in a more complex way than was originally conceived in the classic studies.

In considering the past, this review has gone back some 35 years to White's (1959) theory and forward to the literature on mastery motivation of the mid 1980s. In discussing the present, I will take a somewhat liberal definition and review research conducted since the mid 1980s. The review considers only three issues of current research into mastery motivation, but all involve either a change in perspective from the earlier work or a much greater appreciation of the complexity of this dimension of behavior. The three issues are: transitions in development, new conceptualizations of mastery motivation, and attachment processes. An important feature of these recent perspectives is that they have integrated discussions about mastery motivation with more general issues in developmental psychology.

TRANSITIONS IN DEVELOPMENT AND THE DEVELOPMENT OF MASTERY MOTIVATION

Transitions in Development

There is increasing consensus that during the first two years of life there are several transition points where infants show not just simple and gradual increases in competence, but also the emergence of new and more sophisticated behaviors. These transitions will be outlined before examining their relation to mastery motivation.

An early transitional point seems to be at about five months. Before this time, social interaction is usually based around body games or the reactions of adult and baby to one another—such early social interactions may provide the basis for the reciprocal attunement of adult and baby. At about five months, infant interest broadens to take in more features of their environment such as objects and events. The transition at five months has been identified by authorities such as Kaye (1982), Schaffer (1984) and Trevarthen (1982). A second transition has been located at about nine months involving both cognitive and communicative changes. After this age infants start to use conventional communicative gestures, become more aware of the relevance of adult reactions (e.g., social referencing), and use people to obtain their objectives (e.g., Bates, O'Connell, & Shore, 1987). A third major transition is commonly believed to take place at about 18 months, when there are the beginnings of symbolic play, advances in the ability to sort objects into groups, a rapid expansion in vocabulary, and the beginnings of two-word speech.

In discussing these transitions, Bates et al. (1987) suggested that there may be local homologies between cognition and communication. According to this view, there are widespread changes at certain points in development that are the result of some basic developments in children's ability to process information. A related idea is contained in the specificity hypothesis of Gopnik and Meltzoff (1986). They suggest that there are specific links between related aspects of cognition, such as achievements in object permanence tasks and the use of words like "allgone," rather than widespread changes at particular ages. Is mastery motivation part of these transformations? Do these transformations provide predictions about the development of mastery motivation? Changes in mastery motivation have already been considered in a number of papers (e.g., Barrett & Morgan, this volume; Barrett, Morgan, & Maslin-Cole, 1993; Jennings, 1993; Messer et al., 1986). In the next few pages I will try to bring this material together and integrate it with the claims about general changes in cognition and communication.

The Transition at 5 Months.   In considering the first five months of life, I have argued elsewhere that mastery motivation and attention are closely related dimensions of functioning (Messer, 1993). Furthermore, I also speculate that the dyadic social interaction that occurs up to about five months has consequences for the attentional and mastery systems. My basic argument is that interaction that sustains infant interest in the social actions of another person will enhance mastery behavior because such experience will develop the infant's capacities to attend to social stimuli and thus provide a basis for the later sustained attention to objects and tasks when it is developmentally appropriate. Thus, the way adults manage social interaction to promote infant attention during the first five months of life is predicted to have important consequences for later development.

I also suggest that a related component of infant attention is the ability to habituate to the repeated presentation of the same stimulus and regain interest when a new stimulus is presented. There is the possibility that social interaction in the first five months can enhance this capacity. It is well established that early social interaction is very repetitive, and that much adult behavior consists of variations on a theme (e.g., the repetition of similar utterances, or similar facial expressions like head looming and bobbing). There is the strong possibility that adults who finely tune their social behavior to the attentional capacities of infants will both enhance the baby's informational processing and help them to develop a motivation to sustain their interest in social interaction (see also Stern, 1979). This could be achieved by adults producing changes in their social behaviors when infant interest is flagging. As a result, infants would be given the opportunity to process new information when they become habituated to previous activities, and this should develop their attentional and motivational capacities.

As a result, early adult–infant social interaction could facilitate persistence on mastery tasks and may facilitate the capacity to habituate to familiar stimuli. Such relationships can explain the correlations between faster habituation and later intelligence (Bornstein & Sigman, 1986), and between sustained interest in toys and later scores on the McCarthy scales (Messer et al., 1986). Thus, before five months the characteristics of adult–infant social interaction may have an important influence on the development of attention and persistence. After this age slightly different characteristics of social interaction may influence the development of these abilities as infant interest becomes more focused on the inanimate environment.

From a different perspective, Barrett & Morgan (this volume) and Heckhausen (1993) have both commented on the way that learning contingencies during the first year can be seen as a component process of mastery motivation. The types of behaviors considered by these investigators include the control of external devices, learned helplessness, motivation to produce an effect, and angry/sad reactions to extinction. The presence of these behaviors at ages below five months is especially interesting, as it suggests that even very young infants have a motivation to control their environment, and will react to the success or failure of this control. These feelings of control seem to occur in situations where infants associate their behavior with some outcome—the secondary circular reactions described by Piaget. According to such a view a transition in mastery behavior at five months would not necessarily be expected.

Barrett and Morgan (this volume) have also made the interesting point that although very young infants are unlikely to have the capabilities to identify tasks that have an optimal degree of difficulty, they do show a preference for novelty and that exploration is related to this preference. This should not be seen solely in relation to the physical world. As I have already argued, the social world of the infant may be crucial to fostering feelings of control and providing complex stimuli that enhance infants' information processing. Young infants may be attempting to explore and master this domain.

In discussing the transition at five months it is apparent that the major change involves the orientation to the social and physical worlds. I have argued that the form of social interaction before five months may be important to the initial development of an attentional-mastery system. It is also possible that there is a degree of continuity in the processes relating to the learning of contingencies before and after five months. What is clear from this short review is that we still know very little about mastery motivation during the first half year of life.

A Transition at 9 Months. Evidence has accumulated that a transition in development at about nine months is related to the pattern of mastery motivation on either side of this age. For instance, a longitudinal study examining the relation between mastery motivation and later scores on the McCarthy scales at 30 months revealed the following findings (Messer et al. 1986). At 12 months persistence, as expected, was positively related to later McCarthy scores. However, at six months, exploratory behavior, and not persistence, was related to the later scores. This was interpreted as being due to the 12 month olds' ability to identify the goals appropriate to the characteristics of the toy (e.g. using a manipulandum to produce an effect), whereas 6 month olds simply used their existing repertoire to explore and investigate toys by manipulating, mouthing, and banging. Thus, the change in the pattern of associations between mastery behavior and later competence was explained in terms of the changes at 9 months that concern the development of goal-directed behavior and the understanding of means–ends relations (see Barrett & Morgan, this volume for a more complete description and evaluation of the study).

A different perspective about development has been provided by Jennings (1993; this volume) in her discussion of the relation between changes in children's self concepts and mastery motivation. She makes a distinction between the developing sense of "I," which involves the self as an actor, and the developing sense of "me," which involves a sense of self as a configuration of physical features (e.g., face, hair, size, and so on) together with a sense that others have a perspective about this self. Before nine months, Jennings supposes that infants develop a sense of "I" from the contingent reactions of others and from their effect on the world. Such awareness may result in pleasure when a contingency between their actions and an effect on the environment is detected, as shown in Watson's observations. Jennings concluded that there is only a rudimentary sense of "me" and this is only apparent at nine months as indicated by studies of self-recognition (Harter, 1983).

In relation to this transition it is interesting that both Hobson (1993) and Baron-Cohen (1993) believe that sometime towards the end of the first year infants show an appreciation of the perspective of others. Consequently, they could be considered to start to develop a sense of "me." Hobson suggests that this occurs because adults and infants engage in triadic relationship of joint attention to another referent (i.e. adult, infant, and referent), and during such occasions infants begin to notice that the adult's reaction may be different from their own and consequently start to appreciate that others can have different perspectives from their own (e.g. an adult may react with amusement to something a baby finds frightening). Baron-Cohen (1993) took a very different perspective, but essentially describes a similar process. He believes that infants' ability to form triadic relationships is part of the maturation of a system that enables them to substitute a greater range of items in their representations, whereby they move from simply representing the attentional state of the other person (i.e., where they are gazing) to representing the emotion and interest of the other (i.e., what they are feeling and eventually what they are thinking).

These views have an important implication for mastery motivation in that they suggest that during the second year infants will have a greater appreciation of the viewpoints of others, and may also begin to separate their own standards of achievement from the standards of others. This connects with descriptions of the period of 14–18 months when toddlers start to assert their own authority, reject the help of others, and wish to accomplish tasks by themselves (Jennings, 1993; Stipek, Recchia, & McClintic, 1992).

However, not everyone agrees that the sense of "me" emerges at about nine months. Using evidence from their studies of imitation, Meltzoff and Gopnik (1993) claimed that infants may have some understanding of "me" from a very early age. They claim that newborns are able to imitate adults because they have a "like me" reaction to them. If they are correct, it suggests that there is some rudimentary, but undifferentiated sense of self from a very early age. However, it is important to recognize that these different claims may reflect differing conceptions of "me" and differences about the operationalization of this concept as much as any theoretical difference.

To return to another aspect of Jennings' (1993) work, the suggestion that the transition at 9 months involves infants being able to identify goals, rather than simply respond to the possibilities of a task. She cited the abilities of children of this age to use an indirect strategy to obtain an object in a detour task. Other support for this prediction is provided by Barrett et al. (1993), who argued that below 9 months infants will engage in goal-directed activities on familiar tasks. In contrast, above this age, Barrett et al. supposed that they are able to engage in goal-directed activities with unfamiliar tasks.

If we apply the local homology view of development to mastery motivation, one would expect that changes in mastery behavior would occur at the same age as other changes in cognitive ability. A surprisingly close chronological association has been shown between intentionality and cognitive development on Piagetian tasks (Harding & Golinkoff, 1979), and it would be interesting to establish whether the change from exploration to persistence occurs at a similar age. Some confidence in there being a close association between these dimensions of behavior is provided by Barrett & Morgan's (this volume) review that distinguishes between phase I and phase II behaviors at about this age. Consequently, there seems to be reasonable evidence for a change in the form of mastery behavior at about 9 months, and this may be associated with more general changes in cognitive functioning.

A Transition at 18 Months.   A number of authorities have described a change in representational abilities that occurs at about 18 months. Gopnik and Meltzoff (1986) have argued that this change involves the ability to form hypothetical representations. Similarly, the rapid expansion of vocabulary that often takes place at this age has been explained by new advances in representational abilities (McShane, 1980; Nelson, 1985). From a different perspective, Leslie (1987) proposed that the ability to decouple representations from reality at around 18 months allows the development of pretend play.

Thus, it should be no surprise that the sense of "me" becomes more sophisticated at this point in development (Jennings, 1993; Stipek et al., 1992). For instance, children start to check a mark on their face when they see their own reflection in a mirror (Lewis & Brooks-Gunn, 1979). Nor perhaps should it be surprising that children start at this age to compare their performance with an external standard, a process which will, of course, require more advanced representational abilities (Jennings, 1993), the result being that the sense of success or failure can now be internalized rather than depend on external evaluation. Jennings (1993) believes that this can be seen when children stop activities to regard their accomplishments and when they smile at their own successes.

Redding, Morgan, and Harmon (1988) and Barrett, Morgan, and Maslin-Cole (1993) have provided valuable additional information about these changes. In both studies, children of between 12 and 30 months show more persistence with easy and moderately difficult tasks than with difficult ones. Thus, the findings seem to show that children in their second year are starting to make progress towards organizing their behavior in relation to the difficulty of a task. Interestingly, the 3 year olds in Redding et al.'s (1988) study showed an inverted U-shaped curve, as their persistence was less on the easy and difficult tasks than on the moderately difficult ones. This suggests that by this age children have the representational ability to work out and react to the difficulty of a task.

I have discussed at some length the relation between mastery motivation with children's social and cognitive developments. This is partly because such work provides a way of placing the study of mastery motivation in a more central position in developmental psychology. In addition, such work provides a rich source of hypotheses about the way that mastery motivation develops. It may well be that the transitions identified here are more gradual and less marked, or that changes in mastery are not closely tied to the transitions. However, in testing these ideas we will obtain a much richer understanding of the nature of mastery motivation.

A Broader Conceptualization of Mastery Motivation

As well as considering the relations between mastery motivation and other aspects of development, recent work has provided a broader conceptualization of mastery. This interest can be traced back to earlier research and discussion. For instance,

Jennings (1975) suggested that preschool children show preferences for interacting with people or with objects. In a similar way, Harter, (1978; 1981) in her model of effectance motivation, proposed that three dimensions—motor, interpersonal, and cognitive—could be identified. Observations by MacTurk, Hunter, McCarthy, Vietze, & McQuiston (1985) and MacTurk, Vietze, McCarthy, McQuiston, & Yarrow (1985) led them to identify what they termed social mastery motivation in Down syndrome and nondelayed infants. They regarded this as being concerned with maintaining and influencing interaction.

These ideas have been built on in research by Wachs and his colleagues (see chapter 6, this volume). Wachs (1987) suggested that three different forms of mastery motivation can be distinguished at 12 months: object motivation, social motivation, and social–object mastery motivation that involves obtaining adult attention through the use of objects. The object and social forms of mastery motivation were found to have a zero-order correlation. In addition, Wachs presented findings suggesting that separate aspects of the infant's environment were deferentially correlated with the three forms of mastery motivation. A more recent study by Coombs & Wachs (1993) of 18 month olds suggests that social mastery involves attempts to obtain adult involvement in a task, initiation of social interaction, and more positive affect. In this volume, Wachs and Coombs defined social mastery as "an interest in competently interacting with other people, as shown primarily by persistence of attempts to initiate social interactions and secondarily by attempts to maintain social interactions and by displays of positive affect during interactions."

Given the discussion in the previous section about transitions in development, I would like to speculate about the way social mastery changes with age. A large body of research attests to the attractiveness of people to very young infants (see Messer, 1994), and there are suggestions that from a very early age infants can differentiate people from objects (e.g., Hobson, 1993; Meltzoff & Gopnik, 1993; Trevarthen, 1982). It would also seem likely that the experience of early social interaction could have an important effect on social mastery. For example, research with mothers who are depressed suggests that their infants show lower levels of social behavior (Murray & Stein, 1989), although it is unclear whether there is also depressed activity with objects and object exploration. Thus, during the first five months of life there may be differences between infants in their persistence to initiate and maintain social interactions, and, consequently, the rudiments of social mastery. These differences in mastery might be expected to be more easily detectable after five months when infants' interest in objects becomes more apparent.

From about 9 months the increasing appreciation of the adult as a separate entity may result in different strategies to obtain attention. The literature on early social and referential speech would suggest that there are two different styles; some infants use social games and routines when communicating with adults, while others communicate about objects (Bates et al., 1987; although there have been questions about the basis of this distinction, Bates, Dale, & Thal, in press). The research into language development would suggest that these styles do not emerge until after about nine months. Thus, it would appear that similar object/social styles have been observed in the communication of children and in the mastery classification scheme developed by Wachs and Coombs.

At the 18-month transition there are advances in representational abilities; this seems to involve a further separation of self from others and should change children's ideas about others and the way to interact with them. The other important change is the ability to use language for social contact. The analysis of the way conversation is used by children to obtain and sustain social interaction is a challenging field of enquiry, but one that may need to be tackled if we are to fully understand social mastery motivation at this age.

We can thus see that social and object mastery are likely to change as children become older and new developmental abilities are acquired. It is also worth reflecting that the suggestions about object and social domains of mastery raise several interesting questions about the development of these characteristics, the first and most obvious question being, when do these styles and differences appear? In the first few months? At five months? At nine months? Another important question is the importance of adult responsiveness to the development of social mastery. A further question concerns the stability of these characteristics: Do these styles continue despite cognitive changes in ability, or are there periods of transformation when new abilities emerge and previous ways of dealing with the world are discarded?

In relation to the issue of social mastery it is also important to recognize that the social and object worlds are closely bound together in development. If we look at the acquisition of words, a foundation for later cognitive and social advances, it is becoming increasingly recognized that process is related to the amount of social interaction and speech that involve joint attention between child and mother (Messer, 1994). What is even more interesting for discussions about mastery motivation is that it seems that following a child's interest and labeling objects that are the focus of their attention is positively associated with the acquisition of words, whereas the labeling of objects that infant attention has been directed towards is not associated with the acquisition of the relevant words (Tomasello & Farrer, 1986). This is explained in terms of the increased cognitive demands involved in following another's direction, but it is equally plausible to suggest that when conversation follows the child's interest he or she will have a greater feeling of control and may be more motivated to acquire information about the referent.

In addition, we should remember that social and object mastery may be more complex processes than simple attention to objects or people. For example, social mastery may result in a child initiating social interaction, leading to the investigation of a greater range of objects by adult and child. Alternatively, a child's interest in objects may lead to social interaction, and this could be associated with the acquisition of a better vocabulary. This is similar to the argument being put forward by Wachs & Coombs (this volume) that the goodness of fit between child and environment may be the most important determinant of the development of mastery motivation.

Mastery Motivation and Attachment Processes

It might be expected that there would be a close relationship between mastery motivation and the security of attachment. The type of social experiences that infants experience is commonly believed to influence their attachment to their parents, and this attachment may in turn influence their mastery behavior. For example, Riksen-Walraven, Meij, van Roozendaal, and Koks (1993) expected that there would be a relation between attachment and exploration, as exploration is typically believed to be activated when children feel secure. Consequently, it was predicted that anxious–resistant infants would explore less than secure infants, and that anxious–avoidant infants would be interested in objects, but explore in a less focused manner. However, their study revealed that only one measure was related to the child's security of attachment, and this only occurred for girls, not boys. One way to account for these findings is to suppose that the attachment system has the greatest influence on exploration of distant objects. Consequently, exploration of objects that are comparatively near to the mother, as in this study may be unaffected by the child's type of attachment.

Maslin-Cole, Bretherton, and Morgan (1993) have also failed to find relationships between attachment and mastery at 18 or 25 months. In contrast, maternal scaffolding activities predicted both mastery and competence. This suggests that the moment-to-moment interventions of adults in children's activities may be particularly relevant to mastery motivation, but, somewhat surprisingly, the more general relationships with adults do not have an effect.

A similar conclusion is drawn by Hauser-Cram (1993) in her study of social interaction between parents and children with Down syndrome. High levels of parental involvement (a subscale of the HOME) during infancy were related to lower persistence measures at 3 years. Hauser-Cram suggested that this may be because directive styles of interaction increases dependency. In contrast, the provision of play materials and a cohesive and adaptable family structure was associated with persistence and pleasure at a later age. This study suggests that intrusive parenting may interfere with the development of motivation, but that supportive family characteristics may promote the development of motivation and competence.

Thus, somewhat unexpectedly, the investigations of attachment do not find particularly strong relationships between attachment and mastery (see also the chapter by Wachs & Coombs, this volume). As yet, the reasons for this failure are not entirely clear. In contrast, there are indications that features of adult–child interaction influence mastery motivation. In general it seems that a style that involves an emphasis of technical aspects, direction, and modeling is associated with lower levels of mastery, while the provision of appropriate materials and social support is associated with higher levels of mastery motivation.

FUTURE DIRECTIONS

Gaps in our Knowledge

Before considering the direction of future research, it is worth identifying some of the important gaps in our knowledge about mastery that need to be filled. Much of the research on motivation has been conducted in laboratory settings and, as a result, there is a danger of building a picture of mastery behavior that has little ecological validity. Some remedy to this deficiency has already been provided by Morgan and his colleagues in their development and use of the DMQ questionnaire (Morgan et al., 1993); they find that mothers' perceptions of their child's behavior are related to laboratory observations of the same children's behavior. Further data collection in naturalistic circumstances would be desirable to provide more information about the type of goals that children themselves select, and their persistence in such self-selected tasks.

In addition, our knowledge of causal relationships is limited. This has been a consequence of the frequent use of longitudinal investigations. We can talk of correlations or predictions between variables, but we cannot identify causal relationships. This is a problem common to many areas of developmental psychology. Hauser-Cram and Shonkoff (this volume) have discussed the way mastery motivation could be a focus for interventions with children who have developmental disabilities. The implementation of such programs would allow causal relations between environment and mastery motivation to be evaluated, as well as the relation between changes in mastery motivation and competence. In relation to this, Bryant (1990) has argued that the uses of intervention programs that are based on previous correlation studies are of great practical and theoretical value (but see McCall, 1977 for reservations about this type of approach).

Another gap involves our lack of knowledge about other cultures. It is possible that our ideas of mastery motivation are, in part, a product of Western assumptions about the individual's role in shaping their own destiny. Do other cultures believe children have a motivation for mastery? Are such characteristics valued? Cross-cultural research can help to answer these questions and allow an examination of the role of socialization in the development of mastery motivation. Because of these concerns, the research of Busch-Rossnagel, Vargas, Knauf, and Planos (1993), who have studied children from Hispanic families, is particularly welcome. However, it is also important to note that Busch-Rossnagel et al. also identified problems in drawing conclusions from such work; these problems are caused by any two cultures having many differences between them and, consequently, there is a great difficulty in identifying which cultural characteristic is responsible for the differences between children. This suggests that a useful research strategy may be to look for similarities in the pattern of development, which occur despite large cultural differences—this would at least identify characteristics of development that are largely independent of environmental influences.

Future Ways to Conceptualize Mastery Motivation

In the past, mastery motivation was assessed by measuring persistence on tasks. Present day work suggests that mastery motivation changes in form as children develop and that there may be different domains of mastery motivation. How should we conceptualize mastery motivation in the future?

There are at least three different ways to conceptualize mastery motivation. The first is to suppose an extremely wide provence for mastery motivation so that all processes that influence the production of mastery behavior can be regarded as aspects of mastery motivation; cognitive and perceptual capacities would then be considered as part of a wider motivational component. White (1959) came close to adopting such a position. The difficulty with this conceptualization is that it makes broad assumptions that are very difficult to investigate. It also has the implication that there is very little reason to consider the relationship between motivation and competence; they will measure essentially similar characteristics.

A second approach is to identify different styles of mastery motivation. This involves the assumption that the important differences between children are qualitative rather than quantitative. The success of this methodology can be seen in the attachment classification of secure and insecurely attached children, where the strategy has been to examine different styles of attachment rather than measure the strength of attachment. In the same way different forms of mastery behavior could be identified. An example of this approach is present in the work of Wachs and his colleagues in their proposals about social- and object-related domains of mastery motivation. There are, of course, other dimensions of behavior that may involve different styles. Children might be classified according to whether they persist in task-related activities, explore the possibilities offered by a task, or are uncooperative. A feature of applying this approach to mastery motivation is that concern moves away from measuring the amount of mastery motivation to assessing the style of mastery motivation. An example of this type of argument is that a child who switches goals may have a different style of mastery from a child that persists in one aspect of a task, although the quantity of mastery motivation does not necessarily differ between the children. As a result, future research would be directed to identifying the different types of activities that occur when children engage in a task, and an advantage would be that this might provide an assessment of children who are clearly motivated, but not in an adaptive or cooperative way. Such children can show a form of mastery by refusing to cooperate or by being in opposition to the experimenter's wishes.

A third method of conceptualizing mastery motivation involves identifying criterion behavior such as persistence on a task and assuming that it constitutes a measure of mastery motivation. An advantage of a narrow definition is that at least there can be consistency between different studies, and that issues of measurement may be simplified. However, the use of a narrow definition may be inappropriate because mastery is now being conceptualized in broad terms; a few measures simply may not provide an accurate or valid assessment of this general concept. As we have already seen, it is unlikely that any one behavioral measure can be applied across the development range. Furthermore, it should be borne in mind that there are advantages in assessing mastery by considering a range of different behaviors; changes in the way that mastery develops with age would be more likely to be detected, as would any characteristics that are of relevance to later development.

The assessment of criterion behaviors would allow mastery to be studied in the same way as developmental competence or intelligence, and a major concern would be in obtaining a psychometrically respectable assessment procedure. Once this was achieved, it would be possible to begin to identify influences of external variables on mastery motivation and influences of mastery motivation on other characteristics of children. It would be assumed that mastery motivation could be measured in a way that is uncontaminated by other influences, such as competence, and progress is being made to produce such assessments (see Morgan, MacTurk, & Jennings, this volume). This approach also assumes that mastery motivation can be measured along a dimension, from low to high, but it is questionable whether this is the case. Important differences may be categorical rather than quantitative. Even if scores can be obtained, there remains a difficulty in combining scores from different domains of mastery to give a summary measure. Moreover, the idea of mastery as a specific quantifiable characteristic of individuals does not easily fit with previous theories that treat it as a multidimensional construct (Hunt, 1965; White, 1959; Yarrow & Messer, 1983). There is also a danger that if effort is concentrated on issues of psychometrics, the study of the processes by which mastery motivation influences behavior may become neglected. As McCall (1977) has pointed out, the investigation of individual differences can lead to broad principles of development being ignored.

Of the three possibilities, I prefer the second approach that attempts to classify children's behavior rather than attempt to measure the degree of motivation that is present. It seems to me that our limited knowledge about mastery means that it is unwise, on an a priori basis, to identify behaviors that are the result of mastery motivation. Instead, it may be a better strategy to build up a picture of those behaviors that are conceptually and statistically related. When such a classification system is established, it should be possible to examine the antecedents of mastery and its consequence for later development. However, it may not be necessary to choose between these options. I would like to suggest that by conceptualizing mastery in a slightly different way we may be able to integrate different approaches to measurement.

Constituent Processes in Mastery Motivation

It is clear that mastery motivation cannot be measured directly, rather, it is an internal state that is hypothesized to influence the expression of certain behavior and, consequently, mastery motivation must be inferred from such behavior. Further, it is likely that other internal processes can influence behavior and thereby create errors in measurement. This can occur because of the difficulty of identifying a goal toward which motivated behavior is directed. There may be the same motive force in two individuals, but it is directed toward different ends. For example, two children might possess similar motives for mastery, but one may direct her behavior toward exploration and the other direct his behavior toward completing a task. In both examples it would be extremely difficult to obtain accurate assessments of mastery motivation.

Some of the problems in conceptualizing and assessing mastery motivation might be solved be identifying the constituent processes of *selection, engagement,* and *interest.* In any motivational system there needs to be the selection of an objective (Harter, 1981; White, 1959). Thus, children might be classified according to their selection of activities or according to the type of task they prefer (e.g., motor, verbal, problem-solving, object-related, social-related). This is an important element in motivation and one that most studies of mastery have ignored. Furthermore, there is an interesting question about the ages when such preferences emerge and how this emergence is related to transitions in development.

It might be supposed next that children differ in the way they become engaged in the task that they have selected. Some may engage in persistent focused activities, others in more general exploration. Still others might be discouraged easily but be prepared to return to the problem later. Consequently, behavior might be classified according to the pattern of engagement that children exhibit with a task or a set of tasks. Such a classification might be qualitative rather than quantitative.

Finally, because children differ in the amount of time that they spend on tasks, measurements can be made of this aspect of behavior. It is not clear whether it would be better to obtain the total duration spent with a task or the duration spent in different types of activities with a task; both may be relevant to our understanding of mastery motivation.

By analyzing the selection of activities, the engagement with tasks, and the duration of activity, it should be possible to examine a wide range of behaviors in an integrated fashion (e.g., persistence, curiosity, exploration, preference for optimal challenge). There still remains a difficulty in dealing with confounding factors such as developmental competence, but, as the work of Morgan and his colleagues have shown, considerable progress already has been made in disentangling mastery from competence (see MacTurk, Morgan, & Jennings, this volume).

SUMMARY

The discussion of the past, present and future has dealt with a number of interlocking themes. We have seen that the original idea of mastery motivation as a unidimensional construct has been superseded by an appreciation of the complexity of mastery and its developmental profile. Particularly important have been the moves to integrate mastery with other findings about social and cognitive development. This has resulted in a deeper understanding of the nature of mastery motivation, but has also generated new issues that need to be answered by future research. Further, the recognition that there are different forms of mastery motivation has provided a more realistic picture of children's behavior, but this has complicated issues of measurement. In looking to the future there is likely to continue to be debates about assessment and conceptualization. In many ways it is a strength of this research area that there are different research agendas involving different methodologies, such diversity is more likely to provide a useful and accurate picture of mastery motivation.

The last point that I would like to make is that if future research on mastery motivation is to take an important place in developmental psychology it should continue to be linked with other subject areas. Motivation is at the core (or near to it) of many issues in development psychology. Thus, the study of mastery motivation is relevant to the acquisition of a wide range of skills and abilities, and in this way it is of relevance to our understanding of fundamental processes in developmental whereby children's abilities are changed or transformed.

REFERENCES

Baron-Cohen, S. (1993, March). *Origins of theory of mind: The eye-direction detector*. Paper presented at the Society for Research in Child Development Conference, New Orleans, LA.

Barrett, K. C., Morgan, G. A., & Maslin-Cole, C., (1993). Three studies on the development of mastery motivation in infancy and toddlerhood. In D. J. Messer (Ed.), *Mastery motivation in early childhood: Development, measurement and social processes* (pp. 83–108). London: Routledge.

Bates, E., Dale, P. S., Thal, D. (in press). Individual differences and their implications for theories of language development. In P. Fletcher & B. MacWhinney (Eds), *Handbook of child language*. Oxford: Blackwell.

Bates, E., O'Connell, B., & Shore, C. (1987). Language and communication in infancy. In J. Osofsky (Ed.), *Handbook of infant development*, 2nd ed. (pp. 147–202). New York: Wiley.

Bornstein, M. H., & Sigman, M. D. (1986). Continuity in mental development from infancy. *Child Development, 57,* 251-74.

Bryant, P. (1990). Empirical evidence for causes in development. In G. Butterworth & P. Bryant (Eds.), *Causes of development* (pp. 33-45). Hemel Hempstead: Harvester Wheat Sheaf.

Busch-Rossnagel, N. A., Vargas, M., Knauf, D. E., & Planos, R. (1993). Mastery motivation in ethnic minority groups: the sample case of Hispanics. In D. J. Messer (Ed.), *Mastery motivation in early childhood: Development, measurement and social processes* (pp. 132-148). London: Routledge.

Coombs, T. T., & Wachs, T. D., (1993). The construct validity of measures of social mastery motivation. In D. J. Messer (Ed.), *Mastery motivation in early childhood: Development, measurement and social processes* (pp. 168-185). London: Routledge.

Gaiter, J. L., Morgan, G. A., Jennings, K. D., Harmon, R. J., & Yarrow, L. J. (1982). Variety of cognitively oriented caregiver activities: Relationships to cognitive and motivational functioning at 1 and 3.5 years of age. *Journal of Genetic Psychology. 141,* 49-56.

Goldberg, S. (1975). Developmental differences in the manifestation of mastery motivation on problem-solving tasks. *Child Development, 46,* 370-378.

Gopnik, A., & Meltzoff, A. N. (1986). Relations between semantic and cognitive development in the one-word stage. The specificity hypothesis. *Child Development, 57,* 1040-53.

Harding, C. G., & Golinkoff, R. M. (1979). The origins of intentional vocalization in prelinguistic infants. *Child Development, 50,* 13-40.

Harter, S. (1978). Effective motivation reconsidered: Towards a development model. *Human Development, 21,* 34-64.

Harter, S. (1981). A model of mastery motivation in children. In W. A. Collins (Ed.), *Minnesota symposia on child psychology* (Vol. 14, pp. 215-258). Hillsdale, NJ: Erlbaum.

Harter, S. (1983). Developmental perspectives on the self-system. In M. Hetherington (Ed.), *Carmichael's manual of child psychology: Social and personality development* (pp. 275-386). New York: Wiley.

Hauser-Cram, P. (1993). Mastery motivation in 3-year-old children with Down Syndrome. In D. J. Messer (Ed.), *Mastery Motivation in Early Childhood: Development, Measurement and Social Processes* (pp. 230-250). London: Routledge.

Heckhausen, J. (1993). The development of mastery and its perception within caretaker-child dyads. In D. J. Messer (Ed.), *Mastery motivation in early childhood: Development measurement and social processes* (pp. 55-79). London: Routledge.

Hobson, R. P. (1993) *Autism and the development of mind.* Hove, U. K.: Erlbaum Mitchell.

Hunt, J. McV. (1965). Intrinsic motivation and its role in psychological development. In D. Levine (Ed.), *Nebraska symposium on motivation.* (Vol. 13, pp. 189-276). Lincoln: University of Nebraska Press.

Jennings, K. (1975). People versus object orientation, social behaviour, and intellectual abilitiesin pre-school children. *Developmental Psychology, 11,* 511-9.

Jennings, K. D. (1993) Mastery motivation and the formation of self-concept from infancy through early childhood. In D. J. Messer (Ed.), *Mastery motivation in early childhood: Development, measurement and social processes* (pp. 36-54). London: Routledge.

Jennings, K. D., Harmon, R. J., Morgan, G. A., Gaiter, J. L., & Yarrow, L. J. (1979). Exploratory play as an index of mastery motivation. *Developmental Psychology, 15,* 386-394.

Kaye, K. (1982). *The mental and social life of babies.* Chichester: Harvester.

Leslie, A. M. (1987). Pretence and representation: the origins of "theory of mind". *Psychological Review, 94,* 412-26.

Lewis, M., & Brooks-Gunn, J. (1979). *Social cognition and the acquisition of self.* London: Plenum.

Lewis, M., & Goldberg, S. (1969). Perceptual–cognitive development in infancy: A generalized expectancy model as a function of the mother–infant interaction. *Merrill–Palmer Quarterly, 15,* 81-100.

MacTurk, R. H., Hunter, F., McCarthy, M. E., Vietze, P. M., & McQuiston, S. (1985). Social mastery in Down Syndrome and nondelayed infants. *Topics in Early Childhood Special Education, 4,* 93-109.

MacTurk, R. H., Vietze, P. M., McCarthy, M. E., McQuiston, S., & Yarrow, L. J. (1985). The organization of exploratory behavior in Down syndrome and nondelayed infants. *Child Development, 56,* 573-581.

Maslin-Cole, C. Bretherton, I., & Morgan, G. A. (1993). Toddler mastery motivation and competence: Links with attachment security, maternal scaffolding and family climate. In D. J. Messer (Ed.), *Mastery motivation in early childhood: Development, measurement and social processes* (pp. 205-239). London: Routledge.

McCall, R. (1977). Challenges to a science of developmental psychology. *Child Development, 48,* 333-344.

McShane, J. (1980). *Learning to talk.* Cambridge: Cambridge University Press.

Meltzoff, A. N., & Gopnik, A. (1989). On linking nonverbal imitation, representation, and language learning in the first two years of life. In G. E. Speidel & K. E. Nelson (Eds.), *The many faces of imitation in language learning* (pp. 23-51). New York: Springer-Verlag.

Meltzoff, A. N., & Gopnik, A. (1993). The role of imitation in understanding persons and developing a theory of mind. In S. Baron-Cohen, H. Tager-Flushberg, & D. Cohen (Eds.), *Understanding other minds—perspective from autism* (pp. 335-366). Oxford: Oxford University Press.

Messer, D. J. (1993). Mastery, attention, IQ and parent–infant social interaction. In D. J. Messer (Ed.), *Mastery motivation in early childhood: Development, measurement and social processes* (pp. 19-35). London: Routledge.

Messer, D. J. (1994). *The development of communication.* Chichester: Wiley.

Messer, D. J., McCarthy, M. E., McQuiston, S., MacTurk, R. H., Yarrow, L. J., & Vietze, P. M. (1986). Relation between mastery behavior in infancy and competence in early childhood. *Developmental Psychology, 22,* 366–372.

Messer, D. J., Rachford, D., McCarthy, M. E., & Yarrow, L. J. (1987). Assessment of mastery behavior at 30 months: Analysis of task-directed activities. *Developmental Psychology, 23,* 771–781.

Morgan, G. A., Maslin-Cole, C., Harmon, R. J., Busch-Rossnagel, N. A., Jennings, K. D., Hauser-Cram, P., & Brockman, L. (1993). Parent and teacher perceptions of young children's mastery motivation: Assessment and review of research. In D. J. Messer (Ed.), *Mastery motivation in early childhood: Development, measurement, and social Processes* (pp. 109–131). London: Routledge.

Murray, L., & Stein, A. (1989). The effects of postnatal depression on the infant. *Bailliere's Clinical Obstetrics and Gynaecology, 3,* 921–933.

Nelson, K. (1985). *Making sense: The acquisition of shared meaning.* New York: Academic Press.

Papousek, H. (1969). Individual variability in learned responses in human infants. In R. J. Robertson (Ed.), *Brain and early behaviour* (pp. 45–57). London: Academic Press.

Redding, R. E., Morgan, G. A., & Harmon, R. J. (1988). Mastery motivation in infants and toddlers: Is it greatest when tasks are moderately challenging? *Infant Behavior and Development, 11,* 419–430.

Riksen-Walraven, M. J., Meij, H., van Roozendaal, J., & Koks, J. (1993). Mastery motivation in toddlers as related to quality of attachment. In D. J. Messer (Ed.), *Mastery motivation in early childhood: Development, measurement and social Processes* (pp. 189–205). London: Routledge.

Schaffer, H. R. (1984) *The child's entry into a social world.* London: Academic Press.

Stern, D. (1979) *The first relationship.* London: Fontana.

Stipek, D., Recchia, S., & McClintic, S. (1992) Self-evaluation in young children. *Monographs of the Society for Research In Child Development, 57* (1, Serial No. 226).

Tomasello, M., & Farrar, J. (1986). Joint attention and early language. *Child Development, 57,* 1454–1463.

Trevarthen, C. (1982). The primary motives for cooperative understanding. In G. Butterworth & P. Light (Eds.), *Social cognition* (pp. 77–109). Brighton: Harvester.

Wachs, T. D. (1987). Specificity of environmental action as manifest in environmental correlates of infant's mastery motivation. *Developmental Psychology, 23,* 782–790.

Watson, J. S. (1966). The development and generalization of "contingency awareness" in early infancy: Some hypotheses. *Merrill–Palmer Quarterly, 12,* 123–135.

Watson, J. S. (1972). Smiling, cooing and "The Game." *Merrill–Palmer Quarterly, 18,* 323–329.

White, R. W., (1959). Motivation reconsidered: The concept of competence. *Psychological Review, 66,* 297–333.

Yarrow, L. J., McQuiston, S., MacTurk, R. H., McCarthy, M. E., Klein, R. P., & Vietze, P. M. (1983). Assessment of mastery motivation during the first year. *Developmental Psychology, 19,* 159–171.

Yarrow, L. J., & Messer, D. J. (1983). Motivation & cognition in infancy. In M. Lewis (Ed.), *Origins of intelligence* (2nd ed., pp. 451–477). Hillsdale, NJ: Erlbaum.

14

TOWARD A MULTIFACETED CONCEPTUALIZATION OF MASTERY MOTIVATION: AN ORGANIZED SUMMARY OF RESEARCH*

George A. Morgan

Raymond K. Yang

Colorado State University

Given the volume of research on mastery motivation, a useful step at this time would be to identify the areas that have received the most attention and areas that have been relatively neglected. To provide a systematic way of surveying the literature, we use the conceptualization of mastery motivation outlined in chapters 1–3 of this volume. Because this chapter was written after those that precede it in this volume, it has also been influenced by those chapters.

We begin by summarizing the conceptualizations of mastery motivation, particularly how it is organized. In the second section, we classify the existing empirical mastery motivation research into four age-based tables consistent with Barrett and Morgan's phases (chapter 3, this volume). Within each table, studies are listed and described by the task domains they assessed and by

---

*We wish to acknowledge the assistance of Jonelle Sandel with the tables, references, and statistics presented in this chapter. We also appreciate helpful comments and corrections from several colleagues, especially Karen Barrett, Lois Brockman, Kay Jennings, and Diana Knauf.

whether they measure various aspects of mastery motivation. In the third section, we summarize a few studies that provide support for the multifaceted framework presented in the tables. We also introduce an extensive data set previously unanalyzed for mastery motivation. This reanalyzed data provide multimethod support for the multifaceted conceptualization of mastery motivation. The data also suggest that by 3 years, gender differences in mastery motivation have emerged. In the fourth and final section, we present recommendations for further research, based on the multifaceted conceptualization of mastery motivation, the extant research summarized in the four tables, and the new analysis.

THE ORGANIZATION OF MASTERY MOTIVATION

The several definitions of mastery motivation presented in chapter 1 (Morgan, MacTurk, & Hrncir, this volume) are precursors of the definition by Barrett and Morgan (chapter 3). That definition, which forms one basis for this chapter, is: *"mastery motivation is . . . a multifaceted, intrinsic, psychological force that stimulates an individual to attempt to master a skill or task that is at least somewhat challenging for him or her."* One of the key features of this definition is that mastery motivation is multifaceted and that the facets are dissociable; that is, not necessarily correlated. Barrett and Morgan argued that indicators of mastery motivation can be categorized as either Instrumental or Expressive, with each of these two categories including a number of aspects or facets.

For example, some instrumental aspects are a tendency to persist at tasks that are somewhat difficult or challenging, preference for one's *own* physical and or cognitive control over events, and preference for some degree of challenge and/or novelty. Some of the expressive aspects of mastery motivation include the exhibition of pleasure, interest, pride, and frustration/anger. In the mastery motivation literature, persistence at challenging tasks and task pleasure have been the main indicators of the instrumental and expressive aspects, respectively, of mastery motivation. The tables presented in this chapter show whether these traditional mastery motivation measures (task persistence and pleasure) were used in a study and also whether "other" indicators were reported.

Chapter 1 divides the types of mastery motivation tasks facing infants and young children into three large domains: object-oriented, social, and gross motor. That chapter includes a 3 × 2 table indicating that for each of these three domains, one might expect to find both instrumental and expressive indicators of mastery motivation. That 3 × 2 table forms the basic structure of the tables presented in the next section of this chapter.

In chapter 2, MacTurk, Morgan, and Jennings divided the methods of gathering data about children's persistent task directedness into three main approaches: observations of behavior during structured tasks, observations of behavior during free play, and parent/teacher ratings based on everyday life. This distinction is built into the instrumental aspects of the tables presented in this chapter.

Chapters 1, 2, and, especially, 3 of this volume also indicate the importance of transformations and changes in mastery motivation as the child develops through infancy and the preschool years. In chapter 3, Barrett and Morgan presented a detailed analysis of continuities and changes in mastery motivation over the first three years of life.

A Summary Organization of the Mastery Motivation Literature

In this section, we organize the empirical research reviewed throughout this volume using the conceptualization presented earlier and expanded versions of the 3 × 2 table that was presented in chapter 1. An expanded table is presented here for each of the three age phases described by Barrett and Morgan as well as for the preschool years. Table 14.1 identifies empirical research reports designed to study mastery motivation in infants during phase one, which extends from birth to approximately 8 or 9 months of age. Tables 14.2 and 14.3 are similar, but identify mastery motivation studies of children in phase 2 (approximately 8–9 months to 17–21 months) and phase 3 (approximately 17–21 months to 32–36 months). Table 14.4 lists literature pertaining to mastery motivation during the preschool years.

Note that each of the four tables has the same structure and includes the same *types* of information. Vertically, the tables are divided into the three domains: object, social, and gross motor. Horizontally, the main distinction is between the instrumental and expressive aspects.

Each empirical study is placed in one or more of the three domains and in one or more table(s) depending on the

TABLE 14.1.   EMPIRICAL STUDIES OF THREE DOMAINS AND TWO ASPECTS
OF MASTERY MOTIVATION FOR INFANTS BIRTH TO 8 OR 9 MONTHS

		Aspects of Mastery Motivation				
		Instrumental Aspects				Expressive Aspects	
Citation		TPER	FP	DMQ	OTHERi	TPLS	OTHERe
Mastery Domains:							
a) Object Mastery Motivation							
Barrett et al.	1993	Y	Y	N	Y	Y	N
Hupp & Abbeduto	1992	Y	N	Y	Y	N	N
MacTurk et al.	1985a	Y	N	N	N	Y	N
MacTurk et al.	1985b	Y	N	N	N	Y	N
Messer et al.	1986	Y	N	N	N	N	N
Vietze et al.	1983	Y	N	N	N	N	N
Yarrow et al.	1983	Y	N	N	N	Y	N
b) Social Mastery Motivation							
MacTurk et al.	1985a	Y	N	N	N	Y	N
c) Gross Motor Mastery Motivation							
None							

TPER=Task persistence (duration of independent task-directed behavior at structured
mastery tasks). FP=Free play persistence (engrossment and/or duration of goal-
directed free play). DMQ=Dimensions of Mastery Questionnaire persistence (parent or
teacher ratings of child's persistence). OTHERi=Other instrumental mastery motivation
indicators (e.g., preference for challenge, curiosity, etc). TPLS=Task pleasure (positive
affect during tasks, including from DMQ). OTHERe=Other expressive mastery
motivation indicators (e.g., pride, frustration, etc).

domain(s) of mastery motivation studied and on the age of the
subjects. Thus, a study of 6-month-old children attempting traditional object-oriented mastery tasks (e.g., Yarrow et al., 1983)
would be listed alphabetically by author under "object mastery
motivation" in Table 14.1. Longitudinal or other multiaged studies would be listed in the tables with the appropriate *mental
ages*. For example, the Yarrow et al. (1983) study of 6 and 12
month olds, is listed in both Table 14.1 and 14.2. Studies that
investigated more than one domain (e.g., MacTurk et al., 1985b)
would be listed under all relevant domains.

Under instrumental aspects, each table indicates whether or
not the researcher reported measures of persistence using each
of the major methods (observations of structured tasks performed independently by the child, observations of free play,
and ratings by parents or teachers). The fourth column shows

whether or not other instrumental indicators of mastery motivation (such as curiosity, preference for challenge, executive capacity, or persistence in a cooperative task) were reported. Under expressive aspects, the table indicates whether task pleasure (positive affect during task directed behavior) and/or other expressive indicators of mastery motivation were reported.

Phase 1 (Birth to 8–9 Months)

There has been relatively little research directly aimed at investigating mastery motivation during phase 1. Although Table 14.1 cites several papers, six of them are from a complex National Institutes of Health study that resulted in a number of publications (e.g., Vietze, McCarthy, McQuiston, MacTurk, & Yarrow, 1983; Yarrow et al., 1983). All of the studies in Table 14.1 utilized infants in the older part of this age period (i.e., 5–9 months), and included infants over 9 months; three of these investigations were longitudinal, and three were cross-sectional.

Some of the findings of these studies have been perplexing. Indeed, McCall (this volume) argued that mastery motivation is not present before the infant can distinguish means from ends at about 8 or 9 months. Barrett and Morgan (this volume) disagree with this position, citing other evidence about early mastery motivation obtained from the early learning and emotional development literature. On the other hand, Messer (this volume) implied that mastery motivation can be identified in infants younger than 5 months and that phase 1 should be divided into two distinct phases.

Note that no studies are listed under gross motor mastery motivation, and only one study is listed under social mastery motivation. Also note that few of these studies used free play, parent/teacher ratings, or measures other than task persistence and/or task pleasure. This implies that gaps exist in our current knowledge; we will return to this in the section on recommendations for future research.

Phase 2 (8–9 Months to 17–21 Months)

Most of the published mastery motivation research has been conducted with children in this phase (often at 12 months) and with object-oriented tasks. Thus, the top part of Table 14.2 con-

TABLE 14.2. **EMPIRICAL STUDIES OF THREE DOMAINS AND TWO ASPECTS OF MASTERY MOTIVATION IN INFANTS AND TODDLERS 8–9 MONTHS TO 17–21 MONTHS**

Citation		Instrumental Aspects				Expressive Aspects	
		TPER	FP	DMQ	OTHERi	TPLS	OTHERe
Mastery Domains:							
a) Object Mastery Motivation							
Barrett et al.	1993	Y	Y	N	Y	Y	N
Belsky et al.	1984	N	Y	N	Y	N	N
Blasko et al.	1990	N	Y	N	N	N	N
Brockman	1984	Y	N	Y	N	Y	N
Caruso	1990	Y	N	N	N	N	N
Castaldi et al.	1990	N	Y	N	N	N	N
Combs & Wachs	1993	Y	Y	Y	Y	Y	N
Frodi et al.	1984	Y	Y	N	N	Y	N
Frodi et al.	1985	Y	N	N	N	Y	N
Fung	1984	Y	N	Y	N	Y	N
Gaiter et al.	1982	Y	N	N	N	N	N
Grolnick et al.	1984	Y	N	N	N	Y	N
Harmon & Culp	1981	Y	Y	N	N	Y	N
Harmon et al.	1984	Y	Y	Y	N	Y	N
Hauser-Cram	(in press)	Y	N	N	N	Y	N
Heckhausen	1993	N	N	N	Y	Y	Y
Hrncir et al.	1985	N	Y	N	Y	N	N
Hupp & Abbeduto	1988	Y	N	Y	N	N	N
Hupp & Abbeduto	1991	Y	N	N	N	N	N
Hupp & Abbeduto	1992	Y	N	Y	N	N	N
Hupp et al.	1992b	Y	N	Y	N	N	N
Jennings	1992	Y	Y	N	N	Y	N
Jennings et al.	1979	Y	Y	N	Y	N	N
Jennings et al.	1984	Y	N	N	N	N	N
Jennings	1993a	Y	N	N	Y	Y	Y
Johnson et al.	1993	Y	N	N	N	Y	N
Krenn	1995	N	N	Y	N	Y	N
MacTurk et al.	1987	N	N	N	Y	Y	N
MacTurk & Trimm	1989	Y	N	N	N	Y	N
MacTurk	1992	Y	N	N	N	Y	N
MacTurk	1993	Y	N	N	N	Y	N
Maslin-Cole et al.	1993	Y	Y	Y	Y	Y	N
Messer et al.	1986	Y	N	N	N	N	N
Morgan et al.	1988	N	Y	Y	Y	Y	N
Morgan et al.	1993	N	N	Y	N	Y	N
Popper et al.	1993	Y	N	N	N	N	N
Redding et al.	1988	Y	N	N	N	Y	N
Seifer et al.	1993	Y	N	N	Y	Y	Y
Smith	1993	Y	N	N	Y	N	N
Vondra	1987	N	N	N	Y	N	N
Vondra	1995	N	N	Y	Y	N	N
Wachs	1987	Y	N	N	N	N	N

TABLE 14.2.   CONTINUED

| | Aspects of Mastery Motivation | | | | | |
| | Instrumental Aspects | | | | Expressive Aspects | |
Citation	TPER	FP	DMQ	OTHERi	TPLS	OTHERe
Wachs & Combs (this vol.)	Y	Y	N	N	N	N
Yarrow et al. 1983	Y	N	N	N	Y	N
Yarrow et al. 1982	Y	N	N	N	Y	N
Zeanah et al. 1993	Y	N	N	Y	Y	Y
b) Social & Social-Object Mastery Motivation						
Combs & Wachs 1993	Y	Y	Y	Y	Y	N
Krenn 1995	N	N	Y	N	Y	N
Morgan et al. 1993	N	N	Y	N	Y	N
Popper et al. 1993	Y	N	N	N	N	N
Wachs 1987	Y	Y	N	N	N	N
Wachs & Combs (this vol.)	Y	Y	N	N	N	N
c) Gross Motor Mastery Motivation						
Morgan et al. 1993	N	N	Y	N	Y	N

TPER=Task persistence (duration of independent task-directed behavior at structured mastery tasks). FP=Free play persistence (engrossment and/or duration of goal-directed free play). DMQ=Dimensions of Mastery Questionnaire persistence (parent or teacher ratings of child's persistence). OTHERi=Other instrumental mastery motivation indicators (e.g., preference for challenge, curiosity, etc). TPLS=Task pleasure (positive affect during tasks, including from DMQ). OTHERe=Other expressive mastery motivation indicators (e.g., pride, frustration, etc).

tains many references. Busch-Rossnagel et al. (this volume) provided a useful review of much of the information related to antecedents of object-oriented mastery motivation at this age, as well as in phases 1 and 3. Note that a number of studies used free play assessments, parent ratings, and "other" measures of, especially, the instrumental aspects of mastery motivation during object-oriented tasks.

It is primarily in this phase that social mastery motivation has been studied. Gross motor mastery motivation has been studied only through parent or teacher ratings of children.

Phase 3 (17–21 Months to 32–36 Months)

Studies specifically directed at investigating mastery motivation have been less common at this age, as shown in Table 14.3, than in phase 2. To supplement the relatively few mastery motivation studies, Barrett and Morgan (this volume) discussed research about emotional development and other data from developmental psychology broadly. Messer, (this volume) encouraged this trend toward including broader literature within the mastery motivation framework. Note that in Table 14.3 there are no studies cited for the social or gross motor mastery domains, except the several Dimensions of Mastery Questionnaire, Krenn (1995) and studies

TABLE 14.3. EMPIRICAL STUDIES OF THREE DOMAINS AND TWO ASPECTS OF MASTERY MOTIVATION IN CHILDREN 17–21 TO 32–36 MONTHS

| | Aspects of Mastery Motivation | | | | | |
| | Instrumental Aspects | | | | Expressive Aspects | |
Citation	TPER	FP	DMQ	OTHERi	TPLS	OTHERe
Mastery Domains:						
a) Object Mastery Motivation						
Barrett et al. 1993	Y	N	N	N	Y	N
Busch-Rossnagel et al. 1993	Y	Y	Y	N	Y	N
Caruso 1990	Y	N	N	N	N	N
Hauser-Cram 1993	Y	N	N	N	Y	N
Heckhausen 1993	N	N	N	Y	Y	Y
Hupp et al. 1992b	Y	N	N	Y	Y	N
Jennings 1992	Y	N	Y	Y	Y	Y
Jennings 1993a	Y	N	N	Y	Y	Y
Johnson et al. 1993	Y	N	N	N	Y	N
Krenn 1995	N	N	Y	N	Y	N
Maslin-Cole et al. 1993	Y	Y	Y	Y	Y	N
Maslin-Cole & Spieker 1990	Y	Y	Y	Y	Y	N
Messer et al. 1987	Y	N	N	Y	Y	N
Morgan et al. 1993	N	N	Y	Y	N	N
Redding et al. 1990	Y	N	N	N	Y	N
Redding et al. 1988	Y	N	N	N	Y	N
Riksen-Walraven et al. 1993	N	N	N	Y	N	Y
Sigman et al. 1987	Y	N	N	N	N	N
Vondra 1995	N	N	Y	Y	N	N
b) Social Mastery Motivation						
Krenn 1995	N	N	Y	N	Y	N
Morgan et al. 1993	N	N	Y	N	Y	N
c) Gross Motor Mastery Motivation						
Morgan et al. 1993	N	N	Y	N	Y	N

TPER=Task persistence (duration of independent task-directed behavior at structured mastery tasks). FP=Free play persistence (engrossment and/or duration of goal-directed free play). DMQ=Dimensions of Mastery Questionnaire persistence (parent or teacher ratings of child's persistence). OTHERi=Other instrumental mastery motivation indicators (e.g., preference for challenge, curiosity, etc). TPLS=Task pleasure (positive affect during tasks, including from DMQ). OTHERe=Other expressive mastery motivation indicators (e.g., pride, frustration, etc).

presented in Morgan et al. (1993). Several studies, especially by European investigators and Jennings, have used a variety of measures in addition to or instead of task persistence and pleasure.

Phase 4 (3–5 Years)

Table 14.4 presents research reports on mastery motivation in 3- to 5-year-old children. Barrett and Morgan (this volume) did not

TABLE 14.4. EMPIRICAL STUDIES OF THREE DOMAINS AND TWO ASPECTS OF MASTERY MOTIVATION 3- TO 5-YEAR-OLD CHILDREN

| | | Aspects of Mastery Motivation | | | | | |
| | | Instrumental Aspects | | | | Expressive Aspects | |
Citation		TPER	FP	DMQ	OTHERi	TPLS	OTHERe
Mastery Domains:							
a) Object Mastery Motivation							
Douchette	1993	Y	N	N	Y	N	N
Gaiter et al.	1982	Y	N	N	Y	N	N
Jennings & Connors	1989	N	Y	Y	N	N	N
Jennings et al.	1984	Y	N	N	Y	N	N
Jennings et al.	1985	Y	Y	Y	Y	N	N
Jennings et al.	1988	Y	Y	N	Y	N	N
Krenn	1995	N	N	Y	N	Y	N
Lutkenhaus	1984	N	N	N	Y	N	Y
McGrath et al.	1993	Y	N	N	Y	Y	Y
Morgan et al.	1993	N	N	Y	N	Y	N
Morgan et al.	1994	Y	Y	N	Y	Y	Y
Niccols & Atkinson	1995	Y	N	Y	N	Y	N
Vondra	1987	N	N	N	Y	N	N
Vondra et al.	1990	Y	N	N	Y	N	Y
b) Social Mastery Motivation							
Krenn	1995	N	N	Y	N	Y	N
Morgan et al.	1993	N	N	Y	N	Y	N
Morgan et al.	1994	N	Y	N	Y	Y	Y
Niccols & Atkinson	1995	Y	N	Y	N	Y	N
c) Gross Motor Mastery Motivation							
Morgan et al.	1993	N	N	Y	N	Y	N
Morgan et al.	1994	Y	Y	N	Y	Y	Y

TPER=Task persistence (duration of independent task-directed behavior at structured mastery tasks). FP=Free play (engrossment and/or duration of goal-directed free play). DMQ=Dimensions of Mastery Questionnaire (parent or teacher ratings of child's persistence). OTHERi=Other instrumental mastery motivation indicators (e.g., preference for challenge, curiosity, etc). TPLS=Task pleasure (positive affect during tasks, including from DMQ). OTHERe=Other expressive mastery motivation indicators (e.g., pride, frustration, etc).

describe a phase beyond 3 years, but Jennings (1993b) has. As in phase 3, research directly addressing mastery motivation with children this age is limited, confined primarily to Jennings' work and research with the DMQ. Again, several investigators have used measures other than task persistence and pleasure; that is, they have taken a multifaceted view of mastery motivation.

DATA RELEVANT TO THIS CONCEPTUALIZATION OF MASTERY MOTIVATION

The framework for the tables presented earlier was based, in part, on principal components analyses of the *ratings* of mothers and teachers of 3- to 5-year-old children (Morgan et al., 1993). These analyses yielded four clear orthogonal mastery motivation factors: three instrumental components (persistence at object, social/symbolic, and gross motor tasks) and one expressive component, labeled mastery pleasure. In general, young children who were rated as highly persistent on object-oriented tasks were not necessarily the same ones who were most persistent at social or gross motor tasks, and none of the three instrumental scales was correlated with pleasure when solving tasks. This separation into four factors was also found in the parent ratings of 1- to 3-year-olds, but the factors were somewhat less distinctive, indicating that persistence may be less domain- or type-of-task-specific and more generalized in infancy and toddlerhood.

As can be seen from inspection of the tables, there are relatively few *behavioral* data that cut across two or more of the domains. One series of behavioral studies (Combs & Wachs, 1993; Wachs, 1987; Wachs & Combs, this volume) has been published, and the results support the separation of the instrumental aspects of object and social mastery, which is consistent with the framework in the tables.

At the present time there is insufficient evidence to determine if the expressive aspects of mastery motivation are separable into three domains as implied by the framework of the tables. If an expressive aspect, such as task pleasure, were assessed during tasks from each of the three domains (object, social, and gross motor), would such pleasure measures be relatively uncorrelated across task domains but correlated with pleasure in similar tasks; that is, would the scores produce three factors?

With regard to the multifaceted nature of mastery motivation, the issue we would like to discuss here is whether it is useful to conceptualize mastery motivation as having a number of dissociable (i.e., not necessarily correlated) aspects or behavioral indicators, such as preference for challenge and attention span in addition to persistence. Barrett and Morgan (this volume) proposed such a conceptualization and suggested that studying more aspects would produce a more complete view of mastery motivation. Such an approach, of course, leads to a more complex view of mastery motivation. There have been relatively few studies that directly address this issue, and almost all of them used only tasks in the object domain. Furthermore, most studies with multiple measures (e.g., Ricksen-Walraven et al., 1993; Seifer et al., 1993) have combined the measures into a single (or few) composite mastery motivation measure. Other multi-measure studies (e.g., Jennings et al., 1984, 1988) have developed different types of tasks to assess different aspects (e.g., curiosity and persistence) of mastery motivation. More knowledge about the relationships between various measures and about whether and how to combine them would be useful.

Maslin-Cole, Bretherton, and Morgan (1993) provided such information from a multimethod, multicontext mastery motivation study of 18- and 24-month-old children, which provides support for a multifaceted view of mastery motivation. They performed separate principal components analyses on several instrumental and expressive mastery measures, all in the object mastery domain. Their findings suggest two named components for instrumental mastery at each age: (a) overall task directedness or persistence (on mastery tasks, the Bayley and the DMQ); and (b) free-play engrossment (with symbolic and combinational toys). From the more limited number of expressive measures, one component emerged at 18 months, whereas two emerged at 24 months.

The studies cited in this section are few in number, but support the multifaceted conceptualization of mastery motivation, and they are consistent with the framework presented in Tables 14.1–14.4.

The Bethesda Longitudinal Study Data

Morgan, Sandel, and Yang (1994) have recently reanalyzed data from the National Institute of Mental Health Bethesda Longitudinal study (e.g., Yang & Halverson, 1976; Yang & Moss, 1978), which provided further information regarding the facets of mastery motivation depicted in Tables 14.1–14.4. These Bethesda data came from a sample of 152 3-year-old children who were observed and tested under a variety of conditions during an experimental preschool. Data had been collected from the children and/or their parents at several earlier time periods (e.g., prenatally, during the newborn period, and at 3 and 11 months), but the discussion here considers only findings regarding 3-year-olds.

This very rich data set provided a number of variables related to 3-year-old mastery motivation and the domains presented in Tables 14.1–14.4. For example, children were observed with their mothers, but without peers, in several settings on an initial visit to the nursery school. The children were also observed during the 4 week nursery school with four peers and two teachers. In addition, they were given several standardized tests and presented with experimental procedures, some of which resembled the mastery tasks.[1] From these settings were drawn behavioral observations, teacher ratings, and various scores from the experimental procedures and tests. We assembled about 30 variables that appeared to assess the instrumental aspects of one of the three task domains of mastery motivation (object, social, and gross motor) or the positive expressive aspects.

The settings for the expressive measures were not specified adequately to allow separation of the expressive behaviors by task domains. Because these Bethesda data were not collected with mastery motivation in mind, the available measures did not exactly fit the Barrett and Morgan (this volume) definition of the motive to master challenging tasks. This was especially true in the gross motor and social domains and for the expressive aspects. Nevertheless, we think that the resulting measures are relatively close approximations of several aspects of mastery motivation.

Four principal components analyses (with orthogonal rotation) were run: one for each of the three hypothesized instrumental domains (object, social, and gross motor) and one for

---

[1]We want to thank Charles Halverson, who was PI of the data collected from the 3-year olds, for sharing the data and for advice about it. We also acknowledge the financial support of the Developmental Psychobiology Research Group Endowment in reanalyzing the Bethesda data.

expressive behaviors. In each analysis, one moderately large first factor emerged that fit our conceptualization of that aspect of mastery motivation. However, in each case a second (and in one case a third) factor emerged, which provides support for Barrett and Morgan's contention that mastery motivation has many facets. The second (or third) factor in a domain often included variables assessed in a different context or with a different type of measure. In some cases, the differences mirror variations in how motivation has been measured in previous studies. For example, the first factor from the object-oriented persistence domain is similar to persistence at challenging *tasks*. The second component, labeled *Long Play Bouts*, is somewhat analogous to Jennings et al.'s (1979) continuity of *free play* measure (see chapter 2, this volume) and some other investigators' free play measures. The first factor, which Morgan et al. (1994) call *Persistence at Challenging Tasks and Play Involvement*, is orthogonal to Long Play Bouts. Similarly, in the analysis of the Enthusiasm and Positive Affect domain, the first factor represents enthusiasm and animation during the first day and on a test administered by an unfamiliar person (like the usual measures of mastery pleasure). The second component is positive affect during free play over a four-week period with peers and familiar teachers. Broad affect measures of this type have not usually been considered to be measures of mastery motivation.

Another principal components analysis of all the instrumental components or aspects of mastery motivation derived from the Bethesda Longitudinal data provided some support for three separate instrumental domains (object, social, and gross motor). These results are also consistent with the framework presented in this chapter.

Thus, by 3 years of age, instrumental mastery efforts appear to have differentiated into gross motor, object-oriented, and social domains. At this age, interest in gross motor tasks is usually not compatible with high levels of social interaction because peer play is mostly parallel and adults tend not to participate in gross motor play with young preschoolers. If interaction occurs, it is typically tandem to the task (e.g., walking a balance beam, climbing to the top of a jungle gym). Coincident social exchanges are more likely to occur in object-oriented tasks if the object is small (i.e., manipulable) and another person is nearby. In contrast, the social domain involves interaction initially and directly.

As part of the reanalysis of the Bethesda Longitudinal data Morgan et al. (1994) found that girls and boys differ in several aspects of mastery motivation. For example, girls were higher on attempts to control adults, whereas boys were higher on both persistence at gross motor play and persistence at gross motor tasks. However, there were no gender differences on object–task persistence or initial enthusiasm, a finding consistent with the mastery motivation literature. It seems likely that very few mean gender differences have been found in other studies because investigators have not taken a multifaceted approach to measuring mastery motivation. (See Vondra, this volume, for alternative explanations.)

These differences between boys and girls pertain to specific styles of mastery motivation, not to the total amount of mastery motivation. We doubt that if all possible facets were summed, any sex differences would appear. However, these differences, viewed from the context of early educational settings (e.g., preschool and kindergarten), may have relevance to the well-recognized differences in cognitive/intellective patterns among young boys and girls. The differences in specific facets of mastery motivation may, as distinctive cognative venues, presage girls' verbal and boys' spatial/analytic skills.

In the next section, we discuss recommendations for research based on observable gaps in Tables 14.1 to 14.4 and on the results of the studies described in this section.

RECOMMENDATIONS FOR FUTURE RESEARCH

It is clear from the tables that there are a number of gaps in current research on mastery motivation. First, as mentioned here earlier, phases 1, 3, and 4 (under 8 months and 1½ to 5 years) are relatively understudied. Second, the expressive aspects are less well studied than the instrumental, and it is not clear whether similar measures of the expressive aspects of mastery motivation are as domain- or type-of-task- (e.g., object vs. social) specific as the instrumental aspect of task persistence appears to be. Third, the social and, especially, gross motor domains are grossly underinvestigated, and the field has not reached any consensus about appropriate definitions of and tasks for assessing social mastery motivation and gross motor mastery motivation.

Most importantly, the tables and the data in the last section suggest that there is a need to investigate more fully the usefulness of the multifaceted approach to mastery motivation and the 3 × 2 framework presented in the tables. To do this would require multimethod studies designed to include structured object-oriented, gross motor, and social tasks; such studies should also include free play and parent/teacher rating measures. These studies should be designed to include a wide variety of relevant measures, such as those described by Barrett and Morgan (this volume) in addition to task persistence and task pleasure. The Maslin-Cole et al. (1993) and Morgan et al. (1994) studies approximated this goal, but the former restricted the domain to object mastery and the latter did not have enough emphasis on *challenge*. Studies like those just proposed would provide us with needed information about the interrelationships of task persistence, task pleasure, and other possible indicators of mastery motivation. They would also help us learn how useful other indicators will be, either separately or as part of a pattern/combination.

It is also important to study mastery motivation in children over 5 years of age. As the child grows, mastery motivation may acquire more facets and/or be exhibited in more task domains than the three proposed in chapter 1 (this volume) and supported by the reanalysis of the 3-year Bethesda data. Harter (1985), for example, found five aspects of self-perceived competence, which seem to parallel aspects of motivation, in school-age children. It may also be that there is less clear differention of task domains in infancy. These hypotheses deserve more study.

The gender differences found by Morgan et al. (1994) and discussed previously here are, in some ways, typical of those reported for boys and girls (e.g., Maccoby & Jacklin, 1974). They become important, however, and worth further study when placed in the context of mastery motivation rather than simply differences in styles of play. These findings suggest that 3-year-old boys and girls may preferentially display mastery-relevant behavior in different settings. Although there seem to be few gender differences in persistence at object-oriented tasks, girls seem more likely than boys to seek mastery in social interaction, particularly in their attempts to control adults. Boys, in contrast, seek mastery more often than girls in gross motor tasks. Thus, gender differences in mastery motivation deserve more attention than they have been given in part, because of the implications for early education.

In addition, as discussed extensively by Vondra (this volume) individual differences in mastery motivation may well be substantially influenced by genetic and/or congenital differences. Thus, another reason to examine gender differences, as well as environmental differences, in mastery motivation is because sex seems to be an important congenital characteristic.

In conclusion, we have suggested several areas of research based on inspection of Tables 14.1 to 14.4. We have also proposed research to provide more evidence about the multifaceted approach and the 3 × 2 framework used here for organizing the mastery literature. Finally we (like Vondra, this volume) have suggested additional research on gender differences in mastery motivation.

REFERENCES

Barrett, K. C., Morgan, G. A., & Maslin-Cole, C. (1993). Three studies on the development of mastery motivation in infancy and toddlerhood. In D. Messer (Ed.), *Mastery motivation in early childhood: Development, measurement, and social processes* (pp. 83–108). London: Routledge.

Belsky, J., Garduque, L., & Hrncir, E. (1984). Assessing performance, competence, and executive capacity in infant play: Relations to home environment and security of attachment. *Developmental Psychology, 20,* 406–417.

Blasco, P. M., Hrncir, E. J., & Blasco, P. (1990). The contribution of maternal involvement to mastery performance in infants with cerebral palsy. *Journal of Early Intervention, 14,* 161–174.

Brockman, L. M. (1984, May). *Mastery motivation and competence in young children.* Paper presented at the NIH Workshop on Mastery Motivation, Bethesda, MD.

Busch-Rossnagel, N. A., Vargas, M. E., Knauf, D. E., & Planos, R. (1993). Mastery motivation in ethnic minority groups: The sample case of Hispanics. In D. Messer (Ed.), *Mastery motivation in early childhood: Development, measurement, and social processes* (pp. 132–148). London: Routledge.

Caruso, D. A. (1990). Exploratory behavior, task persistence, and problem-solving ability across the second year of life. *Early Education and Development, 1*(5), 354–370.

Castaldi, J., Hrncir, E. J., & Caldwell, C. B. (1990). Future models for the study of individual differences in motivation during infancy. *Early Education and Development, 1,* 385–393.

Combs, T. T., & Wachs, T. D. (1993). The construct validity of measures of social mastery motivation. In D. Messer (Ed.), *Mastery motiva-*

tion in early childhood: Development, measurement, and social processes (pp. 168–185). London: Routledge.

Douchette, A. C. (1993). Mastery motivation in school-aged children with cognitive deficits. Doctoral dissertation, Boston College, Chestnut Hill, MA.

Frodi, A., Bridges, L., & Grolnick, W. (1985). Correlates of mastery-related behaviors: A short-term longitudinal study of infants in their second year. Child Development, 56, 1291–1298.

Frodi, A., Keller, B., Foye, H., Liptak, G., Bridges, L., Grolnick, W., Berko, J., McAnarney, E., & Lawrence, R. (1984). Determinants of mastery motivation in infants born to adolescent mothers. Infant Mental Health Journal, 5, 15–23.

Fung, A. Y. (1984). The relationship of mother's perception to the child's competence and mastery motivation. Unpublished master's thesis, University of Manitoba, Winnipeg, Canada.

Gaiter, J. L., Morgan, G. A., Jennings, K. D., Harmon, R. J., & Yarrow, L. J. (1982). Variety of cognitively oriented caregiver activities: Relationships to cognitive and motivational functioning at 1 and 3½ years of age. Journal of Genetic Psychology, 141, 49–56.

Grolnick, W., Frodi, A., & Bridges, L. (1984). Maternal control style and mastery motivation of one-year-olds. Infant Mental Health Journal, 5, 72–82.

Harmon, R. J., & Culp, A. M. (1981). The effects of premature birth on family functioning and infant development. In I. Berlin (Ed.), Children and our future (pp. 1–9). Albuquerque: University of New Mexico Press.

Harmon, R. J., Morgan, G. A., & Glicken, A. D. (1984). Continuities and discontinuities in affective and cognitive-motivational development. International Journal of Child Abuse and Neglect, 8, 157–167.

Harter, S. (1985). The self perception profile for children. Manual, University of Denver, Denver, CO.

Hauser-Cram, P. (1993). Mastery motivation in 3-year-old children with Down syndrome. In D. Messer (Ed.), Mastery motivation in early childhood: Development, measurement, and social processes (pp. 230–250). London: Routledge.

Hauser-Cram, P. (In press). Mastery motivation in toddlers with developmental disabilities. Child Development.

Heckhausen, J. (1993). The development of mastery and its perception within caretaker–child dyads. In D. Messer (Ed.), Mastery motivation in early childhood: Development, measurement, and social processes. London: Routledge.

Hrncir, E. J., Speller, G. M., & West, M. (1985). What are we testing? Developmental Psychology, 21, 226–232.

Hupp, S. C., & Abbeduto, L. (1988, March). Comparison of the organization of play by young retarded children who exhibit high and low levels of mastery motivation. Presented at the 21st Annual

Gatlinburg Conference on Mental Retardation/Development Disabilities, Gatlinburg, TN.

Hupp, S. C., & Abbeduto, L. (1991). Persistence as an indicator of mastery motivation in young children with cognitive delays. *Journal of Early Intervention, 15*(3), 219–225.

Hupp, S. C., & Abbeduto, L. (1992). *Comparison of the use of mastery behaviors by eight-, twelve-, and eighteen-month-old children.* Manuscript submitted for publication.

Hupp, S. C., Boat, M. B., & Alpert, A. S. (1992a). Impact of adult interaction on play behaviors and emotional responses of preschoolers with developmental delays. *Education and Training in Mental Retardation. 27*, 145–152.

Hupp, S. C., Lam, S. F., & Jaeger, J. (1992b). Differences in exploration of toys by one-year-old children: A Korean and American comparison. *Behavior Science Research.*

Jennings, K. D. (1992, May). *Development of mastery motivation and sense of agency in toddlers.* Presented at the 8th International Conference on Infant Studies, Miami, FL.

Jennings, K. D. (1993a, March). *Developmental changes in toddler's social orientation and affect during mastery play.* Presented at the Society for Research in Child Development, New Orleans, LA.

Jennings, K. D. (1993b). Mastery motivation and the formation of self-concept from infancy through early childhood. In D. Messer (Ed.), *Mastery motivation in early childhood: Development, measurement, and social processes* (pp. 36–54). London: Routledge.

Jennings, K. D., & Connors, R. E. (1989). Mother's interactional style and children's competence at 3 years. *International Journal of Behavioral Development, 12*(2), 155–175.

Jennings, K. D., Connors, R. E., & Stegman, C. E. (1988). Does a physical handicap alter the development of mastery motivation during the preschool years? *Journal of the American Academy of Child and Adolescent Psychiatry, 27*, 312–317.

Jennings, K. D., Connors, R. E., Stegman C. E., Sankaranarayan, P., & Mendelsohn, S. (1985). Mastery motivation in young preschoolers: Effect of a physical handicap and implications for educational programming. *Journal of the Division for Early Childhood, 9*, 162–169.

Jennings, K., Harmon, R., Morgan, G., Gaiter, J., & Yarrow, L. (1979). Exploratory play as an index of mastery motivation: Relationships to persistence, cognitive functioning and environmental measures. *Developmental Psychology, 15*, 386–394.

Jennings, K., Yarrow, L., & Martin, P. (1984). Mastery motivation and cognitive development: A longitudinal study from infancy to three and one half years. *International Journal of Behavioral Development, 7*, 441–461.

Johnson, D. B., Morgan, G. A., & Yang, R. K. (1993). *The Brazelton neonatal behavioral assessment scale as a predictor of one- and two-year-old mastery behavior.* Paper symposium at the biennial meeting of the Society for Research in Child Development, New Orleans, LA.

Krenn, M. J. (1995). *Mastery motivation and its relation to temperament in childhood: A short-term longitudinal study.* Unpublished doctoral dissertation, University of Manitoba, Winnipeg, Canada.

Lutkenhaus, P. (1984). Pleasure derived from mastery in three-year-olds: Its function for persistence and the influence of maternal behavior. *International Journal of Behavioral Development, 7,* 343–358.

Maccoby, E. E., & Jacklin, C. N. (1974). *The psychology of sex differences.* Stanford, CA: Stanford University Press.

MacTurk, R. (1992). *Relations between mother–infant interaction and the organization of mastery motivation in 9- to 12-month-old deaf and hearing infants.* Poster presented at the 8th International Conference on Infant Studies.

MacTurk, R. (1993). Social and motivational development in deaf & hearing infants. In D. Messer (Ed.). *Mastery motivation in early childhood: Development, measurement, and social processes* (pp. 149–167). London: Routledge.

MacTurk, R. H., Hunter, F., McCarthy, M., Vietze, P., & McQuiston, S. (1985a). Social mastery motivation in Down syndrome and non-delayed infants. *Topics in Early Childhood Special Education, 4,* 93–109.

MacTurk, R. H., McCarthy, M. E., Vietze, P. M., & Yarrow, L. J. (1987). Sequential analysis of mastery behavior in 6- and 12-month-old infants. *Developmental Psychology. 23*(2), 199–203.

MacTurk, R. H., & Trimm, V. M. (1989). Mastery motivation in deaf and hearing infants. *Early Education and Development, 1*(1), 19–34.

MacTurk, R. H., Vietze, P. M., McCarthy, M. E., McQuiston, S., & Yarrow, L. J. (1985b). The organization of exploratory behavior in Down syndrome and nondelayed infants. *Child Development, 56,* 573–581.

Maslin-Cole, C., Bretherton, I., & Morgan, G. A. (1993). Toddler mastery motivation and competence: Links with attachment security, maternal scaffolding, and family climate. In D. Messer (Ed.), *Mastery motivation in early childhood: Development, measurement, and social processes,* (pp. 205–229). London: Routledge.

Maslin-Cole, C. A. & Spieker, S. J. (1990). Attachment as a basis for independent motivation: A view from risk and non-risk samples. In M. T. Greenberg, D. Cecchetti, & E. M. Cummings (Eds.), *Attachment in the preschool years: Theory, research, and intervention* (pp. 245–272). Chicago: The University of Chicago Press.

McGrath, M., Sullivan, M., Brem, F., & Coduri-Rocherolle, K. (1993, March). *Mastery motivation and cognitive development in 4-year-old term and preterm infants.* Presented at the Society for Research in Child Development, New Orleans, LA.

Messer, D. J., McCarthy, M. E., McQuiston, S., MacTurk, R. H., Yarrow, L. J., & Vietze, P. M. (1986). Relation between mastery behavior in infancy and competence in early childhood. *Developmental Psychology, 22,* 336–372.

Messer, D. J., Rachford, D., McCarthy, M. E., & Yarrow, L. J. (1987). Assessment of mastery behavior at 30 months: Analysis of task-directed activities. *Developmental Psychology, 23* (2), 199–203.

Morgan, G. A., Harmon, R. J., Maslin-Cole, C. A., Busch-Rossnagel, N. A., Jennings, K. D., Hauser-Cram, P., & Brockman, L. M. (1993). Parent and teacher perceptions of young children's mastery motivation: Assessment and review of research. In D. Messer (Ed.), *Mastery motivation in early childhood: Development, measurement, and social processes* (pp. 109–131). London: Routledge.

Morgan, G. A., Maslin, C. A., Ridgeway, D., & Kang-Park, J. (1988). Toddler mastery motivation and aspects of mother–child affect communication. *Program and Proceedings of the Developmental Psychobiology Research Group Retreat, 5,* 15–16. (Summary)

Morgan, G. A., Sandel, J. K., & Yang, R. K. (1994). Gender differences in aspects of mastery motivation. *Program and Proceedings of the Developmental Psychobiology Research Group Retreat, 8,* 21–22.

Niccols, A., & Atkinson, L. (1995, March). *Mastery motivation in 5-year-old children with Down syndrome: Relations with attachment, security and competence.* Presented at the Society for Research in Child Development, Indianapolis, IN.

Popper, S. D., Ross, S., Cohn, J. F., & Campbell, S. B. (1993, March). *Social and object mastery play in 12-month olds with depressed and non-depressed mothers: Developmental changes and correlates.* Presented at the Society for Research in Child Development, New Orleans, LA.

Redding, R. E., Harmon, R. J., & Morgan, G. A. (1990). Maternal depression and infants' mastery behaviors, *Infant Behavior and Development, 13,* 391–395.

Redding, R. E., Morgan, G. A., & Harmon, R. J. (1988). Mastery motivation in infants and toddlers: Is it greatest when tasks are moderately challenging? *Infant Behavior and Development, 11,* 419–430.

Riksen-Walraven, M., Meij, H. Th., Van Roozendaal, J., & Koks, J. (1993). Mastery motivation in toddlers as related to quality of attachment. In D. Messer (Ed.), *Mastery motivation in early childhood: Development, measurement, and social processes* (pp. 189–204). London: Routledge.

Seifer, R., Schiller, M., Hayden, L., & Geerher, C. (1993). *Mastery motivation, temperament, attachment, and maternal interaction.* Presented at the Society for Research in Child Development, New Orleans, LA.

Sigman, M., Cohen, S. E., Beckwith, L., & Topinka, C. (1987). Task persistence in two-year-old preterm infants in relation to subsequent attentiveness and intelligence. *Infant Behavior and Development,* *10*, 295–305.

Smith, M. C. (1993, March). *Reconceptualizing the measurement of persistence in an attempt to facilitate prediction of infant problem-solving competence.* Presented at the Society for Research in Child Development, New Orleans, LA.

Vietze, P., McCarthy, M., McQuiston, S., MacTurk, R., & Yarrow, L. (1983). Attention and exploratory behavior in infants with Down syndrome. In T. Field and A. Sostek (Eds.), *Infants born at risk: Perceptual and physiological processes.* New York: Grune and Stratton.

Vondra, J. I. (1987, April). *Early mastery motivation: How can we measure it and what does it mean?* Presented at the Biennial Meeting of the Society for Research in Child Development, Baltimore, MD.

Vondra, J. I. (1995, March). *Early play as an index of competence and motivation.* Presented at the Society for Research in Child Development, Indianapolis, IN.

Vondra, J. I., Barnett, D., & Cicchetti, D. (1990). Self-concept, motivation, and competence among preschoolers from maltreating and comparison families. *Child Abuse and Neglect, 14*(4), 525–540.

Wachs, T. D. (1987). Specificity of environmental action as manifest in environmental correlates of infant's mastery motivation. *Developmental Psychology, 23*, 782–790.

Yang, R. K., & Halverson, C. F., Jr. (1976). A study of the "inversion intensity" between newborn and preschool-age behavior. *Child Development, 47*, 350–359.

Yang, R. K., & Moss, H. A. (1978). Neonatal precursors of infant behavior. *Developmental Psychology, 14*, 607–613.

Yarrow, L. J., McQuiston, S., MacTurk, R. H., McCarthy, M. E., Klein, R. P., & Vietze, P. M. (1983). Assessment of mastery motivation during the first year of life. Contemporaneous and cross-age relationships. *Developmental Psychology, 19*, 159–171.

Yarrow, L. J., Morgan, G. A., Jennings, K. D., Harmon, R. J., & Gaiter, J. L. (1982). Infants' persistence at tasks: Relationships to cognitive functioning and early experience. *Infant Behavior and Development, 5*, 131–142.

Zeanah, C. H., Hirshberg, L., & Miller, D. (1993). *Mastery at 15 months: Maternal correlates in a high risk sample.* Paper symposium at the biennial meeting of the Society for Research in Child Development, New Orleans, LA.

15

CONCLUDING COMMENTS ON MASTERY MOTIVATION: ORIGINS, CONCEPTUALIZATIONS AND APPLICATIONS

Karen Caplovitz Barrett

Colorado State University

Robert H. MacTurk

Gallaudet University

George A. Morgan

Colorado State University

This concluding chapter is divided into three sections. First, the review chapters in this volume (4–11) are briefly summarized, and some comments are made about their implications. Second, we respond in some detail to the commentary chapters by McCall and Messer. Discussion of these two chapters is fairly extensive because these chapters were written as commentaries on the earlier chapters and were aimed, at least partially, at stimulating continued thought and dialogue. Finally, in a third section, we suggest some implications of the previous chapters for future research needs (see also Morgan & Yang, chapter 14, this volume).

The review chapters of this volume describe and discuss several important issues surrounding the existing research on mastery motivation. Several of the chapters review what is currently known about the motivational characteristics of atypical infants and children and, in addition, address the implications of these results for intervention strategies. Other chapters in this middle section are directed toward expanding the theoretical framework of the mastery studies. These chapters serve to substantially broaden our view of this important developmental process.

Insight Into Atypical Populations

In chapters 8–11, Hupp, Jennings and MacTurk, Harmon and Murrow, and Hauser-Cram and Shonkoff address mastery motivation in a broad range of atypical samples. In some respects, their findings are not surprising. Atypical infants and children would be expected to show low persistence with objects and dampened displays of mastery-related pleasure, relative to typical children, according to the existing literature. More importantly, these chapters examine mastery motivation in the context of what Hodapp and Zigler (1990) termed *expanded developmental theory*—the extension of a developmental perspective beyond the classical bounds of cognition and language.

There is some evidence, from studies of several developmental domains in addition to motivation, that children with various types of developmental disorders appear not only to progress through similar sequences of development but to display similar behaviors at each stage of growth (Weisz & Zigler, 1979). In short, the evidence suggests that, in many cases, the primary difference between certain groups of atypical and typical children is that the uncompromised children progress more quickly through the various stages of development, and asymptote at a higher level. Furthermore, investigations of mastery motivation in atypical populations add to our confidence in the validity of the methodology that has been established in the past decade. This latter point is discussed in some detail in chapter 2.

These chapters, especially those by Harmon and Murrow (chapter 10), Hupp (chapter 8), and Hauser-Cram and Shonkoff (chapter 11) make another major contribution through their implications for intervention and assessment. These authors see motivation as an essential *process* that provides the foundation for the development of competence. As such, motivation has essential implications for intervention; strategies should not only be concerned with remediation of specific skills, but with helping foster the motivational process that will induce the children to acquire more skills in the future.

Similarly, Harmon and Murrow pointed out the narrowness of scope of widely used standardized tests. They criticize the long-standing reliance on such tests for assessing atypical children's development, given this narrowness as well as the limited predictive utility of such tests for atypical populations. They suggest that assessments that include motivational measures will provide a more realistic and useful picture of a specific child's developmental status.

Hauser-Cram and Shonkoff voiced the same concern but took a slightly different approach. Their argument is that standardized assessments do not provide a valid estimate of the performance of children with handicaps because of the omission of such children from the normative base. We would point out that if children with handicaps were included in the normative sample, the resulting "deflation" of scores would mitigate against detecting children who are in need of special services. Moreover, it would not be feasible to obtain separate "norms" on large, representative populations of each of the many types of atypical children, and combining across disparate forms of atypical development might poorly represent the expected performance of each form. Nevertheless, it is apparent that traditional assessments of special needs children are problematic and that the inclusion of motivational assessments into standard psychological assessment batteries would add materially to intervention efforts with special populations.

Theoretical Contributions

The Organization/Functionalist Approach. Several of the chapters in the middle section make theoretical contributions as well as reviewing empirical studies. Seifer and Vaughn (chapter 4) examined the theoretical and empirical relationships between mastery motivation and attachment. Both of these concepts are proposed to be aspects of competence within a general organizational model of competence. Seifer and Vaughn used the term competence very broadly, in keeping with the literature on "invulnerability" or competence in the face of stress. According to this approach, "competence" implies "organized patterns of behavior" or adaptive functioning given developmental and environmentally imposed needs. Motivation can thus be construed as a domain of competence.

Like Harmon and Murrow, Hupp, and Hauser-Cram and Shonkoff, then, Seifer and Vaughn pointed to the importance of assessing more than the usual, narrowly defined measures of competence when determining the capabilities of an individual. Seifer and Vaughn highlighted this need for *typical,* as well as *atypical* populations. However, we would support Harmon and Murrow, Hupp, and Hauser-Cram and Shonkoff in suggesting that motivation is a *process,* rather than a product, and believe that the term "competence" suggests a state or product. It is important to note that Seifer and Vaughn did distinguish between mastery motivation and *cognitive* competence in much the same way as we do.

In addition to proposing mastery motivation as a domain of competence, Seifer and Vaughn made the compelling case that mastery motivation should be considered an organizational construct along the lines of attachment. They suggest that many measures of mastery motivation already implicitly treat it as an organizational construct; various discrete behaviors, such as direction of gaze, motor patterns associated with individual objects, and body orientation, make up a single mastery motivation variable such as "persistence," much as a number of discrete behaviors make up each interactive code (e.g., "contact maintaining") in attachment coding. We agree that a variety of discrete behaviors are utilized in coding most mastery motivation measures. However, we think that this organizational (or functionalist) approach needs to be taken a step further: In keeping with the organizational approach, mastery motivation measurement would be improved if researchers investigated patterning among several different relevant measures (e.g., task-directed persistence and choice of somewhat challenging, but soluble, tasks) taking into account the function ("strategy") that the behaviors serve. Most extant research on mastery motivation is too reliant on one or two measures of mastery motivation.

Moreover, we feel that the contributions of organizational approaches to deriving *typologies* could be applied fruitfully to the study of mastery motivation. Mastery motivation is evident in many domains of behavior, including object-directed problem-solving, gross motor tasks, and social interaction. Wachs and Combs (chapter 6) provided empirical evidence and a theoretical rationale for the importance of separating social from object-oriented mastery motivation.

In addition, there are at least two overarching components of mastery motivation (instrumental and expressive), encompassing multiple aspects of mastery motivation. Importantly, various aspects are relatively uncorrelated, within and across domains; thus, different individuals may demonstrate different *patterns* of mastery motivation. When taken together, these more theoretically oriented chapters suggest a rethinking of our traditional, unidimensional approach to the study of individual differences in mastery motivation. Just as attachment classifications are primarily concerned with the organization of the child's proximity seeking, avoidance, contact maintenance, and resistance toward the mother, so might it be more fruitful to recast mastery motivation into a framework that explicitly acknowledges the organization of instrumental and expressive object-related activities, instrumental and expressive socially directed behaviors, and instrumental and expressive gross motor behaviors.

As Seifer and Vaughn pointed out, it is not the frequencies or durations of individual behaviors that determine attachment classifications but, rather, the temporal organization of the child's behavior during the reunion episodes. Likewise, our existing focus on measuring frequencies or duration of discrete acts may serve to mask important differences in how children approach and engage with their environment.

There are some suggestive data that support this possibility. Wachs and Combs (chapter 6) suggested that there are "politicians" and "engineers"; that is, children who are primarily socially oriented and those who are primarily object-oriented. Casual observations of young children's play tend to support this notion. There appear to be children for whom object-related activities serve as an arena for social interaction and others for whom object play is a goal unto itself. Maslin and Morgan (1985) also offered some support for a social/object typology, as did MacTurk, Hunter, McCarthy, Vietze, and McQuiston (1985).

As appealing as this notion may be, the translation into a research agenda presents some problems, the most important being that a significant change in measurement paradigm might be required. As Pedersen suggested in his foreword, the current mastery-motivation assessment situation (i.e., with the child on the mother's lap, facing the examiner) effectively reduces activation of the attachment system. Since the focus has always been on the assessment of the child's self-directed activities, this has been the desirable state of affairs. In fact, Yarrow et al. (1983) treated social behaviors as examples of nonmastery activities and combined them with the off-task measures. When social behaviors are included as an important aspect of motivation, the current situation becomes problematic. For example, differences in the response cost for the infant of various looks compromises our ability to interpret the meaning of those looks. Is looking at mother (high response cost) equivalent to looking at the examiner (low response cost)?

One possible modification of the experimental situation just described might be to move the mother to a position beside and slightly away from the examiner. This would equalize the response cost of looking at the mother and permit a more accurate assessment of the direction of the child's gaze. In addition, the separation of the mother from the infant may serve to moderately activate the attachment system, which would permit an assessment of the infant's strategies to negotiate the competing demands of attachment versus exploration under a condition of low-level stress.

However, other problems remain. Even in this revised situation, is a look at mother or examiner an instance of social referencing, a social bid, or affect sharing? Although each of these different types of looks can be displayed in object mastery, gross motor mastery, or social interaction situations, each serves a different function. Social referencing involves determining *how to react* to novel or ambiguous objects, tasks, or situations and is most relevant to object or gross motor mastery motivation (see Campos & Stenberg, 1981; Klinnert, Campos, Sorce, Emde, & Svejda, 1983). Social bids and affect sharing, in contrast, function primarily to involve other people in one's activities, and are most relevant to social mastery. Information about the child's behavior *following* the look to mother is needed to help determine the function that the look serves.

Despite these problems, we think that work to refine typologies and contexts for measuring them is needed. In keeping with the emphasis of organizational or functionalist approaches on context, such a typology would highlight the role of context (domain) in mastery motivation patterning. It seems reasonable that individual differences in mastery motivation, like individual differences in patterns of attachment, may be better characterized as a typology rather than the unidimensional approach typically applied today.

Moreover, the typological approach could be integrated with

Busch-Rossnagel et al.'s (chapter 5) views on the role of the socializing environment across phases and transitions in development. Investigations of the role of the socializing environment in the development of different types of mastery motivation would be of enormous interest and practical value.

On the other side of the nature–nurture issue, Vondra (this volume) indicated how genetics and temperament could account for many of the findings in the mastery motivation literature. Behavior genetics studies regarding the relative contribution of genetics and environment to mastery motivation types could provide more information about these typologies. For an alternative discussion on the relationships between genetics and performance, we would recommend a provocative article on emergenesis by Lykken, McGue, and Tellegen (1992).

Empirical Relations Between Mastery Motivation and Attachment

Seifer and Vaughn delved more specifically into the relations between attachment and mastery motivation and highlighted some important connections between the attachment and affiliative systems and the exploration/motivational systems. The most clear-cut way in which attachment and mastery systems are theoretically connected is via the *secure base phenomenon,* a central element in the attachment literature. The secure base phenomenon involves the tendency of a securely attached child to use the attachment figure as a base from which to explore the environment. Securely attached infants are predicted to explore the environment more than are insecure infants. However, the empirical relations between attachment classifications and mastery motivation have been weak or nonexistent. There are a number of factors that may be responsible for the paucity of significant relations.

As Pedersen has pointed out in the foreword to this volume, many of these factors may be methodological. In the typical, "home-reared" sample, about 60 to 70% of the babies are classified as Bs ("secure"); whereas only about 20–25% are classified as As ("avoidant"), 10–15% as Cs ("resistant"), and 5–10% as Ds ("disorganized"). For this reason, in the typical sample of 40 or 50 infants, there are insufficient As, Cs, or Ds to maintain the distinction among these three "insecure" classification groups; thus, As, Cs, and Ds are pooled and contrasted with Bs.

Another potential methodological consideration is that mastery motivation is not a unidimensional, metrical phenomenon. Perhaps if the typological approach, alluded to earlier, were taken, empirical relations between attachment and mastery motivation would be revealed more clearly.

However, it also is worth noting, as Maslin-Cole, Bretherton, and Morgan (1993) suggested, that freedom to explore does not ensure high mastery motivation. A child who has a secure attachment to the parent and feels free to explore in the parent's presence may still be relatively unmotivated to *master* the objects being explored. On the other hand, an insecurely attached child may be highly *motivated* to master, and, in a relatively safe context, might manifest this motivation. Thus, it is possible that the relation between attachment and mastery motivation is much more complex than has been acknowledged in investigations conducted to date.

Discussion of the McCall and Messer Chapters

The review chapters that were just discussed provide an empirical and conceptual basis for progress and improvement in research on mastery motivation. Moreover, McCall and Messer's chapters more directly addressed perceived inadequacies in extant research and theory regarding mastery motivation, and, in particular, in chapters 1–3 of this volume. They also proposed remedies for these perceived shortcomings.

In chapter 12, McCall proposed a new definition of mastery motivation, and then indicated a number of difficulties he saw with existing definitions and studies of mastery motivation. This chapter stimulated us to reconsider and evaluate a number of aspects of the models of and research on mastery motivation presented in chapters 1 and 3. Because McCall's chapter was intended to elicit discussion, we would like to respond to a number of points he made, beginning with his definition of mastery motivation.

On the Definition of Mastery Motivation

McCall defined mastery motivation as "the disposition to persistently attempt to attain a goal in the face of moderate uncertainty about whether the goal can be achieved" (this volume, p. 277). He went on to clarify that (a) "disposition" is preferable to "force" or "drive" because it lacks excess meaning, and (b) the goal is some *separate*, desired end state. There is much of value in this definition, but much that we would question. We will proceed through the definition, indicating points of discussion as they occur in sequence.

Disposition Versus Other Terms. First, McCall used the term, "disposition," rather than "drive" or "force," to avoid excess meaning of these latter terms. Ever since behavioristic and social learning theories became prominent, theorists have been trying to avoid many connotations of the term "drive." Like McCall (and White), we believe that traditional drive or instinct theories include a number of assumptions that do not seem appropros to mastery motivation. We doubt that many (if any) mastery motivation researchers believe that there is a fixed amount of mastery motivation that must be released in some fashion. However, does the label "disposition" really remedy the problem of excess meaning? Moreover, does "disposition" best capture the connotations that we *want* to incorporate?

The term "disposition," connotes a relatively static or stable trait. Moreover, "*the* disposition" implies that mastery motivation is a unitary dimension. We believe there is good evidence that mastery motivation is multifaceted, in that several aspects of mastery behavior (e.g., persistence and smiling) (a) are conceptually related to mastery motivation, (b) are empirically related to other conceptually relevant behaviors, and yet (c) are only weakly correlated with one another. Moreover, the nature of each of these aspects of mastery motivation changes with development, and the same measures are only weakly correlated across developmental transitions. Finally, there is evidence that the level of mastery motivation differs across task domains. These data suggest that mastery motivation is not a static, stable, unitary trait, but rather a complex, malleable, process. Thus, although "disposition" is by no means offensive, we fail to see a clear advantage of it over any number of other terms that could be used.

A Separate Goal. McCall holds that in order for behavior to be considered mastery motivation, it must be in pursuit of a "separate goal." Although one might think that "separate" implies that the goal is not intrinsic to the task or activity (and some of McCall's examples are consistent with this interpretation), McCall stated quite clearly that the goal may be intrinsic to the task. To the best of our understanding, what McCall means by *separate* is that the child must understand the difference between the *goal* and the actions taken to achieve the goal. Why is such *understanding* (conscious awareness) necessary?

It has long been a clinical truism that people are not always *aware* of their goals or motives. Yet, their behavior, or the *quality* of the behavior (e.g., its persistent quality) indicates to others what their motives are. A baby (or an adult!) who is not very self-aware or experienced may not know how to accomplish a particular goal, and may try different behaviors, using trial and error, to achieve it. If the person in question is a young baby, the behaviors actually tried may seem totally inappropriate, and the baby may not clearly understand that she is producing the behaviors. Still, why does this mean that the behavior is not *motivated?* As long as the person wants something and acts to achieve it, this seems like motivation to us.

Moderate Uncertainty. We agree with McCall that if one is *completely* certain that the goal will be achieved, then actions taken to achieve the goal are almost never indicators of mastery motivation. We also agree that if one is *completely* certain that the goal will not be achieved, then mastery motivated behavior is unlikely (because the individual almost never would attempt the goal). However, we think that *moderate uncertainty* as a *requirement* for behaviors to be labelled mastery motivation, is fraught with problems.

First of all, degree of uncertainty is subjective; how can a researcher ever know whether a given child is *moderately* or "just a little" or "very" uncertain about whether she or he will realize a particular goal. One can make a somewhat clearer case that something is moderately *difficult* on the basis of how much of it is completed during a set time frame. However, degree of *uncertainty* is dependent on a plethora of factors, including understanding of task requirements, age, self-confidence, and view of intelligence as an "entity . . . (that) is judged through performance" versus "a repertoire of skills that increases through effort" (Dweck & Elliott, 1983, p. 655).

It is beyond the scope of this commentary to address all of these factors, but we shall illustrate the difficulties by elaborating on one particular factor. Dweck's work on learned helplessness and related phenomena highlights that children of *equal ability* differ greatly on whether they see themselves as capable of accomplishing a task (e.g., Dweck & Elliott, 1983). A "helpless" child, who sees a single failure as indicating that she or he is irreparably stupid, may feel high uncertainty about his or her ability to accomplish even a rather unchallenging task. In order to make this child moderately uncertain, one would have to provide an excruciatingly easy task. Would persistence on this too-easy task be considered evidence of mastery motivation?

On the other hand, some children have inappropriately *high* expectations of success. Such children might feel highly certain that they will succeed on a moderately challenging task. According to McCall's definition, persistence on such a task would *not* be considered mastery-motivated. Thus, according to McCall's view, for children who have unrealistic expectations regarding what they can master, mastery motivation would only be possible on tasks that are *unlikely* to promote mastery (because they are too hard or too easy).

It is not clear why McCall defined mastery motivation in terms of subjective uncertainty rather than objective difficulty. It seems possible that he does so to ensure that the person *is aware* that she or he would need to exert some effort to master the task and that the task could, potentially, be mastered if she or he persevered. Such awareness is not part of White's (1959) original conception of effectance motivation; nor is it a necessary feature of our own conception. Again, one may be motivated and be unaware of such motivation. We do think it important to determine individually how difficult a task is, in that different children of the same age will differ in their ability to master a particular task. However, if we see a child persisting at moderately difficult tasks, we would consider that evidence of instrumental mastery motivation regardless of how much uncertainty he or she experiences.

On Methods and Measures

On the Need for Longitudinal Studies. In addition to suggesting a new definition of mastery motivation, McCall suggested methodological shortcomings of current and past research on mastery motivation. One such shortcoming is the absence of longitudinal studies that examine how well infant/early childhood measures of mastery motivation predict outcome measures such as achievement motivation and internal locus of control during middle childhood. Although recently increased attention has been given to potential relations between mastery motivation and achievement motivation (e.g., see Barrett & Morgan, this volume; Dweck & Elliott, 1983), historically, these two literatures have been quite separate.

Mastery motivation, inspired by White (1959), addressed the inclination of infants and young children to engage in behaviors that help them attain competence. For this reason, Yarrow viewed competence as the expected (and desired) result of high mastery motivation and used measures of competence and sometimes mastery motivation as outcome variables in his longitudinal studies (e.g., Jennings, Yarrow, & Martin, 1984; Messer et. al., 1986; Yarrow, Klein, Lomonaco, & Morgan, 1975).

Need for achievement and its descendent, achievement motivation, on the other hand, addressed the needs of children and adults to achieve success and/or avoid failure in socially sanctioned domains such as school. Moreover, current attributional approaches to achievement motivation define achievement motivation in terms of *purposeful* pursuit of *competence* (e.g., see Dweck & Elliott, 1983).

Thus, although mastery motivation and achievement motivation are similar in many ways, they derive from different literatures and are somewhat different in aim. We agree that longitudinal studies assessing the relation between mastery motivation in infancy/early childhood and achievement motivation in middle childhood are needed. It is important to note, however, that there have been a number of studies, some summarized in this book, that have addressed the relation between infant mastery motivation and preschool mastery and competence scores; these studies do suggest that early individual differences in mastery motivation have important implications for future development.

On the Need for Insoluble Tasks.   For methodological reasons, McCall promoted the use of insoluble tasks. Such tasks would be desirable because the child could continue trying to solve them for the full duration of the session without repeating the task. The problem, however, is making an insoluble task that children can work on for a long time while continuing to believe that the task is soluble and not too difficult for them.

Stipek, Recchia, and McClintic (1992) have devised tasks for young children that can be completed partially and yet are insoluble. This does seem to be the best way to devise insoluble tasks. Still, it is very difficult to determine how long a session would need to last in order to determine individual differences in persistence while still not allowing some children to determine that the task is insoluble or too difficult. As mentioned earlier,

McCall acknowledged that "if there is no uncertainty because the organism believes that the goal cannot be obtained, then the organism is not motivated to try to obtain the goal."

One reason why McCall recommended the use of insoluble tasks is that, he claims, otherwise children who are more competent will complete the task sooner, and will thus necessarily have lower or prorated persistence scores (since the session will be over sooner). However, as far as we know, the procedure for mastery tasks has always been to allow and, in fact, encourage subjects to repeat the solutions if they finish the task before the end of the trial. Almost all infants and toddlers readily do so. Thus, persistence duration is not directly and artificially impacted by length of time to solution.

For the individualized method, moreover, tasks are selected so that the children finish part, but not all, of each task during the first half of the trial. Therefore, the first completion (of a multipart task) is not until more than half of the trial elapses, and a child is unlikely to need to repeat the task much if at all. We do agree that with older toddlers it would be desirable to have tasks that cannot be finished within the allotted trial, but much piloting is needed to determine if it is feasible to use insoluble tasks for measures of individual differences in persistence.

On Free Play as a Way of Measuring Mastery Motivation. We agree with McCall that free play has significant problems as a context for measuring mastery motivation. However, we have found, particularly in infants who are about one year old (Barrett, Morgan, Maslin-Cole, 1993) that measures of duration of goal-directed free play are related to the traditional task measures of mastery motivation. There might be some situations in which free play measures would be useful, at least if the selection of available toys is limited (see also Messer, this volume, for more information about the usefulness of free play measures).

Breadth of the Concept

Domains of Mastery Motivation. McCall questioned whether mastery motivation per se varies from one type of task or domain (e.g., social vs. object) to another. He cautioned that differences in persistence (or other measures of mastery motivation) might be due more to the fact that *uncertainty* about solution differs across domains than to the fact that mastery motivation, per se, differs across domains. This illustrates some of the problems with making uncertainty central to the definition of mastery motivation. Yes, one is likely to be more certain about his or her ability to solve some types of tasks than others. This probably stems in part from ability in that domain, and in part from such factors as experience with that task domain. However, one may have less experience and ability in one task domain because one is less motivated to achieve in that domain. Moreover, how will researchers ever be able to determine whether tasks in different domains are equal in subjective uncertainty for preverbal children?

McCall also suggested that measurement of domains of mastery motivation would require holding constant children's desire for the goals on different types of tasks. It seems to us that desire for the goal is affected directly by mastery motivation; one reason one desires a particular goal is that one is motivated to master it. Moreover, one reason that one is motivated to master a particular task is that the goal is something that one desires.

Thus, McCall's point is well taken that differences in uncertainty and desire for goals will enter into differences in mastery motivation across domains. However, these are *reasons for the differences;* they do not imply that differences in motivation do not exist. On the contrary, there is evidence that children differ in their motivation for mastery of tasks in various domains. Separate factors derived from the DMQ ratings indicate that mothers view their children's motivation in such domains as cognition, social interaction, and gross motor behavior as quite distinct (Morgan et al., 1993). Furthermore, Wachs' research (1987; Combs & Wachs, 1993; Wachs & Combs, this volume) on social mastery motivation also indicates that different children are high in the desire for social versus object goals. And, such differences may be important. Perhaps, for example, one wished to capitalize on each child's interests for the purpose of devising individualized curriculum. Perhaps one wished to ensure that children develop in all domains, such that one would increase extrinsic incentives for domains in which intrinsic motivation was low. It may be important to assess differences in motivation across domains despite the multiplicity of factors contributing to those differences. We think that more research on domain-specific measures of mastery motivation is needed.

Developmental Transitions

McCall argued against the developmental transitions described in chapter 3, stating that they seem to be very similar to cognitive changes others have described. Yes, motivational transitions parallel and are affected by cognitive changes, but they go beyond them. It is important to note that we do not see these transitions as suggesting that mastery motivation starts or stops at particular time points. Our point is that there is both change and lack of change in mastery motivation throughout development. Cognitive abilities and socialization change the nature and complexity of mastery motivation. However, they do not *create* mastery motivation.

Concluding Comments About McCall's Chapter

McCall argued that there has been limited definitional methodological and theoretical progress in this area. This may be true, in part, because of lack of consensus on many of the points he raised. However, there has been quite a bit of empirical progress in recent years as pointed out in the middle chapters of this book and in Messer's (1993) edited volume. We also think that Chapter 3 (Barrett and Morgan) makes several important new conceptual and definitional contributions. One contribution is that it ties mastery motivation to broader research literatures such as the development of emotion and achievement motivation. In addition, the position that mastery motivation is multifaceted, and justification for proposing that mastery motivation is present from earliest infancy, are new developments.

Comments on Messer's Chapter

Messer's chapter covered a lot of territory. First, he, like McCall, provided a brief historical overview, from his perspective, that supplements the historical section in chapter 1. The second part of this historical introduction discussed very briefly mastery motivation and similar concepts such as achievement motivation in school-age children. Like McCall (and us), Messer thinks that exploring these connections is an important direction for future research.

Next, Messer discussed broad transitions in development, and more specific transitions in mastery motivation. The phases he proposed and the information he presents about them, however, are flavored by his point of view on probably the two most important issues he raised in this chapter. Messer raised two closely related issues—the issue of just what mastery motivation entails and the thorny issue of how researchers should direct their attention in future studies of mastery motivation.

One approach to the definition and study of mastery motivation that Messer described is positivistic. According to this approach, one would make the *assumption* that a particular behavioral variable (probably, persistence at task-directed behavior) measures mastery motivation, and would constrain oneself to a narrow definition of mastery motivation. Once one makes the assumption that this measure indicates mastery motivation, one can determine its relations to other relevant constructs or measures. In fact, this is not unlike the approach that has been taken in most studies of mastery motivation to date. Messer, like ourselves, however, believes that this is not the preferred direction for future research.

A second approach to defining and investigating mastery motivation, as described by Messer, is to consider *all* influences on mastery behavior to be mastery motivation. This approach, like the first, would be easy to operationalize. However, perhaps even more than the first approach, this definition of mastery motivation would seem invalid, in that it would include skills, abilities, experience, etc., as well as motivational variables.

Messer believes that mastery motivation should be defined in a broader fashion than that suggested by the first approach. However, he is not sure it should encompass *everything* related to mastery behavior, as in the second approach. Messer submitted that we do not yet know enough to determine which behaviors are due to mastery motivation. Instead, in a third approach that he favors most, he suggested focusing on different *styles* of mastery "motivation" (really mastery *behavior*, since he indicated that we don't know which behaviors are caused by mastery motivation). Rather than saying particular children are higher or lower in mastery motivation, one would characterized their *style* of responding to mastery tasks. He went on to indicate:

> An advantage of such a classification is that it might provide an assessment of children who are clearly motivated, but not in an adaptive or cooperative way. Such children can show a form of mastery by refusing to cooperate or by being in opposition to the experimenter's wishes. (p. 309)

Like Messer, we believe that mastery motivation encompasses much more than persistence, and that it is extremely important to determine individual differences in styles of mastery motivation. However, we believe that one can make some a priori conceptual definitions of what should and should not be considered mastery *motivation*. We fail to see how refusal to cooperate, per se, is a form of mastery motivation. A child could devise his or her own mastery task in such a context, and display motivated behavior on that task. However, why is refusal to cooperate necessarily motivated by inclination to master?

Similarly, it is unclear to us that some of the behaviors Messer proposed as indexing mastery motivation, as well as some of the proposed mechanisms for the development of mastery motivation, are apt. This is particularly true for his first stage of mastery motivation (birth to age 5 months).

Messer proposed that, from earliest infancy, social interaction can foster mastery motivation. We agree, and believe that this is an important direction for future research. However, the mechanism Messer proposed for this influence seems more important for enabling the *behaviors used to assess* mastery motivation than mastery motivation itself. For example, he discussed how social interaction may help a baby sustain attention in a stimulus, and also help the baby to habituate to that stimulus. This does seem possible; however, this point raises several issues. First, we wonder whether *sustained* attention to a particular perceptual stimulus indicates increasing mastery motivation. We would argue that prolonged scanning of a simple stimulus might even imply *lower* mastery motivation; once the stimulus has been encoded, further scanning does not aid in mastery. Second, we question whether increased ability to sustain attention or to habituate implies increased mastery motivation. As mentioned in Chapter 3, we believe that preference for moderate novelty is analogous to preference for moderate challenge. However, varying degrees of *ability* to sustain attention or to habituate are *alternative* (in comparison to mastery motivation) sources of individual differences in looking time or habituation. These abilities are not influences on *mastery motivation*, but on *measures* of mastery motivation.

This is why it seems important to place some a priori constraints on what is to be construed as mastery motivation and what is not. No single measure, including persistence at task-directed activity, is a direct indicator of mastery motivation. Perhaps abilities, such as those described by Messer, should be partialled out of habituation measures of the mastery-motivation-relevant dimension of preference for novelty.

In terms of Messer's stages themselves, the analysis is generally consistent with Barrett and Morgan's conceptualization in chapter 3, except that it brings in some additional literature and splits Barrett and Morgan's first phase into two phases by postulating a transition at five months. Messer seems to derive his ages for transitions from literature on broad transitions in development, and to see the 5-month transition as involving increased attention to the outside world. Certainly, greater attention to the outside world has implications for mastery motivation, but it remains an empirical question as to whether there is a marked change in this variable at 5 months or whether attention increases gradually throughout the first 8 or 9 months of life.

In conclusion, we believe that Messer makes a number of very significant points about mastery motivation and its development. As alluded to earlier in this chapter, we endorse his call for a broader definition of mastery motivation, including different *styles* rather than just different *levels*. Also important is his speculation about how the social environment and social processes influence the development of mastery motivation. This discussion expands on the Busch-Rossnagel et al. chapter (this volume), utilizing several studies recently published in Messer (1993). Also significant are Messer's views of future directions in mastery motivation and gaps in our knowledge. In addition to the points alluded to earlier, he points out the paucity of experimental studies on, and our relative lack of knowledge of, other cultures (exceptions being the Busch-Rossnagel, Vargas, & Knauf, 1993 study with Hispanic-American families as well as a number of somewhat similar mastery motivation research studies in Europe). We think that measurement of mastery motivation, like measurement of any "latent construct" will always be a source of controversy, and we agree with Messer that empirical findings need to be an important guide to measurement. However, we believe conceptual definitions must constrain our search for measures if we are to obtain valid measures of *mastery motivation*, as distinguished from the broader domain of *mastery behavior.*

RECOMMENDATIONS FOR FUTURE RESEARCH

The chapters in this volume, taken together, suggest a rather clear-cut vision of needed directions for future research on mastery motivation. First, mastery motivation needs to be viewed more broadly, with research becoming less dependent on one or two measures in a single context. Moreover, some aspects of mastery motivation deserve special attention, given the paucity of research on them to date: Expressive aspects of mastery motivation are understudied in all contexts, as are instrumental and expressive aspects of social and gross motor mastery motivation. (See also Morgan & Yang, chapter 14, this volume).

Second, there is a need to explore a typological approach to patterns or styles of mastery motivation. As a start, it would be sensible to determine whether or not children manifest mastery motivation more through instrumental versus expressive channels, and whether they manifest more mastery motivation in object-related versus social versus gross motor contexts.

Third, there is a need to link the study of mastery motivation with that of achievement motivation and to determine the empirical relation between mastery and achievement motivation using longitudinal investigations. Despite the similarities in these two domains of inquiry, there also are obvious differences. Moreover, clarification is needed regarding how *mastery motivation* during the elementary school years and beyond differs from *achievement motivation* at these same ages.

Fourth, there is a need for additional studies to determine the usefulness of measures of mastery motivation for assessment of developmental progress of typical and atypical groups and for intervention with atypical groups. Development is not static; it is a process, and assessing a child's developmental status at a particular slice of time provides an incomplete picture of how development is proceeding. It seems quite possible that motivational measures will be better predictors of future progress than are measures of competence at a particular time; at the very least, they would seem important attributes to assess in addition to standard developmental tests.

For some 20 years, research on mastery motivation has made slow, but steady progress. It seems that this field of inquiry is coming of age, and is ready to forge its way out in new directions. All of us who have been involved in this research enterprise can feel a glow of mastery pleasure and pride at having made progress in the understanding of mastery motivation. However, many moderately challenging tasks remain for us to conquer. We must persist and meet the challenge.

References

Barrett, K. C., Morgan, G. A., & Maslin-Cole, C. (1993). Three studies on the development of mastery motivation in infancy and toddlerhood. In D. Messer (Ed.), *Mastery motivation in early child-*

hood: Development, measurement, and social processes (pp. 83–108). London: Routledge.

Busch-Rossnagel, N. A., Vargas, M. E., & Knauf, D. E. (1993). Mastery motivation in ethnic minority groups: The sample case of Hispanics. In D. Messer (Ed.), *Mastery motivation in early childhood: Development, measurement, and social processes* (pp. 132–148). London: Routledge.

Campos, J. J., & Stenberg, C. (1981). Perception, appraisal, and emotion: The onset of social referencing. In M. Lamb & L. Sherrod (Eds.), *Infant social cognition: Empirical and theoretical considerations* (pp. 273–314). Hillsdale, NJ: Erlbaum.

Combs, T. T., & Wachs, T. D. (1993). The construct validity of measures of social mastery motivation. In D. Messer (Ed.), *Mastery motivation in early childhood: Development, measurement, and social processes* (pp. 168–185). London: Routledge.

Dweck, C. S., & Elliott, E. S. (1983). Achievement motivation. In P. H. Mussen (Gen. Ed.) & E. M. Hetherington (Vol. Ed.), *Handbook of child psychology: Vol. IV. Socialization, personality, and social development* (pp. 643–691). New York: Wiley.

Hodapp, R. M., & Zigler, E. (1990). Applying the developmental perspective to individuals with Down syndrome. In D. Cicchetti & M. Beeghly (Eds.), *Children with Down syndrome: A developmental perspective* (pp. 1–29) Cambridge: Cambridge University Press.

Jennings, K., Yarrow, L., & Martin, P. (1984). Mastery motivation and cognitive development: A longitudinal study from infancy to three and one half years. *International Journal of Behavioral Development, 7*, 441–461.

Klinnert, M., Campos, J., Sorce, J., Emde, R., and Svejda, M. (1983). Emotions as behavior regulators: Social referencing in infancy. In R. Plutchik & H. Kellerman (Eds.), *Emotion: Theory, research, and experience: Vol. 2.* (pp. 57–86). New York: Academic Press.

Lykken, D. T., McGue, M., & Tellegen, A. (1992). Emergenesis: Genetic traits that may not run in families. *American Psychologist, 47*, 1565–1577.

MacTurk, R. H., Hunter, F. T., McCarthy, M. E., Vietze, P. M., & McQuiston, S. (1985). Social mastery motivation in Down syndrome and nondelayed infants. *Topics in Early Childhood Special Education, 4*, 93–109.

Maslin, C. A., & Morgan, G. A. (1985, April). *Measure of social competence: Toddlers' social and object orientation during mastery tasks.* Presented at the Biennial Meeting of the Society for Research in Child Development, Toronto, Canada.

Maslin-Cole, C., Bretherton, I., & Morgan, G. A. (1993). Toddler mastery motivation and competence: Links with attachment security, maternal scaffolding, and family climate. In D. Messer (Ed.), *Mastery motivation in early childhood: Development, measurement, and social processes* (pp. 205–229). London: Routledge.

Messer, D. (Ed.). (1993). *Mastery motivation in early childhood: Development, measurement, and social processes.* London: Routledge.

Messer, D., McCarthy, M., McQuiston, S., MacTurk, R., Yarrow, L. J., & Vietze, P. (1986). Relation between mastery behavior in infancy and competence in early childhood. *Developmental Psychology, 22,* 366–372.

Morgan, G. A., Harmon, R. J., Maslin-Cole, C. A., Busch-Rossnagel, N. A., Jennings, K. D., Hauser-Cram, P., & Brockman, L. M. (1993). Parent and teacher perceptions of young children's mastery motivation: Assessment and review of research. In D. Messer (Ed.), *Mastery motivation in early childhood:* (pp. 109–131). London: Routledge.

Stipek, D., Recchia, S., & McClintic, S. (1992). Self-evaluation in young children. *Monographs of the Society for Research in Child Development, 57* (1, Serial No. 226).

Weisz, J., & Zigler, E. (1979). Cognitive development in retarded and nonretarded persons: Piagetian tests of the similar sequence hypothesis. *Psychological Bulletin, 86,* 831–851.

White, R. W. (1959). Motivation reconsidered: The concept of competence. *Psychological Review, 66,* 297–333.

Yarrow, L. J., Klein, R., Lomonaco, S., & Morgan, G. (1975). Cognitive and motivational development in early childhood. In B. Z. Friedlander, G. M. Sterritt, & G. E. Kirk (Eds.), *Exceptional infant: Assessment and Intervention* (pp. 491–502). New York: Bruner/Mazel.

Yarrow, L. J., McQuiston, S., MacTurk, R. H., McCarthy, M. E., Klein, R. P., & Vietze, P. M. (1983). Assessment of mastery motivation during the first year of life. Contemporaneous and cross-age relationships. *Developmental Psychology, 19,* 159–171.

AUTHOR INDEX

A

Abe, K., 229, *234*
Abbeduto, L., 149, *162*, 222, 226, 227, *235*, *333*, *334*
Abbott, D., 266, *271*
Ainsworth, M.D.S., 97, 101, 104, *112*, 135, 136, *140*
Allessandri, S., 65, 66, 69, 76, 85, *90*, *92*
Allen, R., 203, 205, 218, 267, *272*
Alpert, A.S., *334*
Altshuler, K., 208, 217
Amaya-Williams, M., 262, *269*
Anderson, E., 101, *112*
Arend, R., 101, 102, *112*, *113*
Atkinson, J.W., 5, *15*
Aydlett, L.A., 183, 193

B

Baak, K., 173, 197
Bakeman, R., 45, *51*
Balla, D., 232, *236*
Ballyguier, G., 150, *161*
Bambara, L.M., 230
Banta, J.T., 36, *51*
Barnard, K.E., 266, *268*
Barnett, D., *337*
Baron-Cohen, S., 300, *312*
Barrera, M.E., 205, 215, 241, 242, *253*
Barrett, K.C., 7, 8, 9, 10, 12, 13, *15*, 20, 29, 30, 31, 32, 33, 41, 45, 48, *54*, 65, 69, 71, 73, 74, 76, 77, 78, 79, 81, 83, 86, *90*, *92*, 98, 105, 118, 124, 125, 126, 127, 132, 133, 134, 138, 139, *140*, *143*, 246, 251, 263, 264, *269*, 274, 281, 285, 293, 297, 298, 301, 302, *312*, 321, 324, 327, 328, 331, *332*, 350, 351, 353, *357*
Barsch, R.H., 203, *215*
Basham, R., 239, *253*
Bates, E., 297, 304, *312*
Bathurst, K., 191, 193
Batshaw, M.L., 203, 215
Baumeister, A.A., 224, *234*
Bayley, N., 73, *90*, 97, *112*, 177, 185, 226, *234*, 238, *253*
Baysinger, C.M., 173, 198
Beckwith, L., 238, 240, 241, 243, *253*, *254*, *255*, *336*
Bell, R.Q., 98, *112*
Belmont, I., 239, *254*
Belsky, J., 6, *15*, *17*, 20, 49, 129, *141*, 169, 177, 184, 186, 193, 198, 207, 215, 282, *290*, *332*
Benesh-Weiner, M., 5, *17*, 22, 55
Berger, J., 27, *51*
Berlyne, D.E., 276, *291*
Bess, F., 207, 215
Biddle, B.J., 192, 193
Birigen, Z., 11, 12, *17*, 20, 38, 48, 54, *55*, 57, *92*, 128, *143*, 150, *163*, 238, 247, *255*
Bjorkland, D.F., iv, *vi*
Blasco, P., *332*
Blasco, P.M., *332*

SUBJECT INDEX

A

Achievement,
  and mastery motivation,
    274, 284-285, 290
Activity level, 168, 170, 174-175
Affect regulation, 96, 106-108
Assessment of mastery motivation,
    19-51, 171-172, 239, 246-
    251, 282-290
  adult ratings, 20, 40-45,
    250-251
  free play, 20, 38-40, 244,
    247-248
  structured tasks, 20-38,
    248
  structured tasks for 6- and
    12-month-olds, 21-30
  structured tasks for 15- to 36-
    month-olds, 30-35
  structured tasks for preschool-
    ers, 35-38
  validity of, 26, 27-30, 222-
    223
Attachment, iv-vi, 96, 101-102,
    106, 305-306
Attention span, 168-169, 180-183

B

Bayley Scales of Infant Develop-
    ment, 239-245, 247-249, 251
  Mental Development Index
    (MDI), 239
  Psychomotor Developmental
    Index (PDI), 239
Behavioral genetics, 169
Behavioral inhibition, 172-174
Behavioral organization, 100, 243-
    245
Bethesda longitudinal study data,
    327-330
Biology, 165, 168-169, 171-192
Blind children, 212-214

C

Caregiving behaviors (see
    Parenting practices)
Cognitive ability, 167, 169, 170,
    177-178
Cognitive development, iv, 96
  development of at-risk infants,
    239-242
Competence as organized patterns
    of behavior, 99-101
Competence in early childhood,
    97-99, 105-108
Competence (prediction of), 60, 69
Competence vs. mastery motiva-
    tion, 7-9, 108-110, 238, 274,
    279-280, 284, 286, 290
Competent child, defined, 97